OXFORD APOSTOLIC FATHERS
General Editors
Paul Foster   Andrew Gregory   Christopher Tuckett

OXFORD APOSTOLIC FATHERS

A series of critical editions of early Christian texts, comprising the text itself in the original language, a facing translation, a substantial introduction, and extensive notes.

2 CLEMENT

Introduction, Text, and Commentary

Christopher Tuckett

OXFORD
UNIVERSITY PRESS

Great Clarendon Street, Oxford OX2 6DP,
United Kingdom

Oxford University Press is a department of the University of Oxford.
It furthers the University's objective of excellence in research, scholarship,
and education by publishing worldwide. Oxford is a registered trade mark of
Oxford University Press in the UK and in certain other countries.

© Christopher Tuckett 2012

The moral rights of the author have been asserted

First published 2012

Impression: 1

All rights reserved. No part of this publication may be reproduced, stored in
a retrieval system, or transmitted, in any form or by any means, without the
prior permission in writing of Oxford University Press, or as expressly permitted
by law, by licence or under terms agreed with the appropriate reprographics
rights organization. Enquiries concerning reproduction outside the scope of the
of the above should be sent to the Rights Department, Oxford University Press, at the
address above

You must not circulate this work in any other form
and you must impose this same condition on any acquirer

British Library Cataloguing in Publication Data

Data available

Library of Congress Cataloging in Publication Data

Data available

ISBN 978–0–19–969460–0

Typeset by RefineCatch Limited, Bungay, Suffolk
Printed in Great Britain
on acid-free paper by
MPG Books Group, Bodmin and King's Lynn

Preface

My interest in *2 Clement* was probably first aroused in a significant way as a result of a conference in Oxford, held in 2004 and arranged by myself and my colleague Andrew Gregory, on the Apostolic Fathers and the New Testament. Many of the papers from the conference were subsequently published in a two-volume collection *The Reception of the New Testament in the Apostolic Fathers* and *Trajectories through the New Testament and the Apostolic Fathers* (Oxford: Oxford University Press, 2005). The *Reception* volume included a set of essays analysing each of the writings of the Apostolic Fathers individually (focusing on the issue of their relation to the writings of the New Testament), and it fell to me (with Andrew Gregory) to write the essay on *2 Clement* for this volume. (I wrote on *2 Clement* and the gospels, he on *2 Clement* and the rest of the NT: see the bibliography here.) Arising out of the conference was also the plan to inaugurate a series of new editions and commentaries on the writings of the Apostolic Fathers. As a result of writing the part of the essay in the *Reception* volume, my own interest in *2 Clement* had been already excited and I volunteered to try to write the volume in the series on *2 Clement*. The present volume is the end result of that process.

I am very grateful to the other editors of the series, Paul Foster and Andrew Gregory, for supporting my proposal to write this volume in the new series and for their unfailing encouragement throughout the time of research and writing. I am grateful too to Tom Perridge at OUP for his constant and continuing support for the project, as well as to the anonymous readers of the initial proposal and the final manuscript for their helpful and constructive comments. However, the shortcomings in the finished volume are of course solely my own. A significant time for work on the volume was undertaken during a period of sabbatical leave from my post in the University of Oxford, which was extended by a further term thanks to extra funding provided by the John Fell Fund of the University: I am very grateful for the extra time and space this provided to enable me to finish the project during this period of freedom from teaching obligations.

Writing a commentary, especially on a text that has not generated a great amount of scholarly interest in the past (commentaries on *2 Clement* are not that numerous!), means that one engages with a few other scholars, past and present, quite intensively. In writing this commentary, I have been constantly aware of how much one owes to others in the past who have worked on the text and I am grateful for all their endeavours as I have interacted with them. In particular, Andreas Lindemann's and Wilhelm Pratscher's fine commentaries have been constant companions with me during the time of research and writing, and I have learnt an enormous amount from them.

Last, but most important, I owe a very great debt of thanks to my wife for her constant support and encouragement throughout the time of preparing for, and writing, this volume. She has been a rock of support for which I am grateful beyond measure. I am grateful too to my children for their support and encouragement, including at one point the suggestion (when I was struggling with the Introduction to this commentary) that all one should say was '*2 Clement* needs no introduction'. For better or worse, I chose to ignore the advice!

Christopher Tuckett

Oxford, May 2011

Contents

Preface   v
Abbreviations and Conventions   viii

I. INTRODUCTION   1

1. Manuscripts   3
2. Attestation   7
3. Authorship   14
4. Genre   18
5. Literary Unity   27
6. Citations   34
7. Opponents   47
8. Place and Date of Writing   58
9. Theology   65

II. TEXT AND TRANSLATION   83

III. COMMENTARY   125

Bibliography   304
Index of Ancient Sources   311
Index of Modern Authors Cited   326

Abbreviations and Conventions

AJT	*American Journal of Theology*
ANRW	*Aufstieg und Niedergang der römischen Welt*
BAG	W. Bauer, W. F. Arndt, and F. W. Gingrich, *A Greek–English Lexicon of the New Testament and Other Early Christian Literature* (Chicago: University of Chicago Press, 1957)
BCNH	Bibliothèque copte de Nag Hammadi
BDF	F. Blass and A. Debrunner, *A Greek Grammar of the New Testament and Other Early Christian Literature. A Translation and Revision of the ninth–tenth German edition by Robert W. Funk* (Chicago: University of Chicago Press, 1961)
BETL	Bibliotheca Ephemeridum Theologicarum Lovaniensium
BHT	Beiträge zur historischen Theologie
BZAW	Beihefte zur Zeitschrift für die alttestamentliche Wissenschaft
BZNW	Beihefte zur Zeitschrift für die neutestamentliche Wissenschaft
FRLANT	Forschungen zur Religion und Literatur des Alten und Neuen Testaments
GCS	Die griechischen christlichen Schriftsteller der ersten Jahrhunderte
HNT	Handbuch zum Neuen Testament
HTR	*Harvard Theological Review*
ICC	International Critical Commentary
JBL	*Journal of Biblical Literature*
JRelS	*Journal of Religious Studies*
JSNTSup	Journal for the Study of the New Testament Supplement Series
KAV	Kommentar zu den Apostolischen Vätern
LCC	Library of Christian Classics
LCL	Loeb Christian Library
LkR	Lukan redaction
LSJ	H. G. Liddell and R. Scott, *A Greek–English Lexicon. Revised and Augmented throughout by Sir Henry Stuart Jones* (Oxford: Oxford University Press, ^{9}1968)
MattR	Matthean redaction
MTS	Marburger Theologische Studien
NHC	Nag Hammadi Codex
NHMS	Nag Hammadi and Manichean Studies

NHS	Nag Hammadi Studies
NovT	*Novum Testamentum*
NovTSup	Supplements to Novum Testamentum
NTS	*New Testament Studies*
RAC	*Reallexicon für Antike und Christentum*
RGG	*Religion in Geschichte und Gegenwart*
SBAW.PH	Sitzungsberichte der bayerischen Akademie der Wissenschaften. Philosophisch-historische Klasse
SC	Sources chrétiennes
Str–B	H. L. Strack and P. Billerbeck, *Kommentar zum Neuen Testament aus Talmud und Midrasch* (6 vols; Munich: C. H. Beck, 1922–61)
SVF	H. von Arnim (ed.), *Stoicorum Veterum Fragmenta* (Leipzig, 1903–24)
TU	Texte und Untersuchungen
TWNT	G. Kittel and G. Friedrich (eds), *Theologisches Wörterbuch zum Neuen Testament* (9 vols; Stuttgart: Kohlhammer, 1932–79)
VC	*Vigiliae Christianae*
VCSup	Supplements to Vigiliae Christianae
WBC	Word Biblical Commentary
WUNT	Wissenschaftliche Untersuchungen zum Neuen Testament
ZKG	*Zeitschrift für Kirchengeschichte*
ZNW	*Zeitschrift für die neutestamentliche Wissenschaft*

All other abbreviations, and conventions for references to ancient literature, are as in P. H. Alexander *et al.* (eds), *The SBL Handbook of Style for Ancient Near Eastern, Biblical, and Early Christian Studies* (Peabody, Mass.: Hendrickson, 1999).

For capitalization, I have followed the OUP's *Guide to Authors* which recommends that capitalization should be kept to a minimum. I have therefore used e.g. 'church' throughout (though I am fully aware that the use of a capitalized 'Church' would not be inappropriate in some places). I have, however, used 'Gnostic' (rather than 'gnostic'): see p. 50 below for explanation.

On the use of inclusive language, I have endeavoured throughout, when presenting my own statements and arguments, to use inclusive language as far as possible. The case of translations of, and references to, ancient texts which are generally not written in inclusive language is clearly more problematic. For the most part, I have not attempted to change the surface wording to make the language inclusive unless this can be done very easily without making the translation too 'free'. In one instance in *2 Clement*, this is important in that the use of the address $\dot{a}\delta\epsilon\lambda\phi o\acute{\iota}$ alone ('brothers', but probably meant inclusively to cover 'brothers and sisters'), as opposed to $\dot{a}\delta\epsilon\lambda\phi o\grave{\iota}$ $\kappa a\grave{\iota}$ $\dot{a}\delta\epsilon\lambda\phi a\acute{\iota}$ ('brothers and sisters'), is an important source-critical indicator of a possible seam in the tradition between chs. 1–18 and chs. 19–20; hence any attempt to use inclusive language in the 'translation' of ἀδελφοί alone (as e.g. 'brothers and sisters') would hide an important aspect of the text. In line with the social realities of the time at which *2 Clement* was written, I have also referred to the author by the masculine pronoun 'he'/'his' etc. rather than 's/he' or 'he/she': since almost all texts in antiquity were written by men rather than women, this is perhaps a reasonable assumption. I am, however, fully aware that these issues are debatable and that others would make different decisions.

For the texts listed in the 'Parallels' sections, I have provided versions of the texts concerned in their 'original' languages where possible. English translations for the *non*-biblical texts (with the exception of *2 Clement* itself, for which an English translation is given in the text section of this volume) are provided in each case. (For biblical texts, it is assumed that the reader will have ready access to good English translations already and providing these would be unnecessary.)

PART I

Introduction

1. MANUSCRIPTS

The text known to us as *2 Clement* survives in only three manuscripts: two in Greek, Codex Alexandrinus (A) and Codex Constantinopolitanus (C), and one in Syriac (S). A few brief comments are given here on each manuscript.[1]

Codex A. Codex Alexandrinus is a manuscript containing the whole Bible with the texts of *1 Clement* and *2 Clement* at the end of the whole codex. It is currently housed in the British Library in London (MS Reg. 1 D VIII).[2] These two works follow immediately after the end of the 'New Testament' section without any break visible, and it would appear that they were regarded as part of the 'New Testament' by the scribe. Its date is 5th century. The text of *2 Clement* starts at the top of column 2 on fol. 168a without any heading, following immediately after the text of *1 Clement* (and its colophon). The significance of the absence of a heading is not clear. The full titles of each book are given in an ornately decorated colophon at the end of each work. Some books are also supplied with a title at the start;[3] however, the text of *2 Clement* here is not. One would expect a title to appear at the end of

---

[1] For a very full description and assessment of the manuscripts, see J. B. Lightfoot, *The Apostolic Fathers. Part 1. S. Clement of Rome* (2 vols; London: Macmillan, 1890), 1.116–47.

[2] For a facsimile edition of the text, see F. G. Kenyon, *The Codex Alexandrinus (Royal MS 1 D V–VIII) in reduced photographic facsimile* (London: British Museum, 1909). Plates are also available online at www.csntm.org/manuscripts.aspx.

[3] The text of *1 Clement* has the superscription . . . ς κορινθιους ᾱ. The numeral might imply that there was a second work (presumably a 'letter' 'to the Corinthians') associated with *1 Clement*, and that this was probably the text immediately following in the codex. However, this is not stated explicitly. On the other hand, the edges of the pages in A are damaged, and the superscriptions where they do not occur (they are not present for all the biblical books) might have originally been in a part of the page which is now lost. Too much should not therefore be read into the absence of a title for *2 Clement* in the text of A as we now have it. The absence of any superscription in A is used by C. Stegemann, 'Herkunft und Entstehung des sogenannten zweiten Klemensbriefes' (Bonn: Doctoral Dissertation, 1974), 36, 105, as part of her evidence that *2 Clement* was always integrally linked with *1 Clement* in the tradition; but the fact that not all the pages in A are fully extant (with some top edges missing) makes this a precarious argument. See also R. Warns, 'Untersuchungen zum 2. Clemensbrief' (Marburg: Doctoral Dissertation, 1989), 4.

the text. Unfortunately, the text breaks off at the end of fol. 169b at *2 Clem.* 12.5a, and the rest of the text (including then the ending) is missing.

The table of contents given on a separate page of the codex gives the list of books under the heading *Η ΚΑΙΝΗ ΔΙΑΘΗΚΗ* ending with the titles:

ΑΠΟΚΑΛΥΨΙΣ[ΙΩΑ]ΝΝΟΥ
ΚΛΗΜΕΝΤΟΣΕ[ΠΙΣΤ]ΟΛΗ Α
ΚΛΗΜΕΝΤΟΣΕ[ΠΙΣΤ]ΟΛΗ Β

It is agreed that this list is not the work of (one of) the original scribe(s) of A, but is a later addition, probably from around the 7th century.[4] At least then for the compiler of this list, the text was known as the second letter of Clement and evidently closely linked with *1 Clement*. But in any case, the fact that the text of *2 Clement* follows so closely immediately after *1 Clement* in the codex suggests that the scribe writing the text at this point probably thought the same.

The quality of the text is generally good. The scribe is at times careless and errors are not infrequent; but they are generally easy to identify as simply slips rather than deliberate changes.[5] Also it is by far the oldest manuscript witness to the text.

Codex C. Codex Constantinopolitanus is a manuscript containing the texts of a number of the so-called 'Apostolic Fathers', including *1 Clement, 2 Clement,* the Letter of Barnabas, the letters of Ignatius, and the *Didache*. It does not contain any text normally assigned to the New Testament. The manuscript is housed in the Library of the Jerusalem Monastery of the Holy Sepulchre, MS 54.[6] A colophon at the end of the codex gives a precise date for the copying of the manuscript, 1056 CE, as well as the name of the scribe ('Leo'). The text of *2 Clement* starts with a title $Κλήμεντος\ πρὸς\ Κορινθίους\ Β$, thus again indicating that the work is known as the second (letter) of Clement to the Corinthians; at the end, there is simply a note of the number of *stichoi*. As

---

[4] See the comment of T. S. Pattie, cited in K. P. Donfried, *The Setting of Second Clement in Early Christianity*, NovTSup 38 (Leiden: Brill, 1974), 20 n. 3.

[5] For one example among many, see e.g. A's reading $αἰών$ (for $ἀγών$) in 7.1. For an overall assessment of the text of A, see Lightfoot, *Apostolic Fathers*, 1.120: 'On the whole this MS appears to give a good text. The short-comings of the scribe are generally such that they can be easily corrected; for they arise from petty carelessness and ignorance, and not from perverse ingenuity.' Also p. 142 (comparing A with the other manuscripts): 'A (if we set aside merely clerical errors, in which it abounds) is by far the most trustworthy.'

[6] It was originally found (in the 1880s) in the library of the sister house of the monastery in Istanbul (Constantinople), but was subsequently moved to Jerusalem. German scholars often refer to the MS by the letter H (for Hierosolymitanus). A photographic reproduction of the leaves of the manuscript containing the texts of *1 Clement* and *2 Clement* is provided in Lightfoot, *Apostolic Fathers*, 1.425–74.

1. Manuscripts

in A, the text of *2 Clement* follows immediately after that of *1 Clement*, indicating that the two texts are considered as belonging closely together.

The quality of the text is perhaps less good than that of A. The manuscript is written carefully in a minuscule hand; but there are several examples of what appear to be changes made to the text, e.g. instances where allusions to biblical texts have been assimilated to make the wording closer to that of the biblical text in question, changes which seem to reflect dogmatic motives, and other attempts to 'improve' the grammar or the style.[7] Clearly it is not as old a manuscript as A, but it does provide us with our only Greek witness to the text for a substantial part of the whole (from 12.5b to the end).

Codex S. Now housed in the University Library, Cambridge, Add. MSS 1700, this manuscript contains the Syriac New Testament with the texts of *1 Clement* and *2 Clement* placed (without any obvious break) after the Catholic epistles (which appear here before the Pauline corpus).[8] The texts of both *1 Clement* and *2 Clement* have a heading at the start and a colophon at the end of each letter: each heading and colophon implies that the text to which it refers is a letter written by Clement to the Corinthians at Rome. As with the Greek manuscripts, the text of *2 Clement* is thus regarded as belonging closely with *1 Clement*, by the same author (Clement), and with the same original audience (the Corinthian church).

The nature of the translation of the text of the Clementine epistles suggests that these have a separate origin from the rest of the NT. The other NT texts follow closely the Harclean version; but the text of the Clementine letters shows a far greater degree of paraphrase and wordiness by comparison.[9] This feature, combined with the obvious fact that the MS only gives us a text in translation and hence inevitably at one step removed from the original Greek, makes this MS of slightly less value than the other two in some respects.[10] Certainly, given the indirect nature of the witness which any text in translation can provide, it would be hazardous to rely too heavily on smaller details of the text in S to reconstruct any 'original'. On the other hand, it remains a

---

[7] Details in Lightfoot, *Apostolic Fathers*, 1.124–8. Most of Lightfoot's evidence is taken from *1 Clement*, but see here e.g. 9.5 and C's reading $λόγος$ for $πνεῦμα$ in the other MSS.

[8] For the full Syriac text of *1 Clement* and *2 Clement* in the MS, see R. L. Bensly, *The Epistles of S. Clement to the Corinthians in Syriac. Edited from the Manuscript with Notes* (Cambridge: Cambridge University Press, 1899).

[9] See Lightfoot, *Apostolic Fathers*, 1.135, who refers to the 'unrestrained indulgence in periphrasis and gloss' in the versions of the Clementine letters in S.

[10] The readings of S are clearly at times highly regarded, and followed, by Wengst in his edition of the text (K. Wengst, *Didache (Apostellehre). Barnabasbrief. Zweite Clemensbrief. Schrift an Diognet. Eingeleitet, hg., übertragen und erläutert* (Darmstadt: Wissenschaftliche Buchgesellschaft, 1984)). However, such a high evaluation of S may be difficult to justify: see W. Pratscher, *Der zweite Clemensbrief*, KAV 3 (Göttingen: Vandenhoeck & Ruprecht, 2007), 11 n. 16; also the critical comments about Wengst's edition of the text in Warns, 'Untersuchungen', 11–14.

valuable witness to the text, especially in the section after 12.5 where A is no longer extant: and given the tendency of C at times to have errors, S provides a valuable further possible witness for the original Greek text.[11] According to Lightfoot, the text of S often agrees with A where A and C differ (though also on occasions it agrees with C against A), though it is clearly an independent witness to the text.[12]

The manuscript evidence is thus unanimous (as far as it goes) in linking *2 Clement* closely with *1 Clement* and regarding it, along with *1 Clement*, as a(nother) 'letter' written by Clement of Rome to the Corinthians. As we shall see, these assumptions are probably wrong, but it may be that *2 Clement* only survived because of this assumed connection.

---

[11] See e.g. 14.2; 19.1, for instances where S may preserve the more original form of the text against C.
[12] See Lightfoot, *Apostolic Fathers*, 1.138–9.

2. ATTESTATION

Apart from manuscripts containing the text, *2 Clement* is attested in references to the text by others, either in the form of explicit references to the existence of the text, or in the form of verbal allusions and/or possible quotations of the wording of the text.[1]

2.1 Irenaeus

One very early possible piece of evidence showing knowledge of the text of *2 Clement* may be provided by Irenaeus. In *Haer.* 3.3.3, Irenaeus gives a summary of the teaching he says is to be found in *1 Clement*; and at one point, in describing the attributes of God as one who called Abraham, led his people at the Exodus, spoke with Moses, sent the law and the prophets, Irenaeus adds that God is the one 'who has prepared fire for the devil and his angels' (qui ignem praeparaverit diabolo et angelis eius). Most of what Irenaeus says about God here can be seen to be based on parts of *1 Clement*; however, the reference to a fiery judgement for the devil cannot. It is argued by some that this might be based on material in *2 Clement* which deals with judgement and the threat of fire (cf. 7.6; 16.3; 17.5); hence this passage might provide evidence that Irenaeus knew *2 Clement* and associated it with *1 Clement* so closely that he confused the two.[2]

The allusion is by no means certain. The possible parallels in *2 Clement* to Irenaeus' statement do not explicitly mention the devil and/or his angels as

---

[1] The categories run into each other, so no attempt is made here to subdivide the references into e.g. explicit citations, implicit allusions, explicit statements about the text, etc. They are presented in (roughly) chronological order.

[2] See e.g. C. Taylor, 'The Homily of Pseudo-Clement', *Journal of Philology* 28 (1903), 201–4; C. C. Richardson, *Early Christian Fathers*, LCC 1 (London: SCM, 1953), 184; A. Rousseau, *Irénée de Lyon. Contre les Hérésies. Livre III. Tome I Introduction, Notes justificatives, Tables*, SC 210 (Paris: Cerf, 1974), 237.

the object of the fiery judgement.³ Hence it is not certain that one needs to postulate knowledge of *2 Clement* explicitly to explain Irenaeus' language here: it may be due to stock ideas being reflected. Nevertheless, it remains a possible, and very early, testimony to the contents of *2 Clement* being known (and implicitly associated with *1 Clement*).

2.2 Origen

Another possible early reference to the text of *2 Clement* occurs in Origen: in *Comm. Jo.* 2.34.207 (GCS 4, 92), Origen speaks of the prophets teaching ἃ δεῖ φρονεῖν περὶ τοῦ υἱοῦ τοῦ θεοῦ. It is possible that this alludes to the language of *2 Clem.* 1.1, though the allusion (if that is what it is) is extremely brief and not absolutely clearly a 'citation' of *2 Clement*.⁴

2.3 Eusebius

Probably the earliest explicit reference to a second letter of Clement is found in Eusebius, *Hist. eccl.* 3.38.4:

ἰστέον δ' ὡς καὶ δευτέρα τις εἶναι λέγεται τοῦ Κλήμεντος ἐπιστολή· οὐ μὴν ἔθ' ὁμοίως τῇ προτέρᾳ καὶ ταύτην γνώριμον ἐπιστάμεθα, ὅτι μηδὲ τοὺς ἀρχαίους αὐτῇ κεχρημένους ἴσμεν.

It must be known that there is also a second letter ascribed to Clement, but we have not the same knowledge of its recognition as we have of the former, for we do not even know if the primitive writers used it (ET from LCL edition).

---

³ Unless it is in the very obscure reference to the divine judgement punishing a 'spirit' and loading it with chains in 20.4 (see the commentary). The lack of precise correspondence between Irenaeus and *2 Clement* is stressed by Warns, 'Untersuchungen', 52–5, who argues that Irenaeus' language is to be explained on the basis of material in *1 Clement* and Irenaeus' own ideas and preferences.

⁴ The allusion is taken as 'eindeutig' ('clear') by Warns, 'Untersuchungen', 34; A. Lindemann, *Die Clemensbriefe*, HNT 17 (Tübingen: Mohr Siebeck, 1992), 189, and Pratscher, *Zweite Clemensbrief*, 11, are more circumspect but regard the allusion as possible.

According to a brief remark by Maximus the Confessor (*Proleg. in Op. Dionys.* (PG 4.20)), Origen knew four letters of Clement. See A. von Harnack, *Geschichte der altchristlichen Litteratur bis Eusebius. II: Die Chronologie der altchristlichen Litteratur bis Eusebius. Band 1: Die Chronologie der Litteratur bis Irenaeus* (Leipzig: J. C. Hinrichs'sche Buchhandlung, 1897), 439; Pratscher, *Zweite Clemensbrief*, 11. (This may be a reflection of the attribution to Clement of two letters to virgins, now extant in a later Syriac translation, but possibly going back to the 2nd or 3rd century: on these, see the brief note in Lightfoot, *Apostolic Fathers*, 1.100.)

Another possible allusion to *2 Clement* in the work of Origen occurs in his *Hom. Jer.* 18 (GCS 3, 151), where Origen's language (on the impossibility of re-forming a pot after it has been fired, used as an image for rescue for human beings after death) is similar to that of *2 Clem.* 8.1–2. However, the agreement is not so close as to make a theory of direct use of *2 Clement* by Origen certain. For the texts, see Lindemann, *Clemensbriefe*, 189; Pratscher, *Zweite Clemensbrief*, 12.

Eusebius seems to know of the work only through hearsay and appears to have no direct knowledge of it himself.[5] Clearly then he knows of the existence of a second 'letter' attributed to Clement; whether it is our text is, however, not capable of proof as Eusebius gives no further information about it. Nevertheless, the reference to a 'second' epistle indicates that, *if* our text is in mind, it is regarded as an 'epistle' and is linked with *1 Clement* as from the same author.

2.4 Jerome

The existence of the text is noted by Jerome in his *Vir. Ill.* 15:

Fertur et secunda ex eius [= Clement] nomine epistula, quae a veteribus reprobatur.

There is also a second letter under his [= Clement] name which is rejected by earlier writers.

Jerome may well be dependent on Eusebius for this note.[6] Again it confirms the picture of others knowing of the existence of a 'second letter of Clement', though perhaps not knowing much about its content, and not ascribing 'canonical' status to it. However, the fact that people like Eusebius and Jerome go out of their way to mention it and to reject any possible 'canonical' status suggests that the work might have been regarded highly and/or as 'genuine', perhaps as canonical, by others at the time.[7]

2.5 *Apostolic Canons*

Such a status is reflected in the 85th of the so-called *Apostolic Canons* (*Apos. Con.* 8.47.85, dated probably towards the end of the 4th century), which mentions at the end of the list of 'our books, that is the books of the New Covenant ... two epistles of Clement': ἡμέτερα δὲ [βιβλία] τουτέστι τῆς καινῆς διαθήκης ... Κλήμεντος ἐπιστολαὶ δύο. Evidently here two epistles of Clement are known and accepted as part of the NT canon (as is also probably implied by the inclusion of *2 Clement* with the other NT texts in Codex A).

---

[5] cf. Harnack, *Chronologie*, 439; Wengst, *Zweite Clemensbrief*, 208; Lindemann, *Clemensbriefe*, 189; Pratscher, *Zweite Clemensbrief*, 12, though Eusebius is not quite explicit on this point.

[6] So Lindemann, *Clemensbriefe*, 189; Pratscher, *Zweite Clemensbrief*, 13. Similar in sentiment to Jerome is Rufinus who, in his 'translation' of Eusebius, has 'Dicitur tamen esse et alia Clementis epistola cuius nos notitiam non accepimus'. ('There is said to be another letter of Clement, whose status we do not accept.')

[7] cf. P. Parvis, '*2 Clement* and the Meaning of the Christian Homily', in P. Foster (ed.), *The Writings of the Apostolic Fathers* (London and New York: T. & T. Clark, 2007), 33.

2.6 Florilegium Edessenum

Explicit quotations from the text are rare, but do occur in some later Syriac writers, where especially the opening statement (about regarding Jesus as God) appears to have been particularly congenial for Monophysite writers. Thus the anonymous *Florilegium Edessenum* (perhaps 6th century, sometimes wrongly attributed to Timotheus of Alexandria (*c*.457 CE)),[8] has:

Of the same [= Clement of Rome] from the beginning of the third[9] epistle.
My brethren, thus it behoves us to think concerning Jesus Christ, as concerning God, as concerning the Judge of the living and the dead. And it is not right for us to think small things concerning our salvation; for by thinking small things concerning it, we also expect to receive small things. And when we hear as concerning small things, we sin, in that we do not know from whence we are called, and by whom, and to what place, and all those things which Jesus Christ suffered for our sakes. [= *2 Clem.* 1.1–2].
Of the same

There is one Christ our Lord, who saved us, who was first spirit, became then in the flesh and thus called us [= *2 Clem.* 9.5a].[10]

2.7 Severus of Antioch

The same passage from *2 Clem.* 1.1–2 is also cited in full by Severus of Antioch, *Adv. Johannem Grammaticum* [*c*.513–18 CE):[11]

Of Clement, the third bishop of Rome after the Apostles, from the Second Epistle to the Corinthians,
My brethren, thus is it right for us to think concerning Jesus Christ, as concerning God, as concerning the Judge of the living and the dead, and it is not right for us to think small things concerning our salvation: for if we think small things concerning it, we hope also to receive small things. And when we hear as concerning small things, we sin, because we do not know from whence we are called, and by whom and to what place; and how much Jesus Christ endured to suffer for us [= *2 Clem.* 1.1–2].

---

[8] cf. I. Rucker (ed.), *Florilegium Edessenum anonymum (syriace ante 562)*, SBAW. PH 1933 Heft 5 (Munich: Verlag der Bayerischen Akademie der Wissenschaften, 1933).

[9] The reference to this as the 'third' epistle is strange, but may reflect the tradition attributing two (or perhaps two considered as one) epistles 'to virgins' to Clement. See e.g. A. von Harnack, *Geschichte der altchristlichen Litteratur bis Eusebius. I: Die Überlieferung und der Bestand* (Leipzig: J. C. Hinrichs'sche Buchhandlung, 1893), 48; full discussion in Warns, 'Untersuchungen', 59–60.

[10] Translations from Lightfoot, *Apostolic Fathers*, 1.181–2, taken from W. Cureton, *Corpus Ignatianum: A Complete Collection of the Ignatian Epistles, genuine, interpolated, and spurious, together with numerous extracts from them, as quoted by ecclesiastical writers down to the tenth century* (London: Rivington, 1849), 244. (I have simply changed Cureton's older English forms such as 'behoveth' to 'behoves').

[11] Lightfoot, *Apostolic Fathers*, 1.182–3 (taken from Cureton, *Corpus Ignatianum*, 246).

2.8 *Excerpta Patrum*

Finally, an anonymous collection, again in Syriac, known as the *Excerpta Patrum* (probably *c.*7th century), has the following:[12]

From the Second Epistle to the Corinthians, from which also the holy Patriarch Severus adduces proofs in many of his writings; the beginning of which is:
My brethren, thus it is right for us to think concerning Jesus Christ, as concerning God, as concerning the Judge of the living and the dead [= *2 Clem.* 1.1].

And let no one of you say that this flesh is not judged nor rises again. Know by what you have been saved, and by what you have seen, if it be not when you are in this flesh. Therefore it is right for you that you should keep your flesh as the temple of God. For as you were called when you were in the flesh, so also in this flesh shall you come. If it be that Christ our Lord, who saved us, who at first indeed was spirit, became flesh, and thus called you; so that we also in the same flesh receive the reward (= *2 Clem.* 9.1–5).[13]

2.9 Photius

Much later (9th century), Photius, the learned Patriarch of Constantinople, *Bibliotheca* c. 126, wrote about *2 Clement*:

ἡ δὲ δευτέρα καὶ αὐτὴ νουθεσίαν καὶ παραίνεσιν κρείττονος εἰσάγει βίου, καὶ ἐν ἀρχῇ θεὸν τὸν Χριστὸν κηρύσσει, πλὴν ὅτι ῥητά τινα ὡς ἀπὸ τῆς θείας γραφῆς ξενίζοντα παρεισάγει· ὧν οὐδ' ἡ πρώτη ἀπήλλακτο παντελῶς. καὶ ἑρμηνείας δὲ ῥητῶν τινων ἀλλοκότους ἔχει. ἄλλως δέ τε καὶ τὰ ἐν αὐταῖς νοήματα ἐρριμμένα πως καὶ οὐ συνεχῆ τὴν ἀκολουθίαν ὑπῆρχε φυλάττοντα.

The second letter contains advice and exhortation to a better life, and at the beginning proclaims Christ as God; however, it also contains some strange expressions as if from Holy Scripture, from which even the first letter is not altogether free. Certain passages are strangely interpreted. The ideas in it are somewhat poor and the sequence [of thought?] is not kept.[14]

Photius clearly seems to know the contents of the text, including both its opening (apparently) high Christological claim and also the way in which it introduces some sayings as apparently scriptural even though they are not

---

[12] Lightfoot, *Apostolic Fathers*, 1.184–5. (I have, however, changed the 'ye' to 'you' throughout.)

[13] The same extracts (from *2 Clem.* 1 and 9) are also found in three further Syriac texts containing extracts from the 8th to 10th century: see Lightfoot, *Apostolic Fathers*, 1.185–6. The combination of precisely the same texts in such an array of evidence suggests a common tradition: see Stegemann, 'Herkunft', 57.

[14] ET partly my own, partly based on J. H. Freede, *The Library of Photius*, vol. I (London: SPCK, 1920), 213.

contained in the (then) canon of the OT or the NT; but he also clearly has a relatively low opinion about its theological value and merit.[15]

The text of 2 Clement was thus not widely known (or at least mentioned) in the early centuries of the Christian church and was variously regarded: evidently highly respected and even 'canonical' for some, it was rejected as 'not used by the ancients' by others.[16] The external evidence suggests that a 'second' letter purporting to be by Clement was known as early as Eusebius: by then it was evidently taken to be a 'letter', and it was linked closely with the other ('first') letter of Clement. The existence of the text, and its (implied) association with 1 Clement, may be attested earlier still by Irenaeus. The first explicit reference to the letter being addressed 'to the Corinthians' does not come until Severus of Antioch in the early 6th century. (On the other hand, such an address may be implicit in the close link assumed with 1 Clement, which in turn is taken as a letter to the Corinthians without question.)

---

[15] I omit here two other possible allusions to the text of 2 Clement which have been claimed in earlier scholarship: some words of Hippolytus (from fragments of his Contra gentes de universo, recorded in the Sacra Parallela, a later collection attributed to John of Damascus) may echo 2 Clem. 17.5; 19.3–4 (see e.g. Lightfoot, Apostolic Fathers, 2.258–9), though the parallel is not exact enough to be certain that Hippolytus knew the text (see e.g. Warns, 'Untersuchungen', 52; Pratscher, Zweite Clemensbrief, 12). Also some words of (Pseudo-)Justin (Resp. ad orthodox. 74) have been seen as similar to those of 2 Clem. 17.5–6 (see the detailed discussion in Lightfoot, Apostolic Fathers, 1.178–80; also Stegemann, 'Herkunft', 53–4; Pratscher, Zweite Clemensbrief, 13); in a way similar to the evidence from Irenaeus noted above, the writer includes this in a summary of what he claims is found in the work of 1 Clement. However, as with Irenaeus, the parallel is perhaps not precise enough to indicate clearly knowledge of the text of 2 Clement.

One further possible instance has been the recent suggestion that the author of the Nag Hammadi text Interpretation of Knowledge (NHC XI.1) knew 2 Clement. This is explicitly claimed by U.-W. Plisch, 'Die Auslegung der Erkenntnis (NHC XI,1)', in H.-M. Schenke, H.-G. Bethge, and U. U. Kaiser (eds), Nag Hammadi Deutsch 2. Band: NHC V,2 – XIII,1, BG 1 und 4, GCS N.F. 12 (Berlin: De Gruyter, 2003), 736. The possibility might provide important evidence of knowledge—and use—of 2 Clement in an Egyptian milieu at an early date. (Though one must not forget that, while the present Coptic manuscript of Int. Know. clearly comes from Egypt, we do not know the precise origin of the (presumed Greek) Vorlage, or 'original', lying behind the extant Coptic version.)

However, Plisch gives no reason or justification there for his claim. In his earlier edition of the text (U.-W. Plisch, Die Auslegung der Erkenntnis (Nag-Hammadi-Codex XI,1), TU 142 (Berlin: Akademie, 1996), 106–7), he notes the similarity between the allusions/citations of NT gospel materials in Int. Know. 9.31–3 and 2 Clem. 9.11 (cf. Matt. 12.50), and Int. Know. 9.33–5 and 2 Clem. 6.2 (cf. Mark 8.36//). But whether these alone are enough to establish a direct literary relationship between the texts must remain very doubtful. In both instances, the text of Int. Know. is in fact rather closer to the parallels in Clement of Alexandria. (See the commentary here; also W.-P. Funk, L. Painchaud, and E. Thomassen, L'Jnterprétation de la Gnose (NH XI,1), BCNH Textes 34 (Louvain: Peeters, 2010), 127–9.)

[16] On the other hand, the attestation for the text seems wider than just Syriac witnesses (as argued by Stegemann, 'Herkunft', who then uses this to argue for Syria as the place of origin of the text: on this, see below §8.1 Place of Writing).

However, despite this external evidence, many of the presumptions here are now widely questioned. For example, the text is widely agreed not to have been originally a 'letter' (see §4. Genre below), nor is it written by the same author as *1 Clement* (see §3. Authorship below). In general terms, the relatively low level of (explicit) interest shown in the text by patristic writers matches the relatively low amount of extant manuscript evidence for the text.

3. AUTHORSHIP

The issue of the authorship of *2 Clement* is probably impossible to resolve in any positive way. Traditionally, the work was ascribed to Clement of Rome and regarded as Clement's second work alongside the text known as *1 Clement*. The manuscript tradition seems to imply this clearly by linking the two texts together and calling *2 Clement* the 'second' (letter) of Clement to the Corinthians; and other references (such as they are) from antiquity about the text either positively support this or at least do not question it (see §1. Manuscripts and §2. Attestation above).

It is almost universally agreed today that this ascription cannot be right. Any connection between *1 Clement* and *2 Clement* is tenuous and ephemeral. The style and outlook of the two texts are quite different. They share one or two intriguing features, the most notable of which is the citation from an otherwise unknown source of the extended saying in *1 Clem.* 23.3–4//*2 Clem.* 11.2–4. There are also a few linguistic common features between the language of *2 Clem.* 19–20 and *1 Clement* (on which see below); and one or two other tiny details can be highlighted as common to the two texts. But generally the two writings are quite different and almost certainly stem from different authors. For example, the author of *1 Clement* is heavily dependent on Paul and makes very little use of Jesus traditions; the author of *2 Clement* shows little if any evidence of knowing Paul but makes extensive use of a range of Jesus traditions. No one today would wish to maintain that *2 Clement* is to be attributed to the same person who wrote *1 Clement*.[1]

During the early years of scholarship on *2 Clement* (i.e. in the late 19th and early 20th centuries) it was quite popular to speculate about the identity of the author of *2 Clement*, with various suggestions linking the text with names of obscure figures about whom very little is otherwise known. In his early

---

[1] Nevertheless, the connection between *2 Clement* and *1 Clement* remains an intriguing puzzle. For further discussion of the possible nature of the connection, see pp. 16, 29–30 (on the theories of Donfried and Stegemann), and also §8.1 Place of Writing below.

studies of the text, Harnack suggested that the author was the 'Clement' mentioned in Herm. *Vis.* 2.4.3, a figure in the Roman church apparently responsible for sending literature out to others: the common name 'Clement' may then have led to the text being associated with *1 Clement*.² Later, he changed his mind and adopted a suggestion (originally proposed by Hilgenfeld) that the author was the Roman bishop Soter (*c.*165–75 CE) mentioned in Eusebius, *Hist. eccl.* 4.23.9–11: here Eusebius records a letter from Dionysius of Corinth, apparently referring to a communication from bishop Soter, alongside a reference to the letter *1 Clement*. The association of Soter's letter with *1 Clement* may then explain the close association subsequently in the tradition linking *1 Clement* with *2 Clement*.³ The suggestion is a bold one, but impossible to prove and in any case may imply a somewhat uncomfortably late date for *2 Clement*. Moreover, the association of the text with Rome which the theory implies may also be problematic (see below §8.1 Place of Writing).

In the early 20th century, Harris made a different suggestion.⁴ He noted the citation in *2 Clem.* 12 of a tradition also used by the (Gnostic) encratite writer Julius Cassianus (according to Clement of Alexandria). Furthermore, Cassianus is said to have written a book entitled Περὶ ἐγκρατείας. Referring to the words of *2 Clem.* 15.1, where the writer says that he has 'given no small piece of advice περὶ ἐγκρατείας', Harris suggested that *2 Clement* itself might be precisely this (otherwise lost) work of Julius Cassianus. The theory has failed to convince others. In particular, the theory encounters difficulties in that the writer does not appear to be Gnostic, or even encratite;⁵ further, the theme of 'self-control' (ἐγκρατεία), although not unimportant in *2 Clement*, is not the main theme of the text as a whole: hence it is hard to see how the whole of *2 Clement* could be described as a text 'about self-control'.⁶

Without necessarily seeking to identify the author with an individual named elsewhere in the Christian tradition, Donfried proposes a fairly

---

² A. von Harnack, 'Über den sogenannten zweiten Brief des Clemens an die Korinther', *ZKG* 1 (1873), 363–4.

³ See Harnack, *Chronologie*, 438–50; A. von Harnack, 'Zum Ursprung des sog. 2. Clemensbriefs', *ZNW* 6 (1905), 67–71. See earlier A. Hilgenfeld, *Clementis Romanae Epistulae. Edidit, commentario critico et adnotationibus instruxit.* (Lipsiae: T. O. Weigel, 1876), xlv–xlvi; Harnack's suggestion is accepted by others such as Lake, in his LCL edition of Eusebius, 383; cf. too E. J. Goodspeed, *The Apostolic Fathers* (New York: Harper, 1950), 83.

⁴ J. R. Harris, 'The Authorship of the so-called Second Epistle of Clement', *ZNW* 23 (1924), 193–200.

⁵ See detailed discussion in the commentary at relevant points, especially on the citation in ch. 12: here it is likely that the author of *2 Clement* interprets the citation very differently from the way it is used by Julius Cassianus (according to Clement). See also §9.7 Ethics below and the question of how 'encratite' the author of *2 Clement* really is.

⁶ See the detailed critique of Harris by H. Windisch, 'Julius Cassianus und die Clemenshomilie (II Clemens)', *ZNW* 25 (1926), 258–62.

specific theory about the authorship of *2 Clement*, and with it a theory about the place and circumstances of its origins.⁷ Donfried postulates a setting for the letter very close in time to *1 Clement*. The latter was sent by the Roman authorities to the church in Corinth to seek to quell some kind of 'rebellion' by some in the Corinthian community which resulted in removing the presbyters there from office. The letter, according to Donfried, was successful and *2 Clement* reflects this situation after *1 Clement* had been read, fully accepted, and taken on board. *2 Clement* then represents an address by one of the elders who might have been ousted by the earlier rebellion but has been reinstated. Donfried seeks to provide support for his theory by arguing that the language used in 7.1 (in particular the use of καταπλέω) makes best sense if the text were written in Corinth.

The theory is ingenious, but lacks any clear support in the text itself. The evidence of the language of 'sailing' in ch. 7 is ambiguous and does not clearly indicate a Corinthian provenance (see the commentary, and §8.1 Place of Writing below). That both texts reflect some kind of situation of divisions within the community addressed is undeniable; but whether it is exactly the same situation which is presupposed is not at all clear. The 'opponents' who seem to be reflected in *2 Clement* pose a particular problem of identification (see §7. Opponents below); but any possible profile which emerges of them only correlates with the possible 'opponents' in *1 Clement* at a high level of generality; conversely, the theme of 'jealousy' and envy which dominates much of *1 Clement* is not a strong theme in *2 Clement*.

Donfried seeks to identify a more substantial literary connection between the language of *2 Clem.* 19.1 (where the author says he is reading an ἔντευξις, so that they may pay heed to 'what is written' (τοῖς γεγραμμένοις)) and *1 Clem.* 63.2 (where the writer seems to refer to his whole work as an ἔντευξις, exhorting the audience to pay heed to 'what has been written by us' (τοῖς ὑφ' ἡμῶν γεγραμμένοις)). However, the connection is at best tenuous. The reference to what is 'written' is not quite the same in the two texts: in *1 Clement* it is explicitly things written 'by us', a clear reference to the rest of *1 Clement*; in *2 Clement* τοῖς γεγραμμένοις is used absolutely: as such it may refer to words of scripture, or perhaps to the words written in *2 Clement* itself (see the commentary below); however, Donfried claims that the reference is to the words of *1 Clement*, and this seems rather forced.⁸ The common use of ἔντευξις may be no more than coincidental: each writer claims he is making a 'plea' to this audience. There are some points of contact between 19.1, and the small section in 19.1–20.4, and *1 Clement*, and these are connected with the issue of the literary unity of the present text of *2 Clement*, in particular whether 19.1–20.4 represents a later addition to the text (see §5. Literary

---

⁷ See Donfried, *Setting*, 1–15, and especially 1–2 where he outlines the gist of this proposal.
⁸ Donfried, *Setting*, 14.

Unity below). But there is very little to connect the substance of most of the rest of *2 Clement* with *1 Clement*. Overall, Donfried's suggestions about the original setting, and the implications for authorship, of *2 Clement* fail to convince.[9]

Probably the search for an individual named elsewhere in the tradition as the author of *2 Clement* is a vain one. Equally, any attempt to link the text with a very precise situation attested elsewhere (e.g. the context of the writing of *1 Clement*) is very difficult.[10] The text itself gives little if any indication of the author's identity. He does refer to himself[11] specifically on a couple of occasions (cf. 15.1; 18.2).[12] He *may* include himself among the 'presbyters' (cf. 17.3), but this is not certain. His style is generally not to speak/write 'at' his readers/hearers, but to associate himself with them: hence first-person plurals (rather than second-person plurals) predominate. And the language of e.g. 1.6 and 3.1, which refers to the past of both the writer and his audience as characterized by worshipping other idols and sacrificing to 'dead gods', is language typical of (Jews and) Christians talking about Gentiles. It therefore suggests that the author was not a Jew before becoming a Christian. But that is about as far as the text allows us to go. For the rest, the author must remain anonymous, a reflection perhaps of his somewhat self-effacing modesty!

---

[9] For critiques of Donfried's theory, see too T. Aono, *Die Entwicklung des paulinischen Gerichtsgedankens bei den Apostolischen Vätern* (Bern: Peter Lang, 1979), 156; Wengst, *Zweite Clemensbrief*, 213–14; Warns, 'Untersuchungen', 25–9; Pratscher, *Zweite Clemensbrief*, 60. Donfried's suggestion of links between *2 Clem.* 19.1 and *1 Clement* is similar (at one level) to part of the theory of Stegemann, 'Herkunft', who argues that the section *2 Clem.* 19.1–20.4 has significant links with *1 Clement*; and this is then used to develop an overall theory about the original occasion for the writing of both *2 Clem.* 1–18 and *2 Clem.* 19–20. On this, see §5. Literary Unity below.

[10] See further §8. Place and Date of Writing below for discussion of the possible geographical and chronological location of the author.

[11] The general social conditions of the time make it likely that the author was male; hence I use the masculine pronoun to refer to him.

[12] Possibly also 19.1 if this is the same author as the rest of the text.

4. GENRE

Determining the genre of *2 Clement* is by no means an easy task. 'Form' (or genre) and content are closely related, so that any attempt to classify the genre of the present text is closely related to a broader understanding of its contents, both in general terms and in relation to specific details.

4.1 *2 Clement* as 'letter'?

Insofar as *2 Clement* is given any kind of 'description' by others in the earliest tradition, it is uniformly referred to as a 'letter'. This is already the case in Eusebius, who evidently knew of the text as the second 'letter' of Clement; so too Jerome and Rufinus agree in this description. In the manuscript tradition, the text in codex A is listed in the (admittedly probably later) list of contents as the 'second letter' of Clement (although the text in the manuscript itself gives no such evidence);[1] and this is supported by C and S (in the title of the work in C, and in the title and colophon in S). Thus the tradition in the early (and later) church presumes that the text is to be classified as a 'letter' with no dissenting voices.

It is, however, almost universally agreed that this description is not appropriate for the text we have.[2] The extant text lacks almost all of the features one would expect to find in any 'letter'. Thus there are no personal greetings at the start or at the end of the text; there is no reference to the personal circumstances of the author, no reference to the identity of the immediate recipients of the text, nothing equivalent to any kind of 'standard'

---

[1] See §1. Manuscripts above. There is no superscription to the text; and the text breaks off mid-way, so that the end (where one would expect, on the basis of the other texts in the codex, to find a colophon with the 'title' for the work) is not extant.

[2] See e.g. Ph. Vielhauer, *Geschichte der urchristlichen Literatur. Einleitung in das Neue Testament, die Apokryphen und die Apostolischen Väter* (Berlin and New York: De Gruyter, 1975), 739; Donfried, *Setting*, 19–25; Wengst, *Zweite Clemensbrief*, 210; E. Baasland, 'Der 2. Klemensbrief und frühchristliche Rhetorik: "Die erste christliche Predigt" im Lichte der neueren Forschung', *ANRW* 2.27.1 (1993), 97–9; Lindemann, *Clemensbriefe*, 190; Pratscher, *Zweite Clemensbrief*, 25.

4. Genre

opening of a letter at the start.³ Further, Donfried has emphasized the importance of the twin themes of absence and presence: an essential feature of letters in the ancient world is that they are sent in a context of physical absence in order to provide a substitute for the presence ($\pi\alpha\rho\text{ou}\sigma\acute{\iota}\alpha$) of the sender with the recipient(s).⁴ Of this there is no hint in *2 Clement*: indeed, if 19.1 is taken as part of the 'original' text, then it implies that the author is present with the recipients and actively *reading* the text in their hearing. The text is thus not any substitute for an absent author, but is the text being addressed to the hearers directly in the physical presence of the author. In short, there is nothing to indicate that the letter is in any sense a 'letter'.⁵

4.2 *2 Clement* as 'sermon'?

The evidence of passages such as 15.2; 17.3; 19.1, suggesting that the text is being 'read' (presumably out loud) and 'heard' directly by the recipients, has led to the very widely held view that the text should be seen in some sense as a 'sermon', an address given in the course of a gathering of Christians together for worship;⁶ and indeed is often referred to as the oldest extant example of a Christian sermon.⁷ On the other hand, it may be that some caution is required. The latter point implicitly highlights the difficulty (or usefulness) of labelling *2 Clement* a 'sermon': for if it is indeed the earliest such (Christian)

---

³ i.e. the equivalent of 'Dear . . .' at the start of a contemporary letter. The Greek equivalent might be a simple $\chi\alpha\iota\rho\epsilon\tilde{\iota}\nu$, or (in the case of Pauline letters and others produced in imitation in early Christianity) a more flowery 'Grace to you and peace from our Lord Jesus Christ . . .' (or equivalent), followed perhaps by a thanksgiving. Of this there is nothing in *2 Clement*.

⁴ See Donfried, *Setting*, 22–3, referring to the study of H. Koskenniemi, *Studien zur Idee und Phraseologie des griechischen Briefes bis 400 n. Chr.* (Helsinki, 1956).

⁵ Even if the status of 19.1 might be debatable (see §5 below on the Literary Unity of the text), 15.2 (and perhaps 17.3) imply the same: the text is being read out as an address to people who are 'hearing' (15.2) what is said. The text of *2 Clement* does not appear to be any kind of substitute for physical absence. This in turn tells against Harnack's theory that the present text of *2 Clement* is perhaps a 'sermon' (in some sense) of bishop Soter, subsequently sent to Corinth with a letter and to be read there. (See §3. Authorship above.) Undoubtedly, the very fact of the preservation (and presumably reuse) of the text of *2 Clement* in written form implies that it may well have been re-read in new contexts where the original author was no longer present. But subsequent practice and use of a text is not the same as its original purpose (and hence, to a certain extent, its genre).

⁶ So e.g. Harnack, *Überlieferung*, 47; Lightfoot, *Apostolic Fathers*, 2.194; R. Knopf, *Die Lehre der zwölf Apostel. Die zwei Clemensbriefe.* (Tübingen: J. C. B. Mohr, 1920), 151; Richardson, *Fathers*, 183; R. M. Grant and H. H. Graham, *The Apostolic Fathers: A New Translation and Commentary*, vol. 2: *First and Second Clement* (New York: Thomas Nelson & Sons, 1965), 109; Wengst, *Zweite Clemensbrief*, 214 ('Mahnrede'); Baasland, '2.Klemensbrief', 99–107 (though recognizing the need for further precision); Lindemann, *Clemensbriefe*, 190; Pratscher, *Zweite Clemensbrief*, 25–6, and many others.

⁷ So Knopf, *Zwei Clemensbriefe*, 151; Richardson, *Fathers*, 183; W. Pratscher, 'Der zweite Clemensbrief', *Die Apostolischen Väter* (Göttingen: Vandenhoeck & Ruprecht, 2009), 83; cf. too Parvis, '*2 Clement*', 34, and many others.

'sermon' we possess, it is potentially without analogy (at least in its relative past and its contemporary present) and hence such a generic description may not tell us very much. Equally, for us, the lack of comparative material may make it difficult to assess the claim that the text is indeed some kind of 'sermon'.[8]

Part of the problem also arises from the fact that the word 'sermon' is potentially very broad, covering a range of different possibilities.[9] A 'sermon' might be a rather different entity depending on its audience: a sermon to a group of already established Christians is probably different from a sermon to catechumens or those preparing to be baptized.[10] So too a sermon might be a fairly general address on a range of possible issues; others might think of a sermon as specifically based on an authoritative text (probably of 'scripture'), so that the sermon involves the explicit interpretation and application of a specific text. Some have then used the term 'homily' for an address that is a close exposition of a (biblical) text, implicitly distinguishing this from a more general 'sermon'.[11]

---

[8] The methodological difficulties are highlighted by Stegemann, 'Herkunft', 29, 108–17. She points out that the only sermon we have from anywhere near the time of 2 Clement is Melito's Paschal Homily (if it is indeed a genuine homily). In other instances, a 'preaching style', or fragments of a sermon, have been postulated; and there are references to preaching activity (e.g. 1 Cor. 2.1–5); but if a sermon is a real address to a real community, it is inevitable that the records of such addresses have not generally survived in verbatim reports.

[9] cf. more negatively Donfried, Setting, 26: 'To define 2 Clement as a "sermon" is not helpful since we know virtually nothing about the contours of such a genre in the first century A.D.' (Though 2 Clement is probably from the 2nd century!)

[10] Reference is often made also to missionary 'preaching', addressing outsiders and seeking to 'convert' them to the Christian faith; such might be yet another kind of preaching activity and 'sermon'. On the other hand, such a direct appeal to non-Christians would be unlikely to take place within the context of a Christian gathering for worship, and hence such 'preaching' might not qualify for the term 'sermon' in the definition suggested above (at n. 6).

[11] See e.g. Baasland, '2.Klemensbrief', 100; Pratscher, Zweite Clemensbrief, 25: 'eine Homilie im altkirchlichen Sinn, d.h. eine Vers für Vers vorgehende Predigt über einen Text' ('a homily in the sense of the early church, i.e. a sermon going verse by verse through a text'. The distinction is perhaps more relevant in German than in English: in (some) English, a 'homily' might be distinguished from a 'sermon' simply by being shorter and less formalized). But equally negatively as in relation to 'sermon', cf. Donfried, Setting, 26: 'the term "homily" is so vague and ambiguous that it should be withdrawn until its literarily generic legitimacy has been demonstrated'. Certainly the Greek word ὁμιλία can be used in a very wide-ranging way. However, the 'definition' proposed above may go some way to making talk about a 'homily' in the present context at least intelligible. Some have used the two words as virtually synonyms (cf. e.g. Lightfoot, Apostolic Fathers, 2.194 ('the work is plainly not a letter, but a homily, a sermon'); Lindemann, Clemensbriefe, 190 (who refers to the text as a 'Homilie' and 'Predigt' alternately); others cited in Baasland, '2.Klemensbrief', 100 n. 165). Stegemann takes a homily (or sermon: she does not distinguish between the two) as the exposition of a biblical text, mostly on the basis of other Christian examples of 'preaching'; hence she excludes 2 Clement from this category. But her prime examples of other 'sermons' and/or preaching are from rather later in Christian history (Origen, John Chrysostom, Augustine) and this may not be helpful for illuminating the situation at the time of 2 Clement.

4. Genre

In relation to early Christian preaching and/or 'sermons', reference is frequently made to Justin's description of early Christian worship gatherings in *1 Apol.* 67:

καὶ τῇ τοῦ ἡλίου λεγομένῃ ἡμέρᾳ πάντων κατὰ πόλεις ἢ ἀγροὺς μενόντων ἐπὶ τὸ αὐτὸ συνέλευσις γίνεται καὶ τὰ ἀπομνημονεύματα τῶν ἀποστόλων ἢ τὰ συγγράμματα τῶν προφητῶν ἀναγινώσκεται, μέχρις ἐγχωρεῖ· εἶτα, παυσαμένου τοῦ ἀναγινώσκοντος, ὁ προεστὼς διὰ λόγου τὴν νουθεσίαν καὶ πρόκλησιν τῆς τῶν καλῶν τούτων μιμήσεως ποιεῖται

And on the day called Sunday, all who live in cities and in the country gather together to one place, and the memoirs of the apostles or the writings of the prophets are read, as long as time permits; then, when the reader has ceased, the president verbally instructs, and exhorts to the imitation of these good things.

Many have deduced from this (relatively) brief description of Justin's that Christian worship assemblies typically took the form of 'scriptural' readings (from Jewish scriptures ('the prophets'), as well as perhaps from Christian texts ('the memoirs of the apostles') starting to gain the same status), which were then expounded in a fairly detailed way in some kind of 'sermon' (or, in the above sense, a 'homily') by a preacher.

Whether *2 Clement* can fit this model and/or pattern precisely is, however, probably doubtful. Many have interpreted the language of 19.1 and the cryptic phrase there 'after the God of truth' as a reference to a reading of scripture which immediately preceded the reading of the text of *2 Clement* itself (see the commentary). As such this would fit the pattern as outlined by Justin.[12] However, it is difficult if not impossible to try to determine what the scriptural texts preceding the reading of *2 Clement* might have been; and it is equally hard to see *2 Clement* as a detailed exposition of a specific scriptural text.[13] It is thus widely agreed that *2 Clement* is not a 'homily' in the sense of

---

[12] Though equally perhaps the evidence of Justin is part of the argument for interpreting the highly cryptic phrase in *2 Clem.* 19 in this way!

[13] The most sustained attempt to explain *2 Clement* in this way is that of R. Knopf, 'Die Anagnose zum zweiten Clemensbriefe', *ZNW* 3 (1902), 266–79. Knopf argued that the preceding scriptural reading was the text of Isa. 54–66, *2 Clement* then being a sermon based on this text. Part of the argument for this was based on the fact that what appears to be a clear citation of Isa. 54.1 appears in 2.1 (the text is then expounded in great detail, phrase by phrase), but with no introductory formula indicating that it is a citation: hence, Knopf argued, the writer could presume this as already known, perhaps because the audience had just heard the text read as part of the preceding scriptural reading. Knopf also appealed to the fact that a number of the other citations elsewhere in *2 Clement* come from Isa. 54–66; moreover, these citations are characterized by being relatively 'accurate', agreeing closely with the text of the LXX. Hence Knopf argued that the preceding scriptural text read just before the reading of the sermon which is *2 Clement* was this section of chapters from Isaiah.

The theory is ingenious but has failed to convince others. The appeal to alleged 'accuracy' in citation is unconvincing: we simply do not know precisely what the text form of the Jewish

being a sustained exposition of a scriptural text.[14] (Hence any attempt to identify a possible scriptural text which might have been read just before in a liturgical gathering is probably doomed to failure.) This is of course not to deny the obvious fact that scripture (however delimited) is clearly important for the author, as witnessed by the frequent citations employed. However, for the most part, the citations serve (simply) to back up and buttress the argument: they do not provide the basis for, or generate, the argument itself.[15] *2 Clement* may then be a 'sermon', but it is not a 'homily' in the stricter sense of being a sermon in the form of detailed interpretation of a specific scriptural text.

As far as its audience is concerned, it would seem that it is addressed to a group of people who have already become Christians. Non-Christians are referred to in 13.3–4, but clearly as a group of people to whom the addressees do not belong: the 'heathen' are a group of 'them' clearly distinct from 'us'. *2 Clement* is thus in no sense an example of 'missionary preaching', addressing non-believers directly.[16] So too, some parts of the text of *2 Clement* look back and refer to the 'salvation' of the audience as something that is past

---

scriptures available to the writer was, and, given the variety in the text forms of Jewish scriptural texts in antiquity (highlighted now by evidence from Qumran), it would be dangerous to assume that the author must have known 'the' LXX text alone (and hence agreements with this imply accurate quotation, and disagreements imply inaccurate quotation). In any case, 'the' LXX text is probably a modern construct as much as anything else! There are too some practical considerations affecting Knopf's theory: he himself said that the reading of Isa. 54–66 would take about an hour. But then the claim that the hearers would remember the text when it was referred to again (in reading *2 Clem.* 2.1) strains the presumed power of audience memory quite considerably (cf. W. Schüssler, 'Ist der zweite Klemensbrief ein einheitliches Ganzes?' *ZKG* 28 (1907), 11). In any case the number of citations of, or allusions to, Isa. 54–66 in *2 Clement* is not that large (in fact only 4 or 5: 2.1 = Isa. 54.1; 7.6 = Isa. 66.24; 15.3 = Isa. 58.9; 17.4 = Isa. 66.18; 17.5 = Isa. 66.24 (though not an explicit citation): cf. Schüssler, ibid.). Further, despite the detailed exposition of the one verse Isa. 54.1 in ch. 2, it cannot be said that the rest of the text of *2 Clement* represents a detailed exposition of the Isaianic text (and even the other citations from these chapters are not treated in as much detail as Isa. 54.1 in 2.1–3).

Schüssler, 'Zweite Klemensbrief', 12–13, suggested instead a text such as 1 Tim. 3.16 as the possible 'base text' for the sermon: he referred to Pliny's description of Christian gatherings as involving singing hymns to Christ 'as to a god', and claimed that perhaps a text such as 1 Tim. 3.16 might then have been used in this context. But there is virtually nothing in *2 Clement* as it now stands that relates directly to this verse; and in any case, the issue of Christology as such is scarcely the main point developed in the text as we now have it (see below on 1.1).

[14] See Baasland, '2.Klemensbrief', 101–2; J. C. Salzmann, *Lehren und Ermahnen, Zur Geschichte des urchristlichen Wortgottesdienstes in den ersten drei Jahrhunderten*, WUNT 2.59 (Tübingen: Mohr Siebeck, 1994), 229; Pratscher, *Zweite Clemensbrief*, 25.

[15] See Salzmann, *Lehren*, 229: 'der Bewegung geht also von der Predigt zum Text und nicht vom Text zur Predigt' ('the movement is from the sermon to the text, not from the text to the sermon'); similarly Stegemann, 'Herkunft', 114. See too §6. Citations below.

[16] This of course does not exclude the fact that the author is sensitive to the needs and/or fate of outsiders, as 13.3–4 makes clear; but such people are not the immediate addressees of what is said.

(cf. 1.4; 2.7; 3.3; 9.7).¹⁷ This suggests that the author is not addressing catechumens, or those preparing say for baptism.¹⁸ Rather it is addressed to those who are already Christians, but whose final destiny is (according to the writer) in doubt because of their possible ethical behaviour. In this sense, therefore, a *Sitz im Leben* of an address in the context of a group of Christians gathered for some kind of liturgical worship (hence some kind of a 'sermon') fits the evidence reasonably well. But any more details about the precise shape or pattern of that worship, and/or the way in which this 'sermon' might fit with other parts of that pattern (or 'liturgy') are probably beyond the scope of the evidence provided by the text of *2 Clement* itself.

4.3 Self-references

At a few points, the author refers to his own work, though whether this will tell us anything further on the question of the genre of the work as a whole is not clear. Thus in 15.1, the author says that he 'does not think that [he] has given a small συμβουλία about self-control (περὶ ἐγκρατείας)'. Some have sought to interpret this as some kind of generic description of the work as a whole, interpreting then the whole as a συμβουλία.¹⁹ Whether this is appropriate as an interpretation of the text may be somewhat doubtful. As noted earlier in another context, it is unlikely that the text as a whole can (or should) be seen as 'about self-control'.²⁰ Hence it seems inappropriate to interpret the reference here as a description of the whole text, as opposed to being (simply) a comment about part of the argument. Thus the word συμβουλία probably has its more usual meaning of referring (just) to some 'advice' contained in the address,²¹ rather than being a generic description of the work as a whole.²²

This is not to deny that *2 Clement* is in some sense 'symbouleutical'. In Aristotle's famous threefold division of types of rhetoric, one can distinguish: deliberative (συμβουλευτικόν), forensic, and epideictic.²³ The argument of *2 Clement* cannot easily be described as 'forensic' (attacking or defending

---

[17] As will be noted many times, the writer's language of 'salvation' is ambiguous, sometimes referring to it as past, sometimes future. But one cannot deny that, in some sense, he is looking *back* to a saving event by God/Christ that has already happened for his readers/hearers.

[18] *Contra* e.g. A. Stewart-Sykes, *From Prophecy to Preaching: A Search for the Origin of the Christian Homily*, VCSup 59 (Leiden: Brill, 2001), 176, 183–4. See e.g. Pratscher, *Zweite Clemensbrief*, 26.

[19] cf. Donfried, *Setting*, 34–6; Warns, 'Untersuchungen', 65.

[20] See §3. Authorship above, and the theory of Harris that the author was Julius Cassianus, with *2 Clement* as his work Περὶ ἐγκρατείας. A significant problem with the theory is that the text as a whole is *not* primarily about 'self-control' as such (though this is one important part of the discussion). Hence it is hard to see the phrase in 15.1 as a (generic) description of the text of *2 Clement* as a whole.

[21] cf. BAG, 785; also LSJ, 1677.

[22] cf. Baasland, '2.Klemensbrief', 104.

[23] Aristotle, *Rhet.* I.3.1 ff. = 1358a.

someone in relation to the past) or 'epideictic' (praising or censuring in relation to the present), and hence is most appropriately seen as 'deliberative' (advising in relation to the future).²⁴ *2 Clement* thus fits quite neatly into Aristotle's general category of deliberative rhetoric, seeking to advise, warn, exhort, etc., since it is clearly concerned with warnings about eschatological judgement if Christians fail to live out their faith in practice.²⁵ However, while this may be a valid categorization of the text in general terms, it is not certain if it adds to our understanding of the text;²⁶ and the term συμβουλία itself may be only a reference to *some* of the 'advice' the author claims to be giving.

The same probably applies to the use of the word ἔντευξις in 19.1. The situation is slightly more complex here, given the uncertain issue of the authorship of this section (see §5. Literary Unity below). But whoever the author of 19.1 itself is, the rest of the text of *2 Clement* is being summarized as an ἔντευξις. However, it is again uncertain whether this is a *generic* description of the text as a whole, or, as with 15.1, simply a general reference to the fact that chs 1–18 are making an 'appeal' to the readers/hearers.²⁷ The word is indeed used in *1 Clem.* 63.2, also in a summarizing way to refer (in some sense) to the whole of the preceding text; but of itself, the word need have no further connotation than describing the text as a whole as an 'appeal' to those who hear it to take what is said to heart.

4.4 *2 Clement* as 'paraenesis'?

One further category possibly relating to the question of the 'genre' of *2 Clement* is that of 'paraenesis'. The precise nature of what should (or should not) be called 'paraenesis' has been hotly debated in recent scholarship.²⁸ It is widely (though not universally!) agreed that 'paraenesis' is perhaps not a generic category in the sense of a literary genre. Nevertheless, it can be usefully employed as an overarching description referring to a distinctive range of exhortatory materials, especially in early Christian texts.

---

[24] See Donfried, *Setting*, 35–6; Warns, 'Untersuchungen', 64–76; Baasland, '2.Klemensbrief', 103.

[25] It is also future-related in the more mundane sense in that it seeks to influence behaviour that is to come in the future, rather than (primarily) dwelling on behaviour in the past. However, see Baasland, '2.Klemensbrief', 104 n. 191, for a warning against making Aristotle's divisions too rigid or schematic: the suggested distinctions do not preclude some overlapping of categories in individual cases.

[26] To a certain extent it is a deduction from our understanding, rather than an aid to further insight.

[27] cf. BAG, 268.

[28] See the essays in J. Starr and T. Engberg-Pedersen (eds), *Early Christian Paraenesis in Context*, BZNW 125 (Berlin: De Gruyter, 2004); also P. Tite, *Valentinian Ethics and Paraenetic Discourse: Determining the Social Function of Moral Exhortation in Valentinian Christianity*, NHMS 67 (Leiden: Brill, 2009), chs 3, 4 (on 'Defining Paraenesis').

4. Genre

What is striking is that, in a number of ways, *2 Clement* fits a possible general description of 'paraenesis' very closely. Two conferences (in Lund, 2000 and Oslo, 2001) culminated in a suggested 'definition' of paraenesis as

a concise, benevolent injunction that reminds of moral practices to be pursued or avoided, expresses or implies a shared world view and does not anticipate disagreement.[29]

The key points are perhaps that paraenesis is primarily 'benevolent', i.e. it is not overtly polemical; it 'reminds', i.e. it uses materials generally already known and does not introduce new demands; it concerns primarily 'moral' issues; it presupposes a 'shared world view', i.e. it is addressed to insiders rather than outsiders; and it 'does not anticipate disagreement'.

All this fits *2 Clement* remarkably well. As will be seen throughout, the approach of the author is primarily 'benevolent' and not polemical: he uses first persons rather than second persons and speaks with his hearers rather than at them. The subject of discussion is always focused on moral behaviour with little explicit 'theology'. The exhortations given are often fairly bland and general and seem uncontroversial and/or already known: certainly there is no attempt to justify or defend the content of the ethical demand, and equally it is often assumed that references to the 'will' of God/Christ, or his/their 'commandments', will be understood without spelling out the contents in detail. So too the context seems to be an address to insiders, not to outsiders (cf. above on *2 Clement* as an address to Christians already within a Christian community). There is no real attempt to challenge any overarching 'world view' of the hearers.[30] Moreover, there is no hint of any possible disagreement arising from what is said. Thus in many ways, *2 Clement* fits the category (possibly 'genre') of 'paraenesis' very well indeed. Though, as with 'deliberative rhetoric',[31] it is not certain whether this actually helps the interpretative process to progress or whether it simply summarizes the interpretation of the text, gained independently, under another modern label.

In conclusion, we can describe *2 Clement* as some kind of 'sermon', addressed to those who are already Christians, and intended to be read in the context of a liturgical gathering for worship. It is, however, not (as it stands) a 'homiletic

---

[29] See the Introduction in Starr and Engberg-Pedersen (eds), *Early Christian Paraenesis*, 4.

[30] Hence in part the difficulty of seeing the text as addressing possible Gnostic opponents (see §7 below): any Gnostic 'world view' is never addressed or challenged in any way. And in texts such as 14.1–4, it seems to be accepted: see the commentary.

[31] The categories of 'deliberative rhetoric' and 'paraenesis' need not be mutually exclusive. *Contra* e.g. M. Mitchell, *Paul and the Rhetoric of Reconciliation* (Louisville, Westminster, 1993), 52–3, who distinguishes sharply between the two, claiming that deliberative rhetoric gives specific instructions for a specific situation, whereas paraenesis consists only of general (moral) exhortations. But this may narrow the scope of paraenesis too sharply.

sermon', i.e. providing a detailed interpretation of a scriptural text, even though it makes extensive use of scripture to seek to back up what is said. In rhetorical terms it may be classified as 'deliberative', seeking to advise, to warn, to help, etc.; and it may well be meaningful to categorize the contents of the work as 'paraenesis'. But beyond that, precision is probably not possible (or helpful!).

5. LITERARY UNITY

Amongst older commentators, the literary unity of *2 Clement* was rarely doubted. However, since the start of the 20th century, a strong body of opinion has developed arguing that the section 19.1–20.4 represents a secondary addition to the text. Whilst the integrity of the extant text[1] continues to be maintained by some in more recent studies,[2] many others have argued that the section 19.1–20.4 is a later addition to the text.[3] The arguments for this position have been rehearsed many times, and the main points are given here: undoubtedly a strong case can be (and has been) made for dividing the text in this way, but it remains true that the argument against the literary integrity of the present text is not completely watertight.[4]

Those arguing in favour of seeing 19.1–20.4 as a section separate from the rest of the letter have appealed to several factors, highlighting a number of differences, at different levels, between chs 1–18 and 19.1–20.4.[5]

(i) A constant factor in the argument has been the change in the address of the recipients, from simply 'brothers' in chs 1–18 (1.1; 4.3; 5.1; 5.5; 7.1; 8.4; 9.11; 10.1; 11.5; 13.1; 14.1, 3; 16.1) to 'brothers and sisters' in 19.1; 20.2.

---

[1] i.e. the text as extant in those MSS which contain the complete text, namely C and S. (A breaks off at 12.5a and is clearly incomplete.) Both C and S contain 19.1–20.4 with no indication of any doubt about the genuineness of this section.

[2] See e.g. Vielhauer, *Geschichte*, 739; Wengst, *Zweite Clemensbrief*, 210; Baasland, '2.Klemensbrief', 116. The integrity of the present text is not explicitly discussed in e.g. Donfried, *Setting*.

[3] See e.g. A. Di Pauli, 'Zum sog. 2. Korintherbrief des Clemens Romanus', *ZNW* 4 (1903), 326; Schüssler, 'Zweite Klemensbrief', 4–5; Stegemann, 'Herkunft', 70–2; Warns, 'Untersuchungen', 145–7; Lindemann, *Clemensbriefe*, 255–6; Salzmann, *Lehren*, 222–4; Pratscher, *Zweite Clemensbrief*, 18–21.

[4] Pratscher provides probably the most comprehensive list of arguments, though many of the points are taken from earlier studies (see previous note). No attempt is made here to identify precisely who has appealed to which particular piece of evidence.

[5] It is widely agreed that the doxology in 20.5 is almost certainly part of the 'original', to be taken with chs 1–18.

(ii) Ch. 18, with its personal self-reference by the author, and the eschatological reference to the final judgement, seems to provide a fitting end to the preceding text (with perhaps a doxology to follow), whereas the presence of 19.1–20.4 in its present context makes for something of an anticlimax and/or disruption in the structure of the rest of the text.

(iii) 19.1–20.4 contains no citations, unlike the rest of the text.

(iv) There are a number of linguistic and/or theological differences between the language and ideas of the small section 19.1–20.4 and chs 1–18. For example,

 (a) The writer calls his work a συμβουλία in 15.1, but an ἔντευξις in 19.1.
 (b) The word ἀντιμισθία, used at some key points in chs 1–18 (cf. 1.3, 5; 9.7; 11.6; 15.2), does not occur in 19.1–20.4.[6]
 (c) 19.1–20.4 uses vocabulary of 'piety' or 'godliness' (εὐσέβεια 19.1; 20.4; εὐσεβής 19.4; 20.4; θεοσέβεια 20.4) relatively frequently in such a short length of text, but this language is missing from chs 1–18.
 (d) Similarly, the vocabulary of 'unrighteousness' (ἀδικία 19.2; ἄδικος 20.1) occurs in 19.1–20.4, but not in chs 1–18.
 (e) There are a number of instances where the author of 19.1–20.4 appears to use different vocabulary, and/or use the same vocabulary differently, from that in chs 1–18 to express the same idea: e.g. φιλοπονεῖν (19.2) instead of σπουδάζειν (10.2; 18.2); σκοτίζεσθαι τὴν διάνοιαν (19.2) instead of πηροὶ ὄντες τῇ διανοίᾳ (1.6); ἐπιθυμίαι μάταιαι (19.2) instead of κοσμικαὶ ἐπιθυμίαι (17.3); πρόσταγμα (19.3) instead of ἐντολή (3.4; 4.5; 6.7; 8.4; 17.3, 6); ἀθάνατος (19.3) instead of ἄφθαρτος (6.6; 7.3); καρπός is used in 19.3; 20.3 very differently from 1.3 (as eschatological reward rather than human response to God now).
 (f) There are also some more 'theological' differences between the two sections. Some have argued that the balance between human response and divine grace in chs 1–18 is lost in 19.1–20.4 where everything seems to relate to human response. The reference to the possibility that some sins might have been done in ignorance (19.2) seems in some tension with chs 1–18, where it is uniformly assumed that all wrongdoing is culpable and human beings will be held responsible for what they have done (cf. e.g. 16.2–3; 18.2). So too the eschatology implied in 19.4, with its hope for the righteous of a life of blessedness 'above' (to come perhaps immediately after death?), may be more 'individualistic', and rather different from the prospect of cosmic judgement as presented in e.g. 16.3; 17.4–7.

---

[6] Pratscher, *Zweite Clemensbrief*, 18, calls it a 'central term' in the main part of the text (i.e. chs 1–18).

5. Literary Unity

(g) Finally, the situation of the community is arguably different in the two sections. Thus in 20.1, there seems to be a clear, apparently fixed, distinction drawn between the 'unrighteous' who are rich (as 'them') and the members of the community ('us') who are then by implication 'poor'. But in earlier passages, warnings about love of money and/or greed, as well as possible exhortations to give money generously (cf. 16.4),[7] appear to presuppose that the recipients do have at least some money; and the whole tenor of the appeals in the text implies that any divisions are capable of being resolved.

With all these factors in mind, it is not surprising that many have argued that the present text of 2 Clement is not a unity, and that 19.1–20.4 represents a section that should be read *not* as part of the rest of 2 Clement. However, opinions differ on how the relationship between the two sections should be seen in more detail. In part this relates to similarities which many have noted between the language of 2 Clem. 19.1–20.4 and that of 1 Clement.[8] There is a possibly striking agreement in language between 2 Clem. 19.1 and 1 Clem. 63.2, where both seem to refer to what has been said as an ἔντευξις with an explicit reference too to what has been 'written'. Other similarities between the two texts concern the use of piety/godliness language already noted: not only is this language suddenly present in 2 Clem. 19–20 where it was absent from chs 1–18, it is also very prominent in 1 Clement (εὐσέβεια 1.2; 11.1; 15.1 etc., εὐσεβής 2.3 etc., εὐσεβῶς 61.2; 62.1). So too the language of 19.3 ('Blessed are those who obey these commandments (προστάγμασιν)') is close to 1 Clem. 50.5 ('Blessed are we if we perform the commandments (προστάγματα) of God'), including the use of πρόσταγμα, which is rare elsewhere in 2 Clement (see above) but common in 1 Clement.[9]

Just what the possible significance of such common features between the two texts might be is uncertain. Perhaps the most original suggestion is that of Stegemann who claims that 2 Clem. 19.1–20.4 was written by the *same* author as that of chs 1–18 to serve as a concluding section when 1 Clement and 2 Clement were put together. The similarities (as well as the differences) between 2 Clem. 19–20 and the rest of 2 Clement have been noted by others (see below), and Stegemann gives full weight to these. A decisive factor for her is that the evidence about the attestation of 2 Clement always links the text with 1 Clement. Hence she argues that 2 Clement was explicitly written as an appendix to 1 Clement, with 19.1–20.4 added when 2 Clem. 1–18 was

---

[7] It is, however, uncertain whether ἐλεημοσύνη in 16.4 should be translated as 'almsgiving' or taken as a reference to more wide-ranging charitable activity: see the commentary.
[8] See especially Stegemann, 'Herkunft', 78–81; Pratscher, *Zweite Clemensbrief*, 20–1; the similarities are also highlighted by Donfried, *Setting*, 14–15.
[9] This feature is particularly emphasized in this context by Di Pauli, 'Korintherbrief', 325, and Stegemann, 'Herkunft', 81.

joined with *1 Clement*, partly to bolster the prestige of *1 Clement* and to assure its acceptance.[10]

Such an overall theory about the origin of *2 Clement* is not convincing. Some connection between *1 Clement* and *2 Clement* is indeed widely (though not universally) assumed in the patristic evidence about *2 Clement*.[11] However, Stegemann's dual claim that 19.1–20.4 is by the *same* author as the rest of *2 Clement*, but also to be considered separate from it, is difficult to sustain: if the differences in vocabulary and ideas are considered significant enough to imply that the section is to be taken as separate from the rest, it is hard then to ascribe both to the same author; conversely, if the sections are by the same author, then the differences in ideas and vocabulary cannot be regarded as that significant. Moreover, the lack of any substantive links between *1 Clement* and *2 Clement* throughout almost the whole of *2 Clem.* 1–18, and the very superficial nature of any possible links involving *2 Clem.* 19.1–20.4, make it very difficult to see *2 Clement* as explicitly defending the status of *1 Clement* in any way.[12]

In fact the verbal links between *2 Clem.* 19.1–20.4 and *1 Clement* are fairly tenuous. As noted earlier (in relation to Donfried's theory about the origin of *2 Clement* as an address by one of the reinstated presbyters after the success of *1 Clement*, with *2 Clem.* 19.1 as a conscious echo of, and reference to, *1 Clement*), the links between *2 Clem.* 19.1 and *1 Clem.* 63.2 may be simply coincidental (and in any case the participle τοῖς γεγραμμένοις may be used differently: see p. 16 above). The common reference to each as an ἔντευξις may be no more than coincidental; the common use of words in the εὐσεβ- group is probably not distinctive enough to show a link between the two texts;[13] and the common agreement in the beatitude in *1 Clem.* 50.5 and *2 Clem.* 19.3 may be again coincidental.[14]

---

[10] See Stegemann, 'Herkunft', *passim*, esp. the summary on 133–5.

[11] Stegemann relies primarily on the evidence from the manuscripts containing *2 Clement* as well as other external attestation. Much of this evidence is quite late and cannot necessarily be used to provide information about the origins of the text; also not all of it is explicit in linking *2 Clement* with *1 Clement* (see Warns, 'Untersuchungen', 30–8, for more detail).

[12] See too the critique of Stegemann in Wengst, *Zweite Clemensbrief*, 210–12; also Warns, 'Untersuchungen', 38. Stegemann's detailed theory may be unconvincing; nevertheless, it remains the case that there is relatively little evidence for the existence of *2 Clement* independent of *1 Clement*. As noted above (p. 14), the nature of the connection between the two texts remains an intriguing puzzle.

[13] The word group is widely used in the Hellenistic world to refer to the behaviour which is pleasing to the gods; it is widespread in e.g. the Pastorals and 4 Maccabees, as well as in *1 Clement*. See M. Dibelius and H. Conzelmann, *The Pastoral Epistles*, Hermeneia (Philadelphia: Fortress, 1972), 39. (Though Stegemann, 'Herkunft', 80, sees this as then only narrowly attested in early Christian texts and hence the agreement with *1 Clement* as all the more striking. But could one use the same argument to postulate a link between *2 Clement* and the Pastorals?!)

[14] The common use of πρόσταγμα seems too weak a link to establish the case: the author of *2 Clement* is capable of varying his nomenclature in relation to 'commands' to be obeyed (see below).

5. Literary Unity

Other suggestions about the origin of the section 2 *Clem.* 19.1–20.4, when taken to be separate from the rest of *2 Clement*, have varied. Most have assumed that the self-reference in 19.1 by the author as the one who is 'reading' a text implies that the author of this small section was then reading a text, or a 'sermon', by someone else. However, some have also claimed that the position of the section is unusual, and that the present tense ἀναγινώσκω in 19.1 is very odd if it refers to the text of a sermon which has already been read out: rather it reads more naturally as a reference to something that is about to come. Hence Lindemann argues that the section in 19.1–20.4 was originally the *introduction* to the sermon in 1–18 and has now been misplaced, perhaps when *2 Clement* was linked with *1 Clement*.[15] However, this is by no means certain: the present tense of 19.1 does not require a future reference, and it could just as easily be referring to a text which has mostly just been read but where the reading is not yet finished. And there is no direct evidence (e.g. in MSS) that the section 19.1–20.4 was situated anywhere other than in its present position.

On the theory that 2 *Clem.* 19.1–20.4 is a later addition to the text, its precise origin and position remain somewhat enigmatic and unknown. On the other hand, the arguments for regarding the section as separate from the rest of *2 Clement*, whilst clearly strong, are not overwhelming.

First, all concede that there are a number of features which serve to unite the language of ideas in 19.1–20.4 with the rest of the text.[16] Thus the exhortation to repent 'with one's whole heart' occurs in 19.1 and also in 8.2; 17.1. The expression 'the God of truth' in 19.1 echoes 'the Father of truth' in 3.1; 20.5. The note that the hearers can save both themselves and the speaker/preacher occurs in 19.1 and 15.1. The metaphor of the athletic contest is used in 20.2, as also in ch. 7. The language of the 'reward' or 'recompense' (μισθός) which God will give to humans (as a reward for right behaviour) is common to 20.4 and a series of passages earlier (e.g. 3.3; 9.5; etc.). So too the first-person-plural exhortations in 19.2, 3; 20.2 reflect a common and distinctive feature of the style of chs 1–18. Thus, if the section 19.1–20.4 is by someone other than the author of the rest of the text, the person concerned has immersed himself quite deeply in the language and ideas of the author of chs 1–18.

Second, one may note that the section in question is very small: hence any statistics about word usages, and alleged differences in usage between the two sections, must remain somewhat inconclusive. Indeed, the whole of *2 Clement* is not large, so that any alleged inconsistencies in vocabulary may be of uncertain value. In any case, such arguments effectively depend on presuppositions which may be difficult to maintain: for they implicitly

---

[15] Lindemann, *Clemensbriefe*, 256; followed by Pratscher, *Zweite Clemensbrief*, 21.

[16] See e.g. Stegemann, 'Herkunft', 73–4; Pratscher, *Zweite Clemensbrief*, 19. For those arguing that the section is a later addition, this shows that the author of 19.1–20.4 knew the rest of *2 Clement* well and was seeking to integrate what was said here with the rest of the text.

assume that an author is consistent in his use of vocabulary and never varies his usage. However, any author can use synonyms and is not always monochrome in his terminology, or indeed strictly consistent in his ideas. At times the alleged differences in vocabulary between 1–18 and 19–20 involve perhaps only a single instance in either section: hence it is hard to determine what might be the author's 'characteristic' (or only) way of writing. Thus while it is true that a word such as καρπός is used differently in 1.3 and in 19.3; 20.3, one cannot easily argue that one author is only allowed to use a word (which in any case is fairly general and capable of a wide range of usages) in one and only one way. Similarly the difference between σκοτίζεσθαι τὴν διάνοιαν (19.2) and πηροὶ ὄντες τῇ διανοίᾳ (1.6), or between ἐπιθυμίαι μάταιαι (19.2) and κοσμικαὶ ἐπιθυμίαι (17.3), may simply reflect a single author's variation in vocabulary. So too the use of πρόσταγμα in 19.3 as opposed to ἐντολή in chs 1–18 must be seen in the light of the use of ἐνταλμάτα in 17.3: the author of chs 1–18 is quite capable of using synonyms! Such differences in language are thus scarcely conclusive.

Indeed it is clear that within chs 1–18 alone, the author does not exhibit an entirely consistent and/or monochrome diction, or set of ideas. There is some variety and change (possibly development) within these chapters. Thus language about 'repentance', which is prominent from 8.1 onwards, does not appear at all in chs 1–7.[17] So too, in relation to some of the evidence cited above, the word ἀντιμισθία may not occur in chs 19–20 (though there is no clear reason why it should: certainly there is no synonym used here when one would expect the word); but even in chs 1–18 it is used in very different ways: in 9.7 it is the required human response to God; in 11.6 it is the divine response to humans.[18] So too at the level of ideas, it may well be that chs 19–20 stress the importance of human response to God and have little idea of divine grace; but one could say the same equally about large parts of chs 1–18! Indeed many have argued that the 'theology' of *2 Clement* as a whole has little if any place for an element of divine grace. (See §9. Theology below.) Similarly, any alleged differences in eschatology between chs 19–20 and 1–18 may be no more (and no less) than similar alleged 'differences' (or 'discrepancies') between the eschatology reflected in different parts of the writings of those such as Paul or Luke in the NT.[19]

---

[17] In the past, this has occasionally led to theories advocating a different origin for chs 1–7 from that of chs 8–20, or perhaps a change of audience: see on 8.1 below.

[18] Hence it is hard to see the word as alone, and on each occasion, expressing 'the central idea' of *2 Clement*: cf. n. 6 above.

[19] Discussions of Luke's eschatology have long had to grapple with ideas and presuppositions in different parts of Luke–Acts which appear somewhat discordant on the surface: cf. the more 'individualistic' ideas reflected in the accounts of the death of Stephen in Acts 7 and the penitent thief in Luke 23.43, alongside the more cosmic picture of the End in passages such as Luke 12, 17, 21. So too Paul's eschatological ideas are notoriously difficult to square with each other and have given rise to theories that his eschatology developed over his letter-writing period (cf. 1 Thess. 4 and 1 Cor. 15 vs. 2 Cor. 5 and Phil. 1.23).

In assessing the evidence one must also not forget the small space which the relevant parts of the text occupy. 19.1–20.4 is a relatively short section; and if one took sections of comparable length from chs 1–18, one might find a similar alleged lack of key features in the text. Thus it is indeed the case that chs 19–20 contain no explicit citations. But then, while there are a number of citations scattered throughout chs 1–18, one can point to passages such as 15.5–17.3, comparable in length to 19.1–20.4, where there is no explicit citation. Even ch. 1, which is comparable in length, has no citation. Thus the absence of citations in this section may not be decisive.

In the end, not a lot may depend on the issue. In one way, the section 19.1–20.4 adds not very much more to what has already been said and functions as a 'résumée' of what precedes it;[20] and presumably that is in some respects its intention whoever was the author. Possibly, *if* one takes the section as a later addition, then the phrase μετὰ τὸν θεὸν τῆς ἀληθείας in 19.1 is not to be taken as part of the 'original' sermon of chs 1–18, in which case this would obviate the need to try to look for a prior (biblical) text on which the ('original') sermon might be based.[21] However, the general picture that one has of early Christian 'preaching' is that it occurred within a general context in which scriptural readings took place. So the issue of the relationship between any 'sermon' and a biblical text which has been read might still remain.

In summary, the case for regarding 19.1–20.4 as not part of the 'original' text of *2 Clement* is probably indecisive. There are some differences, one of the most striking of which remains the address 'brothers and sisters', in place of the earlier uniform 'brothers'. Other differences in language, and possibly ideas, are, however, less compelling: they may be equally explicable as a result of a single writer's ability to vary his diction, as well as from a writer's having perhaps a number of ideas that are not always fully worked out into a consistent and coherent pattern.

---

[20] Although it might be that the language of 19.4 introduces very different ideas about the afterlife and/or attitudes to the 're-creation' of the material world: see the commentary.

[21] Salzmann, *Lehren*, 222. Though it does then raise questions of what the phrase itself is referring to!

6. CITATIONS

One of the most striking features of *2 Clement* is the extensive use of citations. The author cites a large number of texts, many of them identifiable as 'scripture'. These include texts from the 'Old Testament', and from Jesus traditions as reflected in the New Testament canonical gospels. In addition, there are further texts, presented as citations in exactly the same way as the scriptural ones but which correspond to no known text currently in 'scripture'.[1] The citations in *2 Clement* have always been a source of fascination for students of the text, and offer us potential insight into the development of the history of the canon;[2] they also may allow us to see some aspects of early Christian (and Jewish) literature that was suppressed by the later canonizing process. This area of interest is reflected in the commentary here by presenting an analysis of each possible citation in the text in a separate section for each chapter entitled 'Parallels', prior to the commentary itself. Here an attempt is made to identify the possible source and origin of each citation, as well as to consider possible parallels (e.g. in early Christian literature) to see what light this can throw on our understanding of the text of *2 Clement*.

6.1 Introductory formulae

The vast majority of the texts usually identified as citations in *2 Clement* are explicitly signalled as such with a clear introductory formula (19 times).

---

[1] The categories of 'Old Testament', 'New Testament', and perhaps 'scripture', are potentially anachronistic: *2 Clement* probably comes from a time when the precise boundaries of the canon of 'scripture', both Jewish and Christian, were still fluid and there may not have been a fixed, universally recognized body of 'scriptural' texts at all. I use the term 'scripture' here to refer to texts which are regarded as 'sacred' in some way, and 'canon' to refer to the precise delimitation of such texts in a clearly circumscribed and defined list. Cf. J. Barr, *Holy Scripture. Canon. Authority, Criticism* (Oxford: Clarendon, 1983); J. Barton, *Holy Writings, Sacred Text: The Canon in Early Christianity* (London: SPCK, 1997).

[2] Commentators regularly have a section on the citations in the Introduction to the text; and the studies of e.g. Donfried, *Setting*, and Warns, 'Untersuchungen', both devote very long chapters (for Warns over 400 pages) to an analysis of these citations.

6. Citations

On other occasions, the author may well be citing a prior text, but there is no explicit introductory formula as such. The clearest example is probably 2.1, where the words of Isa. 54.1 are (almost certainly) cited. The fact that there is a citation in mind here is shown by the way in which the text is then explicitly broken up into separate clauses, and each one interpreted in turn (see the commentary); further, the continuation of the text in 2.4 introduces another citation (from perhaps Matt. 9.13: see below) as a ἑτέρα γραφή, suggesting that what has gone just before is also a γραφή. Other instances are, however, not so clear. Thus many have seen a 'citation' (but with no introductory formula signalling it as such) in e.g. 11.7 (the wording is very similar to the 'quotation' (of an unknown source) given by Paul in 1 Cor. 2.9), 16.3 (cf. Isa. 34.4), 16.4 (cf. 1 Pet. 4.8), and 17.5 (= Isa. 66.24, cited earlier in 7.6 with an introductory formula).[3] Whether these should be regarded as 'citations' is debatable.[4] So too there are other instances where the wording of the text of *2 Clement* is closely aligned with that of another text, but where one might think that an 'allusion' is a better description of the text in question (see e.g. the parallels in language between *2 Clem.* 16.4 and Tob. 12.8–9, noted in the commentary). Clearly certainty is not possible and judgements are inevitably subjective.

The introductory formulae used vary, as may be seen from the following table:[5]

2 Clement	Possible origin of citation	Ascription	Introductory formula
2.1	Isa. 54.1	—	—
2.4	Matt. 9.13//Mark 2.17	ἑτέρα γραφή	λέγει
3.2	Matt. 10.32//Luke 12.8	αὐτός [= Jesus]	λέγει
3.5	Isa. 29.13 (cf. Matt. 15.8//Mark 7.6// 1 Clem. 15.2)	'he' [= Jesus] or 'it' 'he' [= Jesus]	λέγει ... ἐν τῷ Ἡσαΐᾳ

---

[3] On one occasion, it is not clear whether a text should be regarded as one citation or two: cf. 6.1–2 where 6.1 is closely parallel to Luke 16.13, and 6.2 where the text is close to Mark 8.36//s; but the text runs on without a break from 6.1 to 6.2 and there is a single introductory formula ('he/it says') at the start of the citation in 6.1 only. Is this then to be regarded as a single citation, signalled as such? Or as two citations with an introductory formula lacking for the second?

[4] Some would reserve the word 'citation' for a quotation from another text which is explicitly signalled as such by the writer with an introductory formula; they would then use a term such as 'allusion' or 'echo' to refer to possible quotations not explicitly signalled as such. For a discussion of the broad issues, see A. F. Gregory and C. M. Tuckett, 'Reflections on Method: What Constitutes the Use of the Writings that Later Formed the New Testament in the Apostolic Fathers?', in A. F. Gregory and C. M. Tuckett (eds), *The Reception of the New Testament in the Apostolic Fathers* (Oxford: Oxford University Press, 2005), 61–82.

[5] Some details here are of course debatable and debated, e.g. about the 'origin' of the citation, and also to whom it is attributed (when e.g. the introduction consists of a verb without an explicit subject). For further discussion of each case, see the commentary.

2 Clement	Possible origin of citation	Ascription	Introductory formula
4.2	Matt. 7.21	'he' [= Jesus]	λέγει
4.5	Unknown (?*Gos. Naz.*) + Matt. 7.23//Luke 13.27	ὁ κύριος	εἶπεν
5.2–4	Unknown cf. Matt. 10.16// Luke 10.3 + Matt. 10.28//Luke 12.4–5	ὁ κύριος	λέγει
6.1	Luke 16.13	ὁ κύριος	λέγει
6.2	Mark 8.36//s	[= ὁ κύριος from 6.1?]	[as in 6.1?]
6.8	Ezek. 14.13–20	ἡ γραφή	λέγει . . . ἐν τῷ Ἰεζεκιήλ
7.6	Isa. 66.24	'he/it'	φῆσιν
8.5	Luke 16.10–12	ὁ κύριος	λέγει . . . ἐν τῷ εὐαγγελίῳ
9.11	Mark 3.35//s	ὁ κύριος	εἶπεν
11.2–4	Unknown (cf. *1 Clem.* 23.3–4)	ὁ προφητικὸς λόγος	λέγει
11.7	Unknown (cf. 1 Cor. 2.9; *1 Clem.* 34.8)	—	—
12.2	Unknown (cf. *Gos. Eg.*; *Gos. Thom.* 22)	ὁ κύριος	εἶπεν
13.2	Isa. 52.5	ὁ κύριος	λέγει
13.4	Luke 6.32	ὁ θεός	λέγει
14.1	Jer. 7.11	ἡ γραφή	λεγούσα
14.2	Gen. 1.27	ἡ γραφή	λέγει
15.3	Isa. 58.9	ὁ θεός	λέγοντα
16.3	Cf. Isa. 34.4	—	—
16.4	Tob. 12.8–9	—	—
16.4	??1 Pet. 4.8	—	—
17.4	Isa. 66.18	ὁ κύριος	εἶπεν
17.5	Isa. 66.24		

The introductory formulae are not absolutely uniform, and some variation is clearly visible. On the other hand, one may note that the introductions to citations which appear to be from Jewish scripture are no different generally from those introducing Jesus traditions, and in turn these are no different from those introducing (what one might call, anachronistically) 'apocryphal' citations. The uniform verb that is used is one of 'saying': what is cited is said to be what someone/something 'says' or 'said'. The present tense predominates: of the 19 introductory formulae, only 4 use the aorist εἶπεν: the remaining use (or imply) a present tense λέγει / λεγούσα / λέγοντα / φησιν. Moreover, the four aorists are distributed over the categories of Jewish scripture, Jesus traditions in the 'NT', and 'apocryphal' citations.[6] It is thus hard to distinguish one class of citations from another (in relation to their possible origin) on the basis of the introductory formulae used.

It is noteworthy that none of the introductions uses a verb of writing (cf. Paul's characteristic use of ὡς γέγραπται). The texts cited here are things that are not necessarily 'written' as such (though one or two are described as a γραφή):[7] rather, what is crucial for the writer is that they 'speak'—in the present and to the present.

The subject of the verb varies: the author seems to use a range of different subjects, with ὁ κύριος as the most frequent. Sometimes the text is cited as a γραφή (cf. above), sometimes no subject of the verb is specified (and then it is not certain whether the implied subject is personal ('he', with uncertainty as to who the 'he' is), or impersonal ('it', i.e. the text)).[8] Once it is said to be ὁ προφητικὸς λόγος (11.2). Twice it is 'God' (13.4; 15.3), one (13.4) introducing a saying that appears to be a saying of *Jesus*. With the common use of ὁ κύριος, it is often not certain whether Jesus or God is intended. (See the commentary at the relevant places.) Perhaps, though, for the author himself there is ultimately not a lot to be gained by distinguishing the two: for him, one should 'think of Jesus as of God' (1.1), so that, at least at the functional level, the two are equivalent (see §9.2 Christology and on 1.1 below). What Jesus says is what God says, and vice versa.

Scripture is thus genuinely the word *of God*, and speaks directly to the present and to the author's *Christian* readership/audience. In the citations from Jewish scripture, there is barely a trace of any idea that these texts originally were written for a Jewish, non-Christian readership; it is assumed that they relate, immediately and directly, to the present of the author's own day and to the audience he is currently addressing. Indeed the whole issue of non-Christian Jews and/or Judaism does not really arise in the text anywhere.[9] Further, there is scarcely any idea that the texts concerned come from a past era. Rather, it is assumed as a given that all these texts are

---

[6] cf. 4.5 (semi-'apocryphal'); 9.11 (cf. Mark 3.35//s); 12.2 ('apocryphal'); 17.4 (Isa. 66.18). Pratscher, *Zweite Clemensbrief*, 35, suggests that the aorist εἶπεν occurs relatively more frequently in 'apocryphal' citations (though he includes the εἶπεν of 5.4; but this is probably part of the citation itself, not an introductory formula to an independent citation, at least in its present form). In fact two out of the four 'apocryphal' citations use a present λέγει (5.2; 11.2).

[7] cf. 2.4 (and by implication probably 2.1); 6.8; 14.1; 14.2.

[8] cf. 3.5; 4.2; 7.6.

[9] See §9.6 Jews and Judaism below. The use of scripture in *2 Clement* is thus unlike, say, the use of scripture in a writer like Justin Martyr, where the issue of the competing uses of scripture by Christians and (non-Christian) Jews is very much to the fore.

Christian texts, which address the concerns of the contemporary Christian community directly and immediately.[10]

6.2 *2 Clement* and Jewish scripture

In terms of the range of texts cited from Jewish scripture, it is noteworthy that the majority come from the book of Isaiah. Further, many of the Isaiah citations here agree very closely with the LXX version of the book.[11] What, though, the implications of this might be is not clear. Some have suggested that this implies that the author had access to a manuscript of Isaiah.[12] Others have argued that part of the text of Isaiah might have been the text which provided the basis for the current 'homily' or 'sermon' which is our present *2 Clement*, though this theory is probably not persuasive.[13] Certainly too, given what we now know (especially from Qumran) of the variety of textual forms of scriptural texts in this period, we cannot assume that a writer such as the author of *2 Clement* would have had access to the Greek text of Jewish scripture solely in the form of what we now call 'the' LXX.[14]

The text form of other 'OT' citations is generally uncertain. Most are too short, or represent instances where there is no significant variation between the versions, to draw any firm conclusions about the possible text form presupposed. However, one interesting example in this context occurs in 16.4, where there may be an allusion (though not an explicit citation) to the text of Tob. 12.8–9. There *2 Clement* agrees with one particular form of the text of Tobit, that represented by MSS 106 and 107, in asserting that ἐλεημοσύνη is 'better than' prayer and fasting (see the commentary here). This is, however, the only instance in the work of (even) an allusion to the text of Tobit, so one cannot determine the form in which the rest of the book might have been known to the author of *2 Clement*.

One small negative feature to note is the absence of any clear citation of the Psalms in *2 Clement*.[15] Given the popularity of the Psalms for some Christian writers, such an absence of citations here is perhaps striking (though its significance is unclear).

In relation to the use of these citations from Jewish scripture, they are almost all used for a paraenetic purpose related to the needs and/or

---

[10] cf. Wengst, *Zweite Clemensbrief,* 219.

[11] Though see the form of Isa 29.13 cited in 3.5 where *2 Clement* shows some agreement with *1 Clement*, perhaps attesting to a Greek version of the Isaiah text slightly different from that of the LXX: see the commentary on 3.5 here.

[12] See e.g. Wengst, *Zweite Clemensbrief,* 218.

[13] See §4. Genre above, and discussion of the possible genre of *2 Clement* as a 'homily' or 'sermon', coupled with the theory of Knopf that the text of the sermon was Isa. 54–66.

[14] Hence we cannot assume that instances where a writer agrees closely with the wording of the LXX represent very accurate citations, or conversely that lack of close agreement with the LXX represents a less accurate citation.

[15] Noted by Wengst, *Zweite Clemensbrief,* 218.

expectations of the current Christian audience. Virtually none of them relate to any issues of 'theology' as such (whether e.g. Christology, or ecclesiology):[16] they are not used to bring in support for specific 'theological' claims by the writer. In one way, however, this is simply a reflection of the purpose of the writer generally, which is not to argue for great theological claims as such, but to use any such claims as the basis for paraenetic exhortations about right behaviour in the present by the addressees.

6.3 *2 Clement* and Jesus traditions

A very similar situation arises in relation to the other citations in the text. As noted, many are from Jesus traditions (some of which have parallels in the (later to become) canonical synoptic gospels). For whatever reason, there are no citations of the fourth gospel, and no clear allusions either.[17] So too, of the 'apocryphal' citations, most are of Jesus traditions (or are at least claimed to be).[18]

As already noted, several of the citations have parallels in the synoptic gospels. Whether the writer knew (one or more of) these gospels, and drew his citations from them explicitly is uncertain. Detailed analysis of each one is provided in the commentary. It is, however, noteworthy that, at least at some points, the author of *2 Clement* appears to reflect a stage in the development of the Jesus tradition that presupposes the existence of the redactional activity of at least Matthew and Luke.[19] Thus at these points the author has either drawn his citations from these finished gospels, or he has drawn them from a source which *post*-dates these gospels. And given that this is the case in some

---

[16] One exception in relation to the *immediate* use of a citation might be the use of Gen. 1.27 in *2 Clem.* 14.2, where the text is used to buttress a claim about the pre-existent church; however, the whole line of argument in 14.2–4 makes it clear that, for the author of *2 Clement*, any such speculation is to be channelled into a paraenetic exhortation about appropriate behaviour between men and women. See the commentary below.

[17] Given the very high Christological claim made in 1.1, this silence is perhaps all the more surprising since John's gospel might have provided grist for the author's mill in this respect.

[18] The exception might be 11.2–4, the 'prophetic word' (shared with *1 Clem.* 23.3–4); the reference in the middle of the citation to 'my people' (11.4) is usually taken as more naturally reflecting a citation originally from Jewish scripture; and the use of the same text in *1 Clement* (and the way it is introduced there) would also suggest the same. The example is thus a good illustration of the fact that any form of a canon of Jewish scripture might still be as fluid as any canon of Christian writings at this period. The status of the (possible) citation in 11.7 (where the wording agrees with Paul's apparent 'citation' in 1 Cor. 2.9) in this respect is uncertain. See n. 22 below.

[19] See the detailed section of the commentary on 3.2 (agreement with MattR); 4.5 (possible agreement with LkR); 13.4 (agreement with LkR). For a full analysis of the citations of Jesus traditions with this particular issue to the fore, see H. Köster, *Synoptische Überlieferung bei den Apostolischen Vätern*, TU 65 (Berlin: Akademie, 1957), 62–123; A. F. Gregory and C. M. Tuckett, '*2 Clement* and the Writings that Later Formed the New Testament', in A. F. Gregory and C. M. Tuckett (eds), *The Reception of the New Testament in the Apostolic Fathers* (Oxford: Oxford University Press, 2005), 251–92.

instances where the synoptic parallels enable us to identify such redactional activity with a modicum of certainty, it may also be reasonable to deduce the same in relation to other places where the text of *2 Clement* is parallel to that of the synoptics, but where one cannot necessarily identify the synoptic side of the parallel as explicitly redactional. *2 Clement* is thus a witness to the post-synoptic development of the tradition of the sayings of Jesus reflected here: it is not a witness to an earlier, pre-synoptic form of the tradition.

That said, it is not clear what the immediate source(s) of the synoptic-like sayings in *2 Clement* is/are. It could be that the author knew and used the gospels of Matthew and Luke in something like their present form.[20] It could also be that these texts were known to the author of *2 Clement* indirectly, perhaps in the form of some kind of harmonized version of the texts (similar to that which might have been available to Justin).[21] Alternatively the author might have accessed the text via a collection of citations. The present form of the text simply does not allow us to draw any certain conclusions in this respect.

A further complication is raised by the existence of other citations, clearly marked as such (by the presence of an introductory formula), where there is no parallel in the canonical gospel tradition. In some cases, there may be other parallels in other (non-canonical) texts.[22] In other cases too, there is a partial parallel in the synoptic tradition, but this cannot account for the whole of the citation as it now appears in *2 Clement*.[23] Clearly the author had access to traditions other than those which are now preserved in the present synoptic gospels of the NT. Further, at one point the author specifically says that one such citation is to be found ἐν τῷ εὐαγγελίῳ, 'in the gospel' (8.5, introducing a saying which is partially parallel with Luke 16.10 but which also contains extra material). The usual interpretation is that this refers

---

[20] It goes without saying that the precise form in which such texts might have been known to others is not clear, and e.g. one cannot simply assume that the text of a gospel as known to a writer such as this was identical with that in a modern critical edition such as NA[27].

[21] cf. A. J. Bellinzoni, *The Sayings of Jesus in the Writings of Justin Martyr*, NovTSup 17 (Leiden: Brill, 1967). At some points, there are similarities between the text as cited by the author of *2 Clement* and that cited by Justin, suggesting perhaps a common origin. See e.g. on 5.4 below.

[22] cf. 4.2 (with a parallel in a 'Jewish gospel' glossing a few verses in some MSS of Matthew); 5.2–4 (with a possible parallel in P.Oxy. 4009, which *might* be related to the *Gos. Pet.*); 12.2, 6 (with parallels in *Gos. Eg.* and in *Gos. Thom.*). It is not certain whether 11.7 (cf. 1 Cor. 2.9) should be considered in this category. There is close verbal agreement between the wording here in *2 Clement* and the words which are apparently given as a (scriptural) citation by Paul in 1 Cor. 2.9. But there is no introductory formula in *2 Clement* indicating a citation here. The origin of the citation in 1 Cor. 2 is a notorious crux; the saying appears in a number of other contexts including Ps.-Philo (perhaps then indicating that it is not necessarily of Christian origin) and also as a saying ascribed to Jesus in *Gos. Thom.* 17. But there is nothing to indicate that the author of *2 Clement* knows this as a saying *of Jesus*. For more details, see the commentary here on 11.7.

[23] See e.g. 8.5 (parallel with Luke 16.10 for part of the citation).

to a written *book* called a 'gospel': hence the author has accessed another written *text* for at least this saying. (See the commentary on 8.5.) And clearly then this gospel text cannot have been a form of Matthew or Luke but must have contained other traditions as well or instead.

How much else this gospel text contained is uncertain. Many have assumed that this (one) 'gospel' mentioned in 8.5 was also the source for the other 'apocryphal' citations elsewhere in *2 Clement* and/or for some of the other citations with parallels elsewhere in the canonical gospels.[24] However, this is by no means required by the evidence.[25] It may well be that the author had access to a number of different sources (or 'gospels') for the Jesus traditions which he cites. It is almost certainly a vain cause to try to identify this (one?) gospel text used by the author with a named 'apocryphal' gospel known from elsewhere. Clearly there are links between traditions found here and similar traditions found in other non-canonical gospel texts/traditions. For example, the saying cited in 12.2, 6 has parallels in *Gos. Eg.* and also in *Gos. Thom.* But the detailed analysis of the saying here suggests that neither of these other versions is the origin of the version of the saying in *2 Clement*.[26] Rather, all that we can say is that the tradition of *Gos. Eg.* as relayed by Clement of Alexandria, and the tradition preserved in *Gos. Thom.*, let us see different

---

[24] cf. e.g. Wengst, *Zweite Clemensbrief*, 224, who suddenly summarizes his discussion of the origin of the non-canonical traditions by saying that the author of *2 Clement* '*eine* velorengegange apokryphe Evangelienschrift benutzte' ('used *a* lost, apocryphal gospel writing'; my stress). Cf. too H. von Schubert, 'Der sogen. 2. Clemensbrief, eine Gemeindepredigt', in E. Hennecke (ed.), *Handbuch zu den Neutestamentlichen Apokryphen* (Tübingen: Mohr Siebeck, 1904), 252; Lindemann, *Clemensbriefe*, 194; also E. Schlarb and D. Lührmann, *Fragmente apokryph gewordener Evangelien in griechischer und lateinischer Sprache*, MTS 59 (Marburg: Elwert, 2000), 134–7, who print all the sayings in 'Das Evangelium [sing.] im 2. Clemensbrief' ('the gospel [sing.] in *2 Clement*'; they even give a colophon τὸ εὐαγγέλιον at the end!). The theory is developed in enormous detail by Warns, 'Untersuchungen', who claims that a whole series of texts in *2 Clement* derives from this single apocryphal gospel (3.2; 4.2; 4.5; 5.2–4; 6.1–2; 8.5; 9.11; 11.6b; 12.2, 6; 13.2, 4; 17.4bc, 5a); he also claims to be able to put these into their original sequence in this gospel: 13.4 → 4.2, 5 → 5.2–4 → 3.2 → 13.2 → 9.11 → 8.5 → 6.1, 2 →17.4b, 5a, 4c [=11.6b] →12.2, 6 (see his summary on pp. 466–8). Such precision is, however, perhaps a little optimistic (implied also by Lindemann, *Clemensbriefe*, 194, who says that the reconstruction has a measure of probability but certainty is not possible). Given, however, that Warns himself argues that this gospel is dependent on the gospels of Matthew and Luke, it is hard to see why such a theory is required, rather than positing more use of Matthew/Luke themselves (and Warns is quite ready to presume such dependence elsewhere in *2 Clement*, at times for parallels which are less close verbally to their canonical counterparts (cf. his pp. 283–322, in which he lists a number of cases of claimed 'Zitate aus Mt und Lk' ('citations from Matthew and Luke')).

[25] Lindemann, *Clemensbriefe*, 194, argues on the basis of the parallel between ἐν τῷ εὐαγγελίῳ in 8.5 and ἐν τῷ Ἡσαΐᾳ (in 3.5) as well as ἐν τῷ Ἰεζεκιήλ (in 6.8) that a very specific text must be in mind. This may well be the case for 8.5 itself. But it still does not follow that this (one) gospel is the source for all the other gospel-like citations in *2 Clement*.

[26] See the commentary. Some in the past have suggested that 'the' apocryphal gospel (sing.!) used by *2 Clement* was the *Gos. Eg.* (on the basis of 12.2; so e.g. Lightfoot, Schubert, Bartlet on 4.5; 5.2; and other texts: see the commentary there); but this seems to press the evidence further than it will comfortably go.

points in the development of the history of tradition of the saying (with perhaps the version in *2 Clement* as the oldest).

One other feature of the citations here relates to the status of the Jesus traditions cited here. At one point, the author of *2 Clement* (probably) cites a saying from the Gospel of Matthew (2.4 = Matt. 9.13). This comes immediately after the citation and detailed interpretation of the text from Isa. 54.1 (in 2.1–3), and is introduced as coming from a ἑτέρα γραφή. Not only perhaps does this imply that what precedes is a citation (although there is no introductory formula to the words of Isa. 54.1: see above), it also suggests that the status of the text cited in 2.4 is indeed that of a γραφή and (by implication) on a par with the previous citation. In other words, the saying from the gospel text is being given the status of scripture (γραφή). Whether this is just a slip is not certain.[27] But at face value it does suggest that the process has already started whereby Christian texts are taking their place alongside other texts from Jewish scripture and being considered as part of a developing Christian canon of scripture (which still includes the texts of Jewish scripture, but also supplements them with other Christian texts). This idea is certainly an unusual one in texts from the earliest period of Christian history. Thus, although in one way the authority ascribed to the citations is that of the 'Lord' who speaks through the text(s),[28] it is also the case that the text itself is gaining status and, qua text, is being considered on a par with that of texts of Jewish scripture.

The same idea may be implied by the reference in 14.2 to 'the books and the apostles', brought in as further authorities to back up what the writer wants to say. The 'books' would seem to refer most naturally to books of Jewish scripture.[29] But then the mention of the 'apostles' alongside seems to suggest a Christian supplement being envisaged along with the scriptural texts of Judaism; and the fact that both are mentioned in the equivalent of a single breath implies probably that they are being regarded as having similar, if not equal, status.

The exact referent of 'the apostles' here has always been a problem. In one way, the obvious reference might be to the Pauline corpus of letters. However, one would not necessarily need a reference to 'apostles' (plur.) if the Pauline corpus were in mind; moreover, there is little if any evidence of use of Paul

---

[27] e.g. some have suggested that the author of *2 Clement* may have thought that the citation in 2.4 was in fact a citation of Jewish scripture, or that the absence of a definite article here with γραφή might indicate an implicit awareness that the text cited is not (quite) on a par with 'scripture': see the commentary.

[28] Stressed by Köster, *Synoptische Überlieferung*, 66, though I am not persuaded by his rider that the authority does *not* reside in any way in the text as such.

[29] The Syriac version adds 'of the prophets' which might even be original; though whether this is a reference to specifically *prophetic* books within Jewish scripture, or to all of Jewish scripture which is assumed to be 'prophetic', is not clear: see the commentary below.

elsewhere in *2 Clement* (see below). On the other hand, there is extensive use of 'gospel'-type *Jesus* traditions. It is then at least possible that the reference here to 'the apostles' might be using terminology similar to that of Justin, who refers to 'the memoirs of the apostles' on several occasions, probably referring to gospel texts.[30] Hence it may be that the reference to 'the apostles' in *2 Clem.* 14.2, as an authority alongside 'the books' of Jewish scripture, is to Christian *gospel* texts with traditions about Jesus, some of which are cited by the author in the course of his work.

One may also note that, as with the texts taken from Jewish scripture, the use made of these Jesus traditions is almost always paraenetic, and indeed relatively subsidiary. The exhortations contained in them are mostly those of a generalized ethical exhortation to be good and to obey the commands given by Jesus and/or God. Little is made of them in relation to any 'theology'. And when a tradition appears to be used in such a 'theological' way, as e.g. in 12.2 or 14.2, the use made of the tradition by the author of *2 Clement* is again paraenetic/ethical: the sayings about the two becoming one, and about the church as the body of Christ, are interpreted (perhaps even forced!) by the writer here to serve his own ethical paraenesis.

In addition to what is included here by way of citations, there are some (possibly surprising) gaps in the arsenal of the citations actually used. The absence of any reference to Johannine traditions has already been noted. It is also noteworthy that all the explicit citations are to traditions of the sayings *of Jesus*. There are also no clear citations of, or indeed evidence of use of, any of the epistles of the NT. One or two possible allusions have been noted, but these are by no means certain.

6.4 *2 Clement* and Paul

In relation to Paul and the Pauline corpus, opinions vary; however, it is hard to establish with any certainty that the author of *2 Clement* used, let alone cited, any Pauline texts. Certainly there is no instance of an explicit citation (i.e. with an introductory formula) of a text from the Pauline corpus.[31] Most of the relevant passages are listed below (and discussed in the commentary at the relevant points).

---

[30] See *1 Apol.* 66.3 (where the 'memoirs of the apostles' are explicitly called 'gospels'); 67.3; and on 13 occasions in the section in *Dial.* 100–7. See the discussion in L. Abramowski, 'The "Memoirs of the Apostles" in Justin', in P. Stuhlmacher (ed.), *The Gospel and the Gospels* (Grand Rapids: Eerdmans, 1991), 323–35; G. N. Stanton, *Jesus and Gospel* (Cambridge: Cambridge University Press, 2004), 75–81, 99–105.

[31] The most recent discussions are those by A. Lindemann, *Paulus im ältesten Christentum. Das Bild des Apostels und die Rezeption der paulinischen Theologie in der frühchristlichen Literatur bis Marcion*, BHT 58 (Tübingen: Mohr Siebeck, 1979), 263–72, and the section (by Gregory) in Gregory and Tuckett, '*2 Clement*', 278–89, both concluding that direct knowledge of, or dependence on, the Pauline corpus by the author of *2 Clement* cannot be shown.

(*a*) The most difficult passage to deal with in this context is perhaps *2 Clem.* 14.2, where the author appeals to the claim that 'the . . . church is the body of Christ'. Moreover, this is introduced as something that is evidently well known to the addressees, and hence although it is not given formally as a citation, it is not far off being such. In addition, one may note that the wording of the claim has to be adjusted by the author of *2 Clement* (changing 'body' to 'flesh') to make the point he wishes to make here: hence the case that the original claim (that the church is the 'body' of Christ) is something the author is taking from a prior tradition is strengthened. The close agreement between what is said here and what is said in Eph. 1.23, cf. 2.16; 4.4, 12–16; 5.30, is obvious. (See too, for Paul himself, Rom. 12.5; 1 Cor. 10.16; 12.27; and for deutero-Paul Col. 1.18, 24; 2.19; 3.15.) On the other hand, it is not certain the immediate origin of the claim in *2 Clement* is the text of Ephesians itself. Claims about the church as the body of Christ were developed elsewhere, so it may be that Ephesians is not the *immediate* source of the author's language here.

(*b*) Other possible links with the Pauline corpus are more general. The claim that the addressees are to keep their flesh 'as a temple of God' (9.3) invites comparison with 1 Cor. 3.16; 6.19, though the author here uses 'flesh' rather than 'body' (as in 1 Cor. 6.19), and the analogy may have been commonplace, so that direct dependence on Paul is again uncertain.

(*c*) The use of the imagery of athletic contests in *2 Clem.* 7 also occurs in 1 Cor. 9.24–7, and in both contexts there is a similar concern to deal with the potential 'problem' that the imagery of the 'winner' in a contest only really allows one person to gain the prize, whereas both Paul and the author of *2 Clement* want to encourage all to strive for (and presumably then also gain) the 'prize' here. On the other hand, the imagery of a contest was very widespread in the ancient world (see the commentary on ch. 7), and hence once again direct dependence of *2 Clement* on Paul need not be postulated to make sense of the language used in *2 Clement* within its contemporary context.

(*d*) Both *2 Clem.* 8 and Rom. 9.21 use the image of a pot and the potter (in turn perhaps both echoing the language and imagery of Jer. 18). But the uses differ: in *2 Clement* the analogy is used to stress the need for repentance in the present, whereas in Paul it is used to make a point about the sovereign freedom of God. Once again, there is no need to postulate direct dependence by *2 Clement* on Paul.

(*e*) There are one or two other instances of possible verbal echoes of Pauline language. For example, the language in *2 Clem.* 1.8 about God calling (us) into being from a state of non-existence is similar to Paul's claim in Rom. 4.17, though the idea is by no means peculiar to Paul (see on 1.8). *2 Clement* (11.7; 14.5) shares with Paul (apparently) the citation of unknown origin which Paul uses in 1 Cor. 2.9 (though, as noted above, it is not explicitly indicated as being a citation in *2 Clement*); but there is no evidence that the author of *2 Clement* has taken this from Paul: given the widespread attestation of the saying (cf. above), it is just as likely that the author has accessed the saying (from an unknown source) independently. *2 Clement* also shares with Paul the use of the text from Isa. 54.1 (*2 Clem.* 2.1; Gal. 4.27); but there is no evidence of any awareness of Paul's *use* of the saying by the author of *2 Clement*: and the use here is quite different from that of Paul. (See below on 2.1.)

It is thus hard to establish with any certainty any clear evidence that the author of *2 Clement* knew and used specific Pauline texts. The reference to 'apostles' in 14.2 has sometimes been taken as implying an awareness of authoritative Pauline letters; but, negatively, there is little evidence to indicate actual awareness of Paul's letters, and more positively the author's de facto list of authorities seems to be Jewish scripture and Jesus traditions. Hence the force of the suggestion above that 'the apostles' refers to what Justin calls 'the memoirs of the apostles', i.e. gospels (rather than any apostolic epistles).

6.5 *2 Clement* and the canon

A final point to be noted here concerns the state of any possible canon of scripture presupposed by the author of *2 Clement*. We have already noted the way in which relatively new Christian texts (gospels) are taking their place alongside Jewish texts as a presumed part of scripture.[32] But equally, the author seems just as content to use, apparently as scriptural,[33] other texts which (later) were not regarded as part of any canon (whether Christian or Jewish). Thus texts and/or traditions which might (by later standards) be regarded as 'apocryphal' are treated here with the same respect and value as those which were accepted later as canonical. Wherever these citations have come from, their source is accepted without any qualms as authoritative and on a par with texts from Jewish scripture.

The author of *2 Clement* thus reflects a time of considerable flux and indeterminacy in the state of any developing canon of scripture. Clearly, it seems to be a time when Christian texts are taking their place alongside Jewish texts as scriptural, so that any Jewish canon of scripture is being expanded by Christian additions. But equally, on both the Christian and non-Christian sides, the precise extent of the canon presupposed remains quite fluid (at least as judged by later standards). All this no doubt fits well with

---

[32] The process is presumed and never defended: the author seems to be reflecting an established practice rather than showing any awareness that what is presupposed here might be debatable or controversial.

[33] cf. the introductory formulae, which are used in virtually exactly the same way in relation to texts which might be (anachronistically) regarded as 'canonical' and 'apocryphal'.

other more general theories about the history of the canon (both Jewish and Christian) where the point is frequently made that final decisions, fixing the limits of any canon, come relatively late and that, prior to this, there was considerable fluidity and flexibility about which texts were regarded as 'sacred' (at least in a general sense). The evidence of *2 Clement* certainly reinforces this general picture and places the text very firmly in a period of relative freedom and fluidity in relation to issues about scripture and canonicity.

7. OPPONENTS

That the author of *2 Clement* has some 'opponents' in view is widely assumed. Language such as that used in 10.5, which refers to others teaching 'evil' to innocent people and making not only themselves but also their hearers liable to condemnation in the final judgement, seems too specific to be a general reference to false teachers who might in theory be present in the community (or near by) but equally well might not. Undoubtedly the primary 'problem' which the author seeks to address is at the ethical level: the prime issue at stake is the value given to ethical behaviour in the present, with the author insisting throughout the whole of the text that ethical behaviour now will be rewarded at the final judgement and, conversely, a failure to behave properly now will result in rejection and punishment. The author thus seems to be addressing primarily a 'problem' (as he sees it) of ethical laxity and/or 'freedom', a failure to take seriously the ethical demands of the Christian life. Precisely what lies behind this 'problem' is, however, much less clear. Whether/how others in the writer's community used particular 'theological', or 'doctrinal', arguments to justify a relatively lax approach to ethics is debated. However, the specific warning against any idea that 'this flesh' is not judged or raised in 9.1 seems directed against what is perceived as a specific threat which the hearers are to guard themselves against. Thus most have assumed that the author of *2 Clement* is addressing a fairly specific situation of (what the author regards as) dangerous false teaching going beyond just the general 'ethical' issue on its own.[1]

A widely held view has been that this false teaching, and hence the possible 'opponents', are connected with Gnosticism.[2] The most detailed

---

[1] The statement of Parvis, '*2 Clement*', 38, that 'it is a moral, not doctrinal, evil' which the false teachers of 10.5 teach is true, though there seems to be some 'doctrinal' problem lurking in the background. The difficulty is in identifying it clearly!

[2] See variously H. Windisch, 'Das Christentum des zweites Clemensbriefes', *Harnack-Ehrung. Beiträge zur Kirchengeschichte, ihrem Lehrer Adolf von Harnack zu seinem siebzigsten Geburtstage (7. Mai 1921) dargebracht von einer Reihe seiner Schüler* (Leipzig: Hinrichs'sche Buchhandlung,

presentation of this view is that of Warns, who argues that the specific form of Gnosticism which the author is seeking to argue against is Valentinian Gnosticism, and virtually all of 2 Clement can be seen as explicitly or implicitly addressing this opposition viewpoint. Pratscher provides the clearest summary of the case for identifying the opponents as Gnostic.[3]

(a) In relation to Christology, the author's stress on the importance of the figure of Jesus Christ, perhaps too on the unity between 'Jesus' and 'Christ', as well as on the reality of the incarnation and on the 'becoming flesh' of Christ (cf. 1.1–2; 9.5), can be seen as directed against Gnostic claims which might promote a docetic Christology, denying that the true saviour had really taken 'flesh' fully, and/or possibly driving a wedge between the earthly suffering Jesus and the heavenly figure of Christ. So too the identification made between Jesus Christ and 'the Lord' (cf. 9.5) may be directed against Gnostic unwillingness to use the term 'Lord' for Jesus (cf. Irenaeus, *Haer.* 1.1.3).

(b) In relation to 'theology' (more strictly speaking), the reference to God as the 'Father of truth' (3.1), a term which seems to have been used elsewhere in Gnostic circles (see on 3.1 below), may be used in a mildly polemical way: the writer insists that recognition of God as the 'Father of truth' is not confined to an elite circle of Gnostic initiates, but is available to all.

(c) In relation to ecclesiology, the talk about Christ and the church as some kind of pre-existent syzygy (ch. 14) has its closest parallel in Gnostic speculation and/or mythology about pre-existent aeons (see the commentary here). The insistence by the writer here that the church has become 'fleshly' (as well as being pre-existent and 'spiritual' in the past: see on 14.3 below), as well as the stress on the importance of the 'flesh' in this whole argument, serves then as a powerful argument against any Gnostic (and/or Valentinian) division of human beings in the world into 'pneumatics' and 'psychics'.

(d) In relation to eschatology, the insistence on the importance of the 'flesh', and on the fact that the 'flesh' will be raised and judged at the End-time (cf. especially ch. 9), as well as the insistence on the reality of a future judgement that is to be taken with the utmost seriousness, serve to distinguish the writer sharply from any Gnostic ideas of salvation as something that can be achieved and realized in the present (perhaps through saving

1921), 133; Knopf, *Zwei Clemensbriefe*, 166; Donfried, *Setting*, 112 (and *passim*); Richardson, *Fathers*, 183–7; Wengst, *Zweite Clemensbrief*, 226–7 (though with some reservations); H. Koester, *Introduction to the New Testament*, vol. 2: *History and Literature of Early Christianity* (Philadelphia: Fortress, 1982), 235–6; Warns, 'Untersuchungen', 76–90 (and *passim*); Lindemann, *Clemensbriefe*, 192 (also with caution); C. N. Jefford (with K. J. Harder and L. D. Amezaga Jr.), *Reading the Apostolic Fathers: An Introduction* (Peabody, Mass.: Hendrickson, 1996), 122–7; Pratscher, *Zweite Clemensbrief*, 50–5.

[3] As well as the section of his full commentary, see also Pratscher, 'Zweite Clemensbrief', 97–9 (he states that the view that the opponents are Gnostics is an '*opinio communis*' and mentions no other possibilities).

knowledge).⁴ The author can even use terms which may have been Gnostic, such as ἀνάπαυσις (5.5; 6.7), to describe the future reward in store for the righteous: but it is for the ethically righteous that such 'rest' is promised, not for those possessing saving knowledge.

(*e*) In relation to ethics, the constant insistence by the author of *2 Clement* on the importance of ethical behaviour, of right conduct as the criterion by which final salvation will be bestowed, and on the importance of behaviour in the present life (in the 'flesh', which *will* be raised and judged), all serve to bolster implicitly or explicitly the anti-Gnostic thrust of the text as a whole. Typical of this may be the way in which the author takes up a quotation which may well have its home in Gnostic ideas about ultimate salvation involving the abolition of gender differences (see 12.2) but interprets it in a totally different—ethical—way, to emphasize the importance of moderation and/or propriety in relationships between men and women (12.3–5).

(*f*) In line with all this, there are a number of places where the language used by the author can be seen as particularly pointed if directed against a Gnostic position, serving perhaps to undermine any Gnostic claims. Thus in 3.1, the claim that we 'know' the Father of truth by 'not denying' the person of Jesus, and then interpreting this in terms of ethical behaviour, can be seen as directed against Gnostic claims about 'knowing' God in a radically different way (e.g. through the possession of saving knowledge about one's origins). The taking up of expressions which might have had a home in Gnostic thinking (e.g. about 'rest': cf. 5.5) and interpreting them in terms of the writer's own position, may be another example of the same phenomenon. The claim about the value of saving a soul 'who already knows God' (17.1) may also be all the more pointed if 'erring' Gnostics (claiming to 'know' God) are in mind.⁵

In all, there is then a strong case to be made for the author seeking to correct what he regards as dangerous teaching which may be described as 'Gnostic'.⁶ However, despite the widespread agreement about this broad general picture, one or two reservations may be noted here.

First, there is the general problem of how one defines 'Gnosticism' in this context. Certainly in recent years, some have questioned whether such a

---

⁴ The importance of the futurity of eschatology is vital in Donfried's overall interpretation of the context in which the author of *2 Clement* is writing.

⁵ For other similar examples, see 1.2; 5.5; 9.6; 10.4–5; 17.5 and the commentary there.

⁶ As noted, the most consistent interpretation of *2 Clement* along these lines is that of Warns, 'Untersuchungen', who sees a Valentinian background in almost everything that the author of *2 Clement* says; in particular he claims specifically that the author is attacking Valentinian sacramental ideas and practices in his language of 'strengthening' in 2.7 (combating Valentinian ideas of a sacrament of 'confirmation': see 236–44), or 'redemption' in 17.4 (see 409–16) and a sacrament of the bridal chamber in ch. 12 (448–56).

category is useful as a 'catch all' term to encompass what might have been a very diverse range of different ideas only loosely connected, as well as questioning the validity of some of the church fathers' (polemical) descriptions of such people.[7] In turn, this has led to others arguing (in my view persuasively) that the category may still be meaningful, but nevertheless careful definition and clarification is required about what might be appropriately regarded as 'Gnostic' and what not.[8] In this discussion, it has often been claimed that an essential part of any 'system' or 'group of ideas' that is to merit the term 'Gnostic' should include the idea that the creation of the material world is the work of a being other than the supreme God and that the world is essentially something alien (and 'bad') from which one should seek to escape.

Second, there is also a specific problem in relation to *2 Clement* in that any 'polemic' is very muted, and at best indirect. Several have pointed out that in part this arises from the fact that the author is engaged in a 'conversation' with perhaps three (or more) 'dialogue' partners: there is the author himself, there is the community who are being addressed directly and with whom the author frequently identifies himself (cf. the constant use of the first-person plurals), and there are possible 'false teachers' and outside influences/dangers which are thought to threaten the writer and his community. The author never addresses any false teachers as such. Indeed, only rarely does he seem to address particular 'doctrinal' or 'theological' issues directly. (The issue about the 'flesh' being raised is one exception, but such direct engagement with a particular topic is rare.) Any 'polemic', and/or address to 'opponents', is often implicit at most, and not explicit.

It may be of course that such lack of overt antagonism is explicable. Warns, for example, refers to the author's context, and his audience, as partly explaining the author's reticence. He notes too that, for the author, intra-community harmony is of paramount importance, not only for its own sake but also for the effect it has on outsiders who, if they see Christians failing to show love for one another, will reject the Christian message and thereby 'blaspheme

---

[7] See M. A. Williams, *Rethinking 'Gnosticism': An Argument for Dismantling a Dubious Category* (Princeton: Princeton University Press, 1996); K. L. King, *What is Gnosticism?* (Cambridge, Mass.: Harvard University Press, 2003).

[8] See variously C. Markschies, 'Gnosis/Gnostizismus', *RGG*[4] iii (2000), 1045–53; C. Markschies, *Gnosis: An Introduction* (London: T. & T. Clark, 2003); B. Pearson, 'Gnosticism as a Religion', *Gnosticism and Christianity in Roman and Coptic Egypt* (New York and London: T. & T. Clark International, 2004), 201–23; A. Marjanen (ed.), *Was there a Gnostic Religion?* (Helsinki: Finnish Exegetical Society, 2005), and the general discussion in C. M. Tuckett, *The Gospel of Mary* (Oxford: Oxford University Press, 2007), 45–52. I have therefore retained the word 'Gnostic' in the present discussion; I have also used the capitalized form ('Gnostic' rather than 'gnostic') in light of the tendency among some writers in English to use 'gnostic' to refer sometimes more loosely to more general 'gnosticizing tendencies', rather than to fully developed mythologies about the creation etc. I am, however, fully aware that any decision on capitalization can be questioned!

7. Opponents 51

the name [of God]' (see 13.4). In any case, if the situation is indeed as is proposed, the details would not necessarily need to be spelt out by the writer for his audience since all would know what he is talking about.[9] Nevertheless, the highly indirect nature of any 'polemic' here makes it inevitable that there are questions about the reconstruction of the situation proposed.

First, in relation to 'theo-logy' (ideas about God): if indeed the writer thinks that there is a danger from Gnostic teaching, it is surprising that there is nothing in the text which addresses what some would regard as the essential feature of any Gnostic thinking, namely the idea that the world is essentially evil and has been created by a being who in various Gnostic systems might be regarded as at best ignorant, at worst malevolent, but who is clearly a 'god' of lower status than the supreme God.[10] Indeed the issue of 'theo-logy' (strictly speaking) never really arises explicitly.[11] The uniqueness of God is apparently simply a given throughout the text. Moreover, there is not the slightest suggestion of a possible danger that the one supreme God (the 'Father') might be seen as in any way different from the God of the Hebrew Bible. At one point, the author refers to God explicitly as the creator (15.2: 'God who created us'), with no hint at all that this might be a disputed or polemical claim: the phrase 'who created us' seems in the immediate context to be a somewhat parenthetical comment and in no way controversial.[12] Further, throughout the text the author cites from Jewish scripture in a totally free and unembarrassed way, assuming without any question that the books of the Hebrew Bible are part of Christian scripture which address the Christians of his day with unimpeachable and unquestioned authority. (See §6. Citations above.) The God of Jewish scripture is thus without question the one and only God (20.5). There is not the slightest hint that such a claim might be theologically questionable or disputed (as it might well be in Gnostic circles).[13]

---

[9] See Warns, 'Untersuchungen', 76–8; cf. too his assertion on p. 163 that 'der antivalentinianische Skopus des Ganzen durchweg mehr vorausgesetzt als hervorgekehrt ist' ('the anti-Valentinian scope of the whole is throughout more presupposed than emphasized').

[10] Valentinian Gnosticism and Sethian Gnosticism may differ on how they regard the Creator God: the former may be slightly more sympathetic, regarding the figure as sadly ignorant but not necessarily malevolent; in the Sethian myth, the Creator figure is presented in more hostile terms.

[11] *Pace* e.g. Warns and Pratscher, there is nothing in a text such as 3.1 which suggests that the claim that 'we know the Father of truth' is in any way a contested one, or one put forward in direct competition with claims to the contrary. The claim comes in a subordinate clause as (apparently) something the writer appears to think he can simply assume as a given without any debate or question.

[12] This is then one important sense in which the author and the addressees have a 'shared world view': cf. p. 25 above on 'paraenesis'.

[13] One can contrast the way in which e.g. Ptolemy, in his *Letter to Flora*, takes care to distinguish between different classes of material in the Jewish Law, regarding some parts as clearly invalid, and other parts as having some validity. Equally, there is a refrain running through a number of Gnostic texts, especially those which purport to give an account of the creation of the world, that what (really) happened was 'not as Moses said', i.e. the accounts in

Nor is there any suggestion that the created world might be regarded by possible 'opponents' as inherently evil. Although one might read this into the debate about the value of 'flesh', at most it would seem that the position being addressed by the writer was that the 'flesh' was transitory and perhaps unimportant and a matter of indifference. But in 15.2, the author can apparently take it as common ground that God is the creator of the world, and as such should be 'repaid' for what he is and has done. The writer never seems to have to argue that the created order is inherently good, or that the world is not necessarily evil or even a place to seek escape from. Indeed at one point, the writer seems to urge his readers not to be afraid to undertake precisely this 'escaping' (or at least departing) journey: cf. ch. 5, where the language used by the writer comes very close to what one might call Gnostic (see the commentary). Similarly, on ethics, the exhortation *not* to love the things of this world (cf. 6.3–6) can be almost as world-denying as some Gnostic language. Thus on some matters which might be regarded as absolutely central to any Gnostic thinking, the author is silent (or even tending slightly in a Gnostic direction).

Second, in relation to Christology it is also hard to see what is said here as *necessarily* combating Gnostic ideas. One can (just) read into the language of 1.1–2 an insistence that 'Jesus' and 'Christ' are one and the same, but it is certainly not obvious on a surface reading of the text: the writer simply talks about 'Jesus Christ' as an assumed single person.[14] What is crucial here is that one should not 'think little' of him or the salvation he has brought, which is spelt out as meaning that one should not ignore his (future) position as judge in the final judgement to come. There is no hint of any claims about an alternative 'salvation' brought by a different saviour figure who is not the same as Jesus. Nor is there any stress (in this passage) on the claim that salvation has been brought about by the *suffering* of Jesus and his death on the cross (rather than by bringing saving knowledge). As the commentary will show, there is more than a little ambiguity in the text generally about whether 'salvation' is something that has been achieved already or whether it is still in the future and to be attained. But insofar as it is past, there is little if any discussion on precisely how it has been achieved. It is true that there is a passing reference to Jesus' suffering in 1.2, but it is not at all clear if this is intended to be a pointed attack against an opposing view.[15] It is simply stated

---

the Hebrew Bible are inaccurate and invalid. On this, see C. M. Tuckett, 'Moses in Gnostic Writings', in A. Graupner and M. Wolter (eds), *Moses in Biblical and Extra-Biblical Traditions*, BZAW 372 (Berlin: De Gruyter, 2007), 227–40. Of this there is not a trace, positively or negatively, in *2 Clement*.

[14] See on 1.1, and the lack of any explicit assertion that 'Jesus is the Christ', or 'the Christ is Jesus'.

[15] Elsewhere, references to Jesus' death as atoning or beneficial are striking by their absence: cf. e.g. 16.4 where it is (human) ἐλεημοσύνη which apparently takes away sins, rather than Jesus' death.

as apparently self-evident and capable of being asserted without any discussion or defence of the claim being necessary.[16] Moreover, it comes at the end of a description of 'salvation' that can be read as more Gnostic than anti-Gnostic (see the commentary on 1.2 and the language about knowing one's origins etc.).

In the case of the text at 9.5, it is again unclear how 'polemical' the passage is in relation to Christology. The text is slightly uncertain (see the commentary), though if one follows the reading of all the manuscripts and reads εἷς as the first word rather than εἰ, one could perhaps see the claim that Christ is 'one', and identical with 'the Lord who saved us', as some kind of counter to claims that separated the (heavenly) figure of Christ from Jesus in some way, and/or reflecting an unwillingness to call Jesus Lord;[17] but it can hardly be said that such a claim is the main part of the sentence here. Rather, this statement, along with the assertion that Christ became flesh, seems to be something that can be taken as read by the writer, and assumed as accepted by the readers without question. It is the deduction from this that is the real point at issue, namely the claim that 'we shall receive our reward in this flesh'. The issue is one of Christian behaviour, and/or the nature of Christians' rewards or punishments, not Christology as such.[18]

Third, in relation to ecclesiology, it is indeed striking to note the parallels between what is said in ch. 14 and some Gnostic texts. On the other hand, it is equally striking how *un*polemical the language is in relation specifically to possible Gnostic ideas. And indeed this phenomenon pervades the whole text: the writer seems happy to adopt 'Gnostic' language and terminology at times quite positively and apparently without any embarrassment. He refers to the future state to which Christians can look forward as one of 'rest' (ἀνάπαυσις: 5.5; 6.7), a term characteristic of Gnostic language;[19] he can refer to God as the 'Father of truth' (3.1; 20.5), an epithet that is attested elsewhere in only Gnostic texts (see on 3.1).[20] He can say, again without any apparent

---

[16] This is then another aspect of the 'shared world view': see n. 12 above and p. 25 above on 'paraenesis'.

[17] It is, however, hard to find such an unwillingness reflected anywhere else in *2 Clement*; indeed, almost the opposite seems to be the case. For example, in 4.2 the issue does not seem to be an unwillingness to call Jesus Lord: rather, it is a readiness to say precisely this but without taking seriously enough the ethical implications. See the commentary.

[18] Perhaps ironically, Warns, 'Untersuchungen', 7, 246, adopts the reading εἰ here (when the alternative might have given stronger support to his case); but clearly in the context, the 'if' is not a debated statement: it means 'since it *is* the case that ...', representing a condition that is presumed by all concerned to be in accordance with fact.

[19] The language is characteristic of some Gnostic texts, but not exclusive to them: others can and do use the same terminology. See the commentary on 5.5.

[20] cf. too the reference to the 'God of truth' in 19.1, if this is by the same author; if it is not (see §5. Literary Unity above), then it may be a case of a later writer imitating the same language, whether consciously or unconsciously. In 3.1 the 'Father of truth' is the one whom Christians (including himself) 'know'.

embarrassment, that 'sinning' consists of 'not knowing where we are from', using the terminology attested elsewhere in Gnostic language of self-awareness and identity (see on 1.2). In ch. 12, he uses a text attested elsewhere in (quasi-)Gnostic texts.[21] It is true that he then seeks to interpret the text very carefully in a strictly ethical way. The resulting interpretation that is given is decidedly not Gnostic; but there is no direct indication (unless it is in the artificiality and the tortuousness of the interpretation!) that the writer is consciously opposing a different interpretation of the same text. Similarly in ch. 14, he starts his argument from a statement about Christ and the church as some kind of pre-existent syzygy. Again, with a somewhat forced and tortuous interpretation, he seeks to make the claim into one which serves his overall exhortation for upright ethical behaviour by Christians in the present. But any possible Gnostic reading of the text (e.g. about the pre-existent nature of 'church' and 'Christ' in some kind of unity) is apparently accepted and presupposed: it is certainly not challenged in any way. So too, as already noted, some of the language used in ch. 5 about the need to depart from this world comes very close to Gnostic language (see the commentary).[22] It is of course possible that such language is being used in a quite sophisticated way, either as a means of irony or as a way of seeking to find common ground with any 'opponents'.[23] But this would attribute a degree of sophistication and ingenuity to the writer that may not be justified.

A number of other scholars have noted that any 'polemic' against possible Gnostic views is somewhat muted. Thus Wengst notes that there is 'no explicit polemic'.[24] Further, not all language which might have been congenial to Gnostics is necessarily inherently Gnostic in every instance.[25] At times, Gnostics no doubt took up, and made their own, terminology and language that was more widely used. And hence any apparent agreement between the language of *2 Clement* and that of Gnostics may simply be due to their common use of linguistic and/or religious commonplaces of the time.

It may therefore be more appropriate to see the relationship between *2 Clement* and (incipient) Gnosticism as rather more fluid and less clear-cut than has sometimes been the case in the past. As noted at the start of this section, there do seem to be some 'false teachers' around of whom the writer

---

[21] See below on 12.2 and the parallels in *Gos. Thom.* and *Gos. Eg.* It is of course debated whether *Gos. Thom.* should be regarded as Gnostic. Nevertheless, the saying there seems to reflect Gnostic ideas fairly clearly.

[22] For the (positive) use of 'Gnostic'-type language by the writer, see e.g. Lindemann, *Clemensbriefe*, 192; Wengst, *Zweite Clemensbrief*, 227; Salzmann, *Lehren*, 227.

[23] See above on the possibly pointed nature of some of the writer's language.

[24] Wengst, *Zweite Clemensbrief*, 227 ('keine ausdrückliche Polemik'). See too Lindemann, *Clemensbriefe*, 192.

[25] e.g. the epithet of God as the 'Father of truth' is not inherently Gnostic: it is closely related to the phrase 'God of truth' which does have parallels elsewhere (see on 19.1); similarly, talk of 'rest' as the goal of human existence is by no means confined to Gnostic texts (see on 5.5).

7. Opponents 55

is aware and wishes to guard his community against (cf. 10.5). The issue of the status of the 'flesh', and whether the Christian claims about 'resurrection' involve the resurrection of the 'flesh', is also clearly an important one. But this does not necessarily concern specifically Gnostic claims: issues about the resurrection, and what was believed to be raised, were widespread in the early Christian church, with a variety of answers given.[26]

Above all, the issue facing the writer seems to be a lack of ethical seriousness, including perhaps a failure to respect and accept other Christians (cf. the insistence on Christians exercising love with*in* the community in 13.4). Other ethical exhortations punctuate the whole of the text, though they are often extremely general and unspecific; hence one cannot easily reverse everything that is said here by way of ethical exhortations and assume that some people were claiming (or doing) the opposite.[27] *If* one is permitted to 'mirror read' what is said here (at least in general terms) and postulate 'libertine' tendencies in the community, it does not clearly point to a Gnostic background: not all Gnostics were necessarily libertines, and not all libertines were necessarily Gnostic.[28]

It would be tempting too to tie together closely the apparent eschatological issues addressed and the ethical ones, postulating libertine tendencies arising out of an over-realized eschatology.[29] But whether such ethical laxity is based specifically on beliefs about a *realized* eschatology, and/or claims about a 'salvation' that is already achieved, is not so clear.[30] The analysis of ch. 9, and the discussion of the issue of the resurrection of the flesh, does not clearly point to a fully realized eschatology as being the 'problem' addressed: rather, it is the narrower problem of whether the *flesh* will be included in the resurrection, but the resurrection itself seems to be presumed and accepted

---

[26] See the commentary on 9.1, and Donfried, *Setting*, 133–46.

[27] e.g. there is doubt about the precise interpretation of the exhortations to be 'self-controlled' in relation to sexual activity: whether this refers to abstaining from all sexual activity, or not engaging in extramarital sexual activity, is not certain. See the commentary on 4.3 and §9.7 Ethics below, But whether one can reverse this, and postulate a situation where others were actively promoting, or engaging in, sexual activity which the writer thought to be wrong, is not clear.

[28] The charge of libertinism directed against Gnostics by the church fathers may well be simply the language of polemic. Certainly it has proved very hard to substantiate such charges from texts by Gnostics themselves, e.g. the texts found in the Nag Hammadi library. See Williams, *Rethinking 'Gnosticism'*, 163–88; King, *What is Gnosticism?*, 201–8, and see the commentary on 3.4; 4.3 (though see also what is said there about Epiphanes). On the other hand, what is said in *2 Clement* about ethical behaviour is not at the level of (perhaps fictitious) polemic targeted at others to denigrate their integrity (and perhaps their ideology): a failure to behave properly is, in the author's eyes, apparently a very real danger which is facing his community.

[29] This is argued consistently throughout his study by Donfried (who couples this with a Gnostic framework of thought).

[30] See the detailed discussion of Donfried's theories by Aono, *Entwicklung*, 141–50.

(apparently by all in the discussion) as self-evidently future.³¹ More generally, the author of *2 Clement* himself (notoriously) is quite ambivalent about the timing of any 'salvation' that has happened or will happen. But there is a firm part of the text as a whole³² where the author firmly insists that Christians have already been 'saved' (cf. 1.4, 7; 2.7; 3.3; 9.2, 5). Hence one cannot easily drive a wedge between the author of *2 Clement* as advocating a futurist eschatology and his opponents as proponents of a realized eschatology. If anything, the language of 1.1 suggests that the addressees are in danger of 'thinking (too) *little* of their salvation',³³ not too much (but assigning it to the wrong time frame)!³⁴

Perhaps then one has to be somewhat agnostic about any 'opponents' here. Undoubtedly the writer has in mind some problems which he seeks to address. The presence of traditions such as 12.2 and 14.1–2 also suggests that some Gnostic ideas and/or traditions are 'in the air' for this writer. But it may be then that the text reflects a relatively early time when Gnostics and other Christians coexisted rather more freely and easily than in later periods.³⁵ Certainly, given what is said, as well as what is not said and what seems to be accepted by all sides in the discussion, it is hard to see the 'opponents' here as Gnostics. The author seems able to take up and use language and traditions which were congenial to Gnostics as well. But an explicit focus on key issues of debates and disagreements between Gnostics and other Christians (on the nature of God, the status of the God of the Hebrew Bible, the value of the created order, etc.) is lacking. That *2 Clement* is addressing a situation where the importance of ethical behaviour is perceived to be under threat seems

---

³¹ See the commentary on 9.1. The fact that one does not have to posit a Gnostic background to explain such a denial can be seen from Paul in 1 Cor. 15.50, who explicitly denies that the 'flesh' will participate in the eschatological events!

³² And not just in the opening chapter (where, according to Donfried, the author may be citing a tradition which he wishes to correct: see the commentary on 1.4).

³³ Whether one can 'mirror read' every statement in the text, and for every claim one way postulate an opposition group saying the opposite, is of course questionable and potentially dangerous. Also, 1.1 is directed against the addressees, not the possible 'false teachers' who may be a different group: see above.

³⁴ The evidence of ch. 11, and the use of the citation in 11.2–4 to suggest the 'opponents' had given up all hope for the future, also may need some care. The citation may be used by the author simply to latch on to a couple of key words: those who doubt the promises of God, meaning (in context) specifically the promises of judgement to come, will be shown to be 'double-minded' and hence will be 'miserable' (when they are condemned). But one cannot necessarily transfer all the details of the citation (apparently addressing a situation where people have given up all future hope and are 'miserable' because they are in despair) into the situation being addressed by the author here. See the commentary on 11.1–4.

³⁵ So e.g. H. Lohmann, *Drohung und Verheissung. Exegetische Untersuchungen zur Eschatologie bei den Apostolischen Vätern*, BZNW 55 (Berlin and New York: De Gruyter, 1989), 91. See too Lindemann, *Clemensbriefe*, 192, who simply says that perhaps the evidence only shows that 'es im Umkreis des 2Clem ein gnostisches Christentum gegeben hat' ('there was a Gnostic form of Christianity in the vicinity of *2 Clement*').

clear. That this is connected in some way with teaching activity by some in the community also seems clear (from at least 10.5). But any more precise details, specifically on how 'doctrinal' and/or 'theological' claims might have informed and led to this situation of (apparent) ethical laxity is not certain. The writer focuses almost exclusively on the issue of ethics as such (and even then at a very general level).

8. PLACE AND DATE OF WRITING

Questions about the place and date of writing are ultimately unanswerable, at least with any certainty (or even a degree of high probability). The lack of any concrete details, both concerning the author and the audience, make all these issues extremely unclear.

8.1 Place of writing

The original place of writing of *2 Clement* is unknown. Various suggestions have been made, including Rome, Corinth, Syria, and Egypt.

8.1.1 *Rome*

The theory that *2 Clement* originated in Rome was popular in earlier scholarship, especially when suggestions were made about the authorship of the text: ascribing the text to a Roman author inevitably led to a Roman provenance for the text being proposed. Thus Harnack's suggestion that the author was bishop Soter of Rome, writing *c.*165–170 (see p. 15 above) proved popular with some. Further, it has also been suggested that a Roman provenance might explain the link made in the tradition between *2 Clement* and *1 Clement* if both come from the same geographical location; so too, some links which have been observed between *2 Clement* and both *1 Clement* and Hermas might be explicable if the texts come from the same milieu.[1]

Some of these considerations may, however, be weaker than others. The link with *1 Clement* made in patristic tradition is perhaps the most telling in this context and will be considered shortly. But any substantive links between the contents of *2 Clement* and either *1 Clement* or Hermas are fairly superficial when examined more closely. In relation to *1 Clement*, this was noted earlier when discussing the question of authorship (see p. 14 above): any

---

[1] cf. e.g. Knopf, *Zwei Clemensbriefe*, 152.

8. Place and Date of Writing

similarities in substance are at most fairly tenuous.[2] Equally with Hermas, there is, for example, common language at one level about the church as pre-existent (cf. below on ch. 14) and a common interest in 'repentance'; but *2 Clement* seems to have no idea of the impossibility of post-baptismal sin (as e.g. in Hermas, *Vis.* 2.2.5).[3] Moreover, others have argued that the use of 'apocryphal' texts (as in e.g. 12.2 and elsewhere), as well as the unguarded use of potentially Gnostic ideas and language (cf. the similarity of what is said in ch. 14 with Valentinian speculations about syzygies), are difficult to conceive as emanating from a writer based in Rome, especially at a slightly later date when Valentinus had (perhaps) been expelled from Rome.[4]

On the other hand, the argument about the use of potentially Gnostic language may not be so strong if one posits a slightly earlier date for *2 Clement*, perhaps at a time when Valentinus was in Rome. There is considerable debate about just how much continuity one should posit between Valentinus and his later ('Valentinian') followers, and how far it is right to regard Valentinus himself as a 'Gnostic'.[5] However, it is clear that Valentinus did live in Rome for a time, and enjoyed some popularity: thus his ideas were current there and evidently influential and popular enough for him to arouse some strong opposition. *If* then there is at least a measure of continuity between Valentinus and (possibly later) Valentinian Gnostics, the presence of 'Valentinian' ideas and/or language in *2 Clement* could fit a Roman setting at a slightly earlier time quite plausibly.

There is too the puzzle of the consistent link made in the tradition between *2 Clement* and *1 Clement*. As we have seen, the MS tradition and the great majority of allusions, or references, to *2 Clement* presume a close link with *1 Clement*. Much of this evidence is quite late (and hence not necessarily very valuable as historical evidence about the origin of the text), but it is ubiquitous and consistent; and if the witness of Irenaeus (p. 7 above) is accepted, part of it can be traced back quite early. As noted above, common

---

[2] The most striking is the agreement in the citation of an unknown source in *2 Clem.* 11// *1 Clem.* 23; in addition there are other agreements, e.g. in 3.5; 11.7; 16.4, though all of these also involve citations of other works. Agreements thus focus primarily on other texts, and/or forms of texts, which are known to both authors, rather than on anything that the two authors say for themselves. As noted earlier, the two authors are very different from each other, arguing in very different ways and appealing to different authorities.

[3] See Pratscher, *Zweite Clemensbrief*, 59. For other differences between *2 Clement* and Hermas, see Lightfoot, *Apostolic Fathers*, 2.201.

[4] See Schubert, '2. Clemensbrief', 253; J. V. Bartlet, 'The Origin and Date of 2 Clement', *ZNW* 7 (1906), 125–6; Aono, *Entwicklung*, 157. The precise details of Valentinus' career in Rome are disputed, in particular whether he was forced to leave Rome or not. However, it is clear that he enjoyed considerable popularity for a time, but then engendered some strong opposition.

[5] See e.g. C. Markschies, *Valentinus Gnosticus? Untersuchungen zur valentinianischen Gnosis mit einem Kommentar zu den Fragmenten Valentins*, WUNT 65 (Tübingen: Mohr Siebeck, 1992), and the survey of recent views in I. Dunderberg, *Beyond Gnosticism: Myth, Lifestyle, and Society in the School of Valentinus* (New York: Columbia University Press, 2008).

authorship of the two texts is highly unlikely (see p. 14 above). Nevertheless, a more general model, simply positing a common geographical origin, *may* explain why the two texts were so firmly linked together in the tradition from a very early date; it would also explain the common use of the distinctive citation in *2 Clem.* 11//*1 Clem.* 23, as well as perhaps other smaller agreements which often involved citations rather than substantive points where the two writers are writing freely (see n. 2 above): such agreements may imply a common milieu (rather than any direct relationship between the texts).

The case for a Roman origin for *2 Clement* is not a strong one, but such a theory could fit many of the facts as we have them. Nevertheless, one should certainly also bear in mind other options.

8.1.2 *Corinth*

A number of scholars have argued for the origin of the text in Corinth.[6] A key part of the evidence is often seen in the language of 7.1 and the use of the verb καταπλεῖν, coupled with the athletic imagery. According to some, this verb implies a context of people sailing to take part in athletic contests, which might suggest a reference to the Isthmian games held in Corinth. However, the verb itself will probably not bear the weight of such an interpretation (see below on 7.1). Moreover, the first-person plural καταπλεύσωμεν in 7.3 suggests that the audience (and the author) are those who might make such (probably metaphorical) journeys by sea: they are not necessarily in the place *to* which people sail (i.e. in Corinth as people sail there to take part in the games; see the commentary).

Donfried's further refinement of this overall theory, suggesting that *2 Clement* represents an address by one of the elders ousted in the earlier rebellion in the Corinthian community but now reinstated as a direct result of the reception of *1 Clement*, has already been discussed in relation to the question of authorship. As noted there, any link with the specific situation apparently addressed in *1 Clement* is very tenuous and difficult to sustain. (See §3. Authorship above.)

Without such a global theory as Donfried's, and given the unclear nature of the evidence provided by the verb καταπλεῖν, any attempt to locate the text of *2 Clement* in a situation in Corinth is probably unconvincing.

8.1.3 *Syria*

Arguments have been adduced for locating the text in Syria. The strongest positive argument has been an appeal to the manuscript tradition which is (arguably) most closely connected with Syria, and the possible pattern of the location of references to the text by early church fathers.[7] For example, the

---

[6] cf. Lightfoot, *Apostolic Fathers*, 2.224; Donfried, *Setting*, 1–19.
[7] See Stegemann, 'Herkunft', *passim*.

Syriac manuscript S clearly comes from such a milieu, as might also the manuscript C. However, such manuscript evidence is very late. If one considers other forms of attestation (e.g. allusions to the wording of the text, or references to it by other writers), it is not clear that the text was known exclusively by Syriac writers (cf. the references to the text by Eusebius and later by Jerome and Rufinus, as well as possible allusions to it by Irenaeus and Origen).[8] The (relatively late) attestation of the text in Syriac writers and/or manuscripts may show something about the subsequent history and popularity of the text; it does not show anything very clearly about the origins of the text. Moreover, 'Syria' is probably rather too loose and vague to be specific enough to be helpful in the present context.[9]

8.1.4 Egypt

A fourth context which has gained some popularity in recent years has been Egypt.[10] A number of factors are thought to support such a view. For example, the use of 'apocryphal' texts in general might be more conceivable in Egypt than in, say, Rome. In particular the use of the saying in 12.2, a version of which elsewhere is attributed to the *Gos. Eg.* (and also attested in *Gos. Thom.*, which seems to have circulated in Egypt), indicates the use of a tradition which apparently circulated there. Possible links with Valentinian Gnosticism could point in the same direction: Valentinus came from Alexandria and hence his ideas might have been present in such a milieu; further, alongside the parts of *2 Clement* which appear to criticize Gnostic attitudes, there are some more elements which link more positively with Gnostic language and terminology (see §7. Opponents above), and all this might be best explained if the text originated in a place like Egypt which may have been more tolerant of heterodoxy and/or variations in expressions of Christian thought, including perhaps Gnostic (or 'proto-Gnostic') language and/or ideas. Further, the relatively 'free' ideas presupposed about any canon of Christian scripture, with a number of apocryphal texts (judged by later standards) used without any embarrassment, might also fit better into an Egyptian milieu.[11]

However, we have to admit that our knowledge of Egyptian Christianity in the relatively early period of Christian history from which *2 Clement* probably

---

[8] cf. Warns, 'Untersuchungen', 30–7; Pratscher, *Zweite Clemensbrief*, 60.

[9] See Baasland, '2. Klemensbrief', 91.

[10] Already in earlier scholarship, see Bartlet, 'Origin'; also B. H. Streeter, *The Primitive Church* (London: Macmillan, 1929), 244–53; more recently, see Koester, *Introduction*, 235–6; Vielhauer, *Geschichte*, 744 (Egypt or Syria); Wengst, *Zweite Clemensbrief*, 226; Aono, *Entwicklung*, 158–9; Warns, 'Untersuchungen', 91–5; Lindemann, *Clemensbriefe*, 195 (mostly agnostic, but Egypt or Syria more likely than Rome or Corinth); Pratscher, *Zweite Clemensbrief*, 60–1 (Egypt 'wahrscheinlicher' ('more probable') than Syria or other options).

[11] cf. the relatively free use of a wide range of 'apocryphal' Christian texts, apparently without any embarrassment, by a writer such as Clement of Alexandria.

comes is very limited.¹² The discovery of the Nag Hammadi library has shown us how 'heterodox' and 'orthodox' ideas, language, and texts could apparently coexist in close geographical proximity to each other. In relation to the argument above, the analysis of the saying in 12.2 suggests that the form here is *not* that of the *Gos. Eg.*; the common use of the saying in the two texts *may* suggest a common geographical milieu, but this is by no means demanded.¹³ Further, appeals to a possible environment where (Valentinian) Gnostic ideas and/or language might have been current could point to Egypt, but equally might point to Rome (or indeed elsewhere!), at least at a slightly earlier date (see above). One negative factor which might tell against an Egyptian origin of the text is the lack of any manuscript evidence of the text from Egypt (there are no papyri fragments extant from e.g. Oxyrhynchus as far as we know, and there is no evidence of a Coptic translation of the text).¹⁴ On the other hand, the nature and extent of surviving manuscripts may be due to chance as much as anything else, and arguments from silence are always potentially dangerous.¹⁵

Probably any claim about the geographical origin can be, at the end of the day, no more than an educated guess. An Egyptian origin for the text (probably the most widely held view in current scholarship) is possible, though the lack of firm positive evidence makes it difficult to be certain. The theory of a Roman origin is perhaps more plausible than is often allowed these days, provided one does not date the text too late, perhaps at a time when Valentinus himself was active in Rome and the ideas and language of himself and/or his followers might have been 'in the air'. Certainly too, such a theory might make more plausible the phenomenon of the assumed close link between *2 Clement* and *1 Clement*, as well as the nature of the agreements that exist between these texts.

8.2. Date of writing

Equal uncertainty surrounds the date of the text. A wide range of dates has been proposed over the course of scholarly study, though most would place it at some point in the second century. Donfried's theory about the origin of the text, closely associating it with the reception of *1 Clement* in Corinth, implies a date in the early second century; Harnack's proposal of bishop Soter as

---

¹² cf. Baasland, '2.Klemensbrief', 91; Pratscher, *Zweite Clemensbrief*, 61.

¹³ In any case we do not know for certain the precise geographical origin of the text referred to by Clement as the 'Gospel of the Egyptians'.

¹⁴ Pratscher, *Zweite Clemensbrief*, 61.

¹⁵ Moreover, given the fact that papyri from Oxyrhynchus are still being edited and published, with many more still to appear, it would be hazardous to make any strong claim about an alleged absence from the finds published so far.

the author implies a date *c.*166–74 CE.[16] Most others posit a date somewhere between these two extremes.

Proposals about dating are often connected with theories about other aspects of the text (e.g. on authorship, or on the identity of 'opponents'). They may also be connected with theories about the possible place of writing (see above). Probably the most secure *terminus ad quem* is provided by Eusebius, implying that the text was already in existence by the time he was writing.[17] If the (semi-)parallel between words of Origen and *2 Clem.* 1.1 can be taken as implying knowledge of the text by Origen (p. 8 above), then this would push the *terminus ad quem* back rather earlier and make a date no later than the second century more of a certainty; and if the possible reference to material in *2 Clement* by Irenaeus is also accepted, this would confirm this view even more strongly.[18]

At the other end of the spectrum, a date in the first century seems very unlikely. Analysis of the citations from Jesus traditions in *2 Clement* with parallels in the synoptic gospels indicates that traces of the redactional work of both Matthew and Luke are visible; hence the author of *2 Clement* must post-date the finished works of these evangelists (whether or not he made direct use of these gospels). The author is thus at a point in the development of (at least) the synoptic tradition that post-dates the present synoptic gospels. A date after the end of the first century thus seems most likely.

Having placed the text somewhere in the second century, any more precision is probably guesswork to a certain extent. Some have argued that the relatively free use of (what later became) 'apocryphal' traditions may reflect an earlier, rather than a later, date: the later one gets in the second century, the more likely it is that a developing firm canon, especially the fourfold gospel canon, would have exerted a stronger influence by excluding the citations of apocryphal texts as authoritative.[19] So too, the (probable) absence of allusions to Paul is perhaps easier to fit into an earlier period: by the time of writers like Irenaeus and others, one might expect more reference to Paul. Some kind of awareness of (Pauline?) authoritative texts associated with 'apostles' *may* be implied in the reference to 'the books and the apostles' in 14.2;[20] but the absence of any clear reference to anything specific in this

---

[16] A massively detailed list of proposals is given by Pratscher, *Zweite Clemensbrief*, 62–3.

[17] Though there might be some doubt even here, since Eusebius may not have known the text at first hand, and hence his reference to a second letter of Clement is not unambiguously a reference to our *2 Clement* (given the existence of other letters attributed to Clement in antiquity): see §2. Attestation above.

[18] Although the value of the evidence is debated. See p. 7 above.

[19] On the other hand, even as late a writer as Clement of Alexandria can cite traditions from 'non-canonical' texts very freely. However, the issue may also be connected with the place of writing of the text: use of 'apocryphal' texts may be easier to conceive in an Egyptian milieu, even at a later date, than in a setting such as Rome: see above.

[20] But see also pp. 42–3 above, and also the commentary on 14.2: the reference may be to the gospels as the 'memoirs of the apostles'.

respect in the rest of 2 *Clement* is quite striking. Similarly, the absence of any (clear) allusion to the Gospel of John becomes harder to explain, the later 2 *Clement* is dated.

One factor perhaps indicating a slightly earlier date is the relatively undeveloped idea of any church hierarchy presupposed here. There is no hint of any (monarchical) episcopacy: the one reference to possible authority figures mentions 'presbyters' only (17.3), with no mention of a 'bishop'. Further, any appeals to presbyteral authority are quite muted here (though see 17.3).[21] Such a relatively undeveloped form of any church hierarchy may imply a relatively early date.

One further factor which might bear on the date of the text relates to the 'opponents' presupposed. *If* these are to be identified as associated with Valentinian Gnostics, this might imply a date certainly after Valentinus himself, and perhaps reflecting a time when his followers had developed his ideas to a certain extent.[22] In one way, one could argue that 2 *Clement* might presuppose some development in 'Valentinian' thinking, which would indicate a somewhat later date; on the other hand, the somewhat unreflective use of 'Gnostic' terminology at times by the author of 2 *Clement* himself might indicate a time when clear boundary lines between 'Gnostic' and 'orthodox' had yet to be drawn, and a certain amount of fluidity and interchange was still presupposed. As such, this might indicate a slightly earlier date.[23]

Certainty is clearly not possible. Perhaps all one can say with any confidence is that a date some time around the middle of the second century seems to create the least number of problems.[24] Perhaps though there is some indication to suggest that a date slightly before the middle of the century, rather than after, would fit the evidence (such as it is) better.

As a tentative conclusion, a theory that the text was originally written in Rome at some stage in the early–middle 2nd century might fit the evidence we have reasonably well. But one cannot say more: the evidence is very flimsy and other possibilities (especially for the place of writing) can by no means be excluded.

---

[21] Whether the author himself is one of the presbyters is not clear. His own preferred method of address seems to be to use first-person plurals, not an authoritative second-person address. See further on 17.3 below, also on 1.1. See also p. 25 above on 'paraenesis' and the generally 'benevolent' nature of the exhortation.

[22] See n. 5 above for the issue of how much continuity one should posit between Valentinus himself and his later followers.

[23] Further, if a Roman origin for the text is accepted (see above), a time before Valentinus had become a very controversial figure, and when perhaps at least some of his ideas (*if* they do go back to him) were accepted fairly readily, might fit well.

[24] For similar views, positing a date around the middle of the 2nd century, see e.g. Stegemann, 'Herkunft', 132; Aono, *Entwicklung*, 157; Lindemann, *Clemensbriefe*, 195; B. D. Ehrman, *The Apostolic Fathers I*, LCL (London and Cambridge, Mass.: Harvard University Press, 2003), 160; Parvis, '2 *Clement*', 37; Pratscher, *Zweite Clemensbrief*, 64.

9. THEOLOGY

The 'theology' of 2 Clement is not easy to delineate with any precision. The author does not set out to present a clearly articulated statement about all aspects of his theology: at most, only a part of his 'theology' comes into play. As with so much of the Christian literature of the period, a good deal of what is written stems from a specific historical context and, to a certain extent, is determined by that context. Thus the author of 2 Clement (as also e.g. Paul in many/all of his letters) is writing to address a specific situation. Some things, which might well be of supreme importance to him in another context, might not be mentioned here; some things might not be stressed because they can be taken as read.

It is almost universally agreed that the prime message which the author seeks to convey is the vital importance of proper ethical behaviour by Christians in the present. All other 'theological' themes, if they are introduced, are brought in to bolster and sustain this primary theme. For the present purposes, it may be helpful to divide the material into sections, dealing with the ideas of the writer about God, Jesus, the Spirit, eschatology, etc. But it must be borne in mind that such distinctions are probably artificial, and many of the themes discussed here are treated at most in passing by the writer. This is not to say that they are unimportant; but they are used only in a subsidiary way to buttress his main message of exhorting his audience to take note of the demand for ethical seriousness in their daily lives.

9.1 God

As with so many early Christian texts and writers, the author of 2 Clement rarely if ever appears to reflect in a self-conscious way on the 'doctrine' of God: in almost all his references to God, he apparently thinks that he can take it as read that what he says will be accepted as virtually self-evident. How much of the evidence of 2 Clement is relevant here is also at times not quite clear, especially in relation to things said about 'the Lord': for it is uncertain whether this refers to God or to Jesus. Nevertheless, despite this ambiguity, some things are clearly ascribed to God.

As is so frequently the case with early Christian writers, the Jewish tenet of monotheism is adopted without any question or discussion. At one point, reference is made to the possible polytheistic background of the writer and the addressees (see on 1.6) but this is assumed to be now left behind. God is once referred to as the 'only' God (20.5), but this is in the final doxology and not in a context where much seems to be made of the claim.

In relation to the past, God is presented at one point, and only in passing, as the Creator (15.2). The fact that this is only a passing reference, of which nothing is made as such, is perhaps notable. It does not appear from what the writer says here that the issue is contested in any way: the issue at stake is the proper human *response* to this God, and the notion of God as Creator is assumed without question.[1] Nothing elsewhere is said about the creative activity of God: it is something that can evidently be assumed.

More explicit references to the activity of God relate to the present or future states of the audience (and the author). He is the 'Father' of Jesus (cf. 3.2; 9.11; 12.6: 'my Father'), and also the 'Father' of Christians whom he has called to be 'sons' (1.4; 9.10; 10.1).[2] Further things said about God highlight his goodness, and the way in which human beings experience him mostly in a thoroughly positive way. In relation to the 'salvation' (in general terms) of Christians, God is the one who has 'called us' (10.1; 16.1). He is the one who has sent Jesus to be the saviour and leader of immortality (20.5). A range of similar, positive, attributes and/or activities are ascribed to him: he is one who 'heals' (9.7), who is present and has not deserted his people (2.3; 15.3), is always ready to 'give' (15.4),[3] and as such the source and/or embodiment of 'goodness' (15.5). He is too all-knowing, both of the past and of the 'hearts' of human beings in the present (9.9); he is the 'living' God (20.2); he is unique and invisible (20.5). So, too, the promise in store for the (ethically upright) Christian can be put in terms of entering into his 'kingdom' (9.6; 11.7; 12.1), and experiencing things which are so wonderful that they have not yet been heard or even conceived (11.7).

He is the source of the ethical teaching which is presupposed throughout the text. References to 'the commandments of the Lord/Jesus' or 'his/my commandments' (cf. 3.4; 4.5; 6.7; 8.4; 17.3, 6) may be more Christologically

---

[1] Hence part of the difficulty in seeing the 'opponents' addressed as Gnostic. See §7. Opponents above.

[2] The 'sonship' is past according to 1.4, future according to 9.10. Such ambiguity is thoroughly characteristic of the text: see below.

[3] Though with slight uncertainty here, as in many places, as to whether this is to be attributed to God or to Jesus. However, given the 'functional identity' between God and Jesus (see below on Christology), it may not be necessary, or appropriate, to distinguish between the two in this context.

orientated in immediate terms, in that the 'Lord' may well be Jesus; but obeying such commands is clearly correlated with living in accordance with 'the will' of God (usually as 'Father': cf. 8.4; 9.11; 10.1; 14.1), which is clearly something which must be 'done'. God is thus one who has a clear 'will', demanding specific ethical behaviour on the part of human beings, and Jesus' 'commandments' articulate that 'will' clearly and unambiguously. Again, all this is put forward as almost self-evident: there is no need to argue the case.[4]

Perhaps somewhat surprisingly, almost all of what is explicitly said about God appears in a non-threatening way. As we shall see, warnings about a future judgement, and threats of future punishment for those who are not ethically upright, form an important part of the writer's rhetoric. Yet for the most part, these threats are couched in largely impersonal terms. God is rarely if ever explicitly said to be personally involved in such negative punitive actions. It may be implicit; but it is rarely said. Thus the threat of a coming conflagration (16.3) is in terms of a coming (impersonal) 'day'; the threat of eternal punishment for the wicked in terms of the language of Isa. 66.24 is cast in impersonal terms of their worm not dying, their fire not being quenched, and their being a spectacle to all, but again God as such is not explicitly mentioned as an agent (7.6; 17.5). By contrast, the positive counterparts, expressing the rewards in store for the righteous, are frequently expressed in terms of God's explicit action and involvement: he will 'receive us as sons' (9.10), we will 'enter his kingdom' (11.7).[5] The one exception may be the short sequence in 4.4–5.4, which talks about 'fearing' God, about Jesus as one who positively casts out those who do evil, and fear of the one who has the authority to cast others into hell (presumably God). Yet even here, it may be that the stress is as much on not fearing anyone or anything else (cf. esp. 5.4), with the bit about fearing God as simply the counterpart of this negative plea.[6]

Maybe the author does not explicitly reflect on this in any detail. Certainly there is no hint of the author having in mind a dualistic schema, attributing negative outcomes and/or consequences to a demonic/satanic figure other

---

[4] Again, this might tell against a Gnostic context, since part of the 'theological' claim of the 'orthodox' which Gnostics contested was the idea of God as a lawgiver (i.e. identifying him with the Jewish God of the OT). See §7. Opponents above.

[5] The language of 17.4, referring to the Lord 'rescuing' us, may be similar in this respect. The subject of the action may well be Jesus rather than God (see the commentary), but it is still striking that the author speaks here of human beings being 'ransomed/rescued' at the End. One might expect a verb of judgement (see the commentary and cf. Matt. 16.27). But it is characteristic of the author that, when speaking of the personal activity of God/Christ at the final judgement, he chooses a verb expressing positive saving activity, rather than one which (at least potentially) can include negative rejection.

[6] The other possible counter-example might be the difficult reference in 20.4 to the 'spirit' who *has been* punished and bound in chains. However, (*a*) it is not certain if this is the same author as the rest of the text; and (*b*) even so, it may be significant that the subject of the verb is still not 'God' but the rather more impersonal 'divine judgement'.

than God. Nevertheless, it may be significant that the writer's tendency seems to be to express negative outcomes and threats more in impersonal terms, almost as if they are inevitable consequences, rather than explicitly as the personal activity of God himself.

9.2 Christology (and soteriology)[7]

As with 'theo-logy' strictly speaking, the topic of Christology is not as such central to the writer's concerns, although what he claims about Christ forms the basis for his prime focus, i.e. the appeal for proper ethical behaviour.

Perhaps the most significant thing said about Jesus occurs at the very start: one should think of Jesus as one thinks of God (1.1). The focus is, however, not on Christology in general, nor on what Christ has achieved through his life and death as such (though it is noted briefly in 1.2); rather, the primary focus is on Jesus as the eschatological judge, and on the resulting consequences for practical living for the Christian. The 'identity' between Jesus and God is probably more a functional identity rather than an ontological one.[8] In the case of 1.1, the focus is primarily on the role of Jesus as the judge at the final judgement: as judge, Jesus occupies the role and function of God himself. Elsewhere, there is a free interchange between the person of God and the person of Jesus in relation to a range of different roles and activities, so that what is said of one can also be freely said of the other. Sometimes it is not clear who the author is referring to, especially when he speaks of 'the Lord': this may refer to God or to Jesus. However, in other instances the interchange in activities and/or predicates seems clear. Thus the author can speak of the 'will of Christ' (6.7) and the 'will of our/the Father' (8.4; 9.11; 10.1; 14.1) without any clear distinction in the contents of the 'will' concerned. He can refer to the commands of Jesus/the Lord (3.4; 4.5; 6.7; 17.6) which clearly correlate fully with the 'will' of God (cf. above, especially 8.4): hence in terms of content, there is no distinction between the two. He can talk of the 'appearance' ($\epsilon\pi\iota\phi\acute{\alpha}\nu\epsilon\iota\alpha$) of God (12.1) and of (probably) Christ (17.4: see the commentary). He speaks of both God and Christ 'calling' us (God: 10.1; 16.1; Christ: 1.8; 2.4; 9.5) and 'saving' us (God: 1.4; Christ: 1.7; 2.7; 9.5).[9] So too, sayings from scripture and sayings from the gospel tradition are cited with virtually equal authority, and with almost interchangeable speakers: hence in 13.4 the author can introduce the saying of Jesus (about loving one's enemies) as something that 'God' says; conversely, 'the Lord' who is the speaker in the citation of the words from Isa. 66.18 in 17.4 may be Jesus.

---

[7] In view of the close connection between the two topics for many Christian writers and thinkers, I include 'soteriology' here along with 'Christology'.

[8] cf. Donfried, *Setting*, 99; Lindemann, *Clemensbriefe*, 200–1; Pratscher, *Zweite Clemensbrief*, 66, and see the commentary on 1.1.

[9] The precise identity of the subject of the verb is often unclear.

Clearly then, at one level, there is a functional identity between God and the person of Jesus in that so much is predicated freely and interchangeably of either.[10]

On the other hand, it is not the case of a full personal identity between the two and the writer clearly has in mind a distinction between God and Jesus. Thus Jesus can refer to God as 'my/the Father' (3.2; 9.11; 10.1), obviously as someone other than himself. He is 'sent' by God (20.5), and his purpose is to make known the nature and being of 'the Father of truth' (3.1; cf. 20.5).

In terms of categories important for later Christian 'orthodoxy', the author here seems to presuppose the pre-existence of Jesus: he forms a 'syzygy' with the 'church' in a pre-existent mode of being (see 14.1–2), and he is 'sent' by the Father to be the means of leading other human beings to God (20.5). There is at most one passing reference to the incarnation as such (9.5: 'Christ ... who was first spirit, but became flesh'). The apparent equation made here between Christ and 'Spirit' is also striking; a similar equation seems to be made between the post-Easter (and/or final eschatological) existence of Jesus and 'Spirit' in 14.4: those who abuse the church 'will not receive the Spirit, that is Christ'. But however unusual such an equation might be in terms of later Christian trinitarian theology, it is not unparalleled in NT and second-century Christian writers (see the commentary on 9.5).

Other aspects of the nature and/or 'activity' of Jesus are, however, rarely if ever mentioned. As noted already, the incarnation is referred to only briefly in 9.5. There is also no mention of Jesus' resurrection. There is a discussion of the resurrection of the flesh (i.e. of all Christians, or perhaps of all human beings) in ch. 9; but this is not related to claims about the specific resurrection of Jesus. Perhaps surprisingly, there is also very little reference to the death of Jesus. At just one point the writer reminds his audience not to forget 'how much Jesus Christ endured sufferings for us' (1.2); but this is not developed in any way. It is possible that this note, tacked on to the end of a very 'Gnostic'-like summary of salvation in terms of 'knowing' who we are, where we have come from, and where we are destined for, is intended as a correction of any Gnostic-type tendencies among the audience (see the commentary). But it is still the case that this is not developed, or indeed mentioned, anywhere else in the text. Jesus is indeed presented as 'saving' human beings, using a variety of verbal images (cf. 1.6 and the reference to failing to see properly, being maimed in our understanding, characterized by death, but now having received sight, etc.). But this saving activity is only focused on the cross at 1.2. Further, whereas many other Christians interpreted Jesus' death as atoning for sin in some way, this writer appears to attribute this at

---

[10] See e.g. Aono, *Entwicklung*, 140; Lindemann, *Clemensbriefe*, 201; Pratscher, *Zweite Clemensbrief*, 39–40.

one point to the human activity of 'charity' (ἐλεημοσύνη: 16.4); and in 13.1 his language can be taken as implying that the 'wiping away' of sins is something that 'we' should do ourselves.

The nature, and above all the timing, of the 'saving' activity of Jesus is a notorious crux in the interpretation of *2 Clement*. At one level, there is a range of texts which refer to the saving activity (of Christ, or of God) as something in the past (1.4, 7; 2.7; 3.3; 9.5). Yet alongside these, there are a number of references that clearly imply that salvation is not guaranteed for the Christian, that it depends on the correct ethical response in the present, and definitely lies in the future (cf. 8.2; 13.1; 14.1; 15.1; 17.2; 19.3). How these two ideas relate to each other is not clear. The most extreme view is perhaps that of Donfried. Donfried argues that the language of past salvation comes predominantly in the section 1.4–8 (along with other verbal images of salvation: cf. below), and that this is a statement expressing primarily the views of the 'opponents' being addressed. Thus the author takes up views with which he basically disagrees, in order to correct and modify them. The theory is ingenious but is ultimately unpersuasive simply because there is no such hint in the present text that the author *dis*agrees with what he himself says. (See further the commentary on 1.4.) Further, it is by no means the case that statements about salvation as something in the past are confined to the section 1.4–8: for statements about salvation as something which has already been achieved continue in e.g. 2.7; 3.3; 9.5.[11] In the absence of other indications to the contrary, one has to assume that the author at least thought that he could hold together statements about salvation as past *and* future without any embarrassment.[12] So too the writer can use language other than that of 'salvation' to refer to the gracious action of God in the past or present. Thus he speaks of God/Christ having 'called' us (1.8; 2.4, 7; 5.1; 9.4, 5; 10.1; 16.1), of God as the one who 'heals' (9.7), of Christ as the one who calls us into being (1.8), who has shown 'mercy' to us (3.1), etc.

Further, there is clearly a very real sense in which the author thinks that the demand for ethical behaviour now (and hence the condition to be met if future salvation is to be achieved) is critically related to what has already been achieved (by way of 'salvation'!) in the action of God and/or Christ in the past. Thus the behaviour now demanded of the hearers as the necessary prerequisite for future salvation is not (only) put in terms of obedience to ethical demands which may have existed for ever: rather, it is the appropriate response to grace which has already been given to the hearers in the salvation achieved through Christ. The response is the ἀντιμισθία (1.3, 5; 9.7; 15.2) which Christians must make in response to the gracious and loving God's

---

[11] See Aono, *Entwicklung*, 143–4.

[12] In one way, the situation is not dissimilar in Paul, where statements about a realized and a futurist eschatology sit side by side.

prior act of salvation. Any act of future salvation, and demands for ethical behaviour in order (in some sense) to 'earn' such salvation, takes place within a broader context of the grace of salvation which has already been achieved through the action of Christ. The author may present his statements in a somewhat confused and muddled way at one level (in terms of salvation being both past and future); but he presents a 'pattern of religion' which is very similar in one way to the 'covenantal nomism' as identified by Sanders in relation to both Paul and Palestinian Judaism generally: there are demands on human beings in the present, but these are all in a broader context of divine grace that chooses and elects humans and places them in a context where they are enabled to respond to that prior action of grace and election.[13]

The nature of the text which the author has chosen to write may mean that many things, which might have been part of his overall theological armoury, are not said here. There is nothing really on the 'mechanics' of how past salvation has been achieved, or to a certain extent on what has been achieved: there is simply the note that it *has* happened (at one level), and some verbal images to describe it (cf. the images in 1.6 of being unable to see properly, and in a state of death). In that sense, the 'soteriology' of the author is undeveloped (or at least unstated in the text we have). It is, however, noteworthy that the verbal imagery in 1.6 focuses mostly on the inability of human beings to 'see' and/or understand (cf. the language of being 'maimed in our understanding', being enveloped by 'darkness' and 'mistiness', etc.). It does not speak about 'sin' and/or forgiveness (though 2.4 does talk about Christ coming to call 'sinners'). Hence any 'atonement' in Christ's saving work achieved in the past does not seem to be envisaged generally in relation to nullifying sin and/or its effects (unless this is implicit in the talk about 'repentance': see below).

Jesus is then for the author of *2 Clement* above all the one who has achieved salvation (at least potentially) by placing human beings in the position where they can (and should) respond to that grace by giving back to God the ἀντιμισθία which they owe. In the present, Jesus is above all the one who has given the ethical teaching which Christians are now to obey: the required 'confessing' of Jesus is to be carried out by 'doing what he says' (3.4). Jesus is

---

[13] See the seminal work (on Paul) of E. P. Sanders, *Paul and Palestinian Judaism* (London: SCM, 1975). Paul may have been rather more disciplined in his use of language than the author of *2 Clement*, for example choosing mostly to refer to 'salvation' as something that is future, and reserving language about righteousness and justification for the situation achieved in the past/present by God's saving action (though even Paul can refer to δικαιοσύνη as a future hope in Gal. 5.5); but the basic underlying model remains very similar. One should perhaps give the author the credit for genuinely meaning what he says, rather than simply regarding the statements about past salvation as vestiges of an opposition's theology which the writer disagrees with and wants to correct (Donfried), or as elements which are unintegrated into the wider whole and where the author may simply have not noted the discrepancy (so e.g. Aono, *Entwicklung*, 140).

thus the inaugurator of salvation, but now is primarily the one who provides the required ethical guidance and rules to enable the Christian to respond positively and achieve final salvation.[14]

9.3 The Spirit

The author of *2 Clement* has little to say on the Spirit. Indeed, virtually all that he says is in terms of his Christology, with virtually no idea of the Spirit as an entity in some sense independent of God the Father and/or Jesus. Rather, Jesus himself is said to have been 'spirit' before he 'became flesh' (9.5); and in 14.4, the author seems to imply that, in the present situation of the church, with Jesus absent (in 'heaven'?), Jesus is again equated with the Spirit (see above). Spirit language is thus reserved entirely for the person of Jesus, at least in relation to the past and present.

Perhaps surprisingly (at least at one level), there is nothing in *2 Clement* relating the present existence of Christians to the Spirit, nothing suggesting that Christians possess the Spirit now, or that the activity of the Spirit is an identifiable part of present Christian existence in the church. The church exists in the present, and the church according to 14.4 is the 'flesh', while the 'Spirit' is Christ, and one's behaviour now will be determinative for whether or not one receives the Spirit (= Christ) in the future. Experience of, and possession of, the Spirit is thus exclusively a future hope for the Christian.

All this sets *2 Clement* firmly apart from writers such as Paul or Luke and most other NT writers, as well as the other texts of the 'Apostolic Fathers' (cf. e.g. Ign. *Eph.* 9.1; *Did.* 7.1; 11.7–12; *Barn.* 4.11, etc.), though language about the risen Christ being identified with the Spirit can find precedent in Paul (cf. 1 Cor. 15.45). Maybe this simply shows that the author of *2 Clement* is not Paul or Luke! Whether such usage is determined by the context in which the text is written (e.g. as part of a warning against 'Gnostics' not to value their 'pneumatic' status too highly),[15] is not certain: very little is said about the Spirit, and what is present is related without any apology or argument to the person of Jesus. In no way does it appear that this (to us perhaps) notable lack of mention of any reference to the presence of the Spirit in the present life of the church is in any way a polemical point or that the writer is

---

[14] Whether this 'enabling' process provides the Christian with an ability, or power, to make the required response more successfully is not at all certain. To a certain extent, Christians are expected to do what they have to do by their own efforts, apparently unaided. The writer does not appear to have any idea (as perhaps in Paul) of true obedience only being possible on the basis of the justification achieved for Christians by the Christ event in the past (or by the presence of the Spirit now: see below on the Spirit as solely a future hope in *2 Clement*.) If one makes comparisons between *2 Clement* and other NT writers (which may not be altogether fair!), the soteriological model which *2 Clement* presupposes is perhaps rather closer to that of Matthew than to that of Paul.

[15] cf. Pratscher, *Zweite Clemensbrief*, 42.

9.4 The church

The writer has some things to say about the church[16] which are certainly unusual and striking. For the most part this appears in ch. 14, where the church is presented as a pre-existent entity, as the 'body of Christ', and perhaps as part of a syzygy with the person of Christ, Christ and the church being like man and wife (cf. Gen. 1.27, cited in 14.2). Some hints of similar ideas *may* be reflected in 2.1, which seems to suggest that the present church had some kind of prior existence before it had any (human) members.

Yet, for the most part, again it seems that the writer is not interested in any such 'theological' ideas for their own sake. In ch. 14 he seems to be citing pre-existing traditions or formulations which he can assume are well known to his readers (cf. the introduction in 14.2 to the claim about the church being the body of Christ: 'I do not think that you are ignorant . . .'). And indeed the way in which the author has to struggle to wring the message he wants out of the tradition he cites here suggests that the original claim is not one of his own choosing (see the commentary).

He starts with the claim that the church is pre-existent and 'spiritual' (though this seems to get lost later in the section here!). He then goes on to claim that the church was 'made manifest' in the 'flesh of Christ', and indeed uses language more often associated with the incarnation of Jesus to refer to the church (see the commentary on 14.2). This equation between the church and the flesh is then developed further in a somewhat confusing set of claims (14.3–4: see the commentary), with the further assertion that the 'flesh' is the 'antitype' ($\dot{\alpha}\nu\tau\acute{\iota}\tau\upsilon\pi\sigma s$) of the true reality ($\alpha\dot{\upsilon}\theta\epsilon\nu\tau\iota\kappa\acute{o}\nu$) which is the Spirit: hence there is a close connection (as well as a distinction) between the church and the Spirit which correspond to each other as flesh to spirit. He then makes the claim that Christians must 'guard the flesh', meaning both the church as the flesh of Christ and also the human make-up (cf. 8.6), referring to the need for proper ethical behaviour in the present. It is this to which the whole discussion about the church leads. The way through from the initial claims about the church as the body of Christ is fairly tortuous; however, the aim is not to develop an ecclesiology, but to reiterate the point made throughout the text about the importance of ethical behaviour. Ideas about the church arise probably from the context in which the author is writing and living; they are not necessarily part and parcel of his key ideas.

---

[16] Any discussion of the 'C/church' in English has to decide whether to capitalize the word. I have chosen not to do so throughout here, though a consistent use of 'Church' might be equally appropriate!

9.5 Eschatology

Undoubtedly the writer works with a theological scheme that is dominated by a future eschatology. The demand for proper ethical behaviour in the present is continually buttressed by the threat of future judgement and condemnation for those who fail to do what they should do in the present, and indeed this is the sole sanction which the writer deploys to make his appeal (cf. 6.7, 9; 9.5–6; 11.6–7; 17.3–4).

The author uses a wide range of vocabulary or ideas to express this future expectation and hope. Thus he can talk about the future reward in terms of 'rest' (ἀνάπαυσις: 5.5; 6.7), the 'kingdom' (5.5; 9.6; 11.7; 12.1, 2, 6), 'eternal life' (5.5), receiving the Spirit (14.3), gaining the prize as in an athletics contest (7.2; 20.2), divine sonship (9.10), having 'peace' (10.2), etc. Prior to any rewards (or punishment), he refers to the future as involving the act of (final) judgement (9.1; 16.3; 17.6; 18.2), which will take place before Christ, who is the judge of the living and the dead (1.1).

Precisely when this is to come is not clear. At some points, the writer seems to think in terms of a cosmic end of the whole world with a final judgement, at others he seems to think of the key moment as occurring for each individual at the moment of his/her physical death.[17] Thus references to final judgement (cf. 7.6; 17.4–7) and to worries about the delay in the coming of the End (11.2–4) seem to presuppose an idea of a final cosmic judgement; on the other hand, passages like 5.5; 6.5; 19.3–4 seem to presuppose an idea that the end-events will happen to each individual at the moment of his/her departure from this world. (See the commentary.) Again one can accuse the author of inconsistency, but he is in this respect very similar to authors such as Luke or Paul in the NT in having such a dual eschatology.[18]

Yet, as has been said here repeatedly, such ideas are not brought into the discussion for their own sake; they are introduced to buttress the ethical appeal of the writer for proper ethical behaviour.

9.6 Jews and Judaism

Perhaps surprisingly, the issue of Judaism, and the relationship of Christians and/or Christianity to Judaism, does not appear to be a topic of any concern for the writer of *2 Clement*. As already noted, the author uses Jewish scripture freely, and assumes (without apparently ever questioning it, or seeing it as a potentially problematic, or contested, issue) that all such scriptural texts are basically Christian texts which speak directly and unambiguously to the present Christian community. As an example, one can refer to the use of the text from Isa. 54 in *2 Clem.* 2. The same text is used by both Paul and

---

[17] See Aono, *Entwicklung*, 122–3.   [18] See p. 32 and n. 19 above.

Justin Martyr to stake claims about the superiority (qualitatively or quantitatively) of the Christian church over against non-Christian Judaism (see the commentary below). But of this there is not the slightest hint in *2 Clement* and the text is presumed to refer in its entirety to Christians and the Christian church. So, too, the writer gives no hint that his use of scripture might be contested by competing interpretations (as e.g. in Justin's *Dialogue*). Nor is there any reflection of antagonism, or competition, from non-Christian Jewish (or 'Judaizing') groups, as seems to be reflected in Ignatius or the *Didache*. Neither does the writer evidently feel any need to address the issue of non-Christian Judaism (as e.g. in *Barnabas*). In some respects then, *2 Clement* is somewhat different from writings which are roughly contemporary with it.

In line with this, it is also perhaps striking how little is made in any way of Jewish history, or indeed of any explicitly Jewish ideas. Jewish scripture is used (extensively!) and (Jewish) monotheism is assumed as self-evident. However, no reference to the events of 'salvation history' in the Jewish tradition occurs here: thus there is no mention of the Exodus events, or of the giving of the Law at Sinai. (References to the expressed will and/or commands of God seem to presuppose as self-evident where this will and these commands are to be found and what their contents are.) There is one passing reference to God as Creator (15.2: see above), but no reference to any details of the Genesis story.

The author includes himself with his addressees in 1.6, claiming that their (common) past life was one of worshipping material idols, language which in the biblical tradition (which seems to be consciously echoed here) refers primarily to non-Jews (though seen and interpreted from a Jewish perspective!). And when 'outsiders' are mentioned in ch. 13 as possibly encountering the Christian community in a real way, the language used is again the (biblical!) language of 'Gentiles' ($\tau\grave{\alpha}$ $\check{\epsilon}\theta\nu\eta$): such people might come into contact with Christians, but be put off by the failure of Christians to put into practice their love for each other, and hence will reject the Christian gospel thereby 'blaspheming the name' of God.

It would appear that the author of *2 Clement* is living in a context where non-Christian Jewish neighbours are virtually non-existent. The author sees no need to defend any of his Christian claims against competing ideas from non-Christian Jews. He can assume, apparently without any challenge, that Jewish traditions are to be used for (predominantly Gentile) Christians. And if any Jewish history is to be exploited, it seems limited to the twin notions of providing sayings from scripture which reinforce his overall message, and providing examples from the tradition to show that individual ethical failings cannot be rescued by the actions of others, however righteous (cf. 6.8).

9.7 Ethics

It is the theme of proper ethical behaviour that is absolutely central for the author of *2 Clement*. As we have seen in relation to other 'theological' themes, all the writer says serves to bolster and buttress his appeal to the addressees to behave in an ethically responsible and upright way.

The basis for such appeals occasionally refers to the nature of God as Creator (15.2), and to his goodness and his readiness to 'give' (15.4–5). Reference is often made to the ethical demands of God in terms of his 'will' (5.1; 8.4; 9.11; 10.1; 14.1; 6.7 has 'the will of Christ') or 'commandments' (3.4; 4.5; 6.7; 8.4; 17.1, 3, 6),[19] or more generally what he (God or Christ) 'says' (again either generally, cf. 3.4, or in relation to specific cited texts from scripture). It can, however, apparently be assumed as self-evident what the contents of these commands are and/or where they are to be found. But there is no reference to specific texts to give details.

In some contexts, ethical behaviour is expected/demanded as a response to the gracious activity of God and/or Christ in the past. There is just one reference in this context to the creation as the focus of such gracious activity (15.2),[20] as the addressees are there exhorted to give the appropriate 'return' (ἀντιμισθία) to God. But there is no reference anywhere to the saving activity of God in the events of the Exodus. Rather, for the most part the focus is on the 'salvation' achieved by God/Christ in the coming of Christ himself. Thus in ch. 1, there is extensive reference to the salvation achieved by God/Christ, with then the rhetorical question (to be answered later in the text) about what 'return' (ἀντιμισθία) should be given in response (1.3, 5). Later this is made explicit: the 'return' which is required is 'repentance' (9.7) and/or the 'faith and love' which the Christian must show in his/her everyday life (15.2). But the whole logic is clear (using slightly different language) in the transition from ch. 2 to ch. 3: Christ has called and saved us who were perishing (2.4–7); as a result we have come to true knowledge of God (3.1) and hence must 'confess' him and not 'deny' him (3.1); but then the nature of this 'confessing' is unambiguously clarified in that it is said to involve obeying his (ethical) commands (3.4). Certainly in the first part of the text, it seems clear that obeying the ethical commands of God and/or Christ is a response to the gracious act of God in calling Christians in the first place.

---

[19] For some of these, the commandments are those of Christ (3.4; 4.5; 6.7; 17.6); for some it is not clear (e.g. 'of the Lord' 8.4; 17.3). But given the interchangeability between God and Christ in many contexts, there is probably no difference in substance between such 'commandments' (see above).

[20] The reference in 1.8 to calling 'us' into being from a state of 'non-existence' is probably a reference to the addressees and the author becoming Christians.

Later on in the text, however, a rather different basis for ethical behaviour becomes prominent, if not all-embracing, namely the appeal to final judgement, the prospect of eschatological reward (for the righteous) or punishment (for the unrighteous), and where (notoriously) the idea of a salvific act in the past seems to have been almost forgotten. From ch. 8 onwards, where the idea of 'repentance' is introduced for the first time, the theme of the pressure of time before the End is reiterated: while we are here on earth, we must 'repent' before it is too late (8.1–3; 9.7). In a variety of different verbal descriptions and/or images, the author holds out the prospect of future reward for good behaviour.[21] Thus the promise of 'rest', the 'kingdom', and 'eternal life' are mentioned all together in 5.5 as aspects of the 'great and wonderful promise' of Christ; and the way to achieve these promises is spelt out in the next sentence: 'behave in a holy and upright way' (5.6). In 6.7, it is said that if we 'do the will of Christ', we will achieve 'rest'; if not, eternal punishment. We should all 'love one another', the purpose being 'so that we may all enter the kingdom of God' (9.6). Similarly in 11.7, if we 'do righteousness', we will receive eschatological rewards of the kingdom and the things that human beings have not yet conceived. Conversely, failure to put into practice appropriate ethical behaviour will result in rejection and punishment. Confession of Jesus as Lord (the archetypal Christian confession according to 1 Cor. 12.3) is insufficient for salvation if we do not 'do righteousness' (4.1–2). Those who 'do what is lawless' will be cast out (4.5) into eternal fire and torment (cf. 5.4; 7.6; 17.5, 7). Thus for most of the text, it is assumed that 'salvation' is not a matter of past assurance for the Christian but a matter of future hope, which will only be attained on the basis of a life of ethical uprightness and 'righteousness'. If we 'do', i.e. live out, such a life then we will be saved; if not, we will be finally and definitively rejected.

This is of course not quite the whole story. As well as the exhortations to live a life of righteousness in accordance with the commands and will of God and of Christ, there are also numerous calls for 'repentance' (8.1–3; 9.8; 13.1; 16.1; 17.1). As an exhortation apparently addressed to those who are already Christians in some sense, 'repentance' cannot presumably refer to the total change in religious affiliation implied in any act of 'conversion'. The actual words $\mu\epsilon\tau\acute{a}\nu o\iota a$ and $\mu\epsilon\tau a\nu o\epsilon\hat{\iota}\nu$ in *2 Clement* probably refer to the actual change in behaviour that is expected and demanded (see the commentary on 8.1). But presupposed in any such change is clearly an acknowledgement of past failure, of 'sin' having been committed and needing forgiveness. Hence it implies a recognition of the failure of human beings to live up to the moral standards expected and demanded of them by the Christian faith, but also of the possibility of some kind of resolution of that failure. (The language of 'forgiveness' is not used explicitly; but the

---

[21] See Aono, *Entwicklung*, 119–20; Pratscher, *Zweite Clemensbrief*, 45.

implication of the promise of forgiveness is surely present—otherwise the exhortation to 'repent' would be a mocking empty gesture.)

Further, there is no hint that such 'repentance' involves a radical change which can only be undertaken at 'conversion'. The author here is thus unlike e.g. Hermas (*Vis.* 2.2.5) or the writer of Hebrews for whom there seems to be no possibility of forgiveness for (at least some) post-baptismal sin (Heb. 6.6: the reference is probably to apostasy).[22] For the writer of *2 Clement*, repentance is something he feels he can urge upon his addressees at this point in time—and indeed if there is any possibility of the 'sermon' being reread in another context, the same possibility is still available in the future. Thus, whilst with one breath the author is taking very seriously the importance of the ethical demands on the Christian, and underlining that importance by stressing that one's fate in the final judgement is (at one level) dependent on one's moral success or failure in the present, the constant exhortation to repentance suggests that the author is equally aware of the existence of human failure in this regard and envisages a means by which such failure can be accommodated within the provision of the divine dispensation available to the Christian.

It is also striking that the author evidently regards himself as *not* necessarily assured of salvation, nor does he regard himself as ethically perfect: indeed he calls himself 'completely sinful' ($\pi\alpha\nu\theta\alpha\mu\alpha\rho\tau\omega\lambda\acute{o}s$: 18.2).[23] The author seems to regard his own Christian life as one of constant ethical struggle, and perhaps failure, but still one where such struggle is worthwhile and potentially hopeful, even in the context of the threat of final judgement and condemnation for the 'wicked'. Thus for himself, acknowledging his failures and shortcomings, he can still hold hope for the future. Implicit again is then a belief in divine forgiveness for human failings.

One should not lose sight of the fact that all the demands for (apparent) ethical perfection made by the author are set in the context of the gracious activity of God/Christ having generated and enacted a 'salvation' that is past. Moreover, this is not just something that is mentioned in the first chapter and never again repeated.[24] As noted earlier, the language about the 'saving' (and other) gracious activity by God appears throughout the argument of the text.

Due to the influence (possibly excessive influence?) of the study of Paul, the general ethos of *2 Clement* has often had something of a bad press in the past.

---

[22] Whether such statements are to be taken at face value is questionable: such warnings may in part be intended simply to reinforce the seriousness of the situation as the writer sees it, and the threat is part of the rhetoric without perhaps being intended to be taken with wooden literalness.

[23] Similarly in 15.1, he states that the good ethical behaviour of others will save not only themselves, but also himself as their counsellor: evidently he makes no claim to be ethically perfect himself.

[24] See p. 133 on Donfried's theory about 1.4–8.

In particular the ideas which dominate the text after the opening section, above all the theme of eschatological rewards and punishments being (almost) wholly correlated with ethical behaviour in the present, have given rise to assessments of the overall theology of the writer and his text which are probably not meant in an entirely complimentary way! H. Windisch summarized the theology of the text as '[ein] spätjüdisch verstandenes und spätjüdisch verflachtes synoptisches Christentum' ('a form of synoptic Christianity understood, and made superficial, in a late Jewish way').[25] Bultmann refers to the 'legalism' ('Gesetzlichkeit') of the text; he recognizes the occasional references to the saving action of Christ in the past, but notes too the futurist eschatological thrust of the bulk of the text.[26] Torrance asserts that 'the most distinctive features of the Christian faith (with the exception of a strong emphasis on the deity of Christ) are wanting'; the theology of *2 Clement* 'does not . . . leave any room for a doctrine of grace', and the text 'is the least evangelic of all the writings of the so-called Apostolic Fathers'.[27] Vielhauer claims that the author is propounding 'eine handfeste Werkgerechtigkeit' ('a firm idea of justification by works').[28] Aono also accuses the writer of 'Werkgerechtigkeit' ('justification by works'), and although he recognizes both the references to past salvation and also the situation in which the author is writing as perhaps modifying this, in the end he claims that one cannot fully 'excuse' the author.[29] Wengst, like Bultmann, talks of the writer's 'legalism' ('Gesetzlichkeit'), though noting that this is on a par with many other Christian texts of the period.[30] So, too, Donfried notes the differences between Paul and *2 Clement*, although with one breath acknowledging the dangers of setting Paul up as a norm against which other writers are to be judged, he proceeds to do just that! Thus the author of *2 Clement* provides an 'extreme moralism' which has 'overstressed' the future nature of salvation.[31]

---

[25] Windisch, 'Christentum', 126. The use of 'spätjüdisch' is perhaps not untypical of a German scholar writing in the 1920s, and it is clearly not meant as a positive theological assessment of the text!

[26] See R. Bultmann, *The Theology of the New Testament* (2 vols; London: SCM, 1952–5), 2.169. On p. 170 Bultmann gives a series of examples where the theology and ideas of *2 Clement* differ from those of Paul (e.g. the different meaning, and theological evaluation, of 'flesh', the ideas of 'spirit', 'righteous', 'righteousness', etc.). But maybe that only shows that the author of *2 Clement* is not Paul! And the tendency to assess, and judge, other texts by constant reference to Paul may betray an anachronistic, post-Reformation point of view that is unfair to the non-Pauline partner in the comparison.

[27] T. F. Torrance, *The Doctrine of Grace in the Apostolic Fathers* (London: Oliver & Boyd, 1948), 126, 131, 132. It is clear in Torrance's work that the standard of comparison is the Pauline doctrine of justification by faith alone, as interpreted by the Reformers.

[28] Vielhauer, *Geschichte*, 742.

[29] Aono, *Entwicklung*, 162.

[30] Wengst, *Zweite Clemensbrief*, 235.

[31] K. P. Donfried, 'The Theology of Second Clement', *HTR* 66 (1973), 497.

Yet in all this, there is a danger of reading this ancient Christian text too much through post-Reformation spectacles, and putting Paul and Pauline theology on a pedestal against which all other writers are measured (and usually found wanting!).[32] The nature of the text as a whole has to be taken seriously, without some parts taken out of their context within the whole and given possibly disproportionate significance; and one has to bear in mind the context in which the text appears to have been written. Thus the statements about future rewards and punishments based on present behaviour must be taken alongside the initial references to the saving work of Christ as something that is past, and which informs (and perhaps in a real sense makes possible) the Christian present. Further, the context (of possible ethical licence getting out of hand) may have led the writer to stress more heavily one side of what, even in Paul, is a delicate balancing act between stressing the indicatives of the gospel and the (ethical) imperatives which still govern present Christian existence.[33] The demand for a radical change in one's ethical behaviour in the present ($\mu\epsilon\tau\acute{\alpha}\nu o\iota\alpha$), coupled with the explicit statements about the consequences of one's actions now in a future judgement, can be read in a highly 'legalistic' way and as reflecting 'justification by works' (to use anachronistic terminology!). But looking a little more closely at what the writer says and considering too what is implied, as well as taking into account his probable situation, makes it likely that the overall stance of the text in this respect is rather more nuanced: the demand for 'repentance' in the present, and the threats and promises that go with that, are taken very seriously; but the text also implicitly recognizes that human failings can be, and also will be, accommodated and forgiven—provided these are acknowledged and accepted.

One final point to be noted here concerns the *contents* of the ethical demands made by the writer. We have already noted the stress on the need for 'repentance' in the text and a radical change in behaviour, which in turn presupposes prior failure to do what one was meant to do. But what exactly the writer is urging his addressees to do positively, and what to avoid doing, is not always clear.

In many instances the ethical exhortations in *2 Clement* are very general, with appeals to broad categories but with little or no detail supplied about concrete issues.[34] Thus there are appeals to do the 'will of the Father' (14.1), or the 'will of Christ' (6.7), doing what Christ 'says' (3.4), doing 'righteousness' (4.2; 11.7; 19.3), or (rather unspecific) 'words' (15.5), pursuing 'virtue' (10.1), as well as (equally) general references to 'keeping baptism pure and

---

[32] cf. Baasland, '2.Klemensbrief', 127.
[33] I have developed this further in a forthcoming essay on 'Paul and *2 Clement*'.
[34] See especially Wengst, *Zweite Clemensbrief*, 230–1; also Pratscher, *Zweite Clemensbrief*, 47.

undefiled' (6.9), or keeping 'the flesh pure' and the 'seal undefiled' (8.6 cf. 7.6; 8.4). Conversely, one must not 'do evil' (19.2), one must 'flee from impiety' (10.1), 'not disobey his commandments' (3.4), give up the 'evil desires' of the soul (16.2), etc. But in all this there is little that is very concrete, nor is there any discussion of possible ethical issues which might have been contested at the time (with some regarding a particular course of action as perhaps valid and acceptable, and others not). For large parts of the text of 2 Clement, the ethical exhortations remain very general, and it seems to be assumed as almost self-evident that one knows what is 'right' and what is 'wrong'.[35]

Occasionally, the exhortations become a little more specific. At 4.3 the addressees are exhorted not to be 'lovers of money', and 'love of money' is said to be a feature of 'this age' which the readers should be prepared to renounce (6.4). The list of virtues and vices in 4.3 and in 6.4 is relatively short (certainly compared with other lists in early Christian texts), suggesting perhaps that what is mentioned here does have some significance for the author (see the commentary). The references to money might also tie up with the note in 20.1 about the 'unrighteous' enjoying wealth.[36] On the other hand, the theme of money is not explicitly mentioned elsewhere so it must remain uncertain how important it is for the author.

It would seem that intra-community relations are not unimportant for the author, perhaps specifically in light of his current situation. The first point at which the author spells out just a little bit of what the general appeal to do 'good', or 'obey [God's/Christ's] commandments', might imply comes in 4.3, and the first thing mentioned is 'loving one another'. This would certainly link with the discussion in ch. 13, stressing the importance of being able to show to outsiders that Christians not only have the fine sentiments about loving enemies but also that they put that ethic into practice within their own community. So, too, other exhortations to help and support the community punctuate the text at various points (cf. the references to relate to 'one another': 4.3 love, not slander, sympathize with one another; 9.6 love one another; 12.3 speak the truth to each other; 15.5 not begrudge each other; 17.2 help one another). Perhaps then the situation of a potentially divided community, with the dangers of intra-communal enmities and disputes, may mean that the exhortations to 'love one another' are not just vague generalities but are meant to be taken very seriously in relation to current intra-community life.

---

[35] This is one of the ways whereby 2 Clement fits neatly into the category of 'paraenesis': see p. 25 above.

[36] Possibly too 16.4, extolling the value of $\É\lambda\epsilon\eta\mu\omicron\sigma\acute{\upsilon}\nu\eta$ might be relevant here, if the word refers to giving money to others. But see the commentary for the argument that the word may be referring to acts of 'charity' more generally than simply financial giving.

One other theme which has provoked some discussion relates to the author's (possible) summary of his own work as an appeal for ἐγκράτεια, 'self-control' (15.1). As noted below, ἐγκράτεια can refer to a radical asceticism, particularly in relation to sexual activity, or to a more general ability to control one's own instincts, but in relation to sexual activity not advocating complete abstinence (see on 4.3). The interpretation of the Jesus tradition in 12.2 in terms of the way in which human beings should regard members of the opposite sex could be taken in a radically ascetic way: all men and all women should not regard others as objects of desire. However, while the references to 'adultery' in 4.3 and 6.4 suggest that sexual relations outside marriage are clearly regarded as wrong, such specific exhortations against adultery make little sense if one is presuming that all sexual activity is regarded as wrong. Hence the positive exhortation to 'self-control' must be meant in a less radically ascetic way, and should be taken as a more general exhortation, in relation to sexual activity, to restrict such activity to what is deemed to be its proper sphere, and not to prohibit it completely.[37]

The other place in the text where ethical demands become slightly more concrete is in 16.4, with the sudden discussion of prayer, fasting, and 'charity', with the unusual attempt to put these three activities into a relative order of importance, claiming that fasting is better than prayer but that charity is better than both. In one way, this fits well with the general tone of the text as a whole, which stresses the importance of concrete behaviour. However, little else is said here about the nature of the charitable action in mind: does it relate to helping those in need inside the community? Or those outside? Further, if charitable action might include giving money to others in need, such action, if it were ongoing as a continued action, does presuppose that one has money to dispense! Hence a radical lifestyle of giving up all material possessions does not seem to be in view. Once again, the ethos presupposed does not seem to have been a very radical encratite one.

For the most part, then, the writer seems content to stress the vital importance of properly ethical behaviour, but he seems to feel able to leave many of the specific details unstated, or simply presumed. It is assumed for the most part that what is right and what is wrong can be taken as read. Debates about the ethical problems of life for a Christian within secular society, the extent to which Christians can/should assimilate to broader society, the problems of the relations between Christians and a secular state, etc., all appear not to have arisen here (or if they have they are not explicitly discussed). The putting into practice of a Christian ethic might have been an issue; the content of such an ethic seems to have been remarkably uncontroversial.

---

[37] See Wengst, *Zweite Clemensbrief*, 232; Pratscher, *Zweite Clemensbrief*, 49, and the commentary on 4.3 below.

PART II

Text and Translation

ΚΛΗΜΕΝΤΟΣ ΠΡΟΣ ΚΟΡΙΝΘΙΟΥΣ Β

I

1 Ἀδελφοί, οὕτως δεῖ ἡμᾶς φρονεῖν περὶ Ἰησοῦ Χριστοῦ, ὡς περὶ θεοῦ, ὡς περὶ κριτοῦ ζώντων καὶ νεκρῶν· καὶ οὐ δεῖ ἡμᾶς μικρὰ φρονεῖν περὶ τῆς σωτηρίας ἡμῶν.
2 ἐν τῷ γὰρ φρονεῖν ἡμᾶς μικρὰ περὶ αὐτοῦ, μικρὰ καὶ ἐλπίζομεν λαβεῖν· καὶ οἱ ἀκούοντες ὡς περὶ μικρῶν ἁμαρτάνομεν οὐκ εἰδότες, πόθεν ἐκλήθημεν καὶ ὑπὸ τίνος καὶ εἰς ὃν τόπον, καὶ ὅσα ὑπέμεινεν Ἰησοῦς Χριστὸς παθεῖν ἕνεκα ἡμῶν.
3 τίνα οὖν ἡμεῖς αὐτῷ δώσομεν ἀντιμισθίαν, ἢ τίνα καρπὸν ἄξιον οὗ ἡμῖν αὐτὸς ἔδωκεν; πόσα δὲ αὐτῷ ὀφείλομεν ὅσια;
4 τὸ φῶς γὰρ ἡμῖν ἐχαρίσατο, ὡς πατὴρ υἱοὺς ἡμᾶς προσηγόρευσεν, ἀπολλυμένους ἡμᾶς ἔσωσεν.
5 ποῖον οὖν αἶνον αὐτῷ δώσομεν ἢ μισθὸν ἀντιμισθίας ὧν ἐλάβομεν;
6 πηροὶ ὄντες τῇ διανοίᾳ, προσκυνοῦντες λίθους καὶ ξύλα καὶ χρυσὸν καὶ ἄργυρον καὶ χαλκόν, ἔργα ἀνθρώπων· καὶ ὁ βίος ἡμῶν ὅλος ἄλλο οὐδὲν ἦν εἰ μὴ θάνατος. ἀμαύρωσιν οὖν περικείμενοι καὶ τοιαύτης ἀχλύος γέμοντες ἐν τῇ ὁράσει, ἀνεβλέψαμεν ἀποθέμενοι ἐκεῖνο ὃ περικείμεθα νέφος τῇ αὐτοῦ θελήσει.
7 ἠλέησεν γὰρ ἡμᾶς καὶ σπλαγχνισθεὶς ἔσωσεν, θεασάμενος ἐν ἡμῖν πολλὴν πλάνην καὶ ἀπώλειαν, καὶ μηδεμίαν ἐλπίδα ἔχοντας σωτηρίας, εἰ μὴ τὴν παρ' αὐτοῦ.
8 ἐκάλεσεν γὰρ ἡμᾶς οὐκ ὄντας καὶ ἠθέλησεν ἐκ μὴ ὄντος εἶναι ἡμᾶς.

1 ἡμᾶς (bis)] A S ὑμᾶς C (bis)   2 λαβεῖν] A ἀπολαβεῖν C   ὡς περί] C S ὥσπερ A   ἁμαρτάνομεν] A C ἁμαρτάνουσιν καὶ ἡμεῖς ἁμαρτάνομεν S   3 δέ] A γάρ S om C   ὀφείλομεν] C ὀφίλομεν A   5 ποῖον οὖν] C ποῖον S ποίουν A   αὐτῷ δώσομεν] αὐτῷ δώσωμεν A δώσομεν αὐτῷ C   6 πηροί] A πονηροί C   καὶ χρυσόν] A χρυσόν C S   ἄλλο οὐδέν] A οὐδὲν ἄλλο C   αὐτοῦ θελήσει] A θελήσει αὐτοῦ C θελήσει ἡμῶν S   ἐλπίδα] C ἐλπίδαν A   8 ἐκ] A ἐκ τοῦ C

I

1 Brothers, we must think of Jesus Christ as we think of God, as the judge of the living and the dead; and we must not think little of our salvation.

2 For if we think little about him, we also hope to receive little. And we who listen as though it were something little are sinning if we do not know where we were called from, and by whom, and to what place, and how much Jesus Christ endured sufferings for us.

3 What then shall we give him in return, or what fruit shall we offer that is worthy of what he has given us? How many holy works do we owe him?

4 For he granted us light; as a father, he called us 'sons'; he saved us when we were perishing.

5 What praise, then, shall we give him, or what reward can we give him as a return for what we have received?

6 We were maimed in our understanding, worshipping stones, wood, gold, silver, and copper, the works of human beings, and our whole life was nothing other than death. We were covered in darkness and our sight was clouded by mistiness; but we received our sight, by his will putting aside the cloud that covered us.

7 For he had pity on us and through his compassion saved us, having seen the great error and destruction that was in us, and that we had no hope of salvation at all except from him.

8 For he called us when we did not exist, and he willed us into being from non-existence.

II

1 Εὐφράνθητι, στεῖρα ἡ οὐ τίκτουσα, ῥῆξον καὶ βόησον, ἡ οὐκ ὠδίνουσα, ὅτι πολλὰ τὰ τέκνα τῆς ἐρήμου μᾶλλον ἢ τῆς ἐχούσης τὸν ἄνδρα. ὃ εἶπεν· εὐφράνθητι, στεῖρα ἡ οὐ τίκτουσα, ἡμᾶς εἶπεν· στεῖρα γὰρ ἦν ἡ ἐκκλησία ἡμῶν πρὸ τοῦ δοθῆναι αὐτῇ τέκνα.

2 ὃ δὲ εἶπεν· βόησον, ἡ οὐκ ὠδίνουσα, τοῦτο λέγει· τὰς προσευχὰς ἡμῶν ἁπλῶς ἀναφέρειν πρὸς τὸν θεόν, μὴ ὡς αἱ ὠδίνουσαι ἐγκακῶμεν.

3 ὃ δὲ εἶπεν· ὅτι πολλὰ τὰ τέκνα τῆς ἐρήμου μᾶλλον ἢ τῆς ἐχούσης τὸν ἄνδρα· ἐπεὶ ἔρημος ἐδόκει εἶναι ἀπὸ τοῦ θεοῦ ὁ λαὸς ἡμῶν, νυνὶ δὲ πιστεύσαντες πλείονες ἐγενόμεθα τῶν δοκούντων ἔχειν θεόν.

4 καὶ ἑτέρα δὲ γραφὴ λέγει, ὅτι οὐκ ἦλθον καλέσαι δικαίους, ἀλλὰ ἁμαρτωλούς·

5 τοῦτο λέγει, ὅτι δεῖ τοὺς ἀπολλυμένους σώζειν.

6 ἐκεῖνο γάρ ἐστιν μέγα καὶ θαυμαστὸν οὐ τὰ ἑστῶτα στηρίζειν, ἀλλὰ τὰ πίπτοντα.

7 οὕτως καὶ ὁ Χριστὸς ἠθέλησεν σῶσαι τὰ ἀπολλύμενα, καὶ ἔσωσεν πολλούς, ἐλθὼν καὶ καλέσας ἡμᾶς ἤδη ἀπολλυμένους.

2 ἐγκακῶμεν] A ἐκκακῶμεν C   3 τοῦ] A om C   4 δέ] A S om C   7 οὕτως] A οὕτω C   Χριστός] A S κύριος C;

II

1 'Rejoice, you barren one, you who bear no children; break forth and cry out, you who endure no labour pains. For the woman who is deserted has more children than the one who has a husband.' When it said, 'Rejoice, you barren one who bear no children', it meant us; for our church was barren before children were given to it.

2 When it said, 'Cry out, you who endure no labour pains', it means this: that we should offer up our prayers to God sincerely, and not grow weary as women in labour.

3 And when it said, 'For the woman who is deserted has more children than the one who has a husband', it meant that our people seemed to have been deserted by God; but now we who have believed are more in number than those who seem to have God.

4 And another scripture says, 'I have come not to call the righteous, but sinners'.

5 This means that he had to save those who were perishing.

6 For it is great and wonderful to strengthen not the things that are standing but those that are falling.

7 So Christ wished to save the perishing, and he saved many, having come and called us who were already perishing.

III

1 Τοσοῦτον οὖν ἔλεος ποιήσαντος αὐτοῦ εἰς ἡμᾶς, πρῶτον μέν, ὅτι ἡμεῖς οἱ ζῶντες τοῖς νεκροῖς θεοῖς οὐ θύομεν καὶ οὐ προσκυνοῦμεν αὐτοῖς, ἀλλὰ ἔγνωμεν δι' αὐτοῦ τὸν πατέρα τῆς ἀληθείας· τίς ἡ γνῶσις ἡ πρὸς αὐτὸν ἢ τὸ μὴ ἀρνεῖσθαι δι' οὗ ἔγνωμεν αὐτόν.
2 λέγει δὲ καὶ αὐτός· τὸν ὁμολογήσαντά με ἐνώπιον τῶν ἀνθρώπων, ὁμολογήσω αὐτὸν ἐνώπιον τοῦ πατρός μου.
3 οὗτος οὖν ἐστὶν ὁ μισθὸς ἡμῶν, ἐὰν οὖν ὁμολογήσωμεν δι' οὗ ἐσώθημεν.
4 ἐν τίνι δὲ αὐτὸν ὁμολογοῦμεν; ἐν τῷ ποιεῖν ἃ λέγει καὶ μὴ παρακούειν αὐτοῦ τῶν ἐντολῶν, καὶ μὴ μόνον χείλεσιν αὐτὸν τιμᾶν, ἀλλὰ ἐξ ὅλης καρδίας καὶ ἐξ ὅλης τῆς διανοίας.
5 λέγει δὲ καὶ ἐν τῷ Ἡσαΐᾳ· ὁ λαὸς οὗτος τοῖς χείλεσίν με τιμᾷ, ἡ δὲ καρδία αὐτῶν πόρρω ἄπεστιν ἀπ' ἐμοῦ.

1 ἔλεος] C ἔλαιος A   ἡμᾶς] A C add καὶ ἠλέησεν ἡμᾶς S   καὶ οὐ προσκυνοῦμεν αὐτοῖς] A S om C   γνῶσις] C γνώσεις A   ἡ πρὸς αὐτόν] A S τῆς ἀληθείας C   ἀρνεῖσθαι] A add αὐτόν C S   2 ἐνώπιον τῶν ἀνθρώπων] A C om S   αὐτόν] A S om C   μου] A C om S   3 ἡμῶν] A C μέγας S   οὖν (2°)] A om C S   ὁμολογήσωμεν] A C add αὐτόν S   4 καρδίας] A C add ἡμῶν S   τῆς] A om C   διανοίας] A C δυνάμεως ἡμῶν S   5 αὐτῶν] A S αὐτοῦ C   ἄπεστιν] A ἀπέστην C

III

1 He has shown such mercy to us since, first, we who are living do not sacrifice to dead gods, and we do not worship them, but through him we know the Father of truth. What is the knowledge that is directed towards him but not denying him through whom we have come to know him?

2 And even he himself says 'the one who confesses me before other people, I will confess before my Father'.

3 This then is our reward, if we confess him through whom we were saved.

4 But how do we confess him? By doing what he says, not disobeying his commandments, and by honouring him not only with our lips but with our whole heart and our whole mind.

5 And it also says in Isaiah, 'This people honours me with their lips, but their heart is far from me.'

IV

1 Μὴ μόνον οὖν αὐτὸν καλῶμεν κύριον· οὐ γὰρ τοῦτο σώσει ἡμᾶς.
2 λέγει γάρ· οὐ πᾶς ὁ λέγων μοι· κύριε κύριε, σωθήσεται, ἀλλ' ὁ ποιῶν τὴν δικαιοσύνην.
3 ὥστε οὖν, ἀδελφοί, ἐν τοῖς ἔργοις αὐτὸν ὁμολογῶμεν, ἐν τῷ ἀγαπᾶν ἑαυτούς, ἐν τῷ μὴ μοιχᾶσθαι μηδὲ καταλαλεῖν ἀλλήλων μηδὲ ζηλοῦν, ἀλλ' ἐγκρατεῖς εἶναι, ἐλεήμονας, ἀγαθούς· καὶ συμπάσχειν ἀλλήλοις ὀφείλομεν, καὶ μὴ φιλαργυρεῖν. ἐν τούτοις τοῖς ἔργοις ὁμολογῶμεν αὐτὸν καὶ μὴ ἐν τοῖς ἐναντίοις·
4 καὶ οὐ δεῖ ἡμᾶς φοβεῖσθαι τοὺς ἀνθρώπους μᾶλλον, ἀλλὰ τὸν θεόν.
5 διὰ τοῦτο, ταῦτα ἡμῶν πρασσόντων, εἶπεν ὁ κύριος· ἐὰν ἦτε μετ' ἐμοῦ συνηγμένοι ἐν τῷ κόλπῳ μου καὶ μὴ ποιῆτε τὰς ἐντολάς μου, ἀποβαλῶ ὑμᾶς καὶ ἐρῶ ὑμῖν· ὑπάγετε ἀπ' ἐμοῦ, οὐκ οἶδα ὑμᾶς, πόθεν ἐστέ, ἐργάται ἀνομίας.

1 οὖν] A S om C   3 αὐτόν (1°)] C S αὐτῶν A   ὀφείλομεν] C ὀφίλομεν A   ὁμολογῶμεν] A ὁμολογήσωμεν C   5 ἡμῶν] C S ὑμῶν A   κύριος] A C Ἰησοῦς S   ποιῆτε] A ποιήσητε C

IV

1 Let us then not only call him Lord, for this will not save us.

2 For he says, 'Not everyone who says to me "Lord, Lord" will be saved, but only the one who does righteousness.'

3 So then, brothers, let us confess him by our actions, by loving one another, by not committing adultery or slandering one another or being jealous, but by being self-controlled, merciful, good; and we should sympathize with one another and not be lovers of money. It is by these actions that we confess him, and not by their opposites.

4 And we must not fear other people, but God.

5 For this reason, if we do these things, the Lord said, 'Even if you are gathered together with me in my bosom and do not do my commandments, I will cast you out, and I will say to you, "Depart from me, I do not know you or where you are from, you who do what is lawless."'

V

1 Ὅθεν, ἀδελφοί, καταλείψαντες τὴν παροικίαν τοῦ κόσμου τούτου ποιήσωμεν τὸ θέλημα τοῦ καλέσαντος ἡμᾶς, καὶ μὴ φοβηθῶμεν ἐξελθεῖν ἐκ τοῦ κόσμου τούτου.
2 λέγει γὰρ ὁ κύριος· ἔσεσθε ὡς ἀρνία ἐν μέσῳ λύκων.
3 ἀποκριθεὶς δὲ ὁ Πέτρος αὐτῷ λέγει· ἐὰν οὖν διασπαράξωσιν οἱ λύκοι τὰ ἀρνία;
4 εἶπεν ὁ Ἰησοῦς τῷ Πέτρῳ· μὴ φοβείσθωσαν τὰ ἀρνία τοὺς λύκους μετὰ τὸ ἀποθανεῖν αὐτά· καὶ ὑμεῖς μὴ φοβεῖσθε τοὺς ἀποκτέννοντας ὑμᾶς καὶ μηδὲν ὑμῖν δυναμένους ποιεῖν, ἀλλὰ φοβεῖσθε τὸν μετὰ τὸ ἀποθανεῖν ὑμᾶς ἔχοντα ἐξουσίαν ψυχῆς καὶ σώματος τοῦ βαλεῖν εἰς γέενναν πυρός.
5 καὶ γινώσκετε, ἀδελφοί, ὅτι ἡ ἐπιδημία ἡ ἐν τῷ κόσμῳ τούτῳ τῆς σαρκὸς ταύτης μικρά ἐστιν καὶ ὀλιγοχρόνιος, ἡ δὲ ἐπαγγελία τοῦ Χριστοῦ μεγάλη καὶ θαυμαστή ἐστιν, καὶ ἀνάπαυσις τῆς μελλούσης βασιλείας καὶ ζωῆς αἰωνίου.
6 τί οὖν ἐστιν ποιήσαντας ἐπιτυχεῖν αὐτῶν, εἰ μὴ τὸ ὁσίως καὶ δικαίως ἀναστρέφεσθαι καὶ τὰ κοσμικὰ ταῦτα ὡς ἀλλότρια ἡγεῖσθαι καὶ μὴ ἐπιθυμεῖν αὐτῶν;
7 ἐν γὰρ τῷ ἐπιθυμεῖν ἡμᾶς κτήσασθαι ταῦτα ἀποπίπτομεν τῆς ὁδοῦ τῆς δικαίας.

2 κύριος] A C add ἡμῶν S   4 φοβεῖσθε (bis)] C φοβεῖσθαι A   ἀποκτέννοντας] A ἀποκτένοντας C   πυρός] A C om S   5 ἐπαγγελία] C ἐπαγγελεία A   Χριστοῦ] A C κυρίου S   ἀνάπαυσις] A ἡ ἀνάπαυσις C   7 ἐν γάρ] A γάρ ἐν C   ἐπιθυμεῖν] C ἐπιθυμεῖ A   ταῦτα] A S αὐτὰ C

V

1 So then, brothers, having left behind our stay in the strange land of this world, let us do the will of him who called us, and let us not be afraid to leave this world.

2 For the Lord said, 'You will be like lambs in the midst of wolves.'

3 Peter answered and said to him, 'What if the wolves tear the lambs apart?'

4 Jesus said to Peter, 'Let the lambs not be afraid of the wolves after they have died. And you too must not fear those who kill you and then can do nothing more to you; but fear him who, after you die, has the power over body and soul to cast them into the hell of fire.'

5 Know this too, brothers, that our stay in this world in the flesh is brief and short-lived, but the promise of Christ is great and wonderful, namely rest in the kingdom that is coming and eternal life.

6 What then must we do to attain these things except to behave in a holy and upright way, and regard the things of this world as foreign to us and not desire them?

7 For when we desire to obtain these things, we fall away from the right path.

VI

1 Λέγει δὲ ὁ κύριος· οὐδεὶς οἰκέτης δύναται δυσὶ κυρίοις δουλεύειν. ἐὰν ἡμεῖς θέλωμεν καὶ θεῷ δουλεύειν καὶ μαμωνᾷ, ἀσύμφορον ἡμῖν ἐστίν.
2 τί γὰρ τὸ ὄφελος, ἐάν τις τὸν κόσμον ὅλον κερδήσῃ, τὴν δὲ ψυχὴν ζημιωθῇ;
3 ἔστιν δὲ οὗτος ὁ αἰὼν καὶ ὁ μέλλων δύο ἐχθροί.
4 οὗτος λέγει μοιχείαν καὶ φθορὰν καὶ φιλαργυρίαν καὶ ἀπάτην, ἐκεῖνος δὲ τούτοις ἀποτάσσεται.
5 οὐ δυνάμεθα οὖν τῶν δύο φίλοι εἶναι· δεῖ δὲ ἡμᾶς τούτῳ ἀποταξαμένους ἐκείνῳ χρᾶσθαι·
6 οἰόμεθα ὅτι βέλτιόν ἐστιν τὰ ἐνθάδε μισῆσαι, ὅτι μικρὰ καὶ ὀλιγοχρόνια καὶ φθαρτά, ἐκεῖνα δὲ ἀγαπῆσαι, τὰ ἀγαθὰ τὰ ἄφθαρτα.
7 ποιοῦντες γὰρ τὸ θέλημα τοῦ Χριστοῦ εὑρήσομεν ἀνάπαυσιν· εἰ δὲ μήγε, οὐδὲν ἡμᾶς ῥύσεται ἐκ τῆς αἰωνίου κολάσεως, ἐὰν παρακούσωμεν τῶν ἐντολῶν αὐτοῦ.
8 λέγει δὲ καὶ ἡ γραφὴ ἐν τῷ Ἰεζεκιὴλ ὅτι ἐὰν ἀναστῇ Νῶε καὶ Ἰὼβ καὶ Δανιήλ, οὐ ῥύσονται τὰ τέκνα αὐτῶν ἐν τῇ αἰχμαλωσίᾳ.
9 εἰ δὲ καὶ οἱ τοιοῦτοι δίκαιοι οὐ δύνανται ταῖς ἑαυτῶν δικαιοσύναις ῥύσασθαι τὰ τέκνα αὐτῶν, ἡμεῖς, ἐὰν μὴ τηρήσωμεν τὸ βάπτισμα ἁγνὸν καὶ ἀμίαντον, ποίᾳ πεποιθήσει εἰσελευσόμεθα εἰς τὸ βασίλειον τοῦ θεοῦ; ἢ τίς ἡμῶν παράκλητος ἔσται, ἐὰν μὴ εὑρεθῶμεν ἔργα ἔχοντες ὅσια καὶ δίκαια;

1 κύριος] A C add ἡμῶν S   2 ὅλον] A S om C   4 φθορὰν καί] A C om S χρᾶσθαι] A χρήσασθαι C   6 οἰόμεθα] A C add δὲ ἀδελφοί S   τά (3°)] C καί A
7 γάρ] A S om C   αὐτοῦ] A C add καὶ καταφρονήσωμεν αὐτῶν S 9 οἱ τοιοῦτοι δίκαιοι] A C οὗτοι S   οὐ δύνανται ταῖς ἑαυτῶν δικαιοσύναις ῥύσασθαι τὰ τέκνα αὐτῶν] A ταῖς ἑαυτῶν δικαιοσύναις οὐ δύνανται τὰ τέκνα ῥύσασθαι C

VI

1 The Lord says, 'No servant can serve two masters.' If we wish to serve both God and mammon, it is harmful for us.

2 'For what advantage is there, if someone gains the whole world, but forfeits their soul?'

3 But this age and the age to come are two enemies.

4 This age speaks of adultery, corruption, love of money and deceit; but that age renounces these things.

5 We cannot therefore be friends of both. We must renounce this world to obtain the other.

6 We reckon that it is better to hate the things which are here, since they are brief, short-lived and perishable, and to love those things which are good and imperishable.

7 For in doing the will of Christ, we shall find rest; but if not, nothing will save us from eternal punishment if we disobey his commandments.

8 And the scripture in Ezekiel also says, 'Even if Noah, Job and Daniel were to arise, they would not rescue their children from captivity.'

9 But if even righteous men such as these cannot rescue their children by their own righteousness, with what confidence can we enter into the kingdom of God if we do not keep our baptism pure and undefiled? Or who will be our advocate if we are not found doing what is holy and righteous?

VII

1 Ὥστε οὖν, ἀδελφοί μου, ἀγωνισώμεθα εἰδότες, ὅτι ἐν χερσὶν ὁ ἀγὼν καὶ ὅτι εἰς τοὺς φθαρτοὺς ἀγῶνας καταπλέουσιν πολλοί, ἀλλ' οὐ πάντες στεφανοῦνται, εἰ μὴ οἱ πολλὰ κοπιάσαντες καὶ καλῶς ἀγωνισάμενοι.
2 ἡμεῖς οὖν ἀγωνισώμεθα, ἵνα πάντες στεφανωθῶμεν.
3 ὥστε θέωμεν τὴν ὁδὸν τὴν εὐθείαν, ἀγῶνα τὸν ἄφθαρτον, καὶ πολλοὶ εἰς αὐτὸν καταπλεύσωμεν καὶ ἀγωνισώμεθα, ἵνα καὶ στεφανωθῶμεν· καὶ εἰ μὴ δυνάμεθα πάντες στεφανωθῆναι, κἂν ἐγγὺς τοῦ στεφάνου γενώμεθα.
4 εἰδέναι ἡμᾶς δεῖ, ὅτι ὁ τὸν φθαρτὸν ἀγῶνα ἀγωνιζόμενος, ἐὰν εὑρεθῇ φθείρων, μαστιγωθεὶς αἴρεται καὶ ἔξω βάλλεται τοῦ σταδίου.
5 τί δοκεῖτε; ὁ τὸν τῆς ἀφθαρσίας ἀγῶνα φθείρας τί παθεῖται;
6 τῶν γὰρ μὴ τηρησάντων, φησίν, τὴν σφραγῖδα ὁ σκώληξ αὐτῶν οὐ τελευτήσει καὶ τὸ πῦρ αὐτῶν οὐ σβεσθήσεται, καὶ ἔσονται εἰς ὅρασιν πάσῃ σαρκί.

1 οὖν] A om C S   μου] A S om C   ἀγωνισώμεθα] A S ἁγνισώμεθα C   ἀγών] C S αἰών A   εἰ μή] C οἱ μή A εἰ μὴ μόνον S   3 θέωμεν] S θῶμεν A C   4 εἰδέναι] A εἰδέναι δέ C S   ὁ] A S om C   ἀγωνιζόμενος] A ὁ ἀγωνιζόμενος C S   5 δοκεῖτε] C δοκεῖται A   φθείρας] A φθείρων C S   παθεῖται] A πείσεται C   6 αὐτῶν (2°)] A om C

VII

1 So then, my brothers, let us compete, knowing that the contest is to hand, and that many set sail for perishable contests but not all are crowned, but only those who have laboured greatly and have competed well.

2 Let us then compete, that we may all be crowned.

3 So we should run the straight course, the imperishable contest. Let many of us set sail for it, and let us compete so that we be crowned; and if we cannot all be crowned, let us at least come near it.

4 We must be aware that whoever is caught cheating, while competing in a perishable contest, is flogged and thrown out of the stadium.

5 What do you think? What will someone who cheats in the imperishable contest suffer?

6 For those who have not kept the seal, he says 'Their worm will not die and their fire will not be quenched, and they will be a spectacle for all flesh.'

VIII

1 Ὡς οὖν ἐσμὲν ἐπὶ γῆς, μετανοήσωμεν.

2 πηλὸς γάρ ἐσμεν εἰς τὴν χεῖρα τοῦ τεχνίτου· ὃν τρόπον γὰρ ὁ κεραμεύς, ἐὰν ποιῇ σκεῦος καὶ ἐν ταῖς χερσὶν αὐτοῦ διαστραφῇ ἢ συντριβῇ, πάλιν αὐτὸ ἀναπλάσσει, ἐὰν δὲ προφθάσῃ εἰς τὴν κάμινον τοῦ πυρὸς αὐτὸ βαλεῖν, οὐκέτι βοηθήσει αὐτῷ· οὕτως καὶ ἡμεῖς, ἕως ἐσμὲν ἐν τούτῳ τῷ κόσμῳ, ἐν τῇ σαρκὶ ἃ ἐπράξαμεν πονηρὰ μετανοήσωμεν ἐξ ὅλης τῆς καρδίας, ἵνα σωθῶμεν ὑπὸ τοῦ κυρίου, ἕως ἔχομεν καιρὸν μετανοίας.

3 μετὰ γὰρ τὸ ἐξελθεῖν ἡμᾶς ἐκ τοῦ κόσμου οὐκέτι δυνάμεθα ἐκεῖ ἐξομολογήσασθαι ἢ μετανοεῖν ἔτι.

4 ὥστε, ἀδελφοί, ποιήσαντες τὸ θέλημα τοῦ πατρὸς καὶ τὴν σάρκα ἁγνὴν τηρήσαντες καὶ τὰς ἐντολὰς τοῦ κυρίου φυλάξαντες ληψόμεθα ζωὴν αἰώνιον.

5 λέγει γὰρ ὁ κύριος ἐν τῷ εὐαγγελίῳ· εἰ τὸ μικρὸν οὐκ ἐτηρήσατε, τὸ μέγα τίς ὑμῖν δώσει; λέγω γὰρ ὑμῖν, ὅτι ὁ πιστὸς ἐν ἐλαχίστῳ καὶ ἐν πολλῷ πιστός ἐστιν.

6 ἄρα οὖν τοῦτο λέγει· τηρήσατε τὴν σάρκα ἁγνὴν καὶ τὴν σφραγῖδα ἄσπιλον, ἵνα τὴν αἰώνιον ζωὴν ἀπολάβωμεν.

2 ποιῇ] A ποιήσῃ C   καὶ ἐν] A om C   διαστραφῇ] A καὶ διαστραφῇ C S   ἢ συντριβῇ] A συντριβῇ C   βοηθήσει] A βοηθεῖ C   οὕτως] A οὕτω C   τῆς] A om C   ἕως ἔχομεν καιρὸν μετανοίας] A ὡς ἔτι καιρὸν ἔχομεν C   3 κόσμου] A C σαρκός S   ἢ] A C τὰς ἁμαρτίας καὶ οὐκ S   4 σάρκα] C σάρκαν A add ἡμῶν S   6 αἰώνιον] A C om S ἀπολάβωμεν] A ἀπολάβητε C S

VIII

1 So then, while we are still on the earth, let us repent.

2 For we are clay in the hand of the craftsman. For just as the potter, if he makes a vessel and then it is bent or broken in his hands, he then refashions it; but if he has already put it into the fiery kiln, he can no longer mend it. So too with us: while we are still in this world, let us repent with our whole heart of the evil things we have done in the flesh, so that we may be saved by the Lord, while we have time for repentance.

3 For after we leave this world, we will no longer be able there to confess or repent.

4 So then, brothers, if we do the will of the Father, and keep the flesh pure and observe the commandments of the Lord, we will receive eternal life.

5 For the Lord says in the gospel, 'If you do not keep what is small, who will give you what is great? For I say to you that the one who is faithful in what is very little is also faithful in much.'

6 This then is what he means: keep the flesh pure and the seal undefiled, so that we may receive eternal life.

IX

1 Καὶ μὴ λεγέτω τις ὑμῶν, ὅτι αὕτη ἡ σὰρξ οὐ κρίνεται οὐδὲ ἀνίσταται.
2 γνῶτε· ἐν τίνι ἐσώθητε, ἐν τίνι ἀνεβλέψατε, εἰ μὴ ἐν τῇ σαρκὶ ταύτῃ ὄντες;
3 δεῖ οὖν ἡμᾶς ὡς ναὸν θεοῦ φυλάσσειν τὴν σάρκα·
4 ὃν τρόπον γὰρ ἐν τῇ σαρκὶ ἐκλήθητε, καὶ ἐν τῇ σαρκὶ ἐλεύσεσθε.
5 εἷς Χριστός, ὁ κύριος ὁ σώσας ἡμᾶς, ὢν μὲν τὸ πρῶτον πνεῦμα, ἐγένετο σὰρξ καὶ οὕτως ἡμᾶς ἐκάλεσεν· οὕτως καὶ ἡμεῖς ἐν ταύτῃ τῇ σαρκὶ ἀποληψόμεθα τὸν μισθόν.
6 ἀγαπῶμεν οὖν ἀλλήλους, ὅπως ἔλθωμεν πάντες εἰς τὴν βασιλείαν τοῦ θεοῦ.
7 ὡς ἔχομεν καιρὸν τοῦ ἰαθῆναι, ἐπιδῶμεν ἑαυτοὺς τῷ θεραπεύσοντι θεῷ, ἀντιμισθίαν αὐτῷ διδόντες.
8 ποίαν; τὸ μετανοῆσαι ἐξ εἰλικρινοῦς καρδίας.
9 προγνώστης γάρ ἐστιν τῶν πάντων καὶ εἰδὼς ἡμῶν τὰ ἐν καρδίᾳ.
10 δῶμεν οὖν αὐτῷ αἶνον, μὴ ἀπὸ στόματος μόνον, ἀλλὰ καὶ ἀπὸ καρδίας, ἵνα ἡμᾶς προσδέξηται ὡς υἱούς.
11 καὶ γὰρ εἶπεν ὁ κύριος· ἀδελφοί μου οὗτοί εἰσιν οἱ ποιοῦντες τὸ θέλημα τοῦ πατρός μου.

1 οὐδέ] A οὔτε C   4 ἐλεύσεσθε] C ἐλεύσεσθαι A ἦλθεν S   5 εἷς] A C S Flor Edess εἰ Exc Patr   πνεῦμα] A S λόγος C   οὕτως (1°)] A S οὕτως καί C   ἐκάλεσεν] A C ἐγένετο ἐν σάρκι S   ἀποληψόμεθα] C ἀποληψόμαιθα A   6 οὖν] A S om C   7 θεῷ] A C om S   8 εἰλικρινοῦς] C ἰλικρινοῦς A   9 ἐν καρδίᾳ] A ἐγκάρδια C   10 αἶνον] C S αἰώνιον A   11 ποιοῦντες] C πουντες A

IX

1 And let none of you say that this flesh is not judged and does not rise again.

2 Know this: in what state were you saved, and in what state did you receive your sight, except in this flesh?

3 We must therefore guard the flesh like a temple of God.

4 For just as you were called in the flesh, so too you will come in the flesh.

5 There is one Christ, the Lord who saved us, who was first spirit, but became flesh and in this way called us; so also we will receive the reward in this flesh.

6 Let us then love one another, so that we may all enter the kingdom of God.

7 While we have time to be healed, let us give ourselves to God who heals us, giving him our recompense.

8 What is that? Repentance from a sincere heart.

9 For he knows all things in advance, and knows too what is in our hearts.

10 Let us then give praise to him, not only from our mouth but from our heart as well, so that he may receive us as sons.

11 For the Lord said, 'My brothers are those who do the will of my Father.'

X

1 Ὥστε, ἀδελφοί μου, ποιήσωμεν τὸ θέλημα τοῦ πατρὸς τοῦ καλέσαντος ἡμᾶς, ἵνα ζήσωμεν, καὶ διώξωμεν μᾶλλον τὴν ἀρετήν, τὴν δὲ κακίαν καταλείψωμεν ὡς προοδοιπόρον τῶν ἁμαρτίων ἡμῶν, καὶ φύγωμεν τὴν ἀσέβειαν, μὴ ἡμᾶς καταλάβῃ κακά.
2 ἐὰν γὰρ σπουδάσωμεν ἀγαθοποιεῖν, διώξεται ἡμᾶς εἰρήνη.
3 διὰ ταύτην γὰρ τὴν αἰτίαν οὐκ ἔστιν εὑρεῖν ἄνθρωπον, οἵτινες παράγουσι φόβους ἀνθρωπίνους, προῃρημένοι μᾶλλον τὴν ἐνθάδε ἀπόλαυσιν ἢ τὴν μέλλουσαν ἐπαγγελίαν.
4 ἀγνοοῦσιν γὰρ ἡλίκην ἔχει βάσανον ἡ ἐνθάδε ἀπόλαυσις, καὶ οἵαν τρυφὴν ἔχει ἡ μέλλουσα ἐπαγγελία.
5 καὶ εἰ μὲν αὐτοὶ μόνοι ταῦτα ἔπρασσον, ἀνεκτὸν ἦν· νῦν δὲ ἐπιμένουσιν κακοδιδασκαλοῦντες τὰς ἀναιτίους ψυχάς, οὐκ εἰδότες, ὅτι δισσὴν ἕξουσιν τὴν κρίσιν, αὐτοί τε καὶ οἱ ἀκούοντες αὐτῶν.

1 μου] A om C add καὶ ἀδελφαί S   ἁμαρτίων] A ἁμαρτημάτων C   3 γάρ] A S δέ C   προῃρημένοι] A προαιρούμεθα C προαιρούμενοι S   ἀπόλαυσιν] A S ἀνάπαυσιν C   ἐπαγγελίαν] C ἐπαγγελείαν A   4 ἡλίκην] C ἡλήκην A   ἀπόλαυσις] A S ἀνάπαυσις C   οἵαν τρυφήν] A C ἡλίκην ἀπόλαυσιν S   ἐπαγγελία] C ἐπαγγελεία A   5 ἀναιτίους] C ἀνετίους A

X

1 So then, my brothers, let us do the will of the Father who called us, so that we may live; let us rather pursue virtue, but let us abandon evil as the forerunner of our sins, and let us flee from impiety lest evil overtake us.

2 For if we are eager to do good, peace will pursue us.

3 For this reason, no one can find [peace?] when they bring in human fears, and prefer the pleasures of the present to the promise that is to come.

4 For they do not know how great the torment is which the pleasures of the present entail, or what kind of delight the future promise will bring.

5 And if they alone did these things, it would be bearable; but now they continue to teach evil to innocent souls, not knowing that they will have a double penalty, both they and those who hear them.

XI

1 Ἡμεῖς οὖν ἐν καθαρᾷ καρδίᾳ δουλεύσωμεν τῷ θεῷ, καὶ ἐσόμεθα δίκαιοι· ἐὰν δὲ μὴ δουλεύσωμεν διὰ τὸ μὴ πιστεύειν ἡμᾶς τῇ ἐπαγγελίᾳ τοῦ θεοῦ, ταλαίπωροι ἐσόμεθα.

2 λέγει γὰρ καὶ ὁ προφητικὸς λόγος· ταλαίπωροί εἰσιν οἱ δίψυχοι, οἱ διστάζοντες τῇ καρδίᾳ, οἱ λέγοντες· ταῦτα πάλαι ἠκούσαμεν καὶ ἐπὶ τῶν πατέρων ἡμῶν, ἡμεῖς δὲ ἡμέραν ἐξ ἡμέρας προσδεχόμενοι οὐδὲν τούτων ἑωράκαμεν.

3 ἀνόητοι, συμβάλετε ἑαυτοὺς ξύλῳ· λάβετε ἄμπελον· πρῶτον μὲν φυλλοροεῖ, εἶτα βλαστὸς γίνεται, μετὰ ταῦτα ὄμφαξ, εἶτα σταφυλὴ παρεστηκυῖα.

4 οὕτως καὶ ὁ λαός μου ἀκαταστασίας καὶ θλίψεις ἔσχεν· ἔπειτα ἀπολήψεται τὰ ἀγαθά.

5 ὥστε, ἀδελφοί μου, μὴ διψυχῶμεν, ἀλλὰ ἐλπίσαντες ὑπομείνωμεν, ἵνα καὶ τὸν μισθὸν κομισώμεθα.

6 πιστὸς γάρ ἐστιν ὁ ἐπαγγειλάμενος τὰς ἀντιμισθίας ἀποδιδόναι ἑκάστῳ τῶν ἔργων αὐτοῦ.

7 ἐὰν οὖν ποιήσωμεν τὴν δικαιοσύνην ἐναντίον τοῦ θεοῦ, εἰσήξομεν εἰς τὴν βασιλείαν αὐτοῦ καὶ ληψόμεθα τὰς ἐπαγγελίας, ἃς οὓς οὐκ ἤκουσεν οὐδὲ ὀφθαλμὸς εἶδεν, οὐδὲ ἐπὶ καρδίαν ἀνθρώπου ἀνέβη.

1 δουλεύσωμεν] A C πιστεύσωμεν S   τό] C S τοῦ A   2 ἠκούσαμεν] A ἠκούομεν C S   3 ἀνόητοι] A C add ἄφρονες καὶ τῆς ἐννοίας ἐνδεόμενοι S   φυλλοροεῖ] A φυλλορροεῖ C   μετὰ ταῦτα] A S εἶτα C   σταφυλή] A S βλαστός C   4 μου] A C add πρῶτον S   ἔπειτα] C ἔπιτα A   5 μου] A C om S   ἐλπίσαντες] C ἐλπίσαιτες A   ἵνα] A C om S   7 οὓς οὐκ ἤκουσεν οὐδὲ ὀφθαλμὸς εἶδεν] C οὐκ ἤκουσεν οὐδὲ ὀφθαλμὸς εἶδεν A   ὀφθαλμὸς οὐκ εἶδεν καὶ οὓς οὐκ ἤκουσεν S

XI

1 Let us then serve God with a pure heart, and we shall be righteous; but if we do not serve him, because we do not believe God's promise, we shall be miserable.

2 For the prophetic word also says, 'How miserable are those who are double-minded, who doubt in their hearts, who say "We heard these things long ago, in the time of our fathers, but we have waited day after day and have seen none of these things."

3 Fools! Compare yourselves to a tree. Take a vine: first it sheds its leaves, then a bud comes, after these things an unripe grape, then a full bunch.

4 So too my people has had tumults and afflictions; but then it will receive good things.'

5 So then, my brothers, let us not be double-minded, but let us endure in hope, so that we may receive the reward.

6 For he who has promised to repay to everyone the recompense for their deeds is faithful.

7 If then we do righteousness before God, we will enter into his kingdom and we will receive the promises 'which ear has not heard and eye has not seen, nor has it entered into the heart of man'.

XII

1 Ἐκδεχώμεθα οὖν καθ' ὥραν τὴν βασιλείαν τοῦ θεοῦ ἐν ἀγάπῃ καὶ δικαιοσύνῃ, ἐπειδὴ οὐκ οἴδαμεν τὴν ἡμέραν τῆς ἐπιφανείας τοῦ θεοῦ.
2 ἐπερωτηθεὶς γὰρ αὐτὸς ὁ κύριος ὑπό τινος, πότε ἥξει αὐτοῦ ἡ βασιλεία, εἶπεν· ὅταν ἔσται τὰ δύο ἕν, καὶ τὸ ἔξω ὡς τὸ ἔσω, καὶ τὸ ἄρσεν μετὰ τῆς θηλείας οὔτε ἄρσεν οὔτε θῆλυ.
3 τὰ δύο δὲ ἕν ἐστιν, ὅταν λαλῶμεν ἑαυτοῖς ἀλήθειαν καὶ ἐν δυσὶ σώμασιν ἀνυποκρίτως εἴη μία ψυχή.
4 καὶ τὸ ἔξω ὡς τὸ ἔσω, τοῦτο λέγει· τὴν ψυχὴν λέγει τὸ ἔσω, τὸ δὲ ἔξω τὸ σῶμα λέγει. ὃν τρόπον οὖν σου τὸ σῶμα φαίνεται, οὕτως καὶ ἡ ψυχή σου δῆλος ἔστω ἐν τοῖς καλοῖς ἔργοις.
5 καὶ τὸ ἄρσεν μετὰ τῆς θηλείας, οὔτε ἄρσεν οὔτε θῆλυ, τοῦτο λέγει· ἵνα ἀδελφὸς ἰδὼν ἀδελφὴν οὐδὲν φρονῇ περὶ αὐτῆς θηλυκόν, μηδὲ φρονῇ τι περὶ αὐτοῦ ἀρσενικόν.
6 ταῦτα ὑμῶν ποιούντων, φησίν, ἐλεύσεται ἡ βασιλεία τοῦ πατρός μου.

1 ἐπειδή] A ἐπεί C   ἐπιφανείας] C ἐπιφανίας A τοῦ θεοῦ (2°)] A C αὐτοῦ S   2 ἐπερωτηθείς] A ἐρωτηθείς C   τινος] A C add τῶν ἀποστόλων S   τό (1° et 2°)] A τά C   θηλείας] C θηλίας A   3 δύο δέ] A δὲ δύο C   ἑαυτοῖς] C αὐτοῖς A   δυσί] A δύο C   4 ἔξω] A C ἔσω S   ἔσω] A C ἔξω S   ἔσω (2°)] A S ἔξω C   ἔξω (2°)] A S ἔσω C   δῆλος] A δήλη C γνωστὴ καὶ δήλη S   5 θηλείας] C θηλίας A   φρονῇ (1°)] cj Bryennios φρονεῖ C   μηδέ] C μηδὲ ἀδελφὴ ἀδελφὸν ἰδοῦσα S

XII

1 Let us then constantly await the kingdom of God with love and righteousness, since we do not know the day of the appearance of God.

2 For when the Lord himself was asked by someone when his kingdom would come, he said, 'When the two are one, and the outside like the inside, and the male with the female neither male nor female'.

3 Now 'the two are one' when we speak truth to one another and there is one soul in two bodies without any hypocrisy.

4 And 'the outside like the inside' means this: the soul is the 'inside', and the 'outside' is the body. So then, just as your body is visible, so also let your soul be clearly seen in your good works.

5 And 'the male with the female neither male nor female' means this: that a brother who sees a sister should think nothing about her as female, and she should think nothing about him as male.

6 When you do these things, he says, 'the kingdom of my Father will come'.

XIII

1 Ἀδελφοὶ οὖν, ἤδη ποτὲ μετανοήσωμεν, νήψωμεν ἐπὶ τὸ ἀγαθόν· μεστοὶ γάρ ἐσμεν πολλῆς ἀνοίας καὶ πονηρίας. ἐξαλείψωμεν ἀφ' ἡμῶν τὰ πρότερα ἁμαρτήματα καὶ μετανοήσαντες ἐκ ψυχῆς σωθῶμεν, καὶ μὴ γινώμεθα ἀνθρωπάρεσκοι μηδὲ θέλωμεν μόνον ἑαυτοῖς ἀρέσκειν, ἀλλὰ καὶ τοῖς ἔξω ἀνθρώποις ἐπὶ τῇ δικαιοσύνῃ, ἵνα τὸ ὄνομα δι' ἡμᾶς μὴ βλασφημῆται.

2 λέγει γὰρ ὁ κύριος· διὰ παντὸς τὸ ὄνομά μου βλασφημεῖται ἐν πᾶσιν τοῖς ἔθνεσιν, καὶ πάλιν· οὐαὶ δι' ὃν βλασφημεῖται τὸ ὄνομά μου. ἐν τίνι βλασφημεῖται; ἐν τῷ μὴ ποιεῖν ἡμᾶς ἃ λέγομεν.

3 τὰ ἔθνη γὰρ ἀκούοντα ἐκ τοῦ στόματος ἡμῶν τὰ λόγια τοῦ θεοῦ ὡς καλὰ καὶ μεγάλα θαυμάζει· ἔπειτα καταμαθόντα τὰ ἔργα ἡμῶν ὅτι οὐκ ἔστιν ἄξια τῶν ῥημάτων ὧν λέγομεν, ἔνθεν εἰς βλασφημίαν τρέπονται, λέγοντες εἶναι μῦθόν τινα καὶ πλάνην.

4 ὅταν γὰρ ἀκούσωσιν παρ' ἡμῶν, ὅτι λέγει ὁ θεός· οὐ χάρις ὑμῖν, εἰ ἀγαπᾶτε τοὺς ἀγαπῶντας ὑμᾶς, ἀλλὰ χάρις ὑμῖν, εἰ ἀγαπᾶτε τοὺς ἐχθροὺς καὶ τοὺς μισοῦντας ὑμᾶς· ταῦτα ὅταν ἀκούσωσιν, θαυμάζουσιν τὴν ὑπερβολὴν τῆς ἀγαθότητος· ὅταν δὲ ἴδωσιν, ὅτι οὐ μόνον τοὺς μισοῦντας οὐκ ἀγαπῶμεν, ἀλλ' ὅτι οὐδὲ τοὺς ἀγαπῶντας, καταγελῶσιν ἡμῶν, καὶ βλασφημεῖται τὸ ὄνομα.

1 οὖν] C om S   ὄνομα] C ὄνομα τοῦ κυρίου S   ἡμᾶς] S ὑμᾶς C   βλασφημεῖται] C add δι' ὑμᾶς S   2 πᾶσιν] C om S   πάλιν· οὐαὶ δι' ὅν] S διό C   ἡμᾶς ἃ λέγομεν S] ὑμᾶς ἃ βούλομαι C   3 ἡμῶν] S ὑμῶν C   θαυμάζει] C ταῦτα θαυμάζει S   4 ἐχθρούς] C ἐχθροὺς ὑμῶν S   καί (2°)] C ἆρα καί S   ὄνομα] C add τοῦ Χριστοῦ S

XIII

1 So then, brothers, let us at last repent and be alert for the good, for we are filled with much foolishness and evil. Let us wipe away our former sins from ourselves, and having repented with all our soul, we shall be saved. Let us not be men-pleasers, nor let us wish to please only ourselves, but by our righteousness also those who are outside, so that the name is not blasphemed because of us.

2 For the Lord says, 'Continually my name is blasphemed among all the Gentiles', and again, 'Woe to the one through whom my name is blasphemed.' How is it blasphemed? When we do not do what we say.

3 For when the Gentiles hear from our mouths the oracles of God, they marvel at them as beautiful and great; but afterwards, when they discover that our actions are not worthy of the words we speak, they turn to blasphemy, saying that it is a myth and error.

4 For when they hear from us that God says, 'It is no credit to you if you love those who love you; but it is a credit to you if you love your enemies and those who hate you': when they hear this, they marvel at this extraordinary goodness. But when they see that we do not love not only those who hate us, but even those who love us, they laugh at us and the name is blasphemed.

XIV

1 Ὥστε, ἀδελφοί, ποιοῦντες τὸ θέλημα τοῦ πατρὸς ἡμῶν θεοῦ ἐσόμεθα ἐκ τῆς ἐκκλησίας τῆς πρώτης, τῆς πνευματικῆς, τῆς πρὸ ἡλίου καὶ σελήνης ἐκτισμένης. ἐὰν δὲ μὴ ποιήσωμεν τὸ θέλημα κυρίου, ἐσόμεθα ἐκ τῆς γραφῆς τῆς λεγούσης· ἐγενήθη ὁ οἶκός μου σπήλαιον λῃστῶν. ὥστε οὖν αἱρετισώμεθα ἀπὸ τῆς ἐκκλησίας τῆς ζωῆς εἶναι, ἵνα σωθῶμεν.

2 οὐκ οἴομαι δὲ ὑμᾶς ἀγνοεῖν, ὅτι ἐκκλησία ζῶσα σῶμά ἐστιν Χριστοῦ· λέγει γὰρ ἡ γραφή· ἐποίησεν ὁ θεὸς τὸν ἄνθρωπον ἄρσεν καὶ θῆλυ· τὸ ἄρσεν ἐστὶν ὁ Χριστός, τὸ θῆλυ ἡ ἐκκλησία· καὶ ὅτι τὰ βιβλία [τῶν προφητῶν] καὶ οἱ ἀπόστολοι τὴν ἐκκλησίαν οὐ νῦν εἶναι λέγουσιν ἀλλὰ ἄνωθεν. ἦν γὰρ πνευματική, ὡς καὶ ὁ Ἰησοῦς Χριστὸς ὁ κύριος ἡμῶν, ἐφανερώθη δὲ ἐπ' ἐσχάτων τῶν ἡμερῶν, ἵνα ἡμᾶς σώσῃ.

3 ἡ ἐκκλησία δὲ πνευματικὴ οὖσα ἐφανερώθη ἐν τῇ σαρκὶ Χριστοῦ, δηλοῦσα ἡμῖν, ὅτι ἐάν τις ἡμῶν τηρήσῃ αὐτὴν ἐν τῇ σαρκὶ αὐτοῦ καὶ μὴ φθείρῃ ἀπολήψεται αὐτὴν ἐν τῷ πνεύματι τῷ ἁγίῳ· ἡ γὰρ σὰρξ αὕτη ἀντίτυπός ἐστιν τοῦ πνεύματος· οὐδεὶς οὖν τὸ ἀντίτυπον φθείρας τὸ αὐθεντικὸν μεταλήψεται. ἄρα οὖν τοῦτο λέγει, ἀδελφοί· τηρήσατε τὴν σάρκα, ἵνα τοῦ πνεύματος μεταλάβητε.

4 εἰ δὲ λέγομεν εἶναι τὴν σάρκα τὴν ἐκκλησίαν καὶ τὸ πνεῦμα Χριστόν, ἄρα ὁ ὑβρίσας τὴν σάρκα ὕβρισεν τὴν ἐκκλησίαν. ὁ τοιοῦτος οὖν οὐ μεταλήψεται τοῦ πνεύματος, ὅ ἐστιν ὁ Χριστός.

5 τοσαύτην δύναται ἡ σὰρξ αὕτη μεταλαβεῖν ζωὴν καὶ ἀφθαρσίαν κολληθέντος αὐτῇ τοῦ πνεύματος τοῦ ἁγίου, οὔτε ἐξειπεῖν τις δύναται οὔτε λαλῆσαι ἃ ἡτοίμασεν ὁ κύριος τοῖς ἐκλεκτοῖς αὐτοῦ.

1 οὖν] C ἀδελφοί S   2 ὅτι] C ἔτι S   τῶν προφητῶν] S om C   λέγουσιν] S om C   Χριστὸς ὁ κύριος] S om C   3 αὐτοῦ] S om C   ἀντίτυπος] C τύπος S   τὸ ἀντίτυπον] C τὸν τύπον S   4 σάρκα] C add αὐτοῦ S   ὕβρισεν] C add τὴν σάρκα τοῦ Χριστοῦ S   5 ἀφθαρσίαν] S ἀθανασίαν C

XIV

1 So then, brothers, if we do the will of God our Father, we shall belong to the first church, the spiritual one, which was created before the sun and moon; but if we do not do the will of the Lord, we shall belong to what scripture says, 'My house has become a den of thieves.' So then, let us choose to belong to the church of life, so that we may be saved.

2 I do not think that you are ignorant of the fact that the living church is the body of Christ. For the scripture says, 'God made man male and female.' The male is Christ, and the female is the church; and the books [of the prophets] and the apostles say that the church is not just of the present but has existed from the beginning; for she was spiritual, as was our Lord Jesus Christ, but she [or: he] was made manifest in the last days so that she [or: he] might save us.

3 And the church, being spiritual, was manifest in the flesh of Christ, showing us that any of us who guards her in [their] flesh and does not corrupt her, will receive her back again in the Holy Spirit. For this flesh is an antitype of the Spirit; no one who has corrupted the antitype will receive the true reality which it represents. So then, he means this, brothers: guard the flesh so that you may receive the Spirit.

4 But if we say that the flesh is the church and the Spirit is Christ, then whoever abuses the flesh abuses the church. Such a person will therefore not receive the Spirit, which is Christ.

5 This flesh is able to receive such life and immortality when the Holy Spirit is joined to it, and no one can express or speak of 'the things which the Lord has prepared' for his chosen ones.

XV

1 Οὐκ οἴομαι δέ, ὅτι μικρὰν συμβουλίαν ἐποιησάμην περὶ ἐγκρατείας, ἣν ποιήσας τις οὐ μετανοήσει, ἀλλὰ καὶ ἑαυτὸν σώσει κἀμὲ τὸν συμβουλεύσαντα. μισθὸς γὰρ οὔκ ἐστιν μικρὸς πλανωμένην ψυχὴν καὶ ἀπολλυμένην ἀποστρέψαι εἰς τὸ σωθῆναι.

2 ταύτην γὰρ ἔχομεν τὴν ἀντιμισθίαν ἀποδοῦναι τῷ θεῷ τῷ κτίσαντι ἡμᾶς, ἐὰν ὁ λέγων καὶ ἀκούων μετὰ πίστεως καὶ ἀγάπης καὶ λέγῃ καὶ ἀκούῃ.

3 ἐμμείνωμεν οὖν ἐφ' οἷς ἐπιστεύσαμεν δίκαιοι καὶ ὅσιοι, ἵνα μετὰ παρρησίας αἰτῶμεν τὸν θεὸν τὸν λέγοντα· ἔτι λαλοῦντός σου ἐρῶ· ἰδοὺ πάρειμι.

4 τοῦτο γὰρ τὸ ῥῆμα μεγάλης ἐστιν ἐπαγγελίας σημεῖον· ἑτοιμότερον γὰρ ἑαυτὸν λέγει ὁ κύριος εἰς τὸ διδόναι τοῦ αἰτοῦντος.

5 τοσαύτης οὖν χρηστότητος μεταλαμβάνοντες μὴ φθονήσωμεν ἑαυτοῖς τυχεῖν τοσούτων ἀγαθῶν. ὅσην γὰρ ἡδονὴν ἔχει τὰ ῥήματα ταῦτα τοῖς ποιήσασιν αὐτά, τοσαύτην κατάκρισιν ἔχει τοῖς παρακούσασιν.

1 ἐποιησάμην] C add ὑμῶν S   2 μετὰ πίστεως καὶ ἀγάπης] C μετὰ ἀγάπης καὶ μετὰ πίστεως S   5 χρηστότητος] C add τοῦ θεοῦ S

XV

1 I do not think that I have given a small piece of advice about self-control, and whoever takes this advice will not regret it, but will save both themselves and me, the one who has given the advice; for it is no small reward to turn someone who is going astray and perishing so that they may be saved.

2 For this is the recompense which we can pay back to God who created us, if whoever speaks and hears does so with faith and love.

3 Let us then remain righteous and holy in what we have believed, so that we may with confidence make our requests to God who says, 'While you are still speaking, I will say, "See, here I am."'

4 For this saying is a sign of a great promise, for the Lord says that he is more ready to give than we are to ask.

5 Since we are receiving such generosity, let us not begrudge one another to receive such good things. For these words bring as much pleasure to those who do them as they bring condemnation to those who disobey.

XVI

1 Ὥστε, ἀδελφοί, ἀφορμὴν λαβόντες οὐ μικρὰν εἰς τὸ μετανοῆσαι, καιρὸν ἔχοντες ἐπιστρέψωμεν ἐπὶ τὸν καλέσαντα ἡμᾶς θεόν, ἕως ἔτι ἔχομεν τὸν πατέρα δεχόμενον ἡμᾶς.

2 ἐὰν γὰρ ταῖς ἡδυπαθείαις ταύταις ἀποταξώμεθα καὶ τὴν ψυχὴν ἡμῶν νικήσωμεν ἐν τῷ μὴ ποιεῖν τὰς ἐπιθυμίας αὐτῆς τὰς πονηράς, μεταληψόμεθα τοῦ ἐλέους Ἰησοῦ.

3 γινώσκετε δέ, ὅτι ἔρχεται ἤδη ἡ ἡμέρα τῆς κρίσεως ὡς κλίβανος καιόμενος, καὶ τακήσονταί τινες τῶν οὐρανῶν καὶ πᾶσα ἡ γῆ ὡς μόλιβος ἐπὶ πυρὶ τηκόμενος· καὶ τότε φανήσεται τὰ κρύφια καὶ φανερὰ ἔργα τῶν ἀνθρώπων.

4 καλὸν οὖν ἐλεημοσύνη ὡς μετάνοια ἁμαρτίας· κρείσσων νηστεία προσευχῆς, ἐλεημοσύνη δὲ ἀμφοτέρων· ἀγάπη δὲ καλύπτει πλῆθος ἁμαρτιῶν, προσευχὴ δὲ ἐκ καλῆς συνειδήσεως ἐκ θανάτου ῥύεται. μακάριος πᾶς ὁ εὑρεθεὶς ἐν τούτοις πλήρης· ἐλεημοσύνη γὰρ κούφισμα ἁμαρτίας γίνεται.

2 Ἰησοῦ] C τοῦ κυρίου ἡμῶν Ἰησοῦ Χριστοῦ S

XVI

1 So then, brothers, since we have received no small opportunity to repent, let us, while we have the time, turn back to the God who called us, while we still have the Father who accepts us.

2 For if we bid farewell to these pleasures, and conquer our soul by not doing its evil desires, we shall receive the mercy of Jesus.

3 But you know that the day of judgement is coming like a burning oven and some of the heavens will melt and all the earth will melt like lead in a fire, and then the hidden and open things that people have done will be made visible.

4 Charity is therefore good as repentance from sin. Fasting is better than prayer, but charity is better than both; and love 'covers a multitude of sins', but prayer from a good conscience will rescue someone from death. Blessed is everyone who is found to be full of these things; for charity lightens sin.

XVII

1 Μετανοήσωμεν οὖν ἐξ ὅλης καρδίας, ἵνα μή τις ἡμῶν παραπόληται. εἰ γὰρ ἐντολὰς ἔχομεν καὶ τοῦτο πράσσομεν, ἀπὸ τῶν εἰδώλων ἀποσπᾶν καὶ κατηχεῖν, πόσῳ μᾶλλον ψυχὴν ἤδη γινώσκουσαν τὸν θεὸν οὐ δεῖ ἀπόλλυσθαι;
2 συλλάβωμεν οὖν ἑαυτοῖς καὶ τοὺς ἀσθενοῦντας ἀνάγειν περὶ τὸ ἀγαθόν, ὅπως σωθῶμεν ἅπαντες καὶ ἐπιστρέψωμεν ἀλλήλους καὶ νουθετήσωμεν.
3 καὶ μὴ μόνον ἄρτι δοκῶμεν πιστεύειν καὶ προσέχειν ἐν τῷ νουθετεῖσθαι ἡμᾶς ὑπὸ τῶν περσβυτέρων, ἀλλὰ καὶ ὅταν εἰς οἶκον ἀπαλλαγῶμεν, μνημονεύωμεν τῶν τοῦ κυρίου ἐνταλμάτων καὶ μὴ ἀντιπαρελκώμεθα ἀπὸ τῶν κοσμικῶν ἐπιθυμιῶν, ἀλλὰ πυκνότερον προσερχόμενοι πειρώμεθα προκόπτειν ἐν ταῖς ἐντολαῖς τοῦ κυρίου, ἵνα πάντες τὸ αὐτὸ φρονοῦντες συνηγμένοι ὦμεν ἐπὶ τὴν ζωήν.
4 εἶπεν γὰρ ὁ κύριος· ἔρχομαι συναγαγεῖν πάντα τὰ ἔθνη, φυλὰς καὶ γλώσσας· τοῦτο δὲ λέγει τὴν ἡμέραν τῆς ἐπιφανείας αὐτοῦ, ὅτε ἐλθὼν λυτρώσεται ἡμᾶς, ἕκαστον κατὰ τὰ ἔργα αὐτοῦ.
5 καὶ ὄψονται τὴν δόξαν αὐτοῦ καὶ τὸ κράτος οἱ ἄπιστοι, καὶ ξενισθήσονται ἰδόντες τὸ βασίλειον τοῦ κόσμου ἐν τῷ Ἰησοῦ λέγοντες· οὐαὶ ἡμῖν, ὅτι σὺ ἦς, καὶ οὐκ ᾔδειμεν καὶ οὐκ ἐπιστεύομεν καὶ οὐκ ἐπειθόμεθα τοῖς περσβυτέροις τοῖς ἀναγγέλλουσιν ἡμῖν περὶ τῆς σωτηρίας ἡμῶν. καὶ ὁ σκώληξ αὐτῶν οὐ τελευτήσει καὶ τὸ πῦρ αὐτῶν οὐ σβεσθήσεται, καὶ ἔσονται εἰς ὅρασιν πάσῃ σαρκί.
6 τὴν ἡμέραν ἐκείνην λέγει τῆς κρίσεως, ὅταν ὄψονται τοὺς ἐν ἡμῖν ἀσεβήσαντας καὶ παραλογισαμένους τὰς ἐντολὰς Ἰησοῦ Χριστοῦ.
7 οἱ δὲ δίκαιοι εὐπραγήσαντες καὶ ὑπομείναντες τὰς βασάνους καὶ μισήσαντες τὰς ἡδυπαθείας τῆς ψυχῆς, ὅταν θεάσωνται τοὺς ἀστοχήσαντας καὶ ἀρνησαμένους διὰ τῶν λόγων ἢ διὰ τῶν ἔργων τὸν Ἰησοῦν, ὅπως κολάζονται δειναῖς βασάνοις πυρὶ ἀσβέστῳ, ἔσονται δόξαν διδόντες τῷ θεῷ αὐτῶν λέγοντες, ὅτι ἔσται ἐλπὶς τῷ δεδουλευκότι θεῷ ἐξ ὅλης καρδίας.

1 καρδίας] C add ἡμῶν S   ἔχομεν] C add ἵνα S   πράσσομεν] C πράσσωμεν καί S   3 ἀπαλλαγῶμεν] C add καὶ καταπαύσωμεν ἀπὸ πάντων S   προσερχόμενοι] C προσευχόμενοι S   4 κύριος] C add ἡμῶν S   5 καὶ τὸ κράτος] C ἐν κράτει καὶ ἐξουσία S   ἰδόντες] C εἰδότες S   ἐν τῷ Ἰησοῦ λέγοντες] C τούτου καὶ ἔπειτα ἐροῦσιν S   6 ἡμῖν] S ὑμῖν C   7 ἔσονται] C add ἐν ἀγαλλιάσει S   διδόντες] S δόντες C

XVII

1 Let us then repent with our whole heart, so that none of us may perish. For since we have commandments and obey them, to tear people away from idols and instruct them, how much more must we keep from perishing someone who already knows God?

2 Let us then help one another, and bring back those who are weak in goodness, so that we all may be saved and turn one another around and exhort each other.

3 And let us not only appear to believe and pay attention now while we are being exhorted by the elders, but also when we have returned home, let us remember the commandments of the Lord, and let us not be dragged aside by worldly desires. Rather, by coming here more frequently, let us try to make progress in the commands of the Lord, so that, all thinking the same way, we may be gathered together for life.

4 For the Lord said, 'I am coming to gather together all the nations, tribes and tongues.' This means the day of his appearance, when he will come and rescue us, each one according to their deeds.

5 And the unbelievers will see his glory and power, and they will be astonished when they see the sovereignty of the world given to Jesus, and they will say, 'Woe to us! For you were, and we did not know or believe it, and we did not obey the elders who told us of our salvation.' 'And their worm will not die and their fire will not be quenched, and they will be a spectacle to all flesh.'

6 He means that day of judgement, when they will see those who were ungodly among us and who distorted the commandments of Jesus Christ.

7 But the righteous, who have done good, endured torture, and have hated the pleasures of the soul, when they see those who have gone astray and denied Jesus by words or deeds punished with terrible torment in unquenchable fire, will give glory to God, saying, there will be hope for him who has served God with his whole heart.

XVIII

1 Καὶ ἡμεῖς οὖν γενώμεθα ἐκ τῶν εὐχαριστούντων, δεδουλευκότων τῷ θεῷ, καὶ μὴ ἐκ τῶν κρινομένων ἀσεβῶν.

2 καὶ γὰρ αὐτὸς πανθαμαρτωλὸς ὢν καὶ μήπω φυγὼν τὸν πειρασμόν, ἀλλ' ἔτι ὢν ἐν μέσοις τοῖς ὀργάνοις τοῦ διαβόλου σπουδάζω τὴν δικαιοσύνην διώκειν, ὅπως ἰσχύσω κἂν ἐγγὺς αὐτῆς γενέσθαι, φοβούμενος τὴν κρίσιν τὴν μέλλουσαν.

1 οὖν] C add ἀδελφοί S   εὐχαριστούντων] C add καὶ τὸ ἔλεος λαμβανόντων S
2 φυγών] S φεύγων C

XVIII

1 Let us then also be among those who give thanks, who have served God, and not among the ungodly who are judged.

2 For I myself am completely sinful and have not yet fled from temptation; yet, even while still surrounded by the devil's instruments, I am keen to pursue righteousness, so that I may have the strength to come near it, in fear of the coming judgement.

XIX

1 Ὥστε, ἀδελφοὶ καὶ ἀδελφαί, μετὰ τὸν θεὸν τῆς ἀληθείας ἀνακινώσκω ὑμῖν ἔντευξιν εἰς τὸ προσέχειν τοῖς γεγραμμένοις, ἵνα καὶ ἑαυτοὺς σώσητε καὶ τὸν ἀναγινώσκοντα ἐν ὑμῖν. μισθὸν γὰρ αἰτῶ ὑμᾶς τὸ μετανοῆσαι ἐξ ὅλης καρδίας, σωτηρίαν ἑαυτοῖς καὶ ζωὴν διδόντας. τοῦτο γὰρ ποιήσαντες σκοπὸν πᾶσιν τοῖς νέοις θήσομεν, τοῖς βουλομένοις περὶ τὴν εὐσέβειαν καὶ τὴν χρηστοτήτα τοῦ θεοῦ φιλοπονεῖν.

2 καὶ μὴ ἀηδῶς ἔχωμεν καὶ ἀγανακτῶμεν οἱ ἄσοφοι, ὅταν τις ἡμᾶς νουθετῇ καὶ ἐπιστρέφῃ ἀπὸ τῆς ἀδικίας εἰς τὴν δικαιοσύνην. ἐνίοτε γὰρ πονηρὰ πράσσοντες οὐ γινώσκομεν διὰ τὴν διψυχίαν καὶ ἀπιστίαν τὴν ἐνοῦσαν ἐν τοῖς στήθεσιν ἡμῶν, καὶ ἐσκοτίσμεθα τὴν διάνοιαν ὑπὸ τῶν ἐπιθυμιῶν τῶν ματαίων.

3 πράξωμεν οὖν τὴν δικαιοσύνην, ἵνα εἰς τέλος σωθῶμεν. μακάριοι οἱ τούτοις ὑπακούοντες τοῖς προστάγμασιν· κἂν ὀλίγον χρόνον κακοπαθήσωσιν ἐν τῷ κόσμῳ τούτῳ, τὸν ἀθάνατον τῆς ἀναστάσεως καρπὸν τρυγήσουσιν.

4 μὴ οὖν λυπείσθω ὁ εὐσεβής, ἐὰν ἐπὶ τοῖς νῦν χρόνοις ταλαιπωρῇ· μακάριος αὐτὸν ἀναμένει χρόνος· ἐκεῖνος ἄνω μετὰ τῶν πατέρων ἀναβιώσας εὐφρανθήσεται εἰς τὸν ἀλύπητον αἰῶνα.

1 ἔντευξιν] C add τουτ' ἔστιν νουθεσίαν S   τὸν ἀναγινώσκοντα] C ἐμὲ τὸν ἀναγινώσκοντα S   ἐν ὑμῖν] C add τὰ λόγια τοῦ θεοῦ S   σκοπόν] S κόπον C   φιλοπονεῖν] C^corr φιλοσοφεῖν C*   2 ἐνίοτε] S ἔνια C   καὶ ἀπιστίαν] supra lin. C   ἐπιθυμιῶν] C add τούτων S   3 τούτῳ] C om S   τὸν ἀθάνατον] S τὸ δὲ θάνατον C   τρυγήσουσιν] C τρυφήσουσιν S

XIX

1 So then, brothers and sisters, following the God of truth, I am reading you a plea to pay attention to what is written, so that you may save yourselves and the reader among you. For as a reward, I ask you to repent with all your heart, giving yourselves salvation and life. For when we do this, we shall set a mark for all those who are younger, who wish to devote themselves to piety and the goodness of God.

2 And we who are foolish should not be displeased or indignant if someone admonishes us and turns us away from unrighteousness to righteousness. For sometimes, when we do evil, we do not know it because of the double-mindedness and unbelief in our breasts, and we are darkened in our understanding by vain desires.

3 Let us then do righteousness, so that we may be saved at the end. Blessed are those who obey these commandments; though they may suffer evil for a short time in this world, they will reap the immortal fruit of the resurrection.

4 So then, let not the pious person grieve if he suffers misery at the present time; a blessed time awaits him: he shall live again with the fathers above, and will rejoice in an age that is without sorrow.

XX

1 Ἀλλὰ μηδὲ ἐκεῖνο τὴν διάνοιαν ἡμῶν ταρασσέτω, ὅτι βλέπομεν τοὺς ἀδίκους πλουτοῦντας καὶ στενοχωρουμένους τοὺς τοῦ θεοῦ δούλους.
2 πιστεύωμεν οὖν, ἀδελφοὶ καὶ ἀδελφαί, θεοῦ ζῶντος πεῖραν ἀθλοῦμεν καὶ γυμναζόμεθα τῷ νῦν βίῳ, ἵνα τῷ μέλλοντι στεφανωθῶμεν.
3 οὐδεὶς τῶν δικαίων ταχὺν καρπὸν ἔλαβεν, ἀλλ' ἐκδέχεται αὐτόν.
4 εἰ γὰρ τὸν μισθὸν τῶν δικαίων ὁ θεὸς συντόμως ἀπεδίδου, εὐθέως ἐμπορίαν ἠσκοῦμεν καὶ οὐ θεοσέβειαν· ἐδοκοῦμεν γὰρ εἶναι δίκαιοι, οὐ τὸ εὐσεβές, ἀλλὰ τὸ κερδαλέον διώκοντες. καὶ διὰ τοῦτο θεία κρίσις ἔβλαψεν πνεῦμα μὴ ὂν δίκαιον, καὶ ἐβάρυνεν δεσμοῖς.
5 τῷ μόνῳ θεῷ ἀοράτῳ, πατρὶ τῆς ἀληθείας, τῷ ἐξαποστείλαντι ἡμῖν τὸν σωτῆρα καὶ ἀρχηγὸν τῆς ἀφθαρσίας, δι' οὗ καὶ ἐφανέρωσεν ἡμῖν τὴν ἀλήθειαν καὶ τὴν ἐπουράνιον ζωήν, αὐτῷ ἡ δόξα εἰς τοὺς αἰῶνας τῶν αἰώνων. ἀμήν.

1 ἡμῶν] S ὑμῶν C   2 πιστεύωμεν] S πιστεύομεν C   3 ταχὺν καρπόν] C ταχὺ καρπούς S   αὐτόν] C αὐτούς S   4 εὐσεβές] C θεοσεβές S   δεσμοῖς] S δεσμός C
5 ἀληθείας] C add τοῦ κυρίου ἡμῶν Ἰησοῦ Χριστοῦ S   ἀφθαρσίας] C ζωῆς καὶ εἰς σωτηρίαν ἡμῶν S   ζωήν] C χαρὰν καὶ ζωήν S   αὐτῷ] C add Ἰησοῦ Χριστῳ τῷ κυρίῳ ἡμῶν σὺν τῷ πνεύματι ἁγίῳ S   δόξα] C add καὶ τὸ κράτος καὶ ἡ δύναμις S   ἀμήν] C add ἐτελειώθη Κλήμεντος ἐπιστολὴ δευτέρα πρὸς Κορινθίοις S

XX

1 But neither let it disturb our mind that we see the unrighteous as wealthy and God's servants oppressed.

2 Let us then have faith, brothers and sisters; we are competing in the contest of the living God and being trained in the present life, so that we may be crowned in the life that is coming.

3 None of the righteous receives a reward [*lit. fruit*] quickly, but waits for it.

4 For if God were to pay the reward of the righteous quickly, we would be immediately engaged in commerce and not in godly piety; for we would appear to be righteous when we were pursuing not piety but gain. And for this reason, divine judgement has harmed a spirit that is not righteous and has weighed it down with chains.

5 To the only invisible God, the Father of truth, who sent us the saviour and founder of immortality, through whom he revealed to us the truth and the heavenly life, to him be glory for ever and ever. Amen.

PART III

Commentary

Chapter 1

COMMENTARY

1 The addressees are addressed as ἀδελφοί. The address is typical for *2 Clement*: cf. 4.3; 5.1, 5; 7.1; 8.4; 9.11; 10.1; 11.5; 13.1; 14.1, 3; 16.1. (In 19.1; 20.2 it is ἀδελφοὶ καὶ ἀδελφαί, which may be an indication of a seam in the tradition: see Introduction §5 Literary Unity above.) The use of family kinship language, indicating a close fictive family relationship between Christians, is frequent in the Pauline letters of the NT and continues in the Apostolic Fathers (cf. *1 Clem.* 4.7; 13.1; 33.1; Ign. *Eph.* 1.1; *Rom.* 6.2; *Barn.* 4.14; 5.5; 6.15).[1]

The writer claims here no special position of authority in relation to the addressees (e.g. as that of a 'father' to 'children': cf. 1 Cor. 4.15); and indeed the same is the case throughout *2 Clement*. There are a few places where the writer refers to himself (e.g. 15.1), but almost always in a fairly self-deprecatory way (cf. 15.1; 17.3 and see the commentary there). Rather, first- (not second-) person plurals dominate in the exhortations: 'we' (rather than 'you') should do all that is exhorted.[2] It would seem then that, for this writer, all are 'brothers' and hence equal in the sight of God. The writer seeks

---

[1] For discussion of this language, see W. A. Meeks, *The First Urban Christians: The Social World of the Apostle Paul* (New Haven: Yale University Press, 1983), 83–7; R. Aasgaard, *'My Beloved Brothers and Sisters': Christian Siblingship in Paul*, JSNTSup 265 (London: T. & T. Clark, 2004), and his 'Brothers and Sisters in the Faith: Christian Siblingship as an Ecclesiological Mirror in the First Two Centuries', in J. Ådna (ed.), *The Formation of the Early Church*, WUNT 183 (Tübingen: Mohr Siebeck, 2005), 285–316, with references to earlier literature and also (in 'Brothers and Sisters', 314–16) a survey of the (variable) use of such sibling language in early Christian texts. Perhaps surprisingly, given the prevalance of the language in *2 Clement*, Aasgaard does not devote much space to the text (see his 'Brothers and Sisters', 308, claiming that the usage here 'is not linked to typical sibling motifs'). The use of sibling language reinforces the paraenetic nature of the discourse: see p. 25 above, and also generally R. Aasgaard, '"Brotherly Advice": Christian Siblingship and New Testament Paraenesis', in Starr and Engberg-Pedersen (eds), *Early Christian Paraenesis*, 237–65 (though not in relation to *2 Clement*). For evidence of quite widespread use of the language outside Christian circles, see P. A. Harland, 'Familial Dimensions of Group Identity: Brothers (ΑΔΕΛΦΟΙ) in Associations of the Greek East', *JBL* 124 (2005), 491–513.

[2] cf. Baasland, '2.Klemensbrief', 106.

to exhort his addressees, and there is little evidence of a developing hierarchy, or 'church order', in the community—or if there is (cf. the reference to the 'presbyters' in 17.3), the writer does not appeal to it in any significant way to bolster his own authority (beyond perhaps being the preacher of the sermon).[3]

In keeping with this, it is striking how 'low key' some of the writer's exhortations can be at times: cf. his penchant for understatements (e.g. here his exhortations not to 'think little' of Jesus, or of 'our salvation'),[4] as well as his non-aggressive tone in argumentation. He seeks to persuade, but not in a highly polemical tone. This is an *intra*-community discourse, not a polemical attack on those regarded as 'outsiders'. In line with this, it may be that, in what follows, the writer seeks to find common ground with his hearers, before leading on to develop his own ideas and his own views about what he sees as the 'proper' corollaries of that common ground (see below).[5]

The writer's first exhortation is that the hearers should think of Jesus Christ 'as of God' (οὕτως δεῖ ἡμᾶς φρονεῖν περὶ Ἰησοῦ Χριστοῦ, ὡς περὶ θεοῦ). This apparently very high Christological claim made the text of 2 Clement greatly appealing for later writers, especially those at the time of the Monophysite controversy, and hence led to this text being cited (see Introduction §2. Attestation above). However, it is doubtful if Christology in itself is the main focus of attention here. The address is focused not so much on Christology for its own sake, nor on what Christ has achieved through his life and death as such; rather, it is Jesus' status as judge that is crucial, and the resulting consequences for practical living for the Christian. In any case, the 'identity' between Jesus and God implied here is probably more a functional identity than an ontological one.[6] There are some places later where one can read the text as implying an equation between Jesus and God (e.g. 12.1; 13.3, 4), though even here the writer's language is not completely clear (see the commentary there).

Some have used the language here to infer aspects of the situation being addressed by the author. For example, some have argued from this text that the writer is addressing what were taken to be the dangers of an 'Ebionite' Christology, i.e. seeing Jesus as simply a human.[7] On the other hand, little else

---

[3] cf. Matt. 23.8. The situation seems to be rather different in e.g. the Pastoral epistles or Ignatius, where there is a clearly developed church 'order' and/or hierarchy.

[4] See e.g. Baasland, '2.Klemensbrief', 121, on other examples of litotes (e.g. 15.1; 16.1).

[5] For many of these general points, see p. 25 above on 'paraenesis', e.g. for the 'benevolent' nature of the address, as well as the address being to insiders and those with a 'shared world view'.

[6] cf. Donfried, *Setting*, 99; Lindemann, *Clemensbriefe*, 200–1; Pratscher, *Zweite Clemensbrief*, 66, and see Introduction §9.2 Christology above.

[7] See e.g. Lightfoot, *Apostolic Fathers*, 2.211–12; also still suggested as a possibility by Lohmann, *Drohung*, 95–6. For others in earlier scholarship, see Baasland, '2.Klemensbrief', 134–5.

in the rest of the text seems to support this and the issue of Christology as such does not seem to be the central one for the writer. In the modern era, a consensus view has been that the author is addressing some kind of Gnostic ideas, especially in relation to the importance of ethical behaviour and beliefs about the value of the 'flesh'. In particular, the text here has been seen as a (possibly) direct address to some who might be arguing (similar to at least some Gnostics) for a separation between the heavenly Christ and the earthly Jesus.[8] But, as with the possible Ebionite background, there is little else in the text to suggest that such a possible separation provides the prime focus of any debate and disagreement reflected here. One can read such claims into the argument, but it is not obvious from the text itself: the writer simply talks about 'Jesus Christ' as an assumed single person, with no hint that this might be a contested claim.[9]

The author immediately makes clear what it is specifically about Jesus that is, for him, the key issue: rather than Jesus being 'God' as such, or the heavenly Christ and the earthly Jesus being one and the same, the key aspect of the (functional) identity is that it is as 'judge of the living and the dead' (ὡς περὶ κριτοῦ ζώντων καὶ νεκρῶν) that Jesus is to be considered 'as God'. The claim is found in a number of places elsewhere in early Christian literature: cf. Acts 10.42; 1 Pet. 4.5; 2 Tim. 4.1; *Barn.* 7.2; Pol. *Phil.* 2.1. The focus is thus on the future, eschatological judgement which Christ, as judge, will administer, and it is this that provides the basis for the exhortation to live out one's Christian commitment in appropriate, ethical behaviour. This general theme recurs throughout the text: ethical response is demanded in the light of the threat posed by the eschatological judgement that is to come in the future.

This is then spelt out more in the final phrase here: we should not then think little of our salvation (καὶ οὐ δεῖ ἡμᾶς μικρὰ φρονεῖν περὶ τῆς σωτηρίας ἡμῶν). Here it seems likely that σωτηρία refers to the eschatological future: 'thinking little' of our future salvation will jeopardize it. As we shall see, the writer has a somewhat ambivalent view on the nature, and above all the timing, of 'salvation', i.e. whether it is past or still future, but here it is probably future (cf. the parallel with v. 2a).[10]

---

[8] cf. e.g. Warns, 'Untersuchungen', 253–5; also, apparently sympathetically, Pratscher, *Zweite Clemensbrief*, 66 n. 5; cf. also Lindemann, *Clemensbriefe*, 201. Warns also suggests the exhortation not to 'think little' of Jesus Christ may be directed against (Valentinian) Gnostic views that regarded 'Christ' as a relatively 'low' figure in the Pleroma. More generally, see Introduction §7. Opponents above.

[9] There is, for example, no explicit assertion that 'Jesus is the Christ', or 'the Christ is Jesus'. Warns claims that the same issue is at stake in the charge against 'unbelievers' in 17.4–7 who have 'denied' Jesus. But there it is clear that their 'denying' Jesus is seen in their ethical behaviour, not in any 'doctrinal' claims about the identity (or otherwise) of 'Jesus' and 'Christ'. See p. 76 above.

[10] Lindemann, *Clemensbriefe*, 200; Pratscher, *Zweite Clemensbrief*, 67.

2 The future nature of the 'salvation' of v. 1 is made clear by being related here to how much we 'hope to receive'. To 'think little' of Christ is to think wrongly of our future destiny. And, as will be emphasized throughout, it is the combined promise and threat posed by that future destiny which should (for the writer) determine the behaviour of Christians in the present.

The precise meaning of the next phrase is uncertain because of a textual variant. Both the Greek MSS A and C read καὶ οἱ ἀκούοντες ὡς περὶ μικρῶν ἁμαρτάνομεν ('we who listen as though it were something little are sinning'). The Syriac MS S implies a reading καὶ οἱ ἀκούοντες ὡς περὶ μικρῶν ἁμαρτάνουσιν, καὶ ἡμεῖς ἁμαρτάνομεν ('those who listen as though it were something little are sinning, and we also are sinning'). The A C reading creates an awkward article οἱ with ἀκούοντες qualifying the subject 'we' of the verb. Hence many prefer the longer reading of S which eases this grammatical problem. On the other hand, this longer reading seems to introduce a third party (possible outsiders who 'listen' and are apparently distinct from 'you'), but this seems alien to the rest of the text where, with only rare exceptions (cf. 13.4), only the addressees ('you') seem to be in view. The longer S reading may thus be an attempt to ease the slight grammatical unevenness in the A C reading, and hence the latter is perhaps more original.[11] The awkward definite article may be an example of the somewhat awkward style of the author on which many have commented.[12]

Not taking these things (i.e. the nature of salvation and the role of Christ as the judge of the living and dead) seriously enough is 'sinning'. One may note again the writer's relatively eirenic approach: despite the strong charge (cf. the reference to 'sinning'), it is something that 'we' do, not necessarily simply 'you'. The language is seeking to be inclusive; it is not seeking to create barriers within the community and to exclude others.

The nature of the 'sin' is now spelt out a little further, though one suspects that the real nature of any 'offence' in the eyes of the author will come to light later in the text. Here 'sinning' is said to consist of 'not knowing': οὐκ εἰδότες, πόθεν ἐκλήθημεν καὶ ὑπὸ τίνος καὶ εἰς ὃν τόπον, καί ὅσα ὑπέμεινεν Ἰησοῦς Χριστὸς παθεῖν ἕνεκα ἡμῶν. Some have seen here a

---

[11] The A C reading is followed by O. de Gebhardt, A. von Harnack, and Th. Zahn, *Patrum Apostolicorum Opera. Textum ad Fidem Codicum et Graecorum et Latinorum adhibitis praestantissimis editionibus* (Lipsiae: J. C. Hinrichs, 1900), 35; Wengst, *Zweite Clemensbrief*, 238; Ehrman, *Fathers*, 164; Pratscher, *Zweite Clemensbrief*, 67. The S reading is accepted by Lightfoot, *Apostolic Fathers*, 2.212; H. von Schubert, 'Der sogen. zweite Clemensbrief, eine Gemeindepredigt', in E. Hennecke (ed.), *Neutestamentliche Apokryphen. In Verbindung mit Fachgelehrten in deutscher Übersetzung und mit Einleitungen* (Tübingen: Mohr Siebeck, 1904), 172; Knopf, *Zwei Clemensbriefe*, 154; K. Bihlmeyer, *Die Apostolischen Väter. Neubearbeitung der Funkschen Ausgabe* (Tübingen: J. C. B. Mohr (Paul Siebeck), 1956), 71; K. Lake, *The Apostolic Fathers I*, LCL (London and Cambridge, Mass.: Heinemann and Harvard University Press, 1965), 128; Lindemann, *Clemensbriefe*, 199.

[12] e.g. Photius: see p. 11 above.

clear echo of Gnostic language, especially in the first part of the sentence which has parallels in Gnostic ideas and language: salvation consists in 'knowing' where we have come from, and where we are going. Cf. the often cited quotation of Clement of Alexandria of Gnostic (Valentinian) self-understanding: τίνες ἦμεν, τί γεγόναμεν, ποῦ ἦμεν, ἢ ποῦ ἐνεβλήθημεν, ποῦ σπεύδομεν, πόθεν λυτρούμεθα, τί γέννησις, τί ἀναγέννησις ('who we were, what we became, where we were or where we were placed, where we hasten to, from what we are redeemed, what birth is, what rebirth': *Exc.* 78.2).[13] However, the language is not exclusively Gnostic: other non-Gnostics could stress the importance of the question of what one's origins are;[14] moreover, it is not so much the questions that are Gnostic but the answers which one gives to the questions.[15]

The precise force of the language here is not quite clear. It might be that the author is being deliberately polemical, claiming that his audience do *not* know where they are from, etc.[16] However, as we have already noted, the author's approach is not necessarily to be polemical, at least not directly. It may be then that, *if* the author is seeking to counter some kind of 'Gnostic' thinking, this part of the sentence may function as a *captatio benevolentiae*: presumably his readers/hearers would support what he says here about the nature of 'sin' as a lack of knowledge wholeheartedly.

It is possible that there is a twist at the end of the sentence, together with its sequel: sin also, perhaps above all, consists in ignoring the fact that Christ has suffered and died for us all, and the consequences that must flow from that. The atoning death of Jesus is thus claimed at this point to be central in a way that might not have been the case for Gnostic thinking.[17] Yet even here, it is not Jesus' atoning death as such that is central for the writer. There is nothing spelling out in any detail a 'theory' of the atonement: as is the case with much of the NT evidence, the writer is content to leave it at the level of a very general statement that Jesus' death is 'for our sake'.[18] But the note about Jesus'

---

[13] See e.g. Warns, 'Untersuchungen', 78; Pratscher, *Zweite Clemensbrief*, 68. Cf. too *Gos. Truth* (NHC I.3) 22.5, 14–15; 40.30–42.35; also the questions by the hostile powers in the account of the ascent of the soul in Mary's vision in *Gos. Mary* 15–16, on which see Tuckett, *Gospel of Mary*, 180–5.

[14] See Dunderberg, *Beyond Gnosticism*, 29–30, with reference to A. D. DeConick, *Seek to See Him: Ascent and Vision Mysticism in the Gospel of Thomas*, VCSup 33 (Leiden: Brill, 1996), 46–8: cf. *m. Ab.* 3.1; *Teach. Silv.* (NHC VII.4) 92.11–14.

[15] Dunderberg, *Beyond Gnosticism*, ibid.

[16] cf. Lindemann, *Clemensbriefe*, 200.

[17] Pratscher, *Zweite Clemensbrief*, 68–9. However, Gnostic ideas about the suffering and death of Jesus may have varied considerably: see King, *What is Gnosticism?*, 208–13. Nevertheless, although it is the case that not all 'Gnostics' were docetic and denied the reality of Jesus' death, it is not so clear that it was ever a part of any 'Gnostic' interpretation of the death of Jesus to see it as atoning for sin. For a Gnostic ideology, what was wrong with the world was primarily ignorance, a phenomenon which was to be corrected by saving *knowledge*.

[18] The standard NT preposition used is ὑπέρ; here it is ἕνεκα, but with little difference in meaning.

(atoning) death is not developed at all here:[19] hence it is hard to see this passing reference as a particularly pointed one, directed against Gnostics. Nor is Jesus' death mentioned again in the rest of the text. What is far more central for the writer is the response which Christians must make, in their day-to-day ethical behaviour, to the gift of salvation which they have (in part) received.

3 The author now starts to develop his own particular interpretation of the significance of the Christ event, above all in the theme of the appropriate *response* of the Christian to what Christ has done on his/her behalf. He voices the rhetorical questions: What shall we give him in return (ἀντιμισθία)? What 'fruit' shall we give him?

ἀντιμισθία in the first question occurs occasionally in the NT (Rom. 1.27; 2 Cor. 6.13), but is prominent in *2 Clement* (see also 1.5; 9.7; 11.6; 15.2).[20] The language evokes that of debts and obligations. The second question uses the language of 'fruit': what 'fruit' shall we give him that is 'worthy' (ἄξιος) of what he has given us. The language of 'fruit' here, in conjunction with 'worthy', is reminiscent of Matt. 3.8 par. (cf. too Gal. 5.22; Rom. 6.22),[21] though whether one should think of any direct 'allusion' here is doubtful.

In one way, it might be that the expected answers to these rhetorical questions would be assumed to be 'nothing': the greatness of the gifts given, and the identity of the giver, means that any human response, or attempt to 'pay back', is entirely inappropriate, hopelessly inadequate, or perhaps impossible. Similarly, no 'fruit' that we could give could be deemed to be 'worthy' of the divine nature of the gift received. This is, however, not our author's answer! For him, the 'proper' response is precisely what will dominate the discussion in what follows in the rest of the address. It may be, however, that in part the author is taking up the language of his addressees: they might indeed think that obligatory responses are out of place in light of the knowledge and salvation which they have received, and in part the author here may echo that idea in these questions. However, the final question may shift the ground slightly.

The final question is in terms of how much by way of 'holy works' (ὅσια) do we owe to God? The language seems to be primarily that of the cult and of religious obligations.[22] But now the implied answer is not so clearly 'none',

---

[19] cf. Wengst, *Zweite Clemensbrief*, 228–9.

[20] However, the word is not used in the same way in each place. 1.5 simply raises again the question, what can/should our ἀντιμισθία (to God) be? In 11.6, the word refers to God's response to us. However, in the other two instances, 9.7 and 15.2, a positive human ἀντιμισθία (to God) is enjoined.

[21] cf. Knopf, *Zwei Clemensbriefe*, 154, though this may be simply coincidental: in the gospels, the language is of fruit(s) worthy of human repentance, rather than worthy of prior divine gifts. *Pace* Warns, 'Untersuchungen', 314–18, who sees a clear allusion to the gospel passage here.

[22] cf. Knopf, *Zwei Clemensbriefe*, 154, who refers to 'dem herrschenden griechischen Sprachgebrauche, wonach ὅσιον das ist, was sich auf die Götter bezieht, was man ihnen zu leisten schuldig ist, der Gottesdienst, die religiöse und kultische Pflicht' ('the predominant Greek

but may be rather 'all without limit'! Thus the author might be using as a starting point the position and views of his addressees, but seeking to move the discussion on to his own point of view, claiming that a positive response to the divine gifts already given must be real and substantive.

However, before developing more of his own argument, the author gives a more extended description of the divine salvific activity which has already happened (vv. 4–8).

The section in vv. 4–8 is unusual in some respects in relation to the rest of *2 Clement*. Donfried argues that what we have here is a 'hymnic confession', a preformed unit from the community expressing its beliefs about, and thanks for, its present situation as those who have been saved by God through Christ. Further, he suggests that the ideas in this section are somewhat alien to that of the writer, and they may represent the view of the congregation which the writer wishes to 'correct' and modify.[23] Donfried appeals in part to the strongly realized nature of the eschatology presupposed here, e.g. the references to being already saved (v. 4). It is certainly the case that elsewhere, the writer strongly emphasizes the future aspect of eschatology (and of being 'saved') and the dangers which may result from a refusal to take this into account. On the other hand, the realized eschatological framework presented here is by no means unique in *2 Clement*, and even the use of the aorist of σώζειν is not unparalleled later in the text (see 2.7; 3.3; 9.2, 5). The writer does have a genuinely dual aspect to his eschatology, having both a 'now already' and a 'not yet' aspect (to use more Pauline jargon): it is precisely those who have already experienced the grace of God in the Christ event in the past who now have the obligation to respond properly and whose response will be judged in the future. Thus, it may be the case that the writer is here taking up the (possibly traditional) language of his hearers,[24] perhaps

---

usage, where ὅσιον is that which relates to the gods, what one is obliged to do for them, worship, religious and cultic obligation'). Cf. too the translation of Lindemann and Pratscher 'heilige Leistungen' ('holy works'), or Ehrman 'holy deeds'.

[23] See Donfried, *Setting*, 103–4, and earlier his 'Theology', 488. In the *HTR* essay, Donfried is rather more forthright: the language of this section 'do[es] not represent his theological viewpoint ... the remainder of 2 Clement is an interpretation and correction of this hymnic confession.' Cf. too 489: 'There is a clear difference in style *and theology* between this hymnic fragment and the remainder of 2 Clement.' In his (slightly) later *Setting*, 104, this is softened, keeping only the claim that 'our author is taking over and reinterpreting the confession of his congregation. While he does not necessarily disagree with their assertions, he is definitely suggesting that there is vastly more involved in the Christian faith' (= 'Theology', 489–90). The latter statement (he 'does not necessarily disagree ...') is rather more plausible: any theory that a writer cites a viewpoint which he positively *dis*agrees with, and wishes to 'correct', is somewhat dangerous in the absence of any direct indication of such disagreement. And in general terms, it is methodologically difficult to assert that any writer's thought is *not* represented by parts of the only evidence we have for that thought, namely the writer's own text.

[24] cf. too Wengst, *Zweite Clemensbrief*, 270, who says that there may well be traditional language being used, but not necessarily a clearly defined preformed unit.

again to establish rapport with them; but the ideas expressed are not alien to the author and, if he wishes to add to them, it is by way of expansion and elaboration rather than 'correction'.

4 The statement about the actions of God in the past,[25] establishing the status of the community in the present, is given in threefold form, which in a formal way matches the threefold nature of the exhortations in v. 3 (though it is not possible to make exact parallels between the two units).

The first clause speaks of God as having given us 'light', in one way the counterpoint to the 'darkness' of pre-Christian existence characterized by a life of worshipping other gods (1.6). The language is widespread in early Christian tradition,[26] though this is the only occurrence of the theme in *2 Clement*.[27] The second phrase relates to Christians becoming 'sons' of God. Again this reflects widespread Christian terminology,[28] including some parts of the NT gospel tradition (which has clearly influenced the writer at some level): cf. Matt. 5.45; Luke 11.2, etc. Here, as with the previous clause, the claim relates to what has happened already: the hearers have been called to be sons of God.[29]

The third clause here uses language more frequent elsewhere in the text: God has 'saved us who were perishing' (ἀπολλυμένους ἡμᾶς ἔσωσεν). The language of 'saving' is very frequent in *2 Clement*, in relation both to the past and the future.[30] In one way, the author can be said to be not entirely consistent in assuring the hearers they are already 'saved', but also exhorting them not to jeopardize their (future) salvation; yet in another way, he exemplifies the tension found in many early Christian writers.[31]

5 The author takes up the language of v. 3 again, especially in the use of ἀντιμισθία. (In the slightly unusual phrase μισθὸν ἀντιμισθίας, the

---

[25] Throughout this section it is not always clear who the subject of each verb is. However, the reference to 'he' as the one who as Father called us to be sons suggests that it is God rather than Jesus who is in mind (if indeed there is a great difference in the mind of the author: cf. 1.1!).

[26] For present existence, cf. John 1.4; 8.12; 12.35; 1 Pet. 2.9; *1 Clem*. 6.2; 59.2; in relation to the future, cf. Col. 1.12; Ign. *Rom*. 6.2 etc.

[27] Perhaps then giving support to the view that the writer is here quoting an earlier tradition.

[28] cf. Rom. 8.14; 9.26; Gal. 4.7; John 12.36; 1 John 3.1.

[29] In 9.10, the same verbal image is used but related to the future: Christians *will be* received by God as sons. This too is part of Donfried's evidence that the verse here reflects a viewpoint that is not the author's own (see above). However, even elsewhere, the fatherhood of God is not something that is wholly future: cf. e.g. 10.1 ('the Father who called us') where language of God as Father (in the present) may also imply that the hearers are already sons and daughters of God.

[30] For the past, see above; for the future, see 2.5; 4.1–2; 8.2; 13.1; 14.1, 2; 15.1; 17.2; 19.1, 3.

[31] Similar comments could be made about e.g. Paul's use of 'justification' language: see p. 71 n. 13. In one way Paul might be said to be more consistent, for example in reserving some language mostly for the past ('righteousness' etc.) and other vocabulary for the future ('resurrection' or 'salvation'). But at a deeper level, this could be seen as a semantic quibble. The author of *2 Clement* uses the vocabulary of 'saving' more indiscriminately, of both the past and the future, and hence highlights the tension.

Commentary: Chapter 1   135

ἀντιμισθίας is probably an explicative genitive: 'the reward that consists of a return payment'). As noted on v. 3, the answer to these rhetorical questions is perhaps ambiguous. In one way, it might be that the implied answer is 'nothing at all': we can give nothing in return for the wonderful gift of salvation already received. As already noted, the writer's own answer will be rather different: a response *is* required and is regarded as essential. Nevertheless, if there is any truth in the possibility that the section here may reflect the views (and perhaps the formulation) of the community being addressed, the question form may leave the issue open: all would agree that the question follows from the claims made in v. 4. But whereas some might give one answer to the question (claiming that we can give nothing by way of recompense), the author leaves the issue open, at least for the time being.

6 The author elaborates on the contrast between old, pre-Christian existence and the new standing of the Christian in the present. V. 6a sets out the nature of pre-Christian existence in a number of verbal metaphors and painting stark contrasts.

The first clause says that we were 'maimed in our understanding' (πηροὶ ὄντες τῇ διανοίᾳ). πηρός is a rare word in early Christian literature meaning 'maimed, disabled'.[32] For the inability of Christians prior to their conversion and/or Gentiles to understand, cf. Eph. 4.18, and also (in general terms) Paul's language in Rom. 1.18 ff. (indebted in turn to Wis. 13–14). The situation of being 'maimed' is then explicated in terms of who/what people then worshipped: προσκυνοῦντες λίθους καὶ ξύλα καὶ χρυσὸν καὶ ἄργυρον καὶ χαλκόν, ἔργα ἀνθρώπων. Such language about Gentile gods, and the accusation that the idols which others worship are human creations, is frequent in Jewish literature (cf. Ps. 135.15; Isa. 44.9–20; Wis. 13.10–19; also Rom. 1.18–32 for the more general charge that Gentiles worship the created order rather than the creator). For the list of 'stone, or wood' etc., cf. Dan. 5.4, 23 LXX; Wis. 13.10; Rev. 9.20. The language clearly suggests that the writer and his audience ('we') have come to Christianity from a Gentile background (though equally the echoes of biblical (OT) language indicate that at least the writer here is steeped in the words of Jewish scripture).[33]

The negative aspect of pre-Christian existence is then presented in the strongest possible terms, that of 'death' (καὶ ὁ βίος ἡμῶν ὅλος ἄλλο οὐδὲν ἦν εἰ μὴ θάνατος, cf. Col. 2.13; Eph. 2.1; 5.14; Rev. 3.1), though the death/life contrast is not one used by this writer elsewhere. This is followed by yet another metaphor, using the language of darkness and inability to see, anticipating the assertion in v. 6b that 'we have received our sight' (ἀνεβλέψαμεν).

---

[32] BAG, 662. The rarity of the word may have led to the change in C to πονηροί.
[33] cf. Pratscher, *Zweite Clemensbrief*, 72.

The language is unusual[34] but is part of the wide-ranging verbal imagery used here to emphasize the contrast between pre-Christian and Christian existence.

The end of the verse then presents the positive side of the picture: we have 'received our sight' and put aside the cloud that was covering us. The language takes up two of the preceding verbal metaphors: being in 'darkness', we now 'see'; and being in 'mistiness', we have now discarded the cloud that enveloped us.[35]

7 The nature of the salvation event, as well as further descriptions of the pre-Christian lost state, is now presented with a rich variety of vocabulary and associated verbal images. The lost state is one of 'great error' ($πολλὴ$ $πλάνη$), 'destruction' ($ἀπώλεια$), and 'having no hope of salvation at all' ($μηδεμίαν\ ἐλπίδα\ ἔχοντας\ σωτηρίας$).[36] By contrast, 'he' (= Christ?)[37] had pity on us ($ἠλέησεν$), showed 'mercy' ($σπλαγχνισθείς$), and 'saved' ($ἔσωσεν$) us. As with this whole section in vv. 4–8, and to a certain extent unlike much of what will come later in the address, the idea is solely about the present nature of the gifts of salvation: Christ has already 'saved' (aorist) us in the here and now.

8 The language is further developed with the idea of 'salvation' as comparable to a new creation *ex nihilo*. The language of God creating by 'calling' what is not existent into being occurs in Rom. 4.17, though it is doubtful whether one can deduce that the author is dependent on Paul: the language recurs in Hellenistic Judaism to stress the creative power of God (cf. e.g. 2 Macc. 7.28; Philo, *Spec*. 4.187).[38] However, here the reference is entirely related to the power of the soteriological work of Christ in bringing Christians into a state of (at least potential) 'salvation'.[39] What will be made clear in the later parts of the address is that this 'salvation' can be jeopardized if one does not respond appropriately.

---

[34] $ἀμαύρωσις$ ('dimness of sight') and $ἀχλύς$ ('mistiness') occur only here in early Christian literature.

[35] The language is in one way similar to Heb. 12.1, but the ideas concerned are quite different. P. V. M. Benecke, 'II Clement', in *The New Testament in the Apostolic Fathers: By a Committee of the Oxford Society of Historical Theology* (Oxford: Clarendon Press, 1905), 125–6, claims that the verbal coincidences are so close as to suggest that *2 Clement* here has been 'unconsciously influenced' by the language of Hebrews; but the differences in application may make this unlikely: see Gregory and Tuckett, '2 Clement', 290–1.

[36] It is, however, perhaps noteworthy that in all this, the descriptions of the 'lost' state of human beings do not include any reference to 'sin' or sinfulness: cf. Introduction §9.2 Christology (and soteriology) and p. 69–70 above.

[37] The subject of the verbs is probably intended to be Christ, but it could be God. Perhaps the author is unconcerned about the difference: cf. 1.1.

[38] Any direct dependence on Paul is denied by e.g. Lindemann, *Paulus*, 209; Gregory and Tuckett, '2 Clement', 281.

[39] Hence the subject of the verb is probably Christ, cf. 2.4 (very shortly below) and 9.5 (though elsewhere God can also be the subject of the verb: see 10.1; 16.1).

Chapter 2

PARALLELS

2 Clem. 2.1	Isa. 54.1	Gal. 4.27
		γέγραπται γάρ,
Εὐφράνθητι, στεῖρα ἡ οὐ τίκτουσα, ῥῆξον καὶ βόησον, ἡ οὐκ ὠδίνουσα, ὅτι πολλὰ τὰ τέκνα τῆς ἐρήμου μᾶλλον ἢ τῆς ἐχούσης τὸν ἄνδρα	Εὐφράνθητι στεῖρα ἡ οὐ τίκτουσα, ῥῆξον καὶ βόησον, ἡ οὐκ ὠδίνουσα ὅτι πολλὰ τὰ τέκνα τῆς ἐρήμου μᾶλλον ἢ τῆς ἐχούσης τὸν ἄνδρα	Εὐφράνθητι, στεῖρα ἡ οὐ τίκτουσα, ῥῆξον καὶ βόησον, ἡ οὐκ ὠδίνουσα· ὅτι πολλὰ τὰ τέκνα τῆς ἐρήμου μᾶλλον ἢ τῆς ἐχούσης τὸν ἄνδρα

Justin, *1 Apol.* 53.5 εὐφράνθητι στεῖρα ἡ οὐ τίκτουσα, ῥῆξον καὶ βόησον, ἡ οὐκ ὠδίνουσα ὅτι πολλὰ τὰ τέκνα τῆς ἐρήμου μᾶλλον ἢ τῆς ἐχούσης τὸν ἄνδρα

Rejoice, you barren one, you who bear no children; break forth and cry out, you who endure no labour pains. For the woman who is deserted has more children than the one who has a husband.

The text is clearly a quotation, direct or indirect, from Isa. 54.1 (see the discussion below); the same text is also cited by Paul in Gal. 4.27, and Justin (see above). All three Christian writers agree verbatim with the LXX version in their citations of the verse. There is little, if anything, which can be deduced from the text forms alone in relation to any question of literary dependence or the relative ages of the texts involved.

2 Clem. 2.4	Mark 2.17 = Matt. 9.13	Luke 5.32
καὶ ἑτέρα δὲ γραφὴ λέγει, ὅτι οὐκ ἦλθον καλέσαι δικαίους, ἀλλὰ ἁμαρτωλούς·	οὐκ [γὰρ] ἦλθον καλέσαι δικαίους ἀλλὰ ἁμαρτωλούς.	οὐκ ἐλήλυθα καλέσαι δικαίους ἀλλὰ ἁμαρτωλοὺς εἰς μετάνοιαν.

Barn. 5.9 οὐκ ἦλθεν καλέσαι δικαίους ἀλλὰ ἁμαρτωλούς.

He did not come to call the righteous but sinners.

Justin, *1 Apol.* 15.8 οὐκ ἦλθον καλέσαι δικαίους ἀλλὰ ἁμαρτωλοὺς εἰς μετάνοιαν.
I have not come to call the righteous but sinners to repentance.

[1 Tim. 1.15 Χριστὸς Ἰησοῦς ἦλθεν εἰς τὸν κόσμον ἁμαρτωλοὺς σῶσαι]

The saying in *2 Clem.* 2.4 is all but identical with that in Matt. 9.13//Mark 2.17.[1] The parallel in Luke has the (typically Lukan) reference to 'repentance' at the end which is lacking in *2 Clement*: hence there is no question of any dependence, direct or indirect, of *2 Clement* on Luke here.[2]

The saying, or something very similar, occurs in a number of places in early Christian sources, e.g. in *Barn.* 5.9 (in a form identical to that in *2 Clement* and Matthew/Mark), in Justin, *1 Apol.* 15.8 (in a form very close to that of Luke).[3] This may show that the saying circulated independently; and indeed it may be that the saying in the story of Mark 2//Matt. 9 represents an independent saying that has been incorporated secondarily into the story of Jesus eating with tax collectors and sinners.[4] Thus some have argued that the saying was a floating tradition, and that its occurrence in *2 Clement* is due to the author's use of this common tradition, not necessarily of the synoptic gospels themselves.[5] (On the other hand, the presence of the saying independent of its synoptic context in *Barnabas* and Justin probably represents a post-synoptic development of the tradition.)

However, the author here states that the saying comes from 'another' γραφή (having just cited Isa. 54.1 verbatim). The use of γραφή here suggests that the author is taking his quotation from a written source, and hence not from some free-floating oral tradition.[6] Further, it would seem that the source appears to have the status of 'scripture' (see below). It is possible that this text was a gospel text otherwise unknown to us. But a more economical solution would be to say that *2 Clement* here presupposes the Gospel of

---

[1] Matthew and Mark here are in turn all but identical. Matthew has an extra γάρ at the start of the saying: but such an inconsequential detail can scarcely have any significance in the present discussion.

[2] cf. A. F. Gregory, *The Reception of Luke and Acts in the Period before Irenaeus*, WUNT 2.169 (Tübingen: Mohr Siebeck, 2004), 146.

[3] For the texts, see above. 1 Tim. 1.15 is often also cited in this context, though the vocabulary is by no means as close as in the other texts. E.g. 1 Tim. speaks of 'saving', rather than 'calling', sinners; and the verse lacks the antithetical structure evident in the others which sets the claim about calling/saving sinners over against the negative assertion that Jesus did not come to call/save the 'righteous'. As we shall see, 1 Tim. 1.15 might be closer to the words of *2 Clem.* 2.7 (discussed below). Here it should probably be left out of account.

[4] cf. Donfried, *Setting*, 57, referring to R. Bultmann, *History of the Synoptic Tradition* (Oxford: Blackwell, 1968), 18.

[5] So e.g. Donfried, *Setting*, 59–60.

[6] cf. too Köster, *Synoptische Überlieferung*, 71, though Köster is inaccurate in saying 'zitiert er mit γέγραπται' ('he cites with γέγραπται'): the introductory formula is not γέγραπται but καὶ ἑτέρα δὲ γραφὴ λέγει.

Matthew.⁷ For clearer evidence that *2 Clement* elsewhere seems to presuppose the finished Gospel of Matthew (rather than Matthew's sources), see below (on 3.2). Thus whilst certainty is not possible, some dependence on Matthew (direct or indirect) seems to be the most likely explanation for the agreement here too.⁸

2 *Clem.* 2.7	Luke 19.10
οὕτως καὶ ὁ Χριστὸς ἠθέλησεν σῶσαι τὰ ἀπολλύμενα, καὶ ἔσωσεν πολλούς, ἐλθὼν καὶ καλέσας ἡμᾶς ἤδη ἀπολλυμένους	ἦλθεν γὰρ ὁ υἱὸς τοῦ ἀνθρώπου ζητῆσαι καὶ σῶσαι τὸ ἀπολωλός.

[Matt. 18.11 ἦλθεν γὰρ ὁ υἱὸς τοῦ ἀνθρώπου ζητῆσαι καὶ σῶσαι τὸ ἀπολωλός.]

[1 Tim. 1.15 Χριστὸς Ἰησοῦς ἦλθεν εἰς τὸν κόσμον ἁμαρτωλοὺς σῶσαι]

This 'parallel' is less close than others in the text. It is not signalled by the author as a quotation, and the parallel with the synoptic tradition is at best a fairly loose one. The closest parallel is to be found in Luke 19.10.⁹ However, there is no reference in *2 Clement* to Jesus as 'Son of Man', nor to his 'coming' (at least in this part of the saying). The 'parallel' in 1 Tim. 1.15 is sometimes mentioned in this context, but the agreement in wording is even less close than Luke 19.10 (really only 'save' is common to the two texts: the object of the 'saving' is 'sinners' in 1 Timothy, rather than the 'lost').

It is possible that *2 Clement* here has drawn on the saying in Luke 19.10 (and also, in doing so, adapted it slightly). But one cannot really say more with any degree of confidence. The saying is too general, and the

---

⁷ Theoretically it could be Mark; but there is no other evidence in *2 Clement* indicating knowledge or use of Mark, and Matthew's gospel generally was by far the most popular in the early church. Hence it is surely more likely that, if any synoptic gospel is presupposed here, it is Matthew rather than Mark. Cf. Köster, *Synoptische Überlieferung*, 71. See too Warns, 'Untersuchungen', 278, for the lack of any reference to Mark in *2 Clement*. Lindemann, *Clemensbriefe*, 205, also refers to the use of ἔλεος in 3.1 which might be a reminiscence of the quotation of Hos. 6.6 earlier in the same verse in Matthew (cf. too Warns, 'Untersuchungen', 286; also E. Massaux, *Influence de l'Évangile de saint Matthieu sur la littérature chrétienne avant saint Irénée*, BETL 75 (Leuven: Peeters, 1986), 139). However, as W.-D. Köhler, *Die Rezeption des Matthäusevangeliums in der Zeit vor Irenäus*, WUNT 2.24 (Tübingen: Mohr Siebeck, 1987), 136, points out, the idea occurs elsewhere near by in *2 Clem.* 1.7 and need not be related to Matt. 9 at all.

⁸ cf. Köhler, *Rezeption*, 136, qualifying Massaux, *Influence*, 139, who takes this as an example where dependence on Matthew is 'certain': Köhler takes it as 'gut möglich' ('very possible'). Cf. too Köster, *Synoptische Überlieferung*, 71.

⁹ There is also a parallel in Matt. 18.11, though this is generally regarded as a later interpolation into the text of Matthew, based on the verse in Luke 19.10. The MSS which contain the verse in Matt. 18 vary slightly, with the majority omitting ζητῆσαι καί. The shorter version of Matt. 18.11 is then in fact slightly closer to *2 Clement* here (with no reference to 'seeking'); but one probably cannot build too much on this.

sentiments too widespread, for one to be able to pin down any precise parallel exactly.[10]

COMMENTARY

1 The text continues somewhat abruptly with what is almost certainly a quotation from Isa. 54.1. Scriptural (and other) quotations are frequent in *2 Clement*, though they are mostly clearly indicated as such with an introductory formula. Unusually in this case, there is no introductory formula at all. On the other hand, this is clearly regarded as a quotation: in what follows in vv. 1–3, the text is broken up into three sections and a specific interpretation (with a mini-introductory formula for each interpretation) supplied.

The reason for the absence of an introductory formula for the initial quotation is not clear. Some have suggested that Isa. 54.1 was part of the 'text' for the whole sermon which constitutes *2 Clement*.[11] However, it is difficult to see the rest of the 'letter' (or sermon) as further exposition of this text from Isaiah, or indeed of a wider section of text from Isaiah.[12] The text is expounded here in some detail in vv. 1–3: each phrase is taken up (and its wording repeated) and then expounded separately, not unlike some of the *pesher* commentaries from Qumran. But after v. 3, there is no evidence that Isa. 54 (or Isa. 54–66) provides the basis for the author's further exhortations and arguments. It must therefore remain uncertain why there is no explicit introductory formula here. The author apparently assumes that the words of Isa. 54.1 will be recognized as a (scriptural) quotation without more ado. This might be regarded as somewhat surprising, given the clear implication from e.g. 1.6–8 that the audience (and probably the author himself—cf. the 'we' first-person plural throughout ch. 1) were from a Gentile, not Jewish, background. On the other hand, the author (if not his audience) displays extensive knowledge of both Christian and Jewish traditions. It may be that the theory

---

[10] cf. too J. V. Bartlet, in 'II Clement', *New Testament in the Aposotlic Fathers*, 132; Köhler, *Rezeption*, 141 (at least in relation to Matt. 18.11); Gregory, *Reception*, 146–7. Köster, *Synoptische Überlieferung*, 109, thinks of a possible recollection of the Lukan verse by memory. Lindemann, *Clemensbriefe*, 206, says that 'die Nähe zu der Tradition, die auch in Lk 19,10, 1 Tim 1,15 begegnet, ist deutlich' ('the closeness to the tradition which also occurs in Luke 19.10; 1 Tim 1.15 is clear'), but is no more specific. However, Warns, 'Untersuchungen', 304–5, sees here a clear use of either Luke 19.10 or Matt. 18.11.

[11] See pp. 21–2, and the discussion of the theory of Knopf, *Zwei Clemensbriefe*, 156, and his earlier 'Anagnose', that the text on which the sermon is based is Isa. 54–66, together with the critiques which his theory has produced.

[12] This text seems unrelated to the rest of *2 Clement*. And even the other quotations from Isa. 54–66 which occur here are not interpreted in such a detailed, self-conscious way as this text is.

that Isa. 54.1 constituted (part of) a scriptural reading that preceded the sermon here might explain the situation at one level. But, as noted earlier, the 'sermon' of *2 Clement* cannot easily be regarded as a 'homily' in the sense of being wholly devoted to a detailed exposition of a prior biblical text. (See Introduction §4. Genre above.)

The quotation is from Isa. 54.1, with wording that agrees verbatim with that of the LXX. The text is used by Paul in Gal. 4.27 as well as by other early Christian writers (e.g. Just. *1 Apol.* 53.5; *Dial.* 13.8; *Ep. Apos.* 33; Irenaeus, *Haer.* 1.10.3), and also by Jewish writers.[13] The text is applied by Paul as part of his 'allegory' of the Sarah–Hagar story and is interpreted in relation to the Jew–Gentile controversy which dominates that letter: the barren woman is interpreted as referring to the Christian church in contrast to the non-Christian Jews. Justin's use of the text is similar, using it as a proof text for the claimed numerical superiority of Gentile Christians over against Jewish Christians. However, such ideas seem foreign to the use of the text here: generally, the author does not seem concerned to engage in any way with the relationship between Christians and non-Christian Jews, or between Jews and Gentiles (Christian or otherwise).[14] The barren woman is taken as 'our church'; but it is not clear who the 'woman who has a husband' might be. Certainly any polemic against non-Christian Jews seems remote from the author's viewpoint here.

V. 1b takes up the first line of the Isaiah text which is quoted again and introduced by ὃ εἶπεν, and then given an interpretation ἡμᾶς εἶπεν ('he/it meant us'). This is then spelt out further in the next clause: στεῖρα γὰρ ἦν ἡ ἐκκλησία ἡμῶν πρὸ τοῦ δοθῆναι αὐτῇ τέκνα. In general terms the message is clear: the 'barren woman' of the text is taken as referring to 'us', which the author takes as 'our church': 'our' church was once barren but now has 'children' given to it. It is not clear how far one can press the details of the language here. For example, does the language of 'our' church imply the existence of, and implied differentiation from, another ('your' or 'their') church? If taken literally, it seems to imply a view of the church (or 'our' church) as a pre-existent reality having some kind of existence prior to the presence of any human members, similar perhaps to what may be implied in *2 Clem.* 14.[15] However, the image is then a little strange in that this preexistent church is presented somewhat negatively, i.e. as 'barren'. Lindemann suggests that perhaps what is in mind is a period of some 'stagnation' by the author's own part (cf. 'our') of the church, which is now past;[16] however, as

---

[13] See H. D. Betz, *Galatians*, Hermeneia (Philadelphia: Fortress, 1979), 249; Str–B 3.574–5.

[14] Donfried, *Setting*, 199, suggests a possible link between the use of this text by the author of *2 Clement* and the possible use of the same text by Paul's opponents in Galatia; but this seems unlikely: see Lindemann, *Paulus*, 268; Lindemann, *Clemensbriefe*, 204. For discussion of possible similarities with Justin's use of the Isaiah text, see n. 23 below.

[15] cf. Knopf, *Zwei Clemensbriefe*, 156.   [16] Lindemann, *Clemensbriefe*, 204.

Pratscher points out, such a period would not have been one where the church had no children at all.[17] Perhaps the language and imagery should not be pressed too far and the verbal imagery should not be taken over-literally. The writer is simply keen to emphasize the wonderful nature of the present existence of the church as the beneficiary of divine providence (in having 'children' provided for her).

2 The next phrase from Isa. 54—βόησον, ἡ οὐκ ὠδίνουσα—is now repeated, introduced by ὃ δὲ εἶπεν. It is supplied with an interpretation introduced by τοῦτο λέγει. However, the application is quite different from that of the first clause: here it is applied not to the existence of the church, but as part of an exhortation to Christians to pray to God and not to become weary in doing so.[18] The verb βοᾶν is now interpreted as referring to Christians 'crying' to God in prayer (cf. too Luke 18.7; 1 Clem. 34.7; Barn. 3.5 (citing Isa. 58.9))). The interpretation also adds that this refers to 'offering' (ἀναφέρειν) prayers to God. The language is that of the cult, applied here in a metaphorical way to prayer and praise (cf. too Heb. 13.15; 1 Pet. 2.5; Barn. 12.7). The verbs προσεύχεσθαι and ἐγκακεῖν are also used together in Luke 18.1, though it is doubtful if any allusion to the Lukan verse is intended here.[19]

The interpretation in the last part is somewhat strange: the author appears to downgrade the status of women who do give birth (as ones who 'grow weary') and to identify himself and his readers with women who do not.[20] Maybe though, as with the first clause, it is the application that is driving the interpretation of the text: the key thing for the author is that his hearers, who are identified with the 'barren' woman of the text, should continue to pray (equated with the 'cry' from the Isaiah text) and not 'grow weary', which the writer adds as the opposite to perseverance in prayer which he wants to inculcate; but then since the 'crying' is ascribed to the barren woman, it is assumed that the 'growing weary' is to be ascribed to the 'binary opposite' of the barren woman in the text, i.e. women who give birth. The resulting verbal metaphor is, however, very strained and not entirely felicitous.

3 The last line of the Isaiah quotation is now taken up and interpreted, here returning to the ecclesiological interpretation of the first clause: ἐπεὶ ἔρημος ἐδόκει εἶναι ἀπὸ τοῦ θεοῦ ὁ λαὸς ἡμῶν, νυνὶ δὲ πιστεύσαντες πλείονες ἐγενόμεθα τῶν δοκούντων ἔχειν θεόν.

---

[17] Pratscher, Zweite Clemensbrief, 77.
[18] For the abrupt change in thought, cf. Knopf, Zwei Clemensbriefe, 156 ('besonders gewaltsam' ('particularly violent')); also Wengst, Zweite Clemensbrief, 271, though the ideas fit well with the broader context of 2 Clement as a whole: cf. Pratscher, Zweite Clemensbrief, 78.
[19] Pace Warns, 'Untersuchungen', 320–2.
[20] The claim that those giving birth 'grow weary' is itself somewhat questionable as a general claim: though that may reflect a modern perspective!

A number of interpretative moves are made, though it is not clear whether the resulting wording is intended to be significant down to the smallest detail. The barren woman who was 'deserted' is now 'our people' who 'seem to' (ἐδόκει) have been deserted 'by (ἀπό) God'.[21] But taking up the contrast scheme of 'once . . . now', as in the first clause, a contrasting new situation is portrayed: 'we', who have believed, are now more numerous that those who 'seem' (δοκούντων) to 'have God'. A number of features here are not clear. Is the double use of δοκέω here intentional and are both uses meant to be taken in a relatively strong sense? Were 'our people' (only) seemingly deserted by God (they seemed to be, but in reality were not)? And/or are the contrasting group in the final clause claiming to 'have God', but according to the writer do not? Or are the two verbs meant to be taken rather more loosely? It is also not clear who 'our people' are intended to be, and conversely who the contrasting group, those who 'seem to have God', are.

One interpretation in relation to the last question is that the 'contrast group' are the Jews.[22] The author's use of the Isa. 54 text would then be similar to that of Just. *1 Apol.* 53.5–6, though there Justin interprets the numerical contrast as between Gentile and Jewish *Christians*, not between (Gentile) Christians and Jews.[23] 'Our people' would then presumably be the Christian church over against non-Christian Jews/Judaism. However, there is no clear instance elsewhere in *2 Clement* of an attempt to differentiate the Christian community from Jews, and such issues of Christian identity vis-à-vis Judaism simply do not seem to be on the author's horizon at all.[24]

Another interpretation sees here a reference to the author's opponents, perhaps some Gnostic group within the community.[25] 'Our people' might then be the writer's own group within the Christian community. However, it is not easy either to identify specifically Gnostic language behind the alleged

---

[21] For this use of ἀπό, see BDF §211. The sense may be that of alienation and separation as well as perhaps that of agency.

[22] cf. Lightfoot, *Apostolic Fathers*, 2.215; Donfried, *Setting*, 199; Wengst, *Zweite Clemensbrief*, 271. Reference is often made to the fragment of the *Kerygma Petrou* in Clement, *Strom.* 6.41.2–6 on the Jews: ἐκεῖνοι μόνοι οἰόμενοι τὸν θεὸν γινώσκειν ('they think that they alone know God').

[23] Harnack, 'Ursprung', argued that the uses of the Isa. 54 text in Justin and *2 Clement* were so similar that there must be a relationship between the two texts, and the use of Isa. 54 in *2 Clement* was later than that of Justin: hence *2 Clement* should be dated relatively late, well into the second half of the 2nd century. However, the uses of the text by the two writers are not necessarily the same—and even if they were similar, this does not inevitably show a direct literary relationship, but only perhaps a common exegetical tradition: see Wengst, *Zweite Clemensbrief*, 271.

[24] cf. Pratscher, *Zweite Clemensbrief*, 79; see too Introduction §9.6 Jews and Judaism.

[25] cf. Warns, 'Untersuchungen', 63 (on this phrase, also 488–503 for the whole section in *2 Clem.* 2), and mooted too by Lindemann, *Clemensbriefe*, 205.

claim to 'have God'.²⁶ (He does not, for example, talk about people claiming to 'know' God, which might be more easily interpreted as an implicit attack on Gnostic claims.)

The difficulties of making a very precise interpretation here are such that an alternative, rather looser, interpretation may be more convincing. As with the first clause, the writer may not be giving a precise analysis where each term has a clearly defined meaning or referent; rather, he may be thinking and writing in a somewhat looser way. As before, he wants to stress the positive side of the picture, with the main stress on the invincible power of God in calling the church into existence and establishing the Christian community with all its present numbers; and he wants to extract this claim (if necessary slightly violently!) from his biblical text. Hence he claims that Christians are the children of the 'deserted one' of the Isaianic text, and he now interprets the 'deserted' as 'by God'; but that suggests in turn a lack of compassion (or foresight) by God, so he adds that they (only) 'seemed' to be deserted. With the emphasis on the present situation, which contrasts with the previous one, he now claims (again basing himself on the Isaianic text) that his Christian community ('our people') is very large in number, though the Isaiah text puts this in the form of a comparison with another group: hence the author does the same—'we' are more numerous than 'those who seem to have God'. However, the language may not be meant to be taken too literally word for word: the repeated use of δοκέω may simply be due to repetition from the first half of the sentence for a 'rhetorical' effect, though partly too no doubt to introduce the idea that this is a *contrast* group to that of the author's own group, so that an element of critique and negativity is demanded; and the wording referring to those who (think they) 'have' God may simply derive from the wording of the Isaiah text (which refers to the woman who 'has' a husband), without any precise further meaning or reference in mind.²⁷ A search for a real group (of those who 'seem to have God') in the author's own context may therefore be unnecessary and inappropriate.

4 Having dealt with his detailed exposition of the text from Isa. 54, the author now gives another, supplementary, quotation to back up his main argument, introduced by καὶ ἑτέρα δὲ γραφὴ λέγει. The text cited is

---

[26] Pratscher, *Zweite Clemensbrief*, 79, says that the language is a traditional way of speaking and compares e.g. *2 Clem.* 16.1 as well as texts such as John 8.41; Col. 4.1; *1 Clem.* 46.6; Ign. *Magn.* 12.1 (though not all these provide a real parallel to the language of [simply] 'having God'). Irenaeus talks about Gnostic claims about 'having grace' (*Haer.* 1.6.4), though this is not quite the same.

[27] See e.g. Lindemann, *Clemensbriefe*, 205; Pratscher, *Zweite Clemensbrief*, 79. Perhaps one needs to remember that the author may not have been expecting his own words to be pored over by later interpreters and examined under a microscope with precise meaning and reference sought for each and every word! The author of *2 Clement* may have done this with his scriptural text; but he presumably did not think that he himself was writing 'scripture'!

probably taken from the Gospel of Matthew (see above). The reference to the text from which the saying is taken as 'another' γραφή here, apparently with the same status as the scriptural text from Isa. 54.1, is highly unusual for a writing of this period.[28] It suggests that the NT gospel texts (or at least the Gospel of Matthew) were beginning to acquire the status of scripture alongside the books of the OT.[29]

The precise reason for introducing the Jesus saying here is not quite clear. Whether there is any polemic involved (possibly against Gnostics in the community who might have claimed to be especially 'righteous', or already saved) is not certain. It may be that the author is simply wanting to focus on the addressees and to convince them of the wonderful nature of the salvation which they have, at one level, already experienced—a claim that will then be developed by the writer very soon in relation to the resulting obligations which those who have been 'saved' must show in their lives.

5 The saying is interpreted in a way that is formally similar to the interpretation of the Isa. 54 text (τοῦτο λέγει, cf. v. 2). The initial interpretation is in very general terms and expressed in a very impersonal way: literally 'it is necessary to save those who are perishing'. It is not explicitly said who the implied subject of the verb σώζειν is here, or who those who are 'perishing' are. Some have taken the implied subject to be Christian hearers and seen this as a call to missionary activity,[30] or to deal with Gnostic opponents in the community.[31] However, the activity of 'saving' in *2 Clement* is almost always an activity of God or Christ; moreover, there is only rarely any reference to outsiders, or concern for outsiders, in the rest of *2 Clement* (cf. 13.4). In fact, the immediate context here probably provides the correct interpretation of the claim in v. 5: in v. 7 it is made explicit that it is Christ who saves, and it is 'we' who are 'perishing'. The assertion here is thus not so much a call to missionary activity, or to bring to heel others in the community, but rather to emphasize the marvellous present status of the addressees as people who were 'perishing' but now have been 'saved' by Christ. Further, the description of those who have been saved as 'perishing' highlights the magnitude of what has been achieved: Christ's saving action has rescued those who were not only sinners, but who were also about to perish and die. The focus of attention in this section is thus primarily on the wonderful nature of the divine activity in

---

[28] The only other comparable example, always quoted in this context, is *Barn.* 4.14, where Matt. 22.14 is cited with the introductory formula ὡς γέγραπται.

[29] ἡ γραφή is used by the writer elsewhere to refer to (Jewish) scripture: see 6.8; 14.1, 2. Whether one can distinguish between uses of the noun with and without the definite article (so e.g. Lindemann, *Clemensbriefe*, 205) is not certain: the writer here certainly regards this as a quotation which is significant enough both to quote explicitly and then to interpret in a form and manner similar to the way in which the citation of Isa. 54.1 has just been treated (cf. the τοῦτο λέγει in v. 5, as in v. 2).

[30] Wengst, *Zweite Clemensbrief*, 241.

[31] cf. Warns, 'Untersuchungen', 490–2; Lindemann, *Clemensbriefe*, 205.

relation to the hearers in the past. The obligations which this entails will be spelt out later. The change of verb from 'call' in v. 4 to 'save' here may reflect similar exhortations in sayings such as Luke 19.10 and/or 1 Tim. 1.15. Such language was evidently traditional.

6 'Great and wonderful': the language is traditional in a number of contexts in the ancient world, including the Christian tradition (Rev. 15.1, 3; *1 Clem.* 26.1; 50.1; *Barn.* 6.4, etc.). The author gives a further application of the saying cited in v. 4, now taken as referring to what is 'falling' and 'standing'. In one way it is simply an observation about the everyday situation of affairs in the world. As with this whole section, it is not clear precisely how the observation is related to the situation being addressed by the author. Are the things/people[32] who are 'standing' those of the writer's own group, and those who are 'falling' the (Gnostic?) 'opponents' and/or those seduced by them?[33] However, it seems simpler to see the author as identifying both himself and his audience with those 'falling'. The writer seems to be operating with a clear binary distinction throughout this section: everything seems to be good or bad, positive or negative. Thus in v. 4, there is the contrast between 'righteous' and 'sinners', here between 'standing' and 'falling'; clearly too the negative side of these polarities is related to those who are 'perishing', and in v. 7 it is made clear that this relates to 'us'. Once again the focus is primarily on the author's and audience's (common) situation of people who are 'sinners', 'perishing', 'falling', and in desperate need of God's saving activity—which *has* taken place! It is just possible that the author is quietly seeking to attack others who would claim to be 'standing', *not* 'perishing', and 'righteous'. If so, this may then be part of the quiet polemic running through the letter—though one has to say that it is all quite 'quiet'![34]

7 The verse sums up this section, taking up the language of 'saving' and 'perishing' from v. 5 and the 'calling' from v. 4, and now making it absolutely clear who is being referred to in the previous language: it is 'us' who were 'perishing'; and it is Christ who has 'saved us', an action which is here said to be quite deliberate (cf. ἠθέλησεν). Such action is also here clearly something

---

[32] Strictly speaking the participles are both neuter plurals, not masculine: hence they refer in the first instance to impersonal objects, and the claim need be no more than an observation about the way that objects such as buildings might be treated.

[33] So e.g. Lindemann, *Clemensbriefe*, 206; Pratscher, *Zweite Clemensbrief*, 82, adds possible Gentile non-Christians to the latter group.

[34] Warns, 'Untersuchungen', 493–503, sees in this language of 'strengthening' an implied polemic against Gnostic ideas of 'strengthening' (psychics to become pneumatics: cf. *Ap. John* (NHC II.1) 26.12–19; *Tri. Trac.* (NHC I.5) 87.1–10), and to possible ideas of a Valentinian sacrament of 'confirmation'. But this seems to go beyond what the evidence will clearly show. The verb στηρίζειν is commonly used (cf. Luke 22.32; Acts 18.23; Rom. 16.25; 1 Pet. 5.4; *1 Clem.* 8.5; 13.3; 18.12; Ign. *Eph.* 12.1) and no technical ('sacramental') meaning is required to make sense of what is said here.

that lies in the past: he *has* saved us (ἔσωσεν aorist). As noted above, the saying is fairly general, and similar sentiments can be found in a wide range of other sayings (e.g. Luke 19.10; 1 Tim. 1.15).

This opening section of the 'letter'/sermon, climaxing in a sense in v. 7 here, has made clear the wonderful nature of what Christ has already achieved for the Christian hearers. What this implies for the present life of the Christian will now be developed much more strongly in what follows.

Chapter 3

PARALLELS

2 Clem. 3.2	Matt. 10.32	Luke 12.8
λέγει δὲ καὶ αὐτός·		
τὸν ὁμολογήσαντά	πᾶς οὖν ὅστις ὁμολογήσει	πᾶς ὃς ἂν ὁμολογήσῃ
με ἐνώπιον τῶν	ἐν ἐμοὶ ἔμπροσθεν τῶν	ἐν ἐμοὶ ἔμπροσθεν τῶν
ἀνθρώπων,	ἀνθρώπων,	ἀνθρώπων,
		καὶ ὁ υἱὸς τοῦ ἀνθρώπου
ὁμολογήσω αὐτὸν	ὁμολογήσω κἀγὼ ἐν αὐτῷ	ὁμολογήσει ἐν αὐτῷ
ἐνώπιον τοῦ πατρός μου.	ἔμπροσθεν τοῦ πατρός μου	ἔμπροσθεν τῶν ἀγγέλων
	τοῦ ἐν [τοῖς] οὐρανοῖς·	τοῦ θεοῦ·

Rev. 3.5 καὶ ὁμολογήσω τὸ ὄνομα αὐτοῦ ἐνώπιον τοῦ πατρός μου καὶ ἐνώπιον τῶν ἀγγέλων αὐτοῦ.

The saying in *2 Clem.* 3.2 is introduced explicitly as a saying of Jesus. The closest parallel is undoubtedly the Q saying in Matt. 10.32//Luke 12.8.[1] There is no verbatim agreement down to the last preposition or detail: e.g. *2 Clement* does not have a πᾶς construction, it uses ἐνώπιον rather than ἔμπροσθεν, and it has the object of the 'confessing' in the accusative rather than ἐν + dative. These details are, however, relatively trivial, involving little if any difference in substance.

There is doubt about the presence of the words ἐνώπιον τῶν ἀνθρώπων in the text here: the words are present in both Greek MSS A and C, but absent from the Syriac MS S. Some have argued that the words represent a secondary addition, assimilating the text to the wording of the version of the saying in

---

[1] The 'parallel' often cited here from Rev. 3.5 is somewhat more remote: there is nothing in this verse implying the reciprocal relationship whereby Jesus will 'confess' precisely the one who 'confesses' him. In Rev. 3, the one who will be confessed by Jesus is the one who 'conquers'. Hence *pace* e.g. Gregory, *Reception*, 144–5, who takes the common use of ἐνώπιον in Revelation and *2 Clement* as evidence that there was a version of the saying circulating independently of the synoptics (cf. too Donfried, *Setting*, 61); but such a common synonym for a relatively inconsequential word in the saying can only bear this weight in the argument with difficulty.

the canonical gospels (either Luke 12.8 or Luke 12.9).² However, the absence of the phrase in the syr^s version of Matt. 10.32 may indicate that the Syriac version here represents a 'local' Syriac version of the saying.³ Thus despite the fact that the Syriac variant provides a 'shorter' reading (and some might argue more original on that basis), the combined testimony of both Greek MSS suggests that we should read the phrase here.⁴

The version of the saying here clearly aligns closely with that of Matthew against Luke in (*a*) the first person 'I' (rather than 'Son of Man') as the subject of the future 'confessing', and (*b*) the confessing taking place before 'my Father' (rather than 'the angels of God'). Both features are widely regarded as secondary in Matthew in relation to the Lukan version and due to MattR. Thus Matthew's first-person form of the saying is almost universally taken to be a secondary change by Matthew of an original 'Son of Man' saying in Q;⁵ and Matthew's reference to God as 'my Father' represents a feature which is characteristic and distinctive of Matthew in the synoptic tradition.⁶ The version in *2 Clement* thus agrees with Matthew at just those points where Matthew has redacted the tradition. The saying here thus presupposes the development of the tradition after it has gone through Matthew's editorial hand, and hence presupposes Matthew's finished gospel.⁷ Whether the author of *2 Clement* has derived the saying directly from Matthew is not certain; and indeed the slight differences from Matthew might suggest at least a somewhat loose 'citation', perhaps from memory.⁸ Nevertheless, the form of the saying is 'post-Matthean'.

---

² cf. Lightfoot, *Apostolic Fathers*, 2.216; Lindemann, *Clemensbriefe*, 207; the words are included in the text, but bracketed, in Gebhardt, Harnack, and Zahn, *Opera*, 36. ἐνώπιον occurs in Luke 12.9, ἔμπροσθεν in Luke 12.8//Matt. 10.32.

³ See W. L. Petersen, 'Patristic Biblical Quotations and Method: Four Changes to Lightfoot's Edition of *Second Clement*', VC 60 (2006), 398–400; also for a discussion of Petersen's argument, C. M. Tuckett, 'Lightfoot's Text of *2 Clement*: A Response to W. L. Petersen', VC 64 (2010), 503–4.

⁴ cf. too Pratscher, *Zweite Clemensbrief*, 86. The phrase is also read as part of the text by Bihlmeyer, *Apostolischen Väter*, 72; Lake, *Fathers*, 132; Wengst, *Zweite Clemensbrief*, 242; Ehrman, *Fathers*, 168. (With the exception of Ehrman, all note the S reading in their apparatus.)

⁵ 'Son of Man' is the reading adopted in the reconstruction of the text of Q in J. M. Robinson, P. Hoffmann, and J. S. Kloppenborg, *The Critical Edition of Q* (Minneapolis/Leuven: Fortress Press/Peeters, 2000), 304. For others supporting this, see e.g. Bultmann, *History*, 112; S. Schulz, *Q—Die Spruchquelle der Evangelisten* (Zurich: TVZ, 1971), 68; W. D. Davies and D. C. Allison, *The Gospel according to Saint Matthew*, ICC (3 vols; Edinburgh: T. & T. Clark, 1988–97), 2.216.

⁶ For Luke's 'angels' as preserving the Q version, see Robinson, Hoffmann, and Kloppenborg, *Critical Edition*, ibid.; Schulz, *Spruchquelle*, ibid.; Davies and Allison, *Matthew*, ibid.

⁷ cf. Köster, *Synoptische Überlieferung*, 72; Massaux, *Influence*, 142–3; Köhler, *Rezeption*, 131–2; Lindemann, *Clemensbriefe*, 207. Lightfoot, *Apostolic Fathers*, 2.216, describes the text in *2 Clement* here as 'a free quotation of Matt. x. 32'.

⁸ Pratscher, *Zweite Clemensbrief*, 86–7, argues against too much certainty and leaves the question open between direct use of Matthew and a citation from memory. Donfried, *Setting*,

It is also worth noting that the author's language of 'not denying' Jesus in 3.1, just before the citation in v. 2, may presuppose a longer form of the synoptic saying. In both the canonical gospels (and hence presumably in Q), the saying is a twofold one, promising reward for those who 'confess' Jesus and warning for those who 'deny' him (cf. Matt. 12.33//Luke 12.9). *2 Clement* cites only the positive half in v. 2, but seems to presuppose the fuller form of the saying in the language used in v. 1.

Another possible parallel occurs in *2 Clem.* 3.4, where there may be an allusion to the words of the *Shema* in Deut. 6.5, or to the tradition of Jesus' quotation of the *Shema* in the gospels:

How do we confess him? By doing what he says, not disobeying his commandments, and by honouring him not only with our lips but with our whole heart and our whole mind (ἐξ ὅλης καρδίας καὶ ἐξ ὅλης τῆς διανοίας).[9]

The text is not quite certain: the Syriac MS S seems to presuppose reading 'strength' for 'mind' here.[10] Petersen has argued that this is the original reading which also agrees with a possible 'binary' form of the *Shema* found in Justin (*Dial.* 93.2, 3; *1 Apol.* 16.6): hence *2 Clement* here witnesses to an independent form of the *Shema*, perhaps associated with Rome.[11] However, the Syriac reading may be itself an assimilation to the other (canonical) readings, and in any case leaves the A C reading (of 'heart' and 'mind') unexplained; it is also unclear whether, in the passages noted, Justin is citing very accurately a version of the *Shema* which he knows, or whether he is simply summarizing a longer text.[12] Overall, it is preferable to follow the reading of both the Greek MSS here and read 'heart' and 'mind'.[13]

61, argues on the basis of 'substantial differences' between *2 Clement* and the synoptic versions for dependence on an independent source; cf. too Bartlet, in 'II Clement', *New Testament in the Apostolic Fathers*, 130. This seems unnecessary: the differences are scarcely 'substantial', and in all important respects of substance, *2 Clement* agrees closely with Matthew. Warns, 'Untersuchungen', 333–4, takes it as coming from the (one) apocryphal gospel which he posits as used by 'Clement' for a number of his citations, and argues that it follows closely on from the saying cited in 5.2–4, though this gospel in turn presupposes the gospels of Matthew and Luke. But, as Warns himself argues that the author has used the synoptic gospels themselves (directly), it may be easiest to see this simply as the author's use of Matthew, rather than of another gospel text using Matthew. See p. 41 n. 24 above.

[9] It is a moot point whether to include the words in quotation marks in the ET: they are so marked in Lake, *Fathers*, 133, but not in Ehrman, *Fathers*, 169. Quotation marks are not used here.

[10] See Lightfoot, *Apostolic Fathers*, 2.217; Bensly, *Epistles*, xvii.

[11] See Petersen, 'Patristic Biblical Quotations', 401–9.

[12] See J. Verheyden, 'Assessing Gospel Quotations in Justin Martyr', in A. Denaux (ed.), *New Testament Textual Criticism and Exegesis. Festschrift J. Delobel*, BETL 161 (Leuven: Peeters, 2002), 372–5.

[13] For more detail on Petersen's argument, see Tuckett, 'Response', 505–8. Petersen himself admits that he cannot explain the A C reading here: it is 'something of a puzzle' and 'remains a mystery' ('Patristic Biblical Quotations', 406).

Commentary: Chapter 3

If there is an echo of the words of the *Shema*, it is at most an echo: there is no introductory formula to indicate a quotation explicitly. Hence it is not certain how precise any allusion here is intended to be.[14] However, if the text given is correct (though see above), the author seems to presuppose the version of the *Shema* as placed on the lips of Jesus in the gospels. It is well known that the precise wording of the *Shema* differs in the different gospels, especially in relation to the faculties with which one is to love God. Deut. 6.5 MT has 'heart, soul and strength'. This is repeated in the LXX, though there is variation in the MSS on the equivalent of the Hebrew לבב: some MSS (including A) have καρδία, others (including B) have διάνοια. All three synoptic gospels include both καρδία and διάνοια (Mark has 'soul' and 'strength' as well, as does Luke though in a different order; Matthew just has 'strength'). The occurrence of both καρδία and διάνοια thus aligns with the NT gospel accounts, and not with the LXX versions where the two words are alternatives in the MS tradition.

Insofar as there is an allusion to earlier tradition here, the author of *2 Clement* is presupposing the NT gospel tradition of Jesus' appeal to the *Shema*; but the evidence does not allow us to be any more specific about which gospel he might be using.[15]

2 Clem. 3.5	Isa. 29.13 LXX	Matt. 15.8//Mark 7.6
λέγει δὲ καὶ ἐν τῷ Ἡσαΐᾳ	καὶ εἶπεν κύριος	ὡς γέγραπται [ὅτι]
ὁ λαὸς οὗτος	ἐγγίζει μοι ὁ λαὸς οὗτος	οὗτος ὁ λαὸς
τοῖς χείλεσίν	τοῖς χείλεσιν αὐτῶν	τοῖς χείλεσίν
με τιμᾷ,	τιμῶσίν με	με τιμᾷ,
ἡ δὲ καρδία αὐτῶν	ἡ δὲ καρδία αὐτῶν	ἡ δὲ καρδία αὐτῶν
πόρρω ἄπεστιν ἀπ' ἐμοῦ·	πόρρω ἀπέχει ἀπ' ἐμοῦ	πόρρω ἀπέχει ἀπ' ἐμοῦ·

1 Clem. 15.2: λέγει γάρ που· οὗτος ὁ λαὸς τοῖς χείλεσίν με τιμᾷ, ἡ δὲ καρδία αὐτῶν πόρρω ἄπεστιν ἀπ' ἐμοῦ.

For it says somewhere, 'this people honours me with their lips, but their heart is far from me.'

---

[14] Hence, as with Justin, the fact that only two faculties (heart and mind) are mentioned does not necessarily mean that the author's version of the *Shema* mentioned these two faculties only.

[15] Lindemann, *Clemensbriefe*, 208, suggests that the allusion here is to Mark 12.30, since it is in Mark that the two faculties are mentioned next to each other. Others, however, are doubtful on the grounds that nowhere else does *2 Clement* show knowledge of Mark: cf. Köster, *Synoptische Überlieferung*, 108; Warns, 'Untersuchungen', 301. Pratscher, *Zweite Clemensbrief*, 89, excludes Matthew on the grounds that Matthew uses ἐν rather than ἐξ to introduce each faculty, though whether one can base so much on such a tiny detail is debatable.

The text of *2 Clement* here[16] is explicitly introduced as a text from 'Isaiah', namely Isa. 29.13, a verse which is also cited in Matt. 15.8//Mark 7.6. The text form here shares some features with Matthew's/Mark's citation of the verse against Isa. 29.13 LXX, e.g. in omitting the reference to 'drawing near', and hence using the verb τιμάω in the same way syntactically in the sentence. However, equally noteworthy is the existence of another citation of the same text in *1 Clem.* 15.2 which agrees with the version in *2 Clement* almost verbatim, including the use of ἄπεστιν over against ἀπέχει in both Isa. 29 LXX and the canonical gospel versions. It may be that *2 Clement* attests a version of the verse which was also known to the author of *1 Clement* and which in turn was independent of the synoptic evangelists, though the evidence for this is quite slim (really only the use of ἄπεστιν).[17] Further, *2 Clement* (unlike *1 Clement*) explicitly cites this as a verse from 'Isaiah', not a saying of 'the Lord' or of a Christian gospel text. It thus seems most likely that, although a slight influence from the text of Matthew/Mark might be implied, the primary source for the citation here is the book of Isaiah itself, perhaps in a Greek version differing slightly from the LXX version.[18]

COMMENTARY

1 The author now draws out the consequences which follow from the 'mercy' which he and his audience have received (cf. 1.7). He initially elaborates a little more on what this 'mercy' consists of: first (or above all)[19] it means that 'we who are living' (οἱ ζῶντες) no longer worship or sacrifice to 'dead gods'.[20] Christians have nothing more to do with pagan religions or deities.

---

[16] There are also a number of variants in all the texts. Thus *2 Clem.* 3.5 C reads αὐτοῦ for αὐτῶν, probably assimilating to the surface grammar of the singular subject λαός. In the different readings of the verb in the last phrase, *1 Clem.* 15.2 C has ἀπέχει, though this could well be due to assimilation to the NT versions. *2 Clem.* 3.5 C has ἀπέστην which may simply be a variant for ἄπεστιν. I am therefore taking the texts above as perhaps the closest to the 'originals' in each case. (More details of variants in D. A. Hagner, *The Use of the Old Testament and the New Testament in Clement of Rome*, NovTSup 34 (Leiden: Brill, 1973), 172.)

[17] Hagner, *Use*, ibid., assumes that *2 Clement* is dependent on *1 Clement*, but this seems unlikely.

[18] Köster, *Synoptische Überlieferung*, 105; Lindemann, *Clemensbriefe*, 208. Hence *contra* e.g. Knopf, *Zwei Clemensbriefe*, 158, who claims the author is citing from a gospel tradition; also Wengst, *Zweite Clemensbrief*, 243 n. 28, who asserts that the author may be citing the apocryphal gospel used elsewhere, which in turn is dependent on Matthew: this seems unnecessarily complicated.

[19] There is no δεύτερον after the πρῶτον, nor a δέ after the μέν, though neither is unprecedented: see BDF §447.4 and cf. Rom. 1.8; 3.2; 1 Cor. 11.18 for a similar use of πρῶτον μέν. The πρῶτον here may have a superlative, rather than a comparative, sense.

[20] There is a close parallel in the *Acta Carpi* 12, where those about to be martyred assert: οἱ ζῶντες τοῖς νεκροῖς οὐ θύουσιν ('those who are living do not sacrifice to the dead'). For 'dead gods', see also *Did.* 6.3, and cf. the stock polemic of Judaism against idols, e.g. Ps. 106.28; Wis. 13.10; 15.17.

Commentary: Chapter 3   153

However, although there are occasional references back to the pre-Christian past of the addressees (cf. 1.6, 8), that does not seem to be the main focus of attention for the author here. The reference to not worshipping dead gods is thus probably not an implicit (or semi-explicit) exhortation to guard against a perceived danger: rather, it functions as an agreed presupposition on which the author and his hearers are agreed. Much more important is the *ethical* response of Christians in the present (see v. 4 below).

A second aspect of the 'mercy' which Christians have received is now spelt out: through Christ we 'know' the 'Father of truth'. The designation of God as the 'Father of truth' is unusual in early Christian literature but does appear not infrequently in Gnostic texts.[21] This, coupled with the use of the verb 'know' here, could indicate that the author is working within a context significantly informed by Gnostic language.[22] If he is using language congenial to Gnostics, *and* is aware of this, he may also be reinterpreting it in what follows. For example, some have seen in the 'we' as the subject of the verb 'know' here an implied polemic against gnosticizing claims to have esoteric knowledge confined only to a select few: hence not only a select few 'know', but '*we* (all) know'.[23] True 'knowledge' of the Father of truth[24] consists not in any esoteric knowledge of Gnostic mythology, or of secret passwords enabling the true Gnostic to escape to a higher realm; rather, it consists of a proper 'confessing' of the person of Jesus and this is to be manifested in right ethical behaviour in the present. The author may thus be taking up Gnostic language and attempting to reinterpret it, or at least draw out what he regards as the correct (ethical) implications of it.[25]

How far all this is intended to be overtly polemical is, however, not clear. For example, the subject 'we' is not apparently stressed (there is no emphatic ἡμεῖς for the verb ἔγνωμεν).[26] The explicit address *to* the hearers comes later, in v. 4. Rather, what is said here in v. 1 may be still at the level of stating what is common ground between the author and his audience: the claim to 'know' the 'Father of truth' is not contested on either side but can be assumed as given.[27] Further, 'knowing' here can be (and for the author probably should

---

[21] See *Gos. Truth* (NHC I.3) 16.31–3; *Hyp. Arch.* (NHC II.4) 86.20–2; also *Treat. Seth* (NHC VII.2) 53.3–4; *Odes Sol.* 41.9; cf. too Heracleon's commentary on John, frags 13, 16. See Donfried, *Setting*, 112.

[22] cf. Donfried, *Setting*, 112, and others.   [23] cf. Pratscher, *Zweite Clemensbrief*, 84–5.

[24] In the phrase τίς ἡ γνῶσις ἡ πρὸς αὐτόν, the αὐτόν probably refers to the Father of truth.

[25] cf. Wengst, *Zweite Clemensbrief*, 243 n. 25; Donfried, *Setting*, 112: 'while taking over certain "gnosticizing" phraseology, our author is at the same time reinterpreting it'; Warns, 'Untersuchungen', 345–6.

[26] There is an extra ἡμεῖς at the start of the sentence, but this seems to be related more to the fact that 'we' are the ones who do not worship dead gods, and it is hard to see specifically anti-Gnostic polemic in that claim; as noted above, this seems simply to reinforce an *agreed* view.

[27] cf. p. 25 above on paraenesis and the assumption of a 'shared world view'.

be) interpreted as much more akin to 'knowing' (God) in the biblical tradition, referring to the proper relationship between human beings and God (cf. e.g. John 14.7; 16.3; 17.3; Rom. 1.21, together with many examples in the OT, e.g. Hos. 6.6).[28] A Gnostic background is thus not absolutely necessary to explain the language used here. It *may* be that the language here is quite pointed, and directed against Gnostic opponents; but, as with so much elsewhere in 2 Clement, any such polemic, *if* it exists, remains somewhat muted and at best implicit.

The first elaboration of what this knowledge entails is set out negatively: that 'we should not deny him'.[29] Whether there is any hint of docetic (or quasi-docetic) ideas, suggesting some kind of differentiation between the person of the historical Jesus and the divine Christ is not clear. When the 'real' meaning of 'not denying' (i.e. 'confessing') Jesus is spelt out, it is not put in any terms suggesting that the author is trying to prevent such ideas as wrong; rather it is solely in terms of the ethical behaviour of Christians in the present.

2 The negative aspect of 'denying' is now turned round into an exhortation for the corresponding positive activity of 'confessing' Jesus. The implications are spelt out through the citation of a saying of Jesus: whoever confesses Jesus now will be confessed by Jesus (presumably at the Eschaton). The saying is probably gleaned, directly or indirectly, from the Gospel of Matthew (see above). From now on, it will be emphasized that, however much Christians can (and do) look back to God's/Christ's saving action in the past, there is a very real sense of a future sanction which is still in place and which governs Christian existence.

3 'This' is then said to be 'our reward'. The 'this' is probably the future 'confessing' which will be the resulting reward if we 'confess' him now (though the nature of the latter is yet to be spelt out). The 'reward' is thus probably the divine reward which we will receive, not the response which 'we'

---

[28] Hence *contra* e.g. Knopf, *Zwei Clemensbriefe*, 157: 'die Gnosis Gottes, die II Clem. meint, ist der Monotheismus' ('the knowledge of God which 2 Clement has in mind is monotheism'). Monotheism does not seem to be the point at issue: rather, it is the ethical implications of the Christ event that are key. Donfried's suggestion is also partly doubtful when he says that the opposite view combated by the writer here is that 'now that they have received it [the saving gnosis], the gnosis-bringer is irrelevant' (Donfried, *Setting*, 112–13). Such a view would be hard to find among Gnostic groups; more apposite is (at least part of) his further comment 'The historical person of Jesus and *the obligation demanded by him* are not considered primary' (ibid. my stress): the latter is surely key (even if the former is not so certain).

Perhaps ironically, Warns, 'Untersuchungen', 288, argues that confirmation that the citation in *2 Clem*. 2.4 is indeed from Matt. 9.13 (see above) is shown by the reference here in 3.1 to 'mercy' and 'knowing' since just before, Matthew has cited Hos. 6.6 (in Matt. 9.13a), which brings together 'mercy' and 'knowledge of God'. But if so, then language about 'knowing God' can be readily explained from the biblical background without invoking a Gnostic context.

[29] The language about 'denying' Jesus here suggests that the author knows the fuller version (preserved in the canonical gospels) of the saying cited in v. 2 about 'confessing' Jesus: see Parallels above.

are expected to make (cf. the μισθός of 1.5).³⁰ The author is now starting to develop his firmly futurist eschatology which posits future reward on the basis of present activity. Thus although the act of 'salvation' is still here implied as past (ἐσώθημεν aorist!), the fundamental idea has shifted: implicitly, the 'salvation' which has been achieved and attained through the activity of Christ is now conditional upon a proper response.

4 What 'confessing' Jesus means in practice is now spelt out explicitly: to confess Jesus means 'doing what he says', 'not disobeying his commandments', and 'honouring him not only with our lips but with our whole heart and our whole mind'. All the stress is thus placed on practical ethical behaviour in the present. Precisely what ethical commands are in mind is rarely spelt out in any detail in *2 Clement* (see Introduction §9.7 Ethics above). But the exhortation in general terms will dominate the whole of the rest of the address. The author evidently sees a danger in the situation he is addressing where ethical standards are slipping or perhaps regarded as unnecessary. The exhortation of *2 Clement* is not dissimilar to that in the Johannine epistles where knowledge of God and practical ethical behaviour are strongly linked.³¹

Two features of the language used here are noteworthy. First, the reference to 'doing what he says' may echo the wording of Luke 6.46.³² This is the Lukan parallel to Matt. 7.21, which is echoed in 4.2 (see below). This suggests that the author knew both synoptic versions of the saying. Hence it is most likely that he knew both gospels (since at least one version is probably redactional). Second, it is striking that references to Jesus and references to God interchange quite freely in this section.³³ At the end, the writer urges his addressees to honour Jesus 'with our whole heart and our whole mind'. As noted above, this may be a possible allusion to the words of the *Shema* of Deut. 6.5 (cf. above). However, it is notable that these words, as well as the citation of Isa. 29.13 which follows, relate to the response which is expected to

---

³⁰ Hence *contra* e.g. Knopf, *Zwei Clemensbriefe*, 158; Lindemann, *Clemensbriefe*, 207. See, rightly, Pratscher, *Zweite Clemensbrief*, 87.

³¹ cf. e.g. 1 John 2.3, and see Donfried, *Setting*, 113–14; Lindemann, *Clemensbriefe*, 207. Whether this is to be seen in terms of an anti-Gnostic polemic is not certain. Whether Gnostics themselves were so disdainful of ethical norms and standards is now less certain than it was. On the other hand, it does seem to have been part of a fairly standard anti-Gnostic polemic to paint Gnostics in such terms. See e.g. Williams, *Rethinking 'Gnosticism'*, 163–88; King, *What is Gnosticism?*, 201–8. The difficulty here though is that the language is in many ways so *un*polemical in relation to possible Gnostic terminology: cf. above on v. 1 where language about 'knowing' the 'Father of truth' is used quite freely. Moreover, any possible 'libertinism' is here not simply a matter of polemical abuse with which to smear opponents: it is clearly regarded as a real danger which threatens the Christian group for which *2 Clement* is written.

³² So Lindemann, *Clemensbriefe*, 207 ('offensichtlich' ('clearly')); Pratscher, *Zweite Clemensbrief*, 88.

³³ So much so that Knopf, *Zwei Clemensbriefe*, 157, speaks of a 'naiver Modalismus' ('a naive modalism').

be given to *Jesus* (not God).³⁴ Such interchangeability is, however, quite typical for the writer of *2 Clement* (cf. 1.1).³⁵

5 Another citation is adduced to back up the implied threat against those who do not follow the ethical commands of Jesus. The text is from Isa. 29.13, perhaps from a version of the text differing slightly from that of the LXX (see above). The introduction is unusual in stating explicitly which biblical book the quotation comes from (ἐν τῷ Ἡσαΐᾳ).³⁶ The subject of the introductory λέγει is not quite clear: it may be that Jesus is meant,³⁷ with the author thinking of Christ as pre-existent and speaking through the words of prophetic scripture;³⁸ more probably the subject of the verb is an indefinite 'it' ('it says in Isaiah . . .').³⁹ Nevertheless, the thrust of the passage is clear. True piety and devotion to God cannot just consist of 'lip service': it requires ethical action to establish its reality. Otherwise, verbal 'lip service' alone indicates that people are in reality 'far from' God/Christ.

It is striking too that this verse from Isaiah is applied here directly to a Christian audience. There is no evidence of any awareness of the context in the synoptic gospels, where the verse is applied to the opponents of Jesus (and perhaps by implication to the opponents of Jesus' followers). As with all the scriptural citations in *2 Clement*, the words of scripture are presumed to address the Christian readers directly (see Introduction §6. Citations above).

The tenor of the whole of the rest of the address is now set: what matters above all, and is crucial for final reward in heaven, is a proper response to God and Christ by obeying the ethical commands which have been given.

---

[34] cf. Lindemann, *Clemensbriefe*, 207–8.
[35] See more generally Introduction §9.2 Christology, p. 68 above.
[36] cf. too 6.8 'in Ezekiel'. The explicit reference to 'Isaiah' here suggests that the author at least thinks he is citing Isaiah rather than a gospel text.
[37] In theory, a personal 'he' could be God here; however, the 'him' at the start of v. 4 is Jesus (the one who is 'confessed'), and the text moves seamlessly on referring to a 'he' continuously, so it is natural to assume that the same person is meant throughout, *if* the implied third-person pronoun is masculine rather than neuter ('he' rather than 'it').
[38] So Knopf, *Zwei Clemensbriefe*, 158.
[39] Lindemann, *Clemensbriefe*, 208.

Chapter 4

PARALLELS

The chapter contains two explicit quotations: in 4.2 and 4.5. Some have argued that the two citations are two parts of a single citation, with vv. 3–4 providing the interpretation of the first part.[1] However, the presence of a second explicit introductory formula in v. 5, which differs from that used in v. 2,[2] suggests that at least the author of *2 Clement* thought that the two sayings were separate units.

V. 2 is an explicit quotation (with introductory formula λέγει γάρ) of the Q saying Matt. 7.21//Luke 6.46. A version of the same saying may already have been alluded to slightly earlier in 3.4 ('by doing what he says') where the wording is close to that of Luke 6.46. Here the form of the saying is very close to the Matthean version:

2 Clem. 4.2	Matt. 7.21	Luke 6.46
λέγει γάρ·		
οὐ πᾶς ὁ λέγων μοι·	οὐ πᾶς ὁ λέγων μοι·	τί δέ με καλεῖτε·
κύριε κύριε,	κύριε κύριε,	κύριε κύριε,
σωθήσεται,	εἰσελεύσεται εἰς τὴν	
	βασιλείαν τῶν οὐρανῶν,	
ἀλλ' ὁ ποιῶν τὴν	ἀλλ' ὁ ποιῶν τὸ θέλημα	καὶ οὐ ποιεῖτε ἃ λέγω;
δικαιοσύνην.	τοῦ πατρός μου τοῦ ἐν	
	τοῖς οὐρανοῖς.	

---

[1] cf. Donfried, *Setting*, 62; Aono, *Entwicklung*, 131; Warns, 'Untersuchungen', 325–8, who ascribes the composite saying to his proposed apocryphal gospel used by the author of *2 Clement*. The two sayings in *2 Clem.* 4 do have parallels in Matthew that are close to each other there (Matt. 7.21 and 7.23), but whether this can be used as evidence for the sayings belonging together in another (non-Matthean) source used by *2 Clement* is not clear (unless that source was in turn dependent on Matthew): the sayings are from Q, and in Luke are from widely different contexts (Luke 6 and Luke 13); and it is generally assumed that Luke's order reflects the Q order more faithfully—hence the sayings probably did not occur close to each other in Q.

[2] V. 2 λέγει; v. 5 εἶπεν ὁ κύριος.

The similarity with Matthew is clear: cf. the exact verbal agreement in οὐ πᾶς ὁ λέγων μοι· κύριε κύριε, and ἀλλ' ὁ ποιῶν, as well as the overall structure of the saying. Further, it is widely agreed that Matthew has redacted the Q saying significantly so that the present form of the saying in Matt. 7.21 owes a great deal to MattR. Certainly at most of the points where Matthew differs from Luke here, Matthew's version is characteristically Matthean (cf. the reference to 'kingdom of heaven', and 'my Father in heaven').[3] Insofar then as the version in *2 Clement* agrees with that of Matthew, it would seem that *2 Clement* presupposes the finished Gospel of Matthew.

It is true that the version in *2 Clement* lacks the features that might most obviously be identified as MattR ('kingdom of heaven' and 'my Father in heaven'). Thus some have argued that the version in *2 Clement* may represent an earlier form of the saying which Matthew then redacted.[4] This is possible but perhaps unnecessary since (*a*) there is little reason (apart from the version in *2 Clement* itself) to postulate an earlier form of the saying in Matthew other than the (probable) Q version as now represented in Luke 6.46, and (*b*) the differences between *2 Clement* and Matthew, especially at the points where Matthew seems peculiarly Matthean, can be explained as due to the preferred vocabulary of the author of *2 Clement*.[5] Thus the use of σώζειν in the saying (parallel to Matthew's 'enter the kingdom of heaven') takes up the use of the verb in 4.1, and in turn this vocabulary of 'save'/'salvation' is prominent throughout this section of *2 Clement* (cf. 1.4, 7; 2.5, 7; 3.3; 4.1); also, 'righteousness' is a favourite word for this author (cf. 6.9; 11.7; 12.1; 13.1; 18.2; 19.3).[6]

The simplest solution is that the author of *2 Clement* has drawn the quotation, directly or indirectly, from the Gospel of Matthew.[7] As already noted, *2 Clem.* 3.4 may echo the Lukan version of this saying in Luke 6.46 (see above); further, the language of *2 Clem.* 4.1, referring to 'calling' Jesus Lord, also echoes Luke's language (καλεῖτε) in Luke 6.46. It seems therefore that the author of *2 Clement* knows this saying in both its Matthean and its Lukan forms. Probably then *2 Clement* knows both the gospels of Matthew and Luke.

---

[3] cf. Robinson, Hoffmann, and Kloppenborg, *Critical Edition*, 94; also Bultmann, *History*, 116; U. Luz, *Matthew 1–7* (Minneapolis: Fortress, 1989), 440; Davies and Allison, *Matthew*, 1.711–12.

[4] So e.g. Donfried, *Setting*, 63; Gregory, *Reception*, 141, mentioning the possibility of a 'Q^{Mt}' source used by Matthew alone.

[5] See Köster, *Synoptische Überlieferung*, 81.

[6] This answers the claims of some (e.g. Knopf, *Zwei Clemensbriefe*, 158; Donfried, *Setting*, 63) that there is no clear reason for the author of *2 Clement* to change the Matthean wording, and hence he cannot be using Matthew's version.

[7] See Lightfoot, *Apostolic Fathers*, 2.217; Köster, *Synoptische Überlieferung*, 83; Massaux, *Influence*, 144; Köhler, *Rezeption*, 133; *pace* e.g. Lindemann, *Clemensbriefe*, 209; Pratscher, *Zweite Clemensbrief*, 92, who both express more uncertainty.

The case of the saying cited in 4.5 is more complex.

2 Clem. 4.5	Matt. 7.23	Luke 13.27
εἶπεν ὁ κύριος·		
ἐὰν ἦτε μετ' ἐμοῦ		
συνηγμένοι ἐν τῷ κόλπῳ		
μου καὶ μὴ ποιῆτε τὰς		
ἐντολάς μου,		
ἀποβαλῶ ὑμᾶς		
καὶ ἐρῶ ὑμῖν·	καὶ τότε ὁμολογήσω	καὶ ἐρεῖ λέγων ὑμῖν,
	αὐτοῖς ὅτι	
ὑπάγετε ἀπ' ἐμοῦ,		
οὐκ οἶδα ὑμᾶς, πόθεν ἐστέ,	οὐδέποτε ἔγνων ὑμᾶς·	οὐκ οἶδα [ὑμᾶς] πόθεν ἐστέ·
	ἀποχωρεῖτε ἀπ' ἐμοῦ	ἀπόστητε ἀπ' ἐμοῦ,
ἐργάται ἀνομίας.	οἱ ἐργαζόμενοι τὴν	πάντες ἐργάται ἀδικίας.
	ἀνομίαν.	

Ps. 6.9 (LXX): ἀπόστητε ἀπ' ἐμοῦ πάντες οἱ ἐργαζόμενοι τὴν ἀνομίαν.

Justin *1 Apol.* 16.11: καὶ τότε ἐρῶ αὐτοῖς· Ἀποχωρεῖτε ἀπ' ἐμοῦ, ἐργάται τῆς ἀνομίας.

And then I will say to them, 'Depart from me, you who do what is lawless.'

'Jewish' Gospel (gloss at Matt. 7.5 in MS 1424): ἐὰν ἦτε ἐν τῷ κόλπῳ μου καὶ τὸ θέλημα τοῦ πατρός μου τοῦ ἐν οὐρανοῖς μὴ ποιῆτε, ἐκ τοῦ κόλπου μου ἀπορρίψω ὑμᾶς.

If you were in my bosom and do not do the will of my Father in heaven, I will cast you out of my bosom.

For many modern interpreters, the saying divides into two halves: the second half clearly bears a close relationship to the Q saying in Matt. 7.23// Luke 13.27; the first half has no clear parallel with any synoptic saying. However, it should be noted that such a division of the quotation into two halves has no real basis in the text of *2 Clement* itself: the two halves run straight on without a break.[8]

In the second half of the saying here, there are clear parallels in Matthew and Luke; the saying also echoes the words of Ps. 6.9. The situation is thus complex, with problems of determining the more original form of the synoptic tradition, seeking to identify at what stage assimilation and/or allusion to Ps. 6 might have taken place, and also making allowance for the inevitable crop of textual variants which have occurred.

---

[8] cf. Köhler, *Rezeption*, 144: 'Festzuhalten ist, daβ der Verfasser des II Clem beide Zitathälften als Einheit zitiert.' ('One must emphasize the fact that the author of *2 Clement* cites the two halves of the citation as a unity.')

As the texts stand in the versions given above, the text of *2 Clement* is closer to the Lukan version. Thus both agree (against Matthew) in the use of ἐρῶ/ἐρεῖ (Matthew ὁμολογήσω),[9] οὐκ οἶδα ὑμᾶς[10] (Matthew οὐδέποτε ἔγνων ὑμᾶς), πόθεν ἐστε (no parallel in Matthew), and in ἐργάται (Matthew οἱ ἐργαζόμενοι).[11] The *2 Clement* version is possibly closer to Matthew only in the final use of ἀνομία where Luke uses ἀδικία, though even here there is no certainty as the D text of Luke here has ἀνομίαν.[12] Thus the saying in *2 Clem.* 4.5b could be seen as parallel to (one version of the text of) Luke alone.

Koester and Bellinzoni have sought to use the evidence from Justin (*1 Apol.* 16.11, cf. too *Dial.* 76.5) to argue that Justin here (as elsewhere) is using a version of the tradition which harmonized the texts of Matthew and Luke, and that the similar version in *2 Clement* here shows that this harmony pre-dates its use by Justin.[13] However, it is hard to see a clear 'harmonization' in either Justin or *2 Clement* here; moreover, even if they do harmonize, they do so in different ways. Justin's text is close to that of Matthew,[14] and in the text here, the only common features with Luke are the use of ἐρῶ (also in *Dial.* 76.5) and the use of the noun ἐργάται rather than the participle ἐργαζόμενοι.[15] As Donfried says, 'it is difficult to see any significant relationship between 2 Clement and Justin'.[16]

Whether one can identify elements that are MattR and/or LkR in the parallels here is not certain. However, the phrase πόθεν ἐστέ in Luke 13.27 may be due to LkR, assimilating to the context implied by 13.25.[17] If so, then the version of the saying in *2 Clem.* 4.5 presupposes the redactional activity of Luke and hence the existence of Luke's finished gospel.

---

[9] Though a reading of ἐρῶ in Matthew here may be implied by some Old Latin MSS (a c g h) and sy^c: see Köster, *Synoptische Überlieferung*, 87.

[10] ὑμᾶς is present in some MSS of Luke at this point (D Θ pm) but missing from others.

[11] The last point is scarcely significant, given that the two synoptic versions are all but synonymous in this respect. But in any case, ἐργάται may be the reading implied by some Old Latin MSS (a c h q): see Köster, *Synoptische Überlieferung*, 87.

[12] Also 1424 Marcion. (I owe this observation to Professor W. L. Petersen.) The presence of the reading in Marcion implies it is early. The use of ἀνομία also aligns the saying more closely to the wording of Ps. 6.9 LXX. Thus it could be that any change from a Lukan version which used ἀδικία could be due to a secondary assimilation to the text of Ps. 6, without any reference to Matthew at all.

[13] See Köster, *Synoptische Überlieferung*, 92; H. Koester, *Ancient Christian Gospels* (London: SCM, 1990), 356; Bellinzoni, *Sayings*, 25.

[14] For the fuller context of the text in Justin, see Donfried, *Setting*, 64–5. The case for Justin using a harmonized text is based on parallels to both Matthew and Luke: but the main parallels to Luke come elsewhere (e.g. in 16.11a where Justin refers to 'eating and drinking', as in Luke 13.26 and not in Matt. 7.22). Here Justin agrees with Matthew in using ἀποχωρεῖτε (Luke ἀπόστητε, 2 Clement ὑπάγετε).

[15] It is, however, doubtful whether the latter can bear much weight in the present context (see above).

[16] Donfried, *Setting*, 67.

[17] Köster, *Synoptische Überlieferung*, 83–4; also Robinson, Hoffmann, and Kloppenborg, *Critical Edition*, 412. Cf. too Massaux, *Influence*, 150; Aono, *Entwicklung*, 134.

However, the form in which the saying might have been known to the author here has to take account of the first half of the saying as well. Here there is a well-known close parallel to the version in *2 Clement* in the marginal gloss to Matt. 7.5 found in MS 1424, said to be from 'the Jewish (gospel)' (τὸ Ἰουδαϊκόν). The identity of this 'Jewish (gospel)' is debated. Vielhauer has argued that it is the *Gospel of the Nazarenes*,[18] though there is no positive evidence for this. According to Koester, this gospel 'was essentially an expanded edition of the Gospel of Matthew'.[19] However, as Koester also points out, the text mentioned in the marginal gloss echoes Matthean language (especially in the reference to doing 'the will of my father in heaven') and it is just at this point that the text of *2 Clement* is not parallel (it has 'my commandments').[20] Thus Koester claims that the source of *2 Clement* cannot be the *Gospel of the Nazarenes* itself; rather, the version in the Jewish Christian gospel may be later, assimilating to the text of Matthew, and *2 Clement* witnesses to an earlier form of the tradition.

However, it could as easily be argued that the version in *2 Clement* is later, at least in form-critical terms: the object of the 'doing'/'not doing' is here no longer God's commands, but those of Jesus himself ('my' commandments). Hence the version in *2 Clement* represents a version that is significantly 'higher' Christologically. Whilst it is clearly dangerous to posit too neat a developmental scheme in relation to Christology within early Christianity, it may be that the version of this saying here in *2 Clement* represents a later development than the version preserved in the marginal gloss in MS 1424.[21]

The author apparently then had access to, and used, a form of a saying of Jesus that has no exact parallel in any synoptic gospel, but which was clearly known more widely. Further, there is no evidence that the author thought that the whole of his 'citation' in 4.5 was anything other than a single citation (see above). The source for the saying was probably an unknown 'gospel' (or at least a collection of Jesus traditions), and at this point it appears to have overlapped with (at least) Luke in the second half of the saying. Moreover, the analysis above suggests that this source used the tradition as it had been developed by Luke himself. It thus attests to the later development of the tradition *after* the stage of the synoptic evangelists.[22]

---

[18] See Ph. Vielhauer, 'Jewish Christian Gospels', in E. Hennecke, *New Testament Apocrypha 1* (London: SCM, 1963), 136.

[19] Koester, *Ancient Christian Gospels*, 357; idem, *Synoptische Überlieferung*, 92–3.

[20] Koester, ibid.

[21] So e.g. W. L. Petersen, 'Textual Traditions Examined: What the Text of the Apostolic Fathers tells us about the Text of the New Testament in the Second Century', in A. F. Gregory and C. M. Tuckett (eds), *The Reception of the New Testament in the Apostolic Fathers* (Oxford: Oxford University Press, 2005), 39.

[22] cf. Köhler, *Rezeption*, 144; also Massaux, *Influence*, 150; Warns, 'Untersuchungen', 325–8; Lindemann, *Clemensbriefe*, 210–11. Similarly (though with more scepticism about whether Luke's gospel is presupposed), Donfried, *Setting*, 66–7; Gregory, *Reception*, 141–2. Among older studies, Lightfoot, *Apostolic Fathers*, 2.218, ascribes the saying to the *Gospel of the Egyptians*

A number of other quotations of Jesus traditions in *2 Clement* come from sources which evidently cannot be the canonical gospels (see 5.2–4; 8.5; 12.2). Whether all of these are to be traced back to a single source, i.e. one (and only one) 'apocryphal' gospel, is however not certain. The analysis of 4.2 above suggests that the author here knows both the gospels of Matthew and Luke. It may be, therefore, that he had access to a number of different sources containing traditions of Jesus' sayings. Trying to force them all into a single source may be unjustified.[23]

COMMENTARY

1 The argument continues almost seamlessly across the (artificial) 'chapter' division here. In one way, the author is clarifying exactly what he meant, and what he did not mean, earlier by 'confessing' Jesus. It was said—briefly—in ch. 3 that confessing Jesus meant practical action. Now, with the help of a Jesus citation, the negative side is made explicit: 'confessing' does not mean simply uttering words expressing positive views about Jesus himself (calling him 'Lord'). This, says the writer, will *not* save us (οὐ ... σώσει ἡμᾶς). The use of the future σώσει is striking: up to this point, the 'saving' activity of God/Christ seems to relate to what has already happened to the Christian (1.4, 7; 2.5, 7; 3.3); but from now on, it is made clear that being 'saved' is not something that the Christian can rely on, but will only happen in the future for those who respond 'properly'.[24]

2 The message is now confirmed by the citation of the Jesus saying, probably from Matt. 7.21 (see above). The author may adapt the wording slightly, by replacing 'will enter into the kingdom of heaven' with 'will be saved', and 'doing the will of my father in heaven' with 'doing righteousness'. Neither of the terms apparently deleted from Matthew here are uncongenial to the author of *2 Clement*, but equally the language of being 'saved' and 'righteousness' is very congenial and serves the author's purpose very well (see Parallels above). The message is clear: pious words without ethical action count for nothing.

It may also be noteworthy that the 'pious words' apparently involve calling Jesus 'Lord'. There is thus no evidence that, in the situation addressed, there is any reserve about calling Jesus Lord:[25] indeed the reverse seems to be the case.

(apparently on the basis that this is cited later, probably with 12.2 in mind: see below); also Schubert, '2. Clemensbrief', 252; but whether one has to ascribe all non-canonical traditions to a single source is questionable.

[23] See p. 41 above.

[24] On the consistency of the language of *2 Clement*, see the commentary on 1.4 and n. 31 above.

[25] e.g. reflecting possible Gnostic sensibilities (cf. Irenaeus, *Haer.* 1.1.3). See p. 48 above.

The author is warning against a possible over-*willingness* to call Jesus Lord, but without taking seriously enough the ethical consequences which such a confession entails.

3 So far the message about the importance of ethical behaviour has been clear, but somewhat general. It has not been said what specific ethical issues, if any, might be in mind. It is possible, but not certain, that a little more light might be thrown on the issue in what follows as the author gives greater substance to the demand for ethical 'works'.

A general statement about the importance of 'loving one another'[26] comes first. This is followed by a series of three negative exhortations (not 'committing adultery', not 'slandering one another', or being 'jealous'), apparently matched by three positive ones (being 'self-controlled', 'merciful', and 'good').[27] This is then followed by a further negative and positive exhortation: to 'sympathize' with each other and not to be 'lovers of money'. It is possible to read these exhortations as fairly general, referring to standard vices and virtues and hence giving little insight if any into the specific situation of the author and his community. On the other hand, the list here is relatively short.[28] Hence it may be that these particular issues are singled out for mention here because they do relate to the specific situation, and the 'dangers' (as the author sees them) facing the community he is addressing.

The general exhortation to love is in one way similar to Paul in making 'love' the overriding ethical category (cf. 1 Cor. 13; Gal. 5.14; also *1 Clem.* 49). Here, love is explicitly related to relationships within the community ('one another'). Love for outsiders (or 'enemies') is mentioned elsewhere, but only in passing: cf. 13.4 where the more pressing danger is evidently a failure to show love within the community. So too the concern for good internal relations within the community is underlined here by the threefold reference to 'one another' (loving one another, not slandering one another, sympathizing with one another). Further, small pieces of evidence from elsewhere in *2 Clement* suggest that the author sees the issue of possible tensions within the community as a real danger.[29] If the exhortations here are related to a specific situation being addressed by the speaker/author, it seems that any problems are primarily related to relationships within the community.

---

[26] For the use of ἑαυτούς here (instead of ἀλλήλους), see BDF §287.

[27] How precisely the two sets of three are intended to match each other is not clear. Pace e.g. Knopf, *Zwei Clemensbriefe*, 158 (who claims that the three positive and three negative exhortations correspond closely to each other), it seems that the corresponding elements only relate very loosely.

[28] Contrast the extensive list of vices (and/or virtues) in e.g. Rom. 1.29–31; 1 Cor. 6.9–10; Gal. 5.19–23; *1 Clem.* 30.1; 35.5; *Did.* 5.1–2; *Barn.* 20.1–2; Herm. *Sim.* 6.5.5; *Mand.* 8.3, etc.

[29] cf. 9.6 ('love one another'); 12.3 (speaking the truth to one another); possibly 15.5 (not begrudging one another); 17.2 (helping one another).

The three negative exhortations could be seen as fairly stock vices, and similar language occurs in a number of other texts. Thus for adultery (μοιχᾶσθαι/μοιχεία) cf. *1 Clem.* 30.1; 35.8; *Did.* 3.3; 5.1; *Barn.* 20.1; Herm. *Mand.* 4.1.4–8; 8.3;[30] for 'slandering one another'[31] (καταλαλεῖν/καταλαλία) cf. Rom. 1.30; Jas. 4.11; 1 Pet. 2.1; *1 Clem.* 30.1, 3; *Barn.* 20.2; Herm. *Mand.* 8.4; *Sim.* 6.5.5; for 'jealousy' cf. 1 Cor. 13.4; Jas. 4.2; *1 Clem.* 3–6; 14.1; 43.2; 63.2; *Did.* 5.1. 'Jealousy' was clearly the major problem dealt with by the writer of *1 Clement*.[32] It is, however, not explicitly mentioned elsewhere in *2 Clement*, and hence it is hard to make too much of 'jealousy' as a key problem addressed by the writer.[33] The exhortation not to slander one another may be more pointed, and certainly ties in with the general exhortation to be mindful of 'one another' (cf. above), though the language used (καταλαλεῖν) is very general, and widely used in vice lists (see above), so it is not easy to determine what specific problem might be in mind.

Whether adultery is a live issue for the author and/or the community is not clear. The issue is mentioned again in 6.4 (along with 'love of money'), so a case can be made for seeing this as one of the key features of unethical behaviour about which the author is particularly concerned. So too there is much made later in the text about the importance of keeping the 'flesh' 'pure' (8.4 cf. 14.3). In addition, it may be significant that when the author seeks to interpret part of the saying cited in 12.2, he presses the text (about male and female) to claim that it means that there should be no (probably extramarital) sexually charged friendships and/or relationships between men and women in the community (see the commentary). Issues about possible sexual impropriety might also relate to claims made about Gnostics by their opponents, as well as to occasional claims by Gnostics themselves for a rather 'freer' attitude to sexual relations.[34] Thus it might be that the specific

---

[30] If the related word group based on πορνεία is included, a range of other texts comes into view, e.g. Gal. 5.19; Eph. 5.3; Col. 3.5; *Did.* 3.3; Herm. *Mand.* 4.1.5; 8.3, etc.

[31] As with the love command, it is the relationships within the community (ἀλλήλων) that seem to be paramount for the author here.

[32] Warnings about jealousy dominate large sections of that letter: cf. the references just given.

[33] On the theory of Donfried, *Setting*, that *2 Clement* was written in the light of the immediate aftermath of the receipt of *1 Clement* by the Corinthians (and the collapse of the 'rebellion' there), see p. 16 above.

[34] See Introduction §7. Opponents, and the commentary on 3.4 (with references to Williams and King). Williams, *Rethinking 'Gnosticism'*, 184–7, does note one example of a Gnostic writer advocating more sexual freedom, namely Epiphanes as recorded in Clement, *Strom.* 3.6.1–9.3; he is somewhat dismissive of this on the grounds that the reasons which Epiphanes is reported to have given for his sexual freedom do not relate to Gnostic negative views about the world as the creation of an ignorant or malevolent Demiurge, but to claims about equality and fairness in the universe. Nevertheless, such an example may show that other polemical claims about the sexual (mis)behaviour of Gnostics were not total fabrications, even if the situation may have been very varied across different groups (and with a range of different reasons given to justify such behaviour).

mention of adultery, in an otherwise relatively short 'vice list' here, does reflect a particular concern of the writer.

The three negative exhortations are matched by three positive ones. The last two ('slandering' and being 'jealous') relate only in the most general terms to the last two positive exhortations, being 'merciful' and 'good'. Being 'good' is certainly extremely general. Being 'merciful' as a human quality occurs only here in *2 Clement* (though cf. 3.1; 16.2 for Jesus' action to other humans as one of showing 'mercy').[35]

The exhortation to 'self-control' comes first, and as such may correspond to the charge not to commit adultery. The category of ἐγκράτεια had been a very important one in Greek philosophical and ethical writings ever since the time of Socrates (cf. Xenophon, *Mem.* 1.5.1).[36] Aristotle devotes the seventh book of his *Nichomachean Ethics* to the idea. In this tradition, ἐγκράτεια is what distinguishes human beings from animals; it consists above all in the control over one's emotions which leads to true freedom. The theme is taken up by Jewish writers, especially Philo, though with a more dualistic framework of thought: the word tends towards an idea of excluding all bodily needs which are deemed not necessary to existence. Thus the idea of self-control moves over to the idea of abstinence from anything felt to satisfy purely bodily desires.[37] Hence the word takes on a more ascetic meaning, and became associated over time particularly with sexual activity. In the NT, the word does not occur often (cf. Acts 24.25; Gal. 5.23; 2 Pet. 1.6; the verb in 1 Cor. 7.9; the adjective in Tit. 1.8). The word is, however, more frequent in *1 Clement* (35.2; 62.2; 64.1) and in Hermas (*Vis.* 2.3.2; 3.8.4; *Mand.* 6.1.1). It is not always easy to determine whether the word group refers generally to self-control, or specifically to asceticism (especially in relation to sexual activity). At times it would seem that the former is probably the case,[38] though later the term does come to refer more to an ascetic lifestyle, and in a radical form referring to abstaining from any sexual activity at all. In the case of *2 Clement* generally, a meaning of self-control is probably the most likely. In the present context, the exhortation to be ἐγκρατεῖς comes alongside,

---

[35] It is possible that ἐλεημοσύνη in 16.4 might relate to the more general qualities, perhaps including being ἐλεήμων, rather than referring specifically to 'almsgiving' alone: see the commentary there.

[36] For general treatments, see W. Grundmann, ἐγκράτεια, *TWNT* 2 (1935), 338–40; H. Chadwick, 'Enkrateia', *RAC* 5 (1962), 343–65. Cf. also Paul in Gal. 5.23 and see Betz, *Galatians*, 288. See too the excursus of Lindemann, *Clemensbriefe*, 244–5.

[37] cf. Grundmann, *TWNT* 2, 339; also Donfried, *Setting*, 116; cf. Philo, *Spec.* 1.149, 173; 2.195; 4.112; *Leg.* 3.18; *Virt.* 180.

[38] e.g. in Tit. 1.8, a bishop must be 'self-controlled'; but in 1 Tim. 3.2, it is assumed that a bishop may be married (but should be 'the husband of one wife'). Assuming that Titus and 1 Timothy do not contradict each other (which is not impossible but perhaps unlikely), being 'self-controlled' does not exclude being a good husband (and presumably within a fully consummated marriage).

possibly as the antithesis to, the exhortation not to commit adultery, referring to sexual relations outside marriage; but this would be strange (and unnecessary) if all sexual activity were regarded negatively. Thus the exhortation to be ἐγκρατεῖς probably refers more generally to the idea of 'self-control', without necessarily any expectation that this will lead to complete sexual abstinence (at least within marriage).[39]

The fact that this is put first in the list of positive exhortations here may indicate its importance for the author, and as with the list of negatives, the relative shortness of the list may indicate that what is said here is not simply a list of very general virtues. The importance of 'self-control' is also indicated by what is said in 15.1.[40] Thus this relatively short list of vices and virtues may give a glimpse of some of the main ethical issues which the author is seeking to address.

The last two exhortations are that the hearers should (positively) 'sympathize' with each other and (negatively) not be 'lovers of money'. Again it is not easy to determine whether these are relatively general commonplaces, or whether they relate to what are perceived as specific dangers within the community. The exhortation to sympathize with each other takes up the general theme of mutual concern for the well-being of one's fellow Christians within the community already noted (cf. the repeated 'one another' in this verse). The concern about 'love of money' reappears in 6.4, and some concern about financial inequalities may also be reflected in 20.1.[41] The sentiment is widespread in early Christian literature;[42] however, while these last two exhortations can be taken as simply reflecting ethical commonplaces, it may be again that they receive particular relevance in the situation being addressed.

4 The author now introduces another antithesis: one must fear God rather than other human beings.[43] The allusion is probably to Matt. 10.28, probably

---

[39] See Wengst, *Zweite Clemensbrief*, 231; Lohmann, *Drohung*, 123; Pratscher, *Zweite Clemensbrief*, 191.

[40] See the commentary there. Whether one can regard the whole text as about 'self-control' is another matter: see the theory of Harris and the discussion of this in Introduction §3. Authorship.

[41] Though this section may be separate in origin from the rest of the text: see Introduction §5. Literary Unity. It is not certain whether specifically financial issues are in mind in 16.4 and the very positive evaluation given of ἐλεημοσύνη. If this refers to 'almsgiving', i.e. charitable giving of money to others, this might suggest that the issue of money, and the right use of money within the community, was of particular concern for the author. But this meaning of ἐλεημοσύνη may be too restrictive: see the commentary on 16.4.

[42] cf. Luke 16.14; 1 Tim. 6.10; 2 Tim. 3.2; *Did.* 3.5; Pol. *Phil.* 2.2; 4.3; 6.1.

[43] There seems to be no good reason to take θεόν here as a reference to Jesus (so Stegemann, 'Herkunft', 86–7; Wengst, *Zweite Clemensbrief*, 228). See e.g. Lindemann, *Clemensbriefe*, 210; Pratscher, *Zweite Clemensbrief*, 96.

Commentary: Chapter 4   167

also shown by the (rather awkward) μᾶλλον.⁴⁴ The sentence here prepares the way for what will be developed further in 5.2–4 (see below).

5 The importance of obeying the teaching of Jesus is summed up and emphasized again with a further citation from the Jesus tradition: if we⁴⁵ carry on doing these things (ταῦτα), i.e. the things proscribed in v. 3,⁴⁶ then the saying of 'the Lord'⁴⁷ will come into play and those who do not 'do these things' will find definitively rejected. The saying gives rise to difficult and wide-ranging questions about its precise origin (see Parallels above). It may well be that the author is here using a non-canonical source, albeit one that presupposes the finished gospels (or at least Luke). In the context of the argument, it largely repeats what is said in v. 2 and the citation from the Jesus tradition there. Concrete ethical behaviour is all important and any failure to do what is required will result in rejection by Jesus, the judge of the living and the dead (cf. 1.1) at the final judgement.

---

⁴⁴ The construction οὐ ... μᾶλλον, ἀλλά is a little clumsy and seems to be a mixture of οὐ ... ἀλλά and μᾶλλον ... ἤ: see Knopf, Zwei Clemensbriefe, 159, but cf. Warns, 'Untersuchungen', 289–90: the μᾶλλον may be due to the influence of Matt. 10.28, reflected too in the saying in 5.4 which is about to come.

⁴⁵ The MSS vary: A reads ὑμῶν; C and S read/imply ἡμῶν. The former is read by most earlier commentators and editors, the latter by Wengst, Zweite Clemensbrief, 244; Lindemann, Clemensbriefe, 209; also Pratscher, Zweite Clemensbrief, 96, who argues that it is the harder reading in light of the subsequent second-person plurals in the rest of v. 5. In addition, one should note that all the exhortations in the preceding context are in the first-person plural (cf. v. 3 'let us confess ...', v. 4 'we should not fear ...'). However pointed the author may be in addressing his audience, he does seem to keep the polemic relatively low-key by using a first-person rather than a second-person address: see above on 1.2. Moreover, the tendency of C is generally to change first persons to second persons: thus, if the C reading here were secondary, it would go against the general tendency of C. Overall, it seems preferable to accept the CS reading.

⁴⁶ Rather than fearing other people and not God: see Knopf, Zwei Clemensbriefe, 159 (who calls the language here 'lässig und nicht geschickt' ('careless and not skilful')) and contra e.g. Lindemann, Clemensbriefe, 97. The language of 'doing' (πρασσόντων) fits better if referring to concrete behaviour, rather than just 'fearing'.

⁴⁷ Both Wengst, Zweite Clemensbrief, 244, and Lindemann, Clemensbriefe, 210, follow the S reading here which has 'Jesus' alone. This seems unlikely: nowhere else is a Jesus saying introduced by the simple name 'Jesus'. The agreement with Jesus traditions elsewhere almost certainly means that the S reading is the correct interpretation, i.e. 'the Lord' here is Jesus rather than God. But still, there is no reason to go against the combined witness of A and C.

Chapter 5

PARALLELS

2 Clem. 5.2–4	Matt. 10	Luke
² λέγει γὰρ ὁ κύριος· ἔσεσθε ὡς ἀρνία ἐν μέσῳ λύκων. ³ ἀποκριθεὶς δὲ ὁ Πέτρος αὐτῷ λέγει· ἐὰν οὖν διασπαράξωσιν οἱ λύκοι τὰ ἀρνία; ⁴ εἶπεν ὁ Ἰησοῦς τῷ Πέτρῳ· μὴ φοβείσθωσαν τὰ ἀρνία τοὺς λύκους μετὰ τὸ ἀποθανεῖν αὐτά· καὶ ὑμεῖς μὴ φοβεῖσθε τοὺς ἀποκτέννοντας ὑμᾶς καὶ μηδὲν ὑμῖν δυναμένους ποιεῖν,	¹⁶ ἰδοὺ ἐγὼ ἀποστέλλω ὑμᾶς ὡς πρόβατα ἐν μέσῳ λύκων·	(10.3) ὑπάγετε· ἰδοὺ ἀποστέλλω ὑμᾶς ὡς ἄρνας ἐν μέσῳ λύκων.
	²⁸ καὶ μὴ φοβεῖσθε ἀπὸ τῶν ἀποκτεννόντων τὸ σῶμα, τὴν δὲ ψυχὴν μὴ δυναμένων ἀποκτεῖναι·	(12.4–5) λέγω δὲ ὑμῖν τοῖς φίλοις μου, μὴ φοβηθῆτε ἀπὸ τῶν ἀποκτεινόντων τὸ σῶμα καὶ μετὰ ταῦτα μὴ ἐχόντων περισσότερόν τι ποιῆσαι. ⁵ ὑποδείξω δὲ ὑμῖν τίνα φοβηθῆτε·
ἀλλὰ φοβεῖσθε τὸν μετὰ τὸ ἀποθανεῖν ὑμᾶς ἔχοντα ἐξουσίαν ψυχῆς καὶ σώματος τοῦ βαλεῖν εἰς γέενναν πυρός.	φοβεῖσθε δὲ μᾶλλον τὸν δυνάμενον καὶ ψυχὴν καὶ σῶμα ἀπολέσαι ἐν γεέννῃ.	φοβήθητε τὸν μετὰ τὸ ἀποκτεῖναι ἔχοντα ἐξουσίαν ἐμβαλεῖν εἰς τὴν γέενναν. ναὶ λέγω ὑμῖν, τοῦτον φοβήθητε.

Justin, 1 Apol. 19.7: μὴ φοβεῖσθε τοὺς ἀναιροῦντας ὑμᾶς καὶ μετὰ ταῦτα μὴ δυναμένους τι ποιῆσαι, φοβήθητε δὲ τὸν μετὰ τὸ ἀποθανεῖν δυνάμενον καὶ ψυχὴν καὶ σῶμα εἰς γέενναν ἐμβαλεῖν.

Commentary: Chapter 5 169

Do not fear those who kill you, and afterwards cannot do anything; but fear him who, after death, has the power to cast soul and body into hell.

Ps.-Clem. Hom. 17.5.2: μὴ φοβηθῆτε ἀπὸ τοῦ ἀποκτέννοντος τὸ σῶμα, τῇ δὲ ψυχῇ μὴ δυναμένου ποιῆσαι, φοβήθητε δὲ τὸν δυνάμενον καὶ σῶμα καὶ ψυχὴν εἰς τὴν γέενναν τοῦ πυρὸς βαλεῖν.

Do not fear those who kill the body, but cannot do anything to the soul; but fear him who has the power to cast soul and body into the hell of fire.

The tradition in 2 Clem. 5.2–4 is introduced as a citation (λέγει γὰρ ὁ κύριος), consisting of a saying of Jesus (v. 2), a response by Peter (v. 3), and a further saying of Jesus (v. 4). The situation is extremely complex. There are parallels to what is said here in two synoptic contexts: the saying about lambs in the midst of wolves (v. 2) has a parallel in the mission discourse in Matt. 10.16//Luke 10.3; and the saying about not being afraid of those who kill the body (v. 4) is also found in Matt. 10.28//Luke 12.4–5. However, the intervening response by Peter (v. 3), forming the whole into a dialogue scene, has no parallel in the canonical gospels. The saying about not fearing occurs independently in a number of patristic writers,[1] and it may be that the saying circulated independently. Hence, the tradition here is almost certainly composite, consisting of originally independent traditions. On the other hand, nothing suggests that the author of 2 Clement was responsible for bringing together the separate traditions here.[2] As noted below, the main point which the author draws from the citation here is the focus on 'fear' and who/what one should fear. This only comes in v. 4 (parallel to Matt. 10.28//Luke 12.4–5). The rest of the tradition is somewhat redundant for the author's purposes. Hence it is highly unlikely that the author is himself responsible for creating the whole unit here. More likely, he found the unit as a preformed section which he cited en bloc. Thus many have suggested that the author here is dependent on an apocryphal gospel, now lost, which had already combined the separate sayings into a single unit.[3]

The tradition cited here in 2 Clement seems to presuppose elements from both Matthew and Luke, and to reflect a harmonized version of these two

---

[1] cf. Herm. Mand. 12.6.3; Irenaeus, Haer. 3.18.5; Clement, Exc. 5.3; 14.3, as well as the parallels in Justin and the Pseudo-Clementine Homilies noted above.

[2] The possibility is raised by Lindemann, Clemensbriefe, 213, suggesting that v. 4 might represent a secondary addition to vv. 2–3. However, it seems that vv. 2–3 can only with difficulty have existed on their own as the question of Peter really demands an answer (so rightly Pratscher, Zweite Clemensbrief, 104).

[3] cf. Lightfoot, Apostolic Fathers, 2.219, and Schubert, '2. Clemensbrief', 252 (the Gospel of the Egyptians on the basis of other possible parallels in 2 Clement (cf. 12.2)); Massaux, Influence, 151 ('une source apocryphe' ('an apocryphal source')); Köster, Synoptische Überlieferung, 98 (the Gospel of the Nazarenes on the basis of possible other links elsewhere in 2 Clement (cf. 4.5)); Donfried, Setting, 70 ('a non-canonical source'); Warns, 'Untersuchungen', 330–5; Köhler, Rezeption, 146; Lindemann, Clemensbriefe, 213; Gregory, Reception, 144; Pratscher, Zweite Clemensbrief, 104.

gospels;[4] further, some of these elements may well be redactional in Matthew and/or Luke. Thus in the second saying (v. 4), *2 Clement* has no reference to 'killing the soul' but simply refers to others 'not being able to do anything to you'. The vocabulary agrees closely with that of Luke over against Matthew's parallel, and the Lukan wording here has been widely taken to be LkR, Luke avoiding the language of 'killing the soul'.[5] The version in *2 Clement* also agrees with Luke in speaking about fearing the one 'who has authority' (ἔχοντα ἐξουσίαν, Matthew δυνάμενον) to 'throw' (βαλεῖν, Luke ἐμβαλεῖν, Matthew ἀπολέσαι) you into hell 'after you die' (μετὰ τὸ ἀποθανεῖν ὑμᾶς, Luke μετὰ τὸ ἀποκτεῖναι, no equivalent in Matthew). Yet *2 Clement* agrees with Matthew in the language of 'not being able' to do anything more (Luke: not 'having' more they can do), and in referring to 'body and soul' being cast into/destroyed in hell. Thus the tradition as used by *2 Clement* here almost certainly reflects a post-synoptic development of the tradition of the sayings.

Another possibility raised recently is that the tradition here may be related to a tradition appearing in another text which might be identifiable as a fragment of the *Gospel of Peter*. Thus, Lührmann has suggested that P. Oxy. 4009, a small papyrus fragment from Oxyrhynchus, might represent a fragment of the *Gospel of Peter* which overlaps here with the saying in *2 Clem.* 5.[6] The fragment appears to have a version of the saying 'be wise as serpents and innocent as doves' (only the last half is extant): this has a synoptic parallel in Matt. 10.16b, which is adjacent to the saying about sheep and wolves in Matt. 10.16a and which is parallel to *2 Clem.* 5; it also then has a reference to 'wolves' (possibly including a version of the saying about sheep among wolves). The fragment then reflects a dialogue between someone (presumably Jesus) and a person who refers to him/herself in the first person ('he says to me'). What follows is fragmentary, but can be reconstructed to be close to the saying in *2 Clem.* 5 about not fearing death or its consequences. The other main fragment of the *Gospel of Peter* does, at one point, have Peter refer to himself in the first person (*Gos. Pet.* XIV.60). Lührmann therefore suggests that the fragment offers a version of the same tradition as that reflected in *2 Clem.* 5.2–4; also the equivalence of the 'me' in the fragment and 'Peter' in

---

[4] See Köster, *Synoptische Überlieferung*, 95–6. Cf. too Bellinzoni, *Sayings*, 110–11, who argues on the basis of the version in Justin that Justin and *2 Clement* are dependent on the same harmonized version. Cf. too Aono, *Entwicklung*, 136–8.

[5] cf. Robinson, Hoffmann, and Kloppenborg, *Critical Edition*, 296; see e.g. Aono, *Entwicklung*, 136; Schulz, *Spruchquelle*, 158; Davies and Allison, *Matthew*, 2.206.

[6] See D. Lührmann, *Die apokryph gewordenen Evangelien*, NovTSup 112 (Leiden: Brill, 2004), 73–86 (repeating earlier studies). For the first edition of the fragment (with also a tentative identification as a fragment of the *Gospel of Peter*), see P. J. Parsons and D. Lührmann, '4009. Gospel of Peter?', *The Oxyrhynchus Papyri* 60 (London: Egypt Exploration Society, 1994), 1–5.

2 *Clem.* 5.3 ('Jesus said to Peter') suggests that the fragment might stem from an otherwise unattested section of the *Gospel of Peter*.

The theory is by no means certain. For example, the *Gospel of Peter* is not the only text in ancient literature where Peter is referred to in the first person.[7] In any case, the parallels between the P.Oxy. 4009 and 2 *Clem.* 5 are not quite as close as might appear at first sight. The opening saying in the two texts reflects *different* parts of Matt. 10.16 (though the further reference to 'wolves' in P.Oxy. 4009 may reflect the saying in Matt. 10.16a).[8] Further, the alleged parallel between the fragment and 2 *Clement* in the saying about not fearing death depends in part on the parallel being assumed: since the text of P.Oxy. 4009 is so fragmentary, the reconstruction is heavily based on the text of 2 *Clement* and hence the theory that the two texts agree closely is slightly circular. Nevertheless, the fragment does provide a striking parallel not only to the saying about fear (widely attested and perhaps cited independently as we have seen), but also to a setting of this saying in the context of a dialogue with someone else (possibly Peter), as well as a link with another saying related (via Matthew) to the lambs-wolves saying.

The saying in 2 *Clement* here may well reflect a non-canonical, 'apocryphal' gospel source. It *may* be that P.Oxy. 4009 allows us to see some connection between the source used and the *Gospel of Peter*.[9] As noted, it seems clear that the tradition here reflects developments of the tradition which post-date the synoptic gospels. The author of 2 *Clement* probably uses a tradition which has built on, and harmonized, the versions of the saying about not fearing found in Matthew and Luke and combined this with another saying from the synoptic mission discourse. Thus it may well be that 2 *Clement* is not directly dependent on the canonical gospels themselves; but it almost certainly presupposes their finished forms and uses a version of the saying which has been built up from these canonical versions, perhaps in some harmony.[10]

---

[7] See T. J. Kraus and T. Nicklas, *Das Petrusevangelium und die Petrusapokalypse*, GCS NF. 11 (Berlin: De Gruyter, 2004), 59–63, esp. p. 63.

[8] If P.Oxy. 4009 and 2 *Clem.* 5 reflect the same underlying tradition, then again it probably represents a *post*-synoptic development: the two texts have parallels to Matt. 10.16a and 10.16b respectively; and while the latter (on being wise as serpents etc.) may well be proverbial and/or traditional, the combination of this with the lambs-wolves saying probably reflects Matthew's editorial hand. Hence, if the combined evidence of P.Oxy. 4009 and 2 *Clem.* 5 reflects a tradition where both sayings are combined, this almost certainly reflects Matthew's finished gospel where the two traditions are brought together, perhaps for the first time.

[9] Lührmann himself is careful not to overstate any claim and certainly does not argue that the source of 2 *Clem.* 5 *is* the *Gospel of Peter*: he simply talks of 'der Zusammenhang, aus dem die Fassung des POxy 4009 stammt, die Vorlage gebildet haben kann für diejenige von 2Klem 5,2–4' ('the context from which the version of P. Oxy. 4009 stems could have formed the Vorlage of 2 *Clem.* 5.2–4': Lührmann, *Apokryph gewordenen Evangelien*, 82). For a very critical view about the theory of any link between P.Oxy. 4009 and *Gos. Pet.*, see P. Foster, *The Gospel of Peter. Introduction, Critical Edition and Commentary* (Leiden: Brill, 2010), 69–74.

[10] This may also be the significance here of the similar version of the saying in Justin. Cf. n. 4 above.

COMMENTARY

At a very general level, the line of argument in chapters 5 and 6 is relatively clear: the promises awaiting the Christian in a life to come far outweigh the brief, transitory nature of the present life; hence the Christian must strive to achieve these promises and rewards and, in line with everything said so far in the text, these promises will be achieved by living a life of ethical uprightness and obedience. Nevertheless, if this is the general message, the details when pressed are far from clear. Either the author's logic and/or theology are at times somewhat inconsistent or 'clumsy' in some details, or one has to read in a certain amount between the lines of what is said on the surface. Moreover if, as many assume, the author is engaged in some kind of opposition to, and/or polemic against, a form of Gnosticism, the writer himself comes very near to adopting aspects of the kind of Gnostic position that he may be seeking to oppose.[11]

1 The lack of apparent clarity is already striking in the first phrase here which speaks of the readers (and the author) 'having left behind our stay in the strange land of this world' (καταλείψαντες τὴν παροικίαν τοῦ κόσμου τούτου).

The use of παροικία here is striking. The word refers to the state of living as an alien in a place where one does not belong.[12] Here it seems to refer clearly to the present existence of this world (cf. the genitive τοῦ κόσμου τούτου qualifying παροικίαν) as the place/environment where Christians are 'strangers' or 'aliens' and do not (really) belong.[13]

It is not clear, however, how the author regards the present state of the Christians he is addressing; or rather, his language seems to imply something very different from what might be expected. Partly from what is said elsewhere in the text, one would expect him to presume that the addressees are presently in an earthly existence, and that they are to look ahead to a future time and/or place, after death, when they will be rewarded for their good deeds. However, the language here, in particular the aorist participle κατα-

---

[11] cf. Lindemann, *Clemensbriefe*, 212: 'Auffallend ist, daß sich der Prediger hier erstmals explizit gnostischer Terminologie bedient, diese aber offenbar antignostisch einsetzt ... Dabei ist seine eigene Position von der der Gnosis gar nicht weit entfernt ... ' ('It is striking that the preacher here for the first time uses explicitly Gnostic terminology, though uses it clearly in an anti-Gnostic way ... His own position is thereby not far removed from that of Gnosis', with reference especially to 5.5–6.)

[12] cf. 1 Pet. 1.17, used metaphorically (as here) in relation to Christians' existence in the world. It is used more literally in Acts 13.17 in relation to the situation of Israel in Egypt.

[13] Donfried, *Setting*, 119, cites Philo, *Conf.* 77–80, with similar language of 'wise men' who are 'sojourners' in their life on earth, while their true home is in heaven. The idea is very similar then to the language here.

λείψαντες, seems to presume that the Christian readers/hearers have already made the transition from the present life to the life to come: Christians have already 'forsaken' (καταλείψαντες: aorist participle) the place and/or state of being an alien.[14] Perhaps the author is simply writing loosely and/or carelessly:[15] certainly, as it stands, the text is more than a little startling.

The next exhortation is the general theme that dominates this section, and indeed the whole text: 'let us do the will of him who called us'. The one 'who called us' is probably Christ (cf. 1.8; also 6.7 for the 'doing the will of Christ'). Certainly the exhortation to do the will of Christ and/or God is the leitmotif that comes throughout *2 Clement*. The 'doing' refers primarily to the ethical behaviour required in this life.[16]

Coupled with this now is an exhortation 'not to be afraid to leave this world'. This picks up the general language about 'fear' in 4.4, about not fearing men rather than God, as well as partly anticipating the warnings about fearing God in 5.4. Here the negative side of the picture (who/what not to fear) is developed into an exhortation about not fearing death.[17] Christians should not be afraid to depart from this world, i.e. to die and (by implication) move to their true home elsewhere. (The reference to physical death is explicit in the comparison with lambs and wolves which follows.)[18]

---

[14] Some absorb the participle in the following cohortative imperatives ποιήσωμεν ... καὶ μὴ φοβηθῶμεν so as to imply the same cohortative sense for the καταλείψαντες as well: thus Lake's translation 'let us forsake our sojourning' (Lake, *Fathers*, 135); similarly Lightfoot, *Apostolic Fathers*, 2.308: 'let us forsake our sojourn ...'. But this is not quite what the Greek text says! More accurately, Ehrman's translation is 'having abandoned our temporary residence in this world ...'. But an implied cohortative imperative still creates some difficulties with what follows since it seems to imply that 'doing the will of' Christ/God is then something that takes place *not* in this life (unless one reverses the implied temporal order of the verbs and interprets it as 'let us forsake our sojourning and, *before that*, do the will ...', but this seems even more forced!). The Syriac version seems to imply reading a present participle καταλιπόντες (see Bensly, *Epistles*, xvii), but this may be simply an attempt to resolve what was recognized as a problematic reading here.

[15] Almost the only commentator to have noticed the tension between this exhortation and the participle καταλείψαντες is Pratscher, *Zweite Clemensbrief*, 101, who notes that the text seems to imply that 'die christliche Existenz ... wird erst nach des παροικία-Status der Welt gegenüber verwirklicht, wie καταλείψαντες voraussetzt' ('Christian existence ... is only realized after the status of παροικία in the world, as the use of καταλείψαντες presupposes'), though he goes on immediately to say '2 Clem will vermutlich sagen: wer den Willen Christi erfüllt, ist nicht einmal mehr Gast in dieser Welt—eine durchaus radikale Ethik, die Vf. freilich weder als Realität der Gemeinde voraussetzt noch durchhält.' ('*2 Clement* perhaps wants to say that whoever fulfils the will of Christ is no longer even a guest in this world—a thoroughly radical ethic which the author indeed neither presupposes as reality for the community, nor maintains consistently.')

[16] *Contra* Lohmann, *Drohung*, 99, who claims that the 'doing' refers to the action of leaving the present situation in the world.

[17] For ἐξελθεῖν ἐκ τοῦ κόσμου τούτου as a euphemism for dying, see BAG, 447.

[18] However, as noted earlier, the introductory καταλείψαντες seems to imply that Christians have already left this place of sojourning, i.e. the present life. The writer's grammar and/or thought progression are perhaps somewhat confused!

What specifically the writer may have in mind is not certain. He seems to be talking about physical death; but it is not clear whether he means martyrdom, and is exhorting his readers not to fear the possibility of being killed for one's faith, or whether he is talking about the possibility of death in more general terms and the rewards that will follow after death (with certainty, but only after death). Some have argued that martyrdom is in view.[19] The metaphor which follows immediately (of the lambs among the wolves, with the threat of the wolves tearing apart the lambs) does conjure up a picture of violent death being suffered by the 'lambs', i.e. the Christians. On the other hand, the rest of the language is very general, and there is no hint elsewhere in *2 Clement* of violent persecution being a danger faced by Christians. In fact, the primary point which the author wishes to draw from the quotation which follows (with the verbal picture of the lambs among the wolves) is that there is really only one person to 'fear', and that is *not* (even) someone who might inflict physical death. Hence the language here more probably simply refers to physical death in general.[20]

2–4 The exhortation not to fear is now backed up with a quotation in vv. 2–4 from an unknown, or non-canonical, gospel source (see above). The citation represents a composite unit, made up of originally separate sayings (in vv. 2, 4).[21] However, the unit in its present form seems to have been taken over en bloc by the writer, and some of it may be somewhat irrelevant to his main purpose. Certainly the first saying (about lambs among wolves), which seems to stress the dangerous situation, seems beside the point here.[22] It is the second saying which introduces the motif of 'fear', and it is this which seems to be of primary concern for the writer. Thus the key point (effectively an elaboration of what was said in 4.4) is that one should 'fear' *only* the one (= God)[23] who has the power to cast body and soul into the fires of hell (v. 4), i.e. the power of final judgement. The imagery of violent death comes in only as a negative alternative: one should *not* fear anyone else, not even someone who may kill you. But the latter possibility need only be

---

[19] e.g. Knopf, *Zwei Clemensbriefe*, 159–60, who concedes that the language itself is not necessarily specific to martyrdom, but refers to other anti-Gnostic writers who attack Gnostics for being fearful of martyrdom (cf. Eusebius, *Hist. eccl.* 4.7.7; Irenaeus, *Haer.* 3.18.5; 4.33.9; Tertullian, *Scorp.*). See also Lohmann, *Drohung*, 99.

[20] So Donfried, *Setting*, 118–19; Lindemann, *Clemensbriefe*, 212–13; Pratscher, *Zweite Clemensbrief*, 100.

[21] cf. the parallels to v. 4, apparently derived from Matt. 10.28//Luke 12.4–5 and cited separately in various patristic writers: see above.

[22] So correctly Koester, *Ancient Christian Gospels*, 353; cf. too Pratscher, *Zweite Clemensbrief*, 104. It is this element which provides the strongest evidence that the writer is seeking to encourage martyrdom; but this may be simply a vestige of a tradition being cited primarily for another reason, namely to stress the importance of 'fearing' God/Christ.

[23] In the synoptic gospels, the saying clearly refers to God. In *2 Clement* here, the link with 4.4 (and the insistence that God is the only one to be feared) almost certainly implies the same.

theoretical and does not need to be a real threat for the readers for the writer's rhetoric to work.

'Fear' then should only relate to final, eschatological punishment or destruction and this takes place only after death: hence anything experienced this side of death, perhaps even death itself ('do not fear those who kill you'), should not be the cause for any 'real' fear.[24]

5 The theme of 'fear' gives way to the positive counterpart to any fear. The introduction to the verse exhorts the 'brothers'[25] to 'realize' (literally 'know' γινώσκετε) what this means. The use of γινώσκω may be a slightly underhand way of getting at possible Gnostic opponents: the 'real' 'knowing' which the writer is urging on his audience is that of his own message, and not (by implication) that of any rival Gnostic teachers.[26] On the other hand, if this is the case, one has to say that any 'polemic' is again very understated![27]

The writer refers to 'our stay' (ἐπιδημία), which relates closely in meaning with παροικία in v. 1.[28] Again the idea is evoked whereby Christians are thought of as 'not belonging' in their present existence, with a 'true home' elsewhere. Here the stress is on the shortness of time which Christians have in their present existence: our ἐπιδημία is said to be μικρὰ καὶ ὀλιγοχρόνιος. The latter clearly implies an idea of short duration; μικρά might imply the same (thus forming a hendiadys here); alternatively the word might mean 'small in importance' (rather than 'small in duration') and hence form a contrast with the 'greatness' of the promise of Christ that is said to be in store for the readers in v. 5b.[29] However, if the latter is chosen, the author would seem to be adopting a highly negative attitude to the world (present earthly life as unimportant and of little significance), and one that could be regarded as at odds with his insistence elsewhere on the value and importance of the

---

[24] Pratscher, *Zweite Clemensbrief*, 103, notes that the most natural way to interpret v. 4a (the lambs are not to fear the wolves after their death) in context is to take it as a reference to life after death for the Christian, but claims that the saying is then very 'banal'; and hence takes it as a reference to the state of (metaphorical) 'death' of the baptized Christian now, in the sense of Paul's argument in Rom. 6. This, however, seems to import somewhat alien (Pauline) ideas into the context here for which there is little or no support. It seems better to take the saying at face value (however theologically 'banal' it might then be!).

[25] The vocative ἀδελφοί here may be intended to lay particular stress on what is now said: cf. Lindemann, *Clemensbriefe*, 214; Pratscher, *Zweite Clemensbrief*, 104.

[26] cf. Lindemann, *Clemensbriefe*, 214: 'polemisch bzw. ironisch' ('polemical or ironic'), also with reference to Warns, 'Untersuchungen', 269–72.

[27] One may also note that the content of what the readers are exhorted to 'know' is very similar to what a possible Gnostic teacher might also claim!

[28] Ἐπιδημία is quite rare in early Christian literature (only here, but cf. Philo, *Flacc.* 33; Josephus, *Ant.* 8.102).

[29] Compare the translations of Lindemann, *Clemensbriefe*, 211 ('kurz' ('short')) and Ehrman, *Fathers*, 173 ('brief'), evidently opting for the former, with those of Lake, *Fathers*, 135 ('a little thing') and Pratscher, *Zweite Clemensbrief*, 99, discussion on p. 105 ('unbedeutend' ('unimportant')), opting for the latter.

'flesh' (cf. ch. 9).³⁰ Moreover, it is clear that the author does regard earthly existence as significant in that present behaviour determines one's fate at the final judgement. It is true that, as noted earlier, for all his possible opposition to a Gnostic viewpoint, the author comes quite close to sharing parts of such a viewpoint himself (see also on v. 6 below). But overall it may be simpler to take the alternative meaning for μικρά here as 'brief' (hence slightly repetitive with ὀλιγοχρόνιος).

That 'promise' that is in store for the reader is now spelt out ('namely')³¹ as '(the) rest of the coming kingdom'. ἀνάπαυσις is a word pregnant with huge meaning, especially in Gnosticism.³² On the other hand, the word is used in other texts as well, not necessarily Gnostic. In the Hebrew Bible, 'rest' tends to have a this-worldly connotation, referring for example to rest from one's enemies in war (cf. Josh. 21.43–4). But over the course of time and in differing contexts, the word comes to be used for the eschatological salvation that (hopefully) lies in store in the future, and is often used for the location itself of that salvation in some kind of 'heavenly' existence.³³ Thus in some texts in Hellenistic Judaism, the word is used to refer to the heavenly place where salvation will become a reality (cf. e.g. *Jos. Asen.* 8.9; 15.7). The word becomes especially significant in some Gnostic texts, as referring to the future (or perhaps present) salvation that is available.³⁴

How far the writer here is aware of the Gnostic use of the word is not certain. Texts such as *Joseph and Aseneth* show that the word was in current usage to refer to the eschatological salvation in store outside a Gnostic context; however, it may be that the writer here is deliberately taking up words from a Gnostic context and giving them a particular 'spin' or 'twist' to adapt them to his own message. In this case, it may be that he is taking up a Gnostic idea of 'rest' as a state to which the believer can aspire in the present life and insisting that it is something that will come (only) in a *future* existence: it is the rest of the *coming* kingdom. Equally though, as we have noted on a number of occasions already, any 'polemic' is fairly 'quiet' and understated.³⁵

---

³⁰ There is no absolute contradiction, in that on any showing, it is a comparative claim that is being made: present earthly life is of no value not necessarily in itself, but in comparison with the eternal life that is on offer for the future. Further, what is said in ch. 9 about the resurrection of the flesh need again not directly contradict what is said here: future life will still be 'fleshly' and so one must 'guard the flesh', i.e. behave responsibly, in the present.

³¹ Taking the καί in the phrase καὶ ἀνάπαυσις as epexegetic.

³² On the Gnostic use of the word, see Ph. Vielhauer, 'Anapausis. Zum gnostischen Hintergrund des Thomasevangeliums', *Apophoreta. Festschrift für Ernst Haenchen*, BZNW 30 (Berlin: Töpelmann, 1964), 281–99.

³³ See Donfried, *Setting*, 121, with reference to Von Rad, Käsemann, and others.

³⁴ See e.g. *Gos. Truth* (NHC I.3) 24.20; 40.3; 41.13, etc.; *Ap. John* (NHC II.1) 26.31; *Gos. Thom.* (NHC II.2) 2, 50, 60 (though it is of course debatable whether *Gos. Thom.* should be included among 'Gnostic' texts!); *Odes Sol.* 22.12; 26.12; 28.3; 37.4, and many other references.

³⁵ In any case, several Gnostic texts refer to 'rest' as a future goal, rather than to a present reality: hence an insistence on the futurity of any such 'rest' is not necessarily anti-Gnostic.

6 The writer reverts to his general theme by asking how one is to attain these promises, and the answer is his (by now) standard one: by right ethical behaviour (here put in terms of living in a 'holy and righteous' way).[36] This is then further elaborated in terms of regarding the 'things of this world' as 'foreign to us' (ἀλλότρια).[37] The precise identity of the 'things of this world' is, however, not clear. The writer says that we should not 'desire' them; but whether he means particular attractions and/or activities (cf. e.g. the references earlier in 4.3 to adultery, jealousy, and love of money; cf. too 6.4 shortly below) or physical life itself (cf. the immediately preceding discussion on the need not to fear physical death) is not clear. The immediate context suggests the latter, and there is no restrictive clause suggesting otherwise. What is then striking is that once again the writer's whole attitude to the world and (apparently) all things associated with the world sounds almost Gnostic in its tone![38] But perhaps one should not take the statement out of its context in the text as a whole, where, as with v. 5, the wider context suggests a more positive attitude to the world and its affairs.

7 This completes the exhortation: desiring to obtain 'these things' will result in 'falling'[39] from the right path. As with v. 6, the ταῦτα is very general, but certainly when the author spells out a little more what this might mean (shortly in 6.4), it is not in terms of a negative attitude to the world in toto, but only to particular aspects and/or human attitudes.

---

[36] For these two adjectives, or their related nouns, as linked, cf. Luke 1.75; Eph. 4.24; 1 Thess. 2.10; *1 Clem.* 14.1; 48.4. Cf. too 6.9 below.

[37] There is a striking parallel to this language in Herm. *Sim.* 1.3, 11. There, however, it is rather clearer that the reference is to worldly possessions.

[38] This is the context of the comment of Lindemann, cited in n. 11 above.

[39] The use of the verb ἀποπίπτειν in this metaphorical sense (one does not 'fall' from a road or a path!) is not found elsewhere in early Christian literature (Pratscher, *Zweite Clemensbrief*, 107).

Chapter 6

PARALLELS

2 Clem. 6.1	Matt. 6.24	Luke 16.13
λέγει δὲ ὁ κύριος·		
οὐδεὶς οἰκέτης δύναται	οὐδεὶς δύναται	οὐδεὶς οἰκέτης δύναται
δυσὶ κυρίοις δουλεύειν.	δυσὶ κυρίοις δουλεύειν·	δυσὶ κυρίοις δουλεύειν·
	ἢ γὰρ τὸν ἕνα μισήσει καὶ	ἢ γὰρ τὸν ἕνα μισήσει καὶ
	τὸν ἕτερον ἀγαπήσει, ἢ	τὸν ἕτερον ἀγαπήσει, ἢ
	ἑνὸς ἀνθέξεται καὶ τοῦ	ἑνὸς ἀνθέξεται καὶ τοῦ
ἐὰν ἡμεῖς θέλωμεν	ἑτέρου καταφρονήσει.	ἑτέρου καταφρονήσει.
καὶ θεῷ δουλεύειν	οὐ δύνασθε θεῷ δουλεύειν	οὐ δύνασθε θεῷ δουλεύειν
καὶ μαμωνᾷ,	καὶ μαμωνᾷ.	καὶ μαμωνᾷ.
ἀσύμφορον ἡμῖν ἐστίν.		

Gos. Thom. 47 (NHC II.2, 41.14–17): ⲁⲩⲱ ⲙⲛ̅ ϭⲟⲙ ⲛ̅ⲧⲉ ⲟⲩϩⲙ̅ϩⲁⲗ ϣⲙ̅ϣⲉ ϫⲟⲉⲓⲥ ⲥⲛⲁⲩ ⲏ ϥⲛⲁⲣ̅ⲧⲓⲙⲁ ⲙ̅ⲡⲟⲩⲁ ⲁⲩⲱ ⲡⲕⲉⲟⲩⲁ ϥⲛⲁⲣ̅ϩⲩⲃⲣⲓⲍⲉ ⲙ̅ⲙⲟϥ

And it is impossible to serve two masters; otherwise he will honour the one and treat the other contemptuously.[1]

2 Clem. 6.1a is an explicit quotation (cf. the introductory λέγει δὲ ὁ κύριος) of the saying found also in Matt. 6.24//Luke 16.13 with almost verbatim agreement between the versions. *2 Clement* is slightly nearer the Lukan version in having οἰκέτης, which Matthew omits, and it is possible (though not certain) that this is due to LkR.[2] Hence *2 Clement* appears to presuppose Luke's finished gospel (and either quotes it here directly or cites it via an intermediary source). The second part here (v. 1b) is not so close verbally to the synoptic versions. There is the contrast between 'serving God' and '(serving) mammon', and the explicit reference to 'mammon' suggests that

---

[1] Text and English translations of *Gos. Thom.* from B. Layton (ed.), *Nag Hammadi Codex II, 2–7 together with XIII,2, Brit. Lib. Or. 4926(1) and P. Oxy. 1, 654, 655*, vol. I, NHS 20 (Leiden: Brill, 1989).

[2] cf. Robinson, Hoffmann, and Kloppenborg, *Critical Edition*, 462.

the synoptic saying is still in mind. But the use of the first-person plural (ἐὰν ἡμεῖς θέλωμεν) suggests that this is the author's own paraphrase of the saying, rather than an explicit citation.³

The presence of a possibly independent saying circulating in the tradition might be suggested by the presence of a similar saying in *Gos. Thom.* 47 (also apparently without the equivalent of an οἰκέτης).⁴ However, the whole issue of the relationship between *Gos. Thom.* and the synoptics is still very much an open one, and one cannot build too much on the parallel in *Gos. Thom.* here. More likely, it would seem, the author of *2 Clement* is citing the Gospel of Luke.⁵

2 Clem. 6. 2	Matt. 16.26	Mark 8.36	Luke 9.25
τί γὰρ τὸ ὄφελος,	τί γὰρ ὠφεληθήσεται ἄνθρωπος	τί γὰρ ὠφελεῖ ἄνθρωπον	τί γὰρ ὠφελεῖται ἄνθρωπος
ἐάν τις τὸν κόσμον ὅλον κερδήσῃ, τὴν δὲ ψυχὴν ζημιωθῇ;	ἐὰν τὸν κόσμον ὅλον κερδήσῃ τὴν δὲ ψυχὴν αὐτοῦ ζημιωθῇ;	κερδῆσαι τὸν κόσμον ὅλον καὶ ζημιωθῆναι τὴν ψυχὴν αὐτοῦ;	κερδήσας τὸν κόσμον ὅλον ἑαυτὸν δὲ ἀπολέσας ἢ ζημιωθείς;

Clement *Strom.* 6.112.3: τί γὰρ ὄφελος, ἐὰν τὸν κόσμον κερδήσῃς, φησί, τὴν δὲ ψυχὴν ἀπολέσῃς;

What advantage is it if you gain the world, he says, but lose your soul?

Justin *1 Apol.* 15.12: τί γὰρ ὠφελεῖται ἄνθρωπος, ἂν τὸν κόσμον ὅλον κερδήσῃ, τὴν δὲ ψυχὴν αὐτοῦ ἀπολέσῃ;

For what does it profit a man if he gains the whole world but loses his soul?

Int. Know. (NHC XI.2) 9.33–5:⁶ ⲉⲩ ⲛ̄ⲅⲁⲣ ⲡⲉ ⲫⲏⲩ ⲉⲕϣⲁⲛ †ⲍⲏⲩ ⲙ̄ⲡⲕⲟⲥⲙⲟⲥ ⲛ̄ⲕ†ⲁⲥⲓ ⲛ̄ⲧⲉⲕⲯⲩⲭⲏ

For what use is it if you gain the world and forfeit your soul?

---

³ Köhler, *Rezeption*, 142. In most modern translations, the inverted commas are closed at the end of the first half of the saying (e.g. Lake, Ehrman, Lindemann, Pratscher, etc.).

⁴ But whether one can rely on a version in (Coptic) translation for such a relatively small point of detail is very uncertain.

⁵ For the theory that this saying, together with the saying in 8.5 (which is parallel to Luke 16.10–12), comes from an apocryphal gospel, see Warns, 'Untersuchungen', 358. It is, however, difficult to use (implicitly) the evidence of Luke's gospel to make the case that the two sayings were connected in the source of *2 Clement*, and then to claim that the source in question was not Luke itself but an apocryphal gospel. (The conjunction of the sayings in Luke may well be due to LkR, and hence the alleged apocryphal gospel would presuppose Luke's work.) Dependence on Luke seems a more economical solution.

⁶ Coptic text from the edition of Funk, Painchaud, and Thomassen, *L'Interprétation de la Gnose*.

It is not certain whether this is intended to be a continuation of a 'quotation' of what 'the Lord said' (cf. 6.1),[7] and, if so, whether the saying in v. 2 is regarded as a continuation of the same original saying. Clearly, though, what is said here is close to the saying in the synoptics in Mark 8.36 and pars. It seems likely that the author here is citing a tradition.[8] The version in *2 Clement* is closer to the version in Matthew in having the ἐάν + subjunctive construction, rather than the infinitive as in Mark and Luke, though precise comparisons between the wordings here are made more difficult by some textual variants.[9] Thus *2 Clement* agrees with Matthew precisely where Matthew has redacted Mark. *2 Clement* thus shows agreement with Matthew's redactional activity and hence appears to be based (directly or indirectly) on Matthew's finished gospel.[10]

There are parallels to the saying also in Clement of Alexandria and Justin Martyr (see above), and the two versions in which the saying is quoted there are close to each other (cf. especially the common use of ἀπολέσῃ[ς] at the end of the saying, which *might* also be reflected in the original text of *2 Clement*: see n. 9 above). Further, the opening of the saying in Clement of Alexandria is similar to the opening in *2 Clement* (in the use of τί γὰρ ὄφελος).[11] It is then possible that Clement of Alexandria and *2 Clement* attest a common version of the saying. But the comparison with the synoptic evidence suggests that any such version represents a development of the tradition which post-dates and presupposes Matthew's gospel; and its

---

[7] e.g. Lake, *Fathers*, 137, and Ehrman, *Fathers*, 173, in their translations, use inverted commas; Lindemann, *Clemensbriefe*, 211, and Pratscher, *Zweite Clemensbrief*, 107, do not.

[8] Not all quotations of scripture and/or Jesus traditions in *2 Clement* are marked as such by an explicit introductory formula: cf. the quotation of Isa. 54.1 in *2 Clem.* 2.1.

[9] The ὅλον in the text of *2 Clement* is missing in C; and S implies a reading of ἀπολέσῃ instead of ζημιωθῇ (Bensly, *Epistles*, xvii). Both readings are accepted by Warns, 'Untersuchungen', 398–9, and Petersen, 'Patristic Biblical Quotations', 407–11, partly on the grounds that the alternative readings are secondary assimilations to the canonical versions of the saying. For Petersen, these readings both serve to align the form of the saying here more closely with the version in Clement of Alexandria, with both then reflecting a saying independent of the synoptics. However, Pratscher, *Zweite Clemensbrief*, 110, argues that ζημιοῦσθαι fits the context here (with the talk of reward and punishment) better than ἀπολλύναι (though in any case it is difficult to argue for a precise Greek word here on the basis of a text in translation); also the omission of ὅλον in C cannot be relied on too much as C is prone to making omissions in the text (see Tuckett, 'Response', 510–11).

[10] cf. too Köster, *Synoptische Überlieferung*, 73 f.; Massaux, *Influence*, 145; Köhler, *Rezeption*, 135, observes (against Massaux) that dependence on Matthew is not certain, but is still the most probable solution. Even Donfried, *Setting*, 83, concedes that dependence on Matthew is 'possible' (though he also claims that 'one cannot with certainty assert [such] dependence'). Warns, 'Untersuchungen', 394–400, takes it as part of his proposed apocryphal gospel.

[11] Possibly related too may be the version in *Int. Know.* 9.33–5 (see above); if anything the version here is closer to that in Clement of Alexandria in having the saying in the second person (rather than third person). See Funk, Painchaud, and Thomassen, *L'Interprétation de la Gnose*, 129. The suggestion of Warns, 'Untersuchungen', 396–7, that *2 Clement* also knew the saying in this second-person form and changed it to a third person seems fanciful.

similarity with Matthew suggests that it is a version of the same saying, not an independent different one.[12]

2 Clem. 6.8
λέγει δὲ καὶ ἡ γραφὴ ἐν τῷ Ἰεζεκιήλ ὅτι ἐὰν ἀναστῇ Νῶε καὶ Ἰὼβ καὶ Δανιήλ, οὐ ῥύσονται τὰ τέκνα αὐτῶν ἐν τῇ αἰχμαλωσίᾳ.

The saying is clearly introduced as a citation with reference to scripture (γραφή) and the location within scripture specified (ἐν τῷ Ἰεζεκιήλ). The 'quotation' is, however, more of a summarizing précis of the extended passage in Ezek. 14.13–20. Most of the words used here occur in the Ezekiel passage and appear to be drawn from there, though e.g. the general τέκνα replaces the 'sons and daughters' of Ezek. 14.16, 18, 20. The one word unexplained is the final αἰχμαλωσίᾳ.[13] Precise comparisons about the text form presupposed are almost impossible given the very inexact form of the 'quotation'.

The three people named appear in Ezekiel in the order Noah–Daniel–Job. The order here (with Job moved forward) may reflect an assimilation to the canonical order as they appear in the OT. The Ezekiel passage is also cited by Justin, *Dial.* 44.2; 45.3; 140.3, though with the names Noah, Jacob (not Job), and Daniel, but agreeing with the relative order of Noah and Daniel as here. Some later church fathers also have the order Noah–Job–Daniel (cf. e.g. *Apos. Con.* 2.14.4). It is possible that the author here is dependent on another source, e.g. a testimony book; but it may be simply that the passage is cited from memory.[14]

COMMENTARY

1 The verse provides another explicit citation, this time of a tradition of the saying of Jesus, perhaps from Luke 16.13a; the second half of the verse here provides a paraphrase of the second half of the saying in Luke 16.13b (see above). In the present context, the saying is used to drive a firm wedge between the things of this world (= 'mammon') and the things of the world to come (= 'God'). This is now developed in relation to the theme of the 'two ages/aeons' (v. 3). Much of the language used here is intensely dualistic with

---

[12] The similarities between *2 Clement* and Clement of Alexandria do not necessarily mean that the author of *2 Clement* is citing a saying that is totally independent of the synoptics (as Petersen seems to imply): the version in Clement of Alexandria is probably still a variant of the synoptic saying. For fuller discussion, see Tuckett, 'Response', 508–11.

[13] Warns, 'Untersuchungen', 520–1, sees an allusion here to *Pss. Sol.* 2.6, but this seems unnecessary: the context in Ezekiel is one of the prophet addressing those who are 'in captivity' in exile in Babylon. Cf. Knopf, *Zwei Clemensbriefe*, 162: 'ein in LXX oft vorkommendes Wort' ('a word occurring often in the LXX').

[14] cf. Wengst, *Zweite Clemensbrief*, 218.

much said that could be taken as a denigration and rejection of the present world and all that is in it.[15] As such, the writer once again shows close affinities at one level with quasi-Gnostic ideas. Whether this is intentional is not clear!

2 The author continues with what appears to be a further citation (though it is not signalled explicitly as such) of the Jesus tradition (see above). Once again, the main point of the citation appears to be to drive a wedge between this world and the world to come: gaining 'the whole world' (evidently, in context, this is the present world order) is worthless if one loses one's 'soul' (where ψυχή, in context, seems to be the life of the world to come:[16] there is no suggestion here of a body–soul anthropological dualism and indeed such would be alien to what the author says elsewhere).

3 The dualism is now spelt out in uncompromising terms: there are two 'ages', this age and the age to come, and the two are 'enemies' of each other. The author takes up language and ideas from apocalyptic in talking about this age and the age to come (cf. *4 Ezra* 7.50; 8.1; *2 Bar.* 44.9–12; Eph. 1.21; Mark 10.30 pars; cf. also many examples in the NT of negative reference to 'this world/age' in texts such as Gal. 1.4; 2 Cor. 4.4). The radical dualistic outlook expressed in the language of the two ages being 'enemies' of each other is distinctive here. This is the only time when the author of *2 Clement* uses this language (of this age and the age to come) quite so explicitly; and the idea of the two ages being 'enemies' is not developed here significantly: certainly, whilst such language is potentially open to dualistic ideas, with cosmic powers engaged in supra-mundane battles in which human beings are mere pawns in the struggle,[17] the author makes it clear that human responsibility is paramount: human beings must choose which side they are on (and put here in terms of ethical behaviour). Nevertheless, it is still not entirely clear from what the writer says whether he regards 'this age' as irredeemably lost (i.e. a fairly radical cosmological dualism) or whether he is being negative about only some aspects of the present world order. The next verse suggests the latter, but a great deal of the rest of this section (e.g. vv. 3, 5, 6) is couched in more general terms. Thus Donfried's comment, that the ideas in the context here are 'clearly "gnosticizing"',[18] is in one way justified. The next verse seems to reflect a limitation on the cosmological dualism but the language elsewhere in the context is much more open-ended: either the author is being somewhat 'loose' in his use of language, or his ideas are somewhat confused!

---

[15] Donfried, *Setting*, 124, refers to 'the . . . radical cosmological and ethical dualism' here.
[16] See Lindemann, *Clemensbriefe*, 215.
[17] Such ideas may lie behind some of Paul's language at times.
[18] Donfried, *Setting*, 71.

4 This responsibility in terms of human ethical behaviour is now spelt out more explicitly in terms of what 'this age' is taken to mean in practice. 'This age' is associated with the list of vices given here. Thus many argue that any potentially cosmological dualism here is clearly seen to be (only) an 'ethical' dualism, and the similarity with a text such as Jas. 4.4 ('friendship with the world is enmity with God') is regularly noted.[19] Such a limitation would mesh well with the broader context in the rest of the text where the emphasis is on human responsibility and the importance of ethical behaviour.

The list of vices here is very similar to those mentioned earlier in 4.3, especially the references to adultery and love of money. It is also, like 4.3, very short (certainly compared with other vice lists). Whether the activities (or attitudes) mentioned are of particular concern to the author, or whether the list is simply traditional, is not clear (see on 4.3 above).[20] However, the relative brevity here may indicate that at least some of these particular issues were of concern to the author, as in 4.3: sexual behaviour and attitudes to, and use of, money may be issues of particular concern. It is, however, not clear if the vices mentioned are related to each other: e.g. $\phi\theta o\rho\acute{a}$ may be a very general reference to 'corruption', or may be related to the preceding $\mu o\iota\chi\epsilon\acute{\iota}a$ and have a specific reference to sexual violence, i.e. rape.[21] But whether 'deceit' ($\dot{a}\pi\acute{a}\tau\eta$) is related to love of money is not at all clear. Unlike 4.3, there is no list of virtues corresponding with the vices mentioned here.

5 The language reverts to the potentially radically dualistic tone of v. 3: belonging to 'this world' is incompatible with belonging to 'that' one, and we must 'renounce' this world to obtain the other. The language of temporal succession is dropped: it is just 'this' world and 'that' (one), and the two seem to be totally incompatible with each other. The dualism may be primarily an ethical dualism, but the language is perilously close to a position where there seems to be radical denial and rejection of everything to do with the present world order.

6 The introductory $o\iota\acute{o}\mu\epsilon\theta a$ is unexpected, though not impossible, given the author's tendency elsewhere to seek to be not too confrontational in his language.[22] The sentence develops the message from the previous verse: the radical disjunction between the two ages determines what our attitude should be. It is 'better'[23] to 'hate' the things that are present, on the basis that they are

---

[19] cf. Wengst, *Zweite Clemensbrief*, 271 n. 47; Lohmann, *Drohung*, 101; Lindemann, *Clemensbriefe*, 215; Pratscher, *Zweite Clemensbrief*, 111.

[20] e.g. Lohmann, *Drohung*, 101, says that the list is simply a traditional one.

[21] See BAG, 865, and Lindemann, *Clemensbriefe*, 215; Pratscher, *Zweite Clemensbrief*, 111.

[22] In 14.2; 15.1, the author uses the first-person singular $o\ddot{\iota}o\mu a\iota$. Lightfoot, *Apostolic Fathers*, 2.221, emends the text to $o\iota\acute{\omega}\mu\epsilon\theta a$, but there is no MS support for this. The author's general tendency to seek to find as much common ground as possible with his audience would fit the unanimous reading of the MSS here.

[23] The comparative $\beta\acute{\epsilon}\lambda\tau\iota o\nu$ is probably meant as a superlative: see BDF §244,3.

brief,[24] short-lived, and perishable, by contrast with the things that are 'there', which are 'good' and 'imperishable'. The language of 'hating' and 'loving' may well come from the saying about two masters cited in v. 1 above. It may be that the author's primary concern is that the audience should reject specific vices in their ethical behaviour; but he has almost got carried away with his own rhetoric so that the language now is such that it seems to refer to a more radical rejection of everything to do with the present world order.

7 The author now reverts to his more usual theme of exhorting his addressees to be ethically upright and to obey the ethical commands they have received, here expressed as doing 'the will of Christ' (cf. 5.1). As before, the prime motivation is in terms of reward or punishment at the final judgement which is to come. The reward side here is put in terms of 'finding rest'. The language of 'rest' as the eschatological reward has occurred already in 5.5 (see above), *possibly* (though not certainly) echoing Gnostic language about the nature of the desired final state of human beings. Talk of 'finding' rest also echoes the language of Matt. 11.29 (which seems to be a semi-citation of Jer. 6.16 LXX, though replacing ἁγνισμόν with ἀνάπαυσιν). It is possible that *2 Clement* here is dependent on Matthew: certainly there is evidence elsewhere that the author presupposes Matthew's gospel (see above e.g. on 3.2).[25] However, the possible echo is at best very allusive. The alternative to finding rest is to be recipient of 'eternal punishment' (κόλασις αἰώνιος: again a reminiscence of language from Matthew is possible, cf. Matt. 25.46, but it is not certain that the language is distinctive enough to make such a theory fully convincing).[26]

8 The argument takes a slightly different turn with the assertion that no third party can act to benefit individuals other than themselves. To make the point, the author gives what he appears to regard as an exact citation: he prefaces it with an explicit introductory formula referring to scripture as ἡ γραφή (cf. 2.4; 14.1, 2), and explicitly giving the source of the 'citation' as 'in Ezekiel' (cf. 3.5 for a similar reference to Isaiah). The 'citation' is, however, a fairly free, and short, précis of the material found in Ezek. 14.13–20, perhaps from memory, without being an exact quotation of any section as such (see above). The main point being made is that not even the supremely righteous figures of Noah, Job, and Daniel could rescue their children.

---

[24] The language is almost identical with that in 5.5. In both places there is ambiguity as to whether μικρά means 'brief' or 'unimportant'. It was argued above that it may mean 'brief' in 5.5; hence it is taken here in the same sense. However, the addition of φθαρτά to the list of attributes characterizing the present age does introduce a more negative picture than in the earlier context.

[25] Köhler, *Rezeption*, 137 ('möglich' ('possible')); but regarded as not certain by e.g. Lindemann, *Clemensbriefe*, 216; Pratscher, *Zweite Clemensbrief*, 113.

[26] Gregory and Tuckett, '*2 Clement*', 276.

The reference to 'captivity' here is slightly unusual. The word does not derive from the Ezekiel passage (see above). It is just possible that there is a quiet allusion here to Gnostic claims about human beings being held in a form of 'captivity' in the present world: the author would then be taking up the language of the people he may be addressing in the text as a whole; but this is not certain.

9 The application is now made clear: scripture itself says that such righteous people cannot save their own children; so much more then is it the case that only we ourselves can do what is required for salvation. Some of the language used here is slightly unusual. Δικαιοσύναι (plur.) is here used for 'righteous acts': such a usage is not attested in the NT, though it is common in the LXX (Deut. 9.20; Ezek. 3.20; 33.13; etc.). It is also perhaps striking that there is no reference to any saving work of Christ at this point![27] Reference is then made to the difficulty of entering into the βασίλειον of God. Strictly this might mean 'palace', though perhaps it may be synonymous with kingdom/βασιλείαν.[28]

The failure to have confidence about entering the kingdom arises if 'we do not keep our baptism pure and undefiled'. This is the first explicit mention of baptism in the text. The general point is clear: one cannot rely on any 'automatic' salvation, but must maintain one's position by good works. The reference to baptism here may suggest that what the author is addressing is a way of thinking that presumed that, with baptism, one had already achieved such an assured state of (or hope of) salvation that ethical behaviour was no longer important.[29] The stress on the provisional nature of future salvation, and the implicit denial of any reliance on baptism, may reflect the claim evidently made by at least some Gnostics that linked belief in resurrection in the present with baptism.[30] 'Keeping our baptism pure and undefiled' evidently means keeping the ethical obligations undertaken when making the baptismal vows.[31]

The alternative is that we shall have no 'advocate' (παράκλητος) if we do not display 'pious and righteous works'. What is said is in striking contrast

---

[27] As indeed is the case throughout almost the whole of *2 Clement*. Apart from a brief, general reference in 1.2 to Christ suffering a great deal 'for us', *2 Clement* does not explicitly say that Christ's saving work has dealt with the problems created by human sinfulness, or ethical failings (unless it is implicit in the references to 'repentance': cf. p. 78 above.)

[28] Pratscher, *Zweite Clemensbrief*, 116, who compares also 17.5 where 'kingdom' or 'kingly rule' is demanded as the meaning of βασίλειον. Cf. too Eusebius, *Hist. eccl.* 3.28.2; 7.17.2.

[29] See Donfried, *Setting*, 126–8.

[30] e.g. Menander as in Irenaeus, *Haer.* 1.23.5. However, an over-reliance on baptism may also be reflected in e.g. 1 Cor. 1.14–17; 10.1–13 without necessarily implying a Gnostic background.

[31] For 'keeping the baptism', cf. too *Acts of Paul and Thecla* 6 μακάριοι οἱ τὸ βάπτισμα τηρήσαντες. Language of 'pure' and 'undefiled' takes over cultic language and, as so often in early Christianity, applies it to the ethical sphere. Cf. too *1 Clem.* 29.1 for similar use of such terminology.

formally with what is said in 1 John 2.1, where the promise is made that whenever a Christian sins s/he will have a παράκλητος who is Jesus himself. Whether the author of *2 Clement* is deliberately echoing (and 'correcting') the language of 1 John is not certain: on the one hand, the language of a 'paraclete' (whether Jesus or the Spirit) is not that common in early Christianity; on the other hand, there is little other evidence of knowledge and use of Johannine texts in *2 Clement*. But in any case the message is clear: there seems to be a clear statement advocating 'judgement by works' (to put it in what is probably an anachronistic way). Whether there is direct or indirect reference to Paul here must remain uncertain.[32]

---

[32] Warns, 'Untersuchungen', 523–9, argues that the author has in view Valentinians who based themselves on Paul, and Rom. 3.24–31 in particular, denying the value of works on the basis of belief in justification already achieved. But any specifically Pauline language of justification is not visible here: see Lindemann, *Clemensbriefe*, 217; also his *Paulus*, 270–1.

Chapter 7

PARALLELS

The language here is in one way very similar to that of Paul in 1 Cor. 9.24–7 in the use of the athletic contest as a metaphor for the Christian life. Whether the author here is dependent on Paul is uncertain: the athletic metaphor was used very widely in the Graeco-Roman world (see below) so that dependence on Paul is not necessary to explain the language and imagery here.[1] It is though striking that both the author of *2 Clement* and Paul use the contrast φθαρτός ... ἄφθαρτος, though the contrast is applied by Paul to the different 'crowns' which are won, and by the author here to the different contests.

In 7.6 there is a citation of Isa. 66.24 with a very general introductory φησίν (and where the subject is not clear). The verse is also cited in the NT gospel tradition in the Gospel of Mark alone.

2 *Clem.* 7.6	Isa. 66.24	Mark 9.48
ὁ σκώληξ αὐτῶν οὐ τελευτήσει καὶ τὸ πῦρ αὐτῶν οὐ σβεσθήσεται καὶ ἔσονται εἰς ὅρασιν πάσῃ σαρκί	ὁ γὰρ σκώληξ αὐτῶν οὐ τελευτήσει καὶ τὸ πῦρ αὐτῶν οὐ σβεσθήσεται καὶ ἔσονται εἰς ὅρασιν πάσῃ σαρκί	ὅπου ὁ σκώληξ αὐτῶν οὐ τελευτᾷ καὶ τὸ πῦρ οὐ σβέννυται.

The text form in *2 Clement* provides no evidence of influence from the NT gospel text: the version here agrees almost verbatim with that of Isa. 66.24 LXX and shows no agreement at all with any of the (small) differences in the

---

[1] Knopf, *Zwei Clemensbriefe*, 163, speaks of the Pauline passage as one 'die II Clem. vorzuschweben scheint' ('which *2 Clement* seems to have in mind'); cf. too Grant and Graham, *Apostolic Fathers*, 118. Others are less inclined to see any knowledge of the Pauline passage presupposed here: cf. Wengst, *Zweite Clemensbrief*, 271 n. 50; Lindemann, *Paulus*, 265, though slightly more open in Lindemann, *Clemensbriefe*, 218; Gregory and Tuckett, '*2 Clement*', 283; Pratscher, *Zweite Clemensbrief*, 119.

shorter Markan version. There is thus no warrant for concluding that the author is doing anything other than citing Isa. 66 LXX alone.

COMMENTARY

1 The introductory Ὥστε οὖν, ἀδελφοί μου is textually slightly uncertain: the longer text (as here) is read by A, but C (with some support from S) omits both the οὖν and the μου. Such an introduction is at one level stereotypical for the author (cf. 4.3; 10.1; 11.5), though the precise wording varies with sometimes the οὖν omitted (10.1; 11.5), sometimes the μου (4.3).[2] Whether this introduction implies that the author is wanting to lay particular stress on the following exhortation[3] is not certain.

The use of the metaphor of an athletic contest to describe some of the struggles in life was widespread in the ancient world, especially among Stoic and Cynic philosophers.[4] Latching on in part to the widespread disillusionment with the games, many philosophers and other teachers used the imagery of the athletic contest to talk about the struggle in the moral life which was demanded of the true sage.[5] So too the language and imagery was taken up in Hellenistic Judaism, especially in the writings of Philo (cf. *Spec.* 2.91; *Leg.* 3.72; *Agr.* 119–21).[6] The imagery was also exploited by early Christian writers (e.g. 1 Cor. 9.24–7; Phil. 3.13–14; 2 Tim. 2.5; 4.7–8; Heb. 12.1; *1 Clem.* 2.4; 5.5; 35.4).[7]

As with Paul in 1 Cor. 9, the metaphor here is somewhat strained, especially in relation to how many receive prizes for their endeavours, though the author of *2 Clement* and Paul try to evade the force of the metaphor at this point in slightly different ways. The general thrust of the section though is clear: the Christian life is like an athletic contest with rewards at the end: but rewards will only be given to those who strive and 'compete', which in the

---

[2] The longer text is read by e.g. Lightfoot, *Apostolic Fathers*, 2.223; Knopf, *Zwei Clemensbriefe*, 163; the shorter text is read by Wengst, *Zweite Clemensbrief*, 246; Lindemann, *Clemensbriefe*, 218; Pratscher, *Zweite Clemensbrief*, 118. Other variants in 7.1 include αἰών in A for ἀγών, which is probably a clear mistake, as is ἁγνισώμεθα in C for ἀγωνισώμεθα (the reading is not noted in any other editions or apparatus of the text of *2 Clement*, but is clear from the facsimile in Lightfoot); both readings take up the vocabulary of the previous chapter.

[3] So Pratscher, *Zweite Clemensbrief*, 118.

[4] The most detailed study is V. C. Pfitzner, *Paul and the Agon Motif: Traditional Athletic Imagery in the Pauline Literature*, NovTSup 16 (Leiden: Brill, 1967).

[5] cf. e.g. Dio Chrysostom 8.11–12; 9.11–12; Epictetus 3.22.57; Diogenes Laertius 6.70; Seneca, *Ep.* 78.16; see Pfitzner, *Paul and the Agon Motif*, 28, and Donfried, *Setting*, 128–9, with further evidence.

[6] See Pfitzner, *Paul and the Agon Motif*, 38–48.

[7] Given then the widespread use of this language both inside and outside Christian circles, it would probably be precarious to claim any direct link between *2 Clement* and one particular user of the same imagery, such as 1 Cor. 9, too quickly: see p. 44 above.

author's eyes is interpreted as performing good works and succeeding in the struggle to behave ethically.

The exhortation is made to engage in the contest, knowing that the contest is 'to hand' (ἐν χερσίν). The thought is probably not that the contest is imminent but still future, but rather that it is 'to hand' in the sense of being already under way in the present:[8] the 'struggle', or 'contest', in which the Christian is engaged is the present life, not a time to come in the future.

In setting up the parallel between athletic contests and the struggles of the ethical life, the author speaks of many taking part in the contests, and doing so by sailing (καταπλέουσιν, presumably to the relevant places). A number of scholars in the past have seen in this language a possible indication of the geographical location of the author of 2 Clement. If the verb means 'to land', i.e. at a port, but with the port unspecified, this may be because the specific port was felt to be superfluous to mention; further, given the context here of taking part in games, the implied reference may be to the famous Isthmian games held in Corinth, so that the language may indicate that 2 Clement originates in Corinth.[9] It is, however, doubtful if the verb καταπλέω can bear the weight of such an argument. Several have pointed out that the verb is very general, and need only mean to 'land' (i.e. to come from the sea to land) in general terms: it does not necessarily mean to 'travel *to us* by sea'.[10] In any case, others have argued from the same evidence that the reference here is to travel on the Nile and arrival at Alexandria for the games there.[11] One should perhaps also note the first-person plural cohortative καταπλεύσωμεν in v. 3, apparently implying (in a rather strained use of the metaphor) that 'we' should also undertake the same sea travel: but this would be rather odd if the author or the audience were already in Corinth and the verb really implied landing in the port of Corinth! The evidence seems inconclusive to enable us to determine anything about the geographical location of the author, though the evidence of v. 3 might suggest that Corinth is *not* where the author or audience are situated.

The analogy with real athletic contests is acknowledged as only an analogy with the difference that real contests are 'perishable' (φθαρτούς),[12] so that by implication the contest in which the Christian is engaged is qualitatively different (cf. v. 3: ἀγῶνα τὸν ἄφθαρτον).

---

[8] See BAG, 888; Lindemann, *Clemensbriefe*, 218.

[9] See e.g. Lightfoot, *Apostolic Fathers*, 2.197; Donfried, *Setting*, 2–7, with references to other literature. See Introduction §8.1 Place of writing.

[10] See Knopf, *Zwei Clemensbriefe*, 163; Wengst, *Zweite Clemensbrief*, 225, 271–2; Lindemann, *Clemensbriefe*, 219; Pratscher, *Zweite Clemensbrief*, 119–20. In more detail, G. R. Stanton, '2 Clement VII and the Origin of the Document', *Classica et Mediaevalia* 28 (1967), 314–20.

[11] Warns, 'Untersuchungen', 103–5. See also Stegemann, 'Herkunft', 129–31: the language need only imply going to some games, not necessarily the Isthmian games.

[12] Ehrman's translation 'earthly' (Ehrman, *Fathers*, 175) no doubt captures an important part of the sense, but may be a little too paraphrastic.

The author then goes on to what is clearly for him the real issue: the reward or prize available for those who take part in this 'contest'. As with Paul in 1 Cor. 9, the author of *2 Clement* struggles with the analogy of the contest in relation to who will be rewarded. The author does not get quite as far as Paul in conceding that the prize only goes to one competitor, the winner (cf. 1 Cor. 9.24). Here he simply says that 'not all are crowned', but only those who have laboured much and competed well. In general terms, the thrust of the exhortation is clear: Christians should strive (by implication in their moral life and their ethical behaviour) to take part 'well' in the 'contest' in which they are engaged in this life and, as such, they will be 'crowned' and rewarded.

2 This last idea is then explicitly stated. All should strive and work, so that they may be rewarded. The analogy is clearly strained, given that not all competitors in a competition are rewarded: usually it is only the winner (though there is a little evidence of prizes being available for others apart from the outright winner in some games in the ancient world).[13] However, the author's exhortation is clearly logically prior, and the analogy of the competition is evidently accepted as not a precise description of the reality he is seeking to illuminate.

3 The exhortation continues now with reference to the 'real' struggle with which the Christian is engaged. The first exhortation, to 'run'[14] the straight course', takes up language used elsewhere (and slightly mixes metaphors in doing so). The language of the 'straight' way is used quite often in paraenetic tradition to refer to morally upright behaviour as approved by God.[15] The straightness of the course is here clearly an indication of the moral behaviour that is required of the Christian participant in this particular 'race'. The exhortation which follows, to 'set sail for it' (ϵἰς αὐτὸν καταπλεύσωμεν), produces a slightly strange order in the sentence (strictly speaking one presumably sails to get to the start of the race and only then does one run); so too the implied quasi-metaphorical sense of the verb καταπλέω is not evidenced elsewhere and the author's language seems to be driven by the analogy he has developed.

The aim is then made explicit: 'that we may be crowned' (ἵνα καὶ στεφανωθῶμεν). The author seems to realize at this point that the metaphor has become almost too strained since in real life, at most only a few competitors,

---

[13] cf. Josephus, *B.J.* 1.415; Philo, *Agr.* 120–1.

[14] A C read θῶμεν which is extremely difficult, if not impossible; S implies a reading θέομεν (from θεῖν 'to run') which fits much better and hence is universally adopted by editors and commentators.

[15] cf. Wengst, *Zweite Clemensbrief*, 247; Pratscher, *Zweite Clemensbrief*, 121. See e.g. Prov. 2.13; 20.11 LXX; Ps. 106.7 LXX; Acts 13.10; 2 Pet. 2.15.

Commentary: Chapter 7 191

and perhaps only a single winner, will receive a prize or 'crown'. Quite what the author means by the last clause, apparently acknowledging that 'we cannot all be crowned' but still exhorting his readers to 'come near' it, is not clear. Perhaps it is simply a recognition that the parallel with athletic games is not an exact parallel. Clearly though the author wants to emphasize that any 'prize' or reward is not given to all as a matter of right: those who receive a reward in a 'contest' must earn the right to do so. In more prosaic terms (of the author's 'theology'), Christians cannot necessarily rely on their final salvation, but must strive to work for that reward in their efforts now.

4 This thought is developed negatively in what follows, still sticking with the chosen metaphor of the games for a moment longer. The analogy is now drawn with the competitor who cheats, breaks the rules, or who acts unfairly. The appeal is then to the everyday experience of what happens in such a case: the competitor is thrown out of the competition and punished.

5 The author then moves from the situation of the analogy to that of the real 'contest' in which the Christian is engaged in the present life, claiming that comparable punishment awaits those who 'cheat' at this level too (presumably what is in mind is a failure to live an ethical life).

6 The identity and the punishment of those who fail in this way is now spelt out in more detail. Those in mind are said to be those who 'have not kept the seal'. The precise reference in the 'seal' is disputed. The background of the term is probably to be found in Greek and Roman piety where a 'seal' is a gift from a deity guaranteeing protection as well as ownership and a guarantee of belonging.[16] In some contexts, a 'seal' would be a concrete object, something visible and/or tangible. At times, circumcision can be called a 'seal' for Jews (cf. Rom. 4.11; *Barn.* 9.6). Early Christians clearly exploited the language, though applying it to things that were in some ways less tangible entities. Paul in 1 Cor. 9.2 calls the community itself the 'seal' of his apostleship. Other references in the NT clearly link the gift of the Spirit with Christians being 'sealed' (2 Cor. 1.22; Eph. 1.13; 4.30). For some it is very natural, given the evidently close connection between Spirit reception and baptism (cf. Acts 2.38, etc.), to see a reference to baptism in these texts. The language was then exploited in later, second-century texts, e.g. in Hermas where at times the baptismal reference is clear (cf. *Sim.* 8.2.2–4; 9.16.3–7 (4: ἡ σφγραγὶς οὖν τὸ ὕδωρ ἐστίν); 9.17.4, and also in some Gnostic texts (cf. *Ap. John* (NHC II.1) 31.23–5).

Precisely how *2 Clement*'s use of 'seal' here should be interpreted is not absolutely clear. Many see a reference to baptism, though others have disputed

---

[16] See Knopf, *Zwei Clemensbriefe*, 162.

this.[17] The parallel between 6.9 (keeping 'our baptism pure and undefiled') and the present verse (keeping 'the seal', cf. too 8.6 keeping 'the seal undefiled') suggests that the 'seal' and baptism should be identified. On the other hand, the author does also speak later of 'keeping the flesh' (8.4, 6; cf. 9.3 'guard the flesh'), and some have suggested on the basis of 8.6 where the author speaks of keeping the flesh pure and the seal undefiled, that, as the natural 'companion' to flesh is πνεῦμα, the 'seal' is understood in 2 Clement as the Spirit.[18] However, the language of 'keeping' the Spirit (and in 8.6 keeping it 'undefiled') seems rather unusual (if πνεῦμα means God's Holy Spirit rather than a/the human spirit). Others have noted that the close connection in Christian thought between baptism and Spirit may mean that there might not be a great difference in the end between these differing suggestions.[19] However, 2 Clement does not share the view of many other early Christians that the Spirit is a possession of Christians in the present (and hence necessarily received at baptism).[20]

Perhaps the close parallelism between what is said here and in 6.9 is decisive: the author thinks of the 'seal' as baptism.[21] However, the 'seal' is clearly not some kind of magical power which guarantees safety or salvation: as in 6.9, the whole point of the claim here is to tell the hearers, via the negative statement about what is in store for those who do not 'keep the seal', that they must 'keep' it, clearly in a context referring to appropriate ethical behaviour.

The threat of what awaits those who do not do so is spelt out via a quotation of scripture. The introductory formula is a very vague 'he/it says': it is not clear if the subject is God, Jesus, or 'the scripture'. The text is from Isa. 66.24, a verse which is cited also in the NT in Mark 9.48. However, as noted above, the text here agrees almost verbatim with Isa. 66 LXX and shows no evidence of having been influenced by Mark's form of the citation. Its function here is to paint in lurid terms the fate (of eternal punishment) awaiting those who do not 'keep the seal', i.e. 'keep their baptism pure and undefiled' by behaving in an ethically upright way.

---

[17] In favour, see e.g. Lightfoot, *Apostolic Fathers*, 2.226; Knopf, *Zwei Clemensbriefe*, 162, 164; G. W. H. Lampe, *The Seal of the Spirit* (London: SPCK, 1967), 103–4; Donfried, *Setting*, 125; Jefford, *Reading*, 125; Pratscher, *Zweite Clemensbrief*, 123. For more doubt, see G. Fitzer, σφραγίς κτλ., *TWNT* 7 (1964), 952; Lindemann, *Clemensbriefe*, 220–1.

[18] cf. Fitzer, σφραγίς, 952; Wengst, *Zweite Clemensbrief*, 272; also Lindemann, *Clemensbriefe*, 221 (though acknowledging that baptism and Spirit are closely connected: cf. too Pratscher, *Zweite Clemensbrief*, 123).

[19] e.g. Donfried, Lindemann, and Pratscher as in n.17.

[20] See Introduction §9.3 The Spirit above, and below on 14.3.

[21] Both Lake and Ehrman in their translations go as far as to 'translate' σφραγῖδα here as 'seal of [their] baptism': how far interpretative glosses rightfully belong within a 'translation' is clearly debatable!

Chapter 8

PARALLELS

2 Clem. 8.5	Luke 16.12, 10
λέγει γὰρ ὁ κύριος ἐν τῷ εὐαγγελίῳ· εἰ τὸ μικρὸν οὐκ ἐτηρήσατε, τὸ μέγα τίς ὑμῖν δώσει; λέγω γὰρ ὑμῖν, ὅτι ὁ πιστὸς ἐν ἐλαχίστῳ καὶ ἐν πολλῷ πιστός ἐστιν.	¹²καὶ εἰ ἐν τῷ ἀλλοτρίῳ πιστοὶ οὐκ ἐγένεσθε, τὸ ὑμέτερον τίς ὑμῖν δώσει; ¹⁰ὁ πιστὸς ἐν ἐλαχίστῳ καὶ ἐν πολλῷ πιστός ἐστιν, καὶ ὁ ἐν ἐλαχίστῳ ἄδικος καὶ ἐν πολλῷ ἄδικός ἐστιν.

Irenaeus, *Haer.* 2.34.2: et ideo dominus dicebat ingratis existentibus in eum: si in modico fideles non fuistis, quod magnum est, quis dabit vobis?

And therefore the Lord said to those who showed themselves to be ungrateful to him, 'If you have not been faithful in a small thing, who will give you what is great?'

Hilary, *Epistula seu libellus* 1: si in modico fideles non fuistis, quod maius est, quis dabit vobis?

If you have not been faithful in a small thing, who will give you what is greater?

This saying in *2 Clement* is of interest as it is the only one which is said to be 'in the gospel' (ἐν τῷ εὐαγγελίῳ). The word 'gospel' is notoriously ambiguous in Christian usage in the first two centuries CE. However, the most obvious intepretation of the word here is that it refers to a written text containing words attributed to Jesus.[1] The identification of that text is, however, not

---

[1] Köster, *Synoptische Überlieferung*, 11, referring also to the present tense λέγει, as well as the absence of an αὐτοῦ with εὐαγγέλιον: he claims that the present tense is more readily interpreted as referring to words of Jesus (now) recorded in a written text and reproduced, rather than to words of Jesus spoken in the past. Cf. too Lindemann, *Clemensbriefe*, 224; Pratscher, *Zweite Clemensbrief*, 132 (though Donfried, *Setting*, 81, argues that the author of *2 Clement* varies between aorist and present in his introductory verbs of saying to citations).

explicitly specified. What is said here is presented as a single saying (rather than two sayings joined together), with just one introductory formula.[2]

The second half of the saying here is very close in wording to Luke 16.10a. The verse has no parallel in the other synoptic gospels and hence cannot easily be identified as a Lukan redactional creation. In terms of content, it constitutes a kind of proverbial saying.

The first part of the saying here has no clear parallel in the synoptic tradition (its sentiments are not far removed from Luke 16.12, but there is no clear verbal agreement). The presence of a very similar saying in Irenaeus and Hilary may suggest that a saying in this form circulated independently in Christian circles.[3] The differences from Luke in the first part, together with the parallels elsewhere, suggest that the author here has not derived the saying directly from Luke's gospel. It must then come from another, unknown, gospel text.[4] The absence of any clear LkR elements means that one cannot say with any certainty whether the form of the saying here represents a post-Lukan development of the tradition, or a point on a trajectory which bypasses Luke's gospel and reaches back to the pre-Lukan tradition.

COMMENTARY

1 Without any apparent break, the author continues his exhortation, though now with what some have seen as a significant change in terminology: for the first time in the text there is a plea to 'repent' ($\mu\epsilon\tau\alpha\nu o\eta\sigma\omega\mu\epsilon\nu$), a theme which comes frequently from now on in the text (cf. 8.2–3; 9.8; 13.1; 16.1; 17.1; 19.1). Some have seen this as so abrupt, and perhaps as directly contradicting the earlier emphasis on the necessity of practical ethical behaviour (cf. the summary statements about keeping 'our baptism pure and undefiled' in 6.9, or 'keeping the seal' in 7.6, with apparently no allowance being made for those who fail in their attempt to behave ethically), that they have

---

[2] Though there may be other instances in *2 Clement* where separate sayings have been joined and introduced by a single introductory formula: cf. on 6.1 and 6.2 above.

[3] The difference between their *fideles non fuistis* and *2 Clement*'s οὐκ ἐτηρήσατε could be explained by the latter author's preference for the verb τηρεῖν, especially in the immediate context: cf. 6.9; 7.6; 8.4, 6. Hence the wording in *2 Clement* may well be due to the author's assimilation to the wording of his context: see Köster, *Synoptische Überlieferung*, 100; Donfried, *Setting*, 73, and n. 30 below.

[4] Bartlet, in 'II Clement', *New Testament in the Apostolic Fathers*, 133; Schubert, '2. Clemensbrief', 252, again takes it as coming from *Gos. Eg.*; Donfried, *Setting*, 73; Koester, *Ancient Christian Gospels*, 355; Lindemann, *Clemensbriefe*, 224; Gregory, *Reception*, 137; Pratscher, *Zweite Clemensbrief*, 132. Warns, 'Untersuchungen', 354–64, argues that the saying here was linked in the source with the citation in 6.1. Even Massaux, *Influence*, 153, takes it as 'vraisemblable' ('probable') that *2 Clement* is here dependent on 'une source apocryphe' ('an apocryphal source') rather than Luke's gospel.

postulated a change of audience at this point: the author may have switched from addressing baptized Christians to addressing those who have not yet become Christians (and been baptized) as part of missionary preaching.[5] However, there is no clear evidence for such a change: the text continues seamlessly from the previous chapter; also the first-person plural form of the verb here, as well as the reference to the audience as ἀδελφοί in v. 4, suggests that the implied audience has remained unchanged and the author is continuing to address those who are already within the community as baptized Christians.[6] Hence whatever modern commentators may claim about the apparent lack of logic and/or theological consistency in the text, the author evidently felt no problem in insisting on the necessity of 'good works' as the prerequisite for salvation and also on the possibility of—and need for—'repentance' for those who fail to 'do' everything that is required.

Implicit in the author's approach seems to be a distinction between an attitude which might say that ethical demands are irrelevant and/or inappropriate for Christian existence (an attitude which the author vehemently rejects, leading to the firm insistence on the importance of ethical behaviour as a criterion for final salvation), and one which might acknowledge ethical lapses albeit within a broad context of affirming the importance of ethical behaviour (an attitude which the author accepts—hence his insistence on the importance of ethical demands, but coupled with an equally firm insistence on the need for repentance). Despite some of the language used at times, the author of *2 Clement* is not an ethical perfectionist, but a realist!

Yet what precisely is the μετάνοια, or the action of μετανοεῖν, referred to here? Clearly, if addressed to Christians, it is not the 'conversion' which is required as the response to an initial reception of (Christian) kerygmatic preaching (cf. Mark 1.15; Acts 2.38; etc.). When addressed to Christians post-baptism (as here), it has clearly been ethicized and related to the failure of Christians to behave in a morally upright way: rather than referring to any kind of religious 'conversion', it is now related to ethical behaviour (and/or failure to achieve the ethical standards expected).[7] Yet there are different nuances to the word-group. For some, it implies primarily a backward-looking act of remorse, acknowledging as wrong, and being sorry for, actions in the past; as such, this act of 'repentance' is then logically followed (hopefully!) by forgiveness, with a resolve to do better in the future. However, the Greek μετανοι- word-group can also be rather more forward-looking and refer to the change being undertaken to put into practice the new behaviour

---

[5] See e.g. Knopf, *Zwei Clemensbriefe*, 164–5.

[6] See Donfried, *Setting*, 130–1; Wengst, *Zweite Clemensbrief*, 272 n. 58; Lindemann, *Clemensbriefe*, 221; Pratscher, *Zweite Clemensbrief*, 126.

[7] The use of μετάνοια language in this context is prevalent in later strands of early Christian writings: cf. e.g. 2 Tim. 2.25; Rev. 2.5, 16, 21; *1 Clem.* 57.1; 62.2; *Did.* 15.3. See Pratscher, *Zweite Clemensbrief*, 127.

itself (or in the case of 'religious conversion', the new commitment undertaken). Rather than referring to an act of remorse about the past, μετάνοια can mean the act of turning away from the past.[8] It is perhaps this meaning that dominates in *2 Clement*. There is rarely any reference to 'forgiveness' following the act of 'repentance'. Maybe it is implied, and perhaps an expression of genuine remorse for things done wrong in the past is presupposed; but the primary reference in the exhortation to 'repent' is to the actual change required in one's (ethical) way of life and starting to behave differently. μετανοεῖν might then be just as well translated here 'turn, change one's ways', as 'repent'.[9]

Moreover, it is presumably assumed that, once this 'turning' has happened, almost by definition the ethical standards required will be met. (Otherwise, the μετάνοια would not be genuine.) Hence the issue of further 'repentance' required, or whether the Christian life is one of continuous 'repentance and forgiveness', does not arise. Such issues are probably foreign to the author.

The one qualification on the demand for repentance is that such repentance must take place before it is too late, which in the author's perspective seems to mean while Christians are still alive on this earth. Hence the first phrase here 'while[10] we are on the earth', and also (negatively) in v. 3 below. With this proviso, the exhortation to repent now becomes all the more urgent.

2 The author seeks to illustrate the exhortation with the analogy of a pot and potter. The closest parallel here seems to be the language of Jer. 18.4–6 which also talks about a pot being spoiled in the potter's hand. A similar image is used by Paul in Rom. 9.21, but with such a different application that it is not possible to deduce any relationship between *2 Clement* and Paul.[11] In any case, the image was widely used by a range of writers in the ancient world,[12] so one should not deduce anything too quickly about possible dependence between any two such writers.

---

[8] See e.g. BAG, 513–14: as well as meaning a 'change of mind' or 'remorse', μετάνοια is used 'mostly of the positive side of repentance, as the beginning of a new relig. and moral life'. Cf. e.g. Heb. 6.1 μετάνοια ἀπὸ νεκρῶν ἔργων: the μετάνοια is change to the new behaviour itself, not the remorse which precedes it. Cf. too Acts 26.20 ἄξια τῆς μετανοίας ἔργα: BAG 'deeds that are consistent with repentance' (rather than deeds which are worthy of a prior act of remorse).

[9] I have kept 'repent' in the English translation as the traditional translation equivalent, though I am aware that this might be slightly misleading if one does not take account of the different possible nuances of 'repentance'.

[10] For the use of ὡς in this sense, cf. Gal. 6.10; BDF §455.

[11] In Paul, the language is used to illustrate the idea of the sovereign freedom of God as the potter; in *2 Clement*, it is used to develop the idea of human repentance. See Lindemann, *Paulus*, 208.

[12] cf. *T. Naph.* 2.2–5; Epictetus 4.11.27; for Jewish texts, cf. Str–B 3.211; for other Christian texts, cf. Athenagoras, *Leg.* 15.2–3; Theophilus, *Autol.* 2.26; for Gnostic texts, cf. *Orig. World* (NHC II.5) 103.22. See further Pratscher, *Zweite Clemensbrief*, 127–8.

In general terms, the use of the imagery by the author of *2 Clement* here is clear: just as a potter cannot change a piece of pottery once it has been fired in an oven, so it will not be possible to try to change the situation if one leaves any repentance, or change in ethical behaviour, too late. It is the implied temporal deadline for repentance that is the prime point of comparison here.

Whether one should try to allegorize the picture further is not clear: and if one does, one would probably run into difficulties.[13] In one way, the language of the potter 'putting it into the fiery kiln' recalls the language of 7.6 and the image of the 'unquenchable fire' of final judgement, so that the potter is perhaps God. On the other hand, the action required in the application of the image is not that of God but of human beings who are bidden to 'repent': it is up to human beings to 'mend' the 'bent or broken' 'pot' by their 'repenting', i.e. by changing their ethical ways.[14] But this is not easy to reconcile with the clear statement at the start that 'we' are the 'clay in the hand of the craftsman' (who is presumably the 'potter' and/or God). Perhaps it is inappropriate to try to press the details of the verbal picture to be too precise.[15]

The reference to the 'breaking' of the vessel is slightly unclear due to a textual variant: it is not certain whether the vessel is 'made' in the hand of the craftsman (so C) or 'bent or broken' there (so A).[16] In one way, the latter fits the image better, though it might fit the possible application less well if the craftsman is thought of as God. Given the rather loose application of the imagery to the general point being made, it is probably best to take the reading that fits the imagery better, i.e. the A reading here.

The application comes clearly in the second half of this verse with the exhortation to repent, with the proviso 'while we are still in this world', and 'while we have time for repentance'.[17] The addressees are bidden to repent 'with [their] whole heart'[18] of all the wicked deeds they have done 'in

---

[13] Knopf, *Zwei Clemensbriefe*, 165, talks about a 'leise Allegorisierung' ('slight allegorization') here.

[14] See e.g. Donfried, *Setting*, 85; Wengst, *Zweite Clemensbrief*, 272; Lindemann, *Clemensbriefe*, 222.

[15] Lohmann, *Drohung*, 107, even goes so far as to suggest the existence of a later gloss in the text here on the basis of the ill-fitting nature of the image with the application, though he concedes that there is no manuscript evidence to support this.

[16] The word order differs in the two Greek MSS: A has καὶ ἐν ταῖς χερσὶν αὐτοῦ, taking 'in his hands' with the verbs that follow; C has ταῖς χερσὶν αὐτοῦ καί, taking the phrase with the ποιῇ of the preceding phrase. The former is followed by e.g. Lightfoot, *Apostolic Fathers*, 2.226; Lindemann, *Clemensbriefe*, 222; Pratscher, *Zweite Clemensbrief*, 128; the latter by Wengst, *Zweite Clemensbrief*, 249.

[17] There is again slight textual uncertainty: the explicit reference to repentance in the final phrase is read by A but omitted by C (which has an extra ἔτι earlier in the phrase). The difference in meaning is not great; in favour of the A reading might be the author's tendency to repeat key words in any section quite frequently, so that the (slightly redundant) reference to repentance here would fit the author's general style.

[18] This is possibly another (cf. 3.4) echo of the words of the *Shema*, though it is at most a somewhat distant echo.

the flesh'. The issue of the status of the 'flesh' will be of direct concern in the chapter that follows; here, however, 'flesh' seems to be used in a theologically and ethically neutral way simply to refer to existence in this life prior to physical death.[19]

The aim is then ultimately to secure salvation 'by the Lord'. Thus despite the possible implications of some of the author's language whereby salvation seems almost to be something that one 'earns' by one's own efforts, salvation is here ultimately something that comes from God/Christ, not oneself.[20]

3 The thought is then clarified negatively: after death[21] there will be no more opportunity for repentance, no chance to change one's ethical lifestyle. The author has the extra verb ἐξομολογήσασθαι with μετανοεῖν here. Its precise nuance is not certain, but probably has the meaning of confessing sins.[22] The two here may thus be complementary (rather than forming a hendiadys): the 'confessing' may be the retrospective remorse for sins in the past, the 'repenting' being then prospective, referring to the change in lifestyle which is now being undertaken.

The problem posed by post-baptismal sin, and the issue of whether such sin was forgivable, was one that concerned a number of early Christians, especially Hermas. The writer here seems in one way to be relatively 'lax' in that he appears to assume without question that 'repentance', at least in this life, is possible (and if appropriate mandatory) for Christians. And the very existence of his appeal here, as throughout the text, is that such a change is possible at almost any time in the life of the Christian prior to physical death. His line is thus unlike the highly rigorous line apparently adopted in Heb. 6.6. In relation to Christians, he is also perhaps less rigorous than the line adopted in Hermas, which seems to allow one act of 'repentance' up to the moment of the revelation received by Hermas, but not thereafter (cf. Herm. *Vis.* 2.2.4–5; *Mand.* 4.1.8; 4.3.5); however, he does not seem to envisage a chance for repentance after death.[23]

4 The author reverts to his earlier language exhorting the audience to act ethically and correctly. The explicit language of 'repentance' disappears. One is back with the language of the earlier sections of the text but the substance

---

[19] The phrase 'in the flesh' may be used simply to avoid repetition of 'in this world', just used.

[20] See Pratscher, *Zweite Clemensbrief*, 128.

[21] The same language of 'leaving this world' as a euphemism for physical death occurs in 5.1.

[22] cf. Mark 1.5; *Did.* 4.14; *1 Clem.* 51.3; *Barn.* 19.12 (though mostly such a meaning is clear from an explicit object of 'sins', or similar, for the verb).

[23] Unlike Herm. *Vis.* 3.7.5–6, though, this may be for unbaptized people. For the complex issue of the theme in Hermas, see N. Brox, *Der Hirt des Hermas*, KAV 9 (Göttingen: Vandenhoeck & Ruprecht, 1991), 476–85; also C. Osiek, *The Shepherd of Hermas*, Hermeneia (Minneapolis: Fortress, 1999), 28–30.

Commentary: Chapter 8

of what is said remains constant.[24] The correct behaviour required is spelt out in three, apparently synonymous (but somewhat vague) phrases: doing the will of the Father, keeping the flesh pure, and keeping the commandments of the Lord. For doing the will of the Father, cf. 9.11; 10.1; 14.1; earlier the author has spoken of 'the will of the one who called you' (5.1) and of 'the will of Christ' (6.7), probably with no great difference in meaning (certainly at the level of the content of the 'will' concerned).[25] Earlier references to 'commandments' in *2 Clement* (3.4; 4.5; 6.7) refer to these as Jesus': hence here the 'Lord' is probably Jesus rather than God (insofar as the author distinguishes the two).

The reference to 'keeping the flesh pure' probably means the same as the similar language used in 6.9 ('keeping our baptism pure and undefiled') and 7.6 ('keeping the seal'). All three references probably refer to the same demand to keep the ethical requirements arising from one's baptismal vows. Whether there is any more precise reference intended here (beyond the general exhortation to behave in a morally upright way) is not certain. Knopf argues that the language of 'keeping the flesh pure' is to be interpreted in a radically ascetic way which would exclude any sexual activity at all, even within marriage.[26] However, this seems unpersuasive. The language in *2 Clement* is very general,[27] and, for example, the explicit reference to μοιχεία in 4.3 would suggest that normal (full) sexual activity within marriage was not regarded as problematic. (See on 4.3 above.) Rather, what is in mind here is probably a much more general reference to obeying the ethical requirements included in the 'will of the Father' and the 'commandments of the Lord', but without being any more specific.[28]

The promise for the future that is held out here is that 'we will receive eternal life'. The precise language used for the promised future rewards in store for the Christian varies, though in 5.5 the author has already used the phrase 'eternal life'. The verb ληψόμεθα used here can be seen in one way as expressing again the gift character of the future reward (cf. also v. 3 above): 'eternal life' is something that is 'received', not necessarily earned as of

---

[24] *Contra* Lohmann, *Drohung*, 107, who says that the way in which the author here draws the conclusion he does is 'etwas gewaltsam' ('somewhat forced'). However, if the interpretation of the μετανοι- word-group given here is correct, then the exhortation to behave 'correctly' is simply another way of expressing the exhortation to 'repent', i.e. change one's ethical ways.

[25] cf. what has been said earlier about the writer's relatively naive 'functional identity' between God and the person of Jesus (see on 1.1 above).

[26] Knopf, *Zwei Clemensbriefe*, 165, appealing in part to the language of *Acts of Paul and Thecla* 5: μακάριοι οἱ ἁγνὴν τὴν σάρκα τηρήσαντες ... μακάριοι οἱ ἐγκρατεῖς ... μακάριοι οἱ ἔχοντες γυναῖκας ὡς μὴ ἔχοντες ('blessed are those who keep the flesh pure ... blessed are those who are self-controlled ... blessed are those who have wives as not having them').

[27] Unlike *Acts of Paul and Thecla* where the encratite thrust of the text as a whole is clear.

[28] cf. Lindemann, *Clemensbriefe*, 223; Pratscher, *Zweite Clemensbrief*, 130. See also Introduction §9.7 Ethics.

right.[29] On the other hand, one should not necessarily read back later issues anachronistically into the text. The author seems to be working with a model which is (in one way) fairly 'automatic': good behaviour will be rewarded, almost as of right; bad behaviour will lead to punishment. Hence in one way, it may be appropriate to talk of 'earning' one's salvation: certainly human commitment and endeavour are integral to the process!

5 The author then seeks to back up his claims with a quotation of 'the Lord' from 'the gospel'. This is the only citation in *2 Clement* that is said to be 'in the gospel', probably indicating that it is taken from a written text, though with no clear indication as to the identity of that text (see above). The application of the saying seems clear: the 'great' which the hearers may be 'given' is the gift of eternal life; the 'small' which they are to 'keep' or 'guard' is the doing of the will of the Father, keeping the flesh pure,[30] and keeping the commandments of the Lord.

6 The citation is now given an explicit interpretation, which partly repeats what has been said in v. 4 about keeping the flesh pure. This is now glossed here with the command to keep the seal undefiled; also the overall hope of receiving eternal life is repeated here. The reference to the 'seal' adds another instance to the small complex of closely related sayings in 6.9; 7.6; 8.4 about keeping the seal/baptism/flesh pure and undefiled. Probably, as in 7.6, the 'seal' refers to baptism.[31] More generally, all refer to the same demand, implicit in one's baptismal vows, to behave in this life in an ethically upright way.

---

[29] cf. Lindemann, *Clemensbriefe*, 223.

[30] Perhaps the language of 'keeping' the flesh pure in vv. 4, 6 has influenced the wording of the citation here with the reference to 'keeping' what is small: cf. the difference in wording at this point from the versions of the saying in Irenaeus and Hilary and see the discussion above.

[31] As in 7.6, both Lake and Ehrman again 'translate' σφραγῖδα here as 'seal *of baptism*'.

Chapter 9

PARALLELS

2 Clem. 9.11	Matt. 12.50	Mark 3.35	Luke 8.21
καὶ γὰρ εἶπεν ὁ κύριος·			ὁ δὲ ἀποκριθεὶς εἶπεν πρὸς αὐτούς,
ἀδελφοί μου οὗτοί εἰσιν οἱ ποιοῦντες τὸ θέλημα τοῦ πατρός μου	ὅστις γὰρ ἂν ποιήσῃ τὸ θέλημα τοῦ πατρός μου τοῦ ἐν οὐρανοῖς αὐτός μου ἀδελφὸς καὶ ἀδελφὴ καὶ μήτηρ ἐστίν.	ὃς [γὰρ] ἂν ποιήσῃ τὸ θέλημα τοῦ θεοῦ, οὗτος ἀδελφός μου καὶ ἀδελφὴ καὶ μήτηρ ἐστίν.	μήτηρ μου καὶ ἀδελφοί μου οὗτοί εἰσιν οἱ τὸν λόγον τοῦ θεοῦ ἀκούοντες καὶ ποιοῦντες.

Gos. Eb. (as in Epiphanius, *Pan.* 30.14.5): οὗτοι εἰσιν οἱ ἀδελφοί μου καὶ ἡ μήτηρ καὶ ἀδελφαί, οἱ ποιοῦντες τὰ θελήματα τοῦ πατρός μου

For these are my brothers, my mother and my sisters: those who do the will of my Father.

Clement of Alexandria, *Ecl.* 20.3: ἀδελφοί μου γάρ, φησὶν ὁ κύριος, καὶ συγκληρονόμοι οἱ ποιοῦντες τὸ θέλημα τοῦ πατρός μου

For my brothers, says the Lord, and my fellow companions are those who do the will of my Father.

Gos. Thom. 99 (NHC II.2, 49.23–5): ⲛⲉⲧⲛ̄ⲛⲉⲉⲓⲙⲁ ⲉⲧϯⲣⲉ ⲙ̄ⲡⲟⲩⲱϣ ⲙ̄ⲡⲁⲉⲓⲱⲧ ⲛⲁⲉⲓⲛⲉ ⲛⲁⲥⲛⲏⲩ ⲙⲛ̄ ⲧⲁⲙⲁⲁⲩ

Those here who do the will of my Father are my brothers and my mother.

Int. Know. (NHC XI.1, 9.31–3): ⲛⲁⲥⲛⲁⲩ ⲁⲩⲱ ⲛⲁϣⲃⲣ̄ ⲕⲟⲓⲛⲱⲛⲟⲥ ⲛⲉⲧϯⲣⲉ ⲙ̄ⲡⲟⲩⲱϣⲉ ⲙ̄[ⲡ]ⲉⲓⲱⲧ

They are my brothers and my fellow companions who do the will of the Father.

2 Clement here probably reflects a harmonized version of the saying that appears in the (now) canonical gospels, agreeing in part with both Matthew's and Luke's adaptation of the saying in Mark 3.35. Thus *2 Clement* agrees with Luke in the ἀδελφοί μου οὗτοί εἰσιν οἱ (...) ποιοῦντες construction (against Mark's/Matthew's ὅστις ἂν ποιήσῃ); and it agrees with Matthew's reference (in typical Matthean vocabulary) to the will 'of my Father' (Matthew also has 'in heaven'). Matthew and Luke are both redacting Mark's version. Thus the version in *2 Clement* presupposes the redactional activity of both Matthew and Luke and hence presupposes their finished gospels.

On the other hand, we may also note the presence of a similar harmonized version of the saying in *Gos. Eb.* and in Clement of Alexandria (see above).[1] Hence it may well be that *2 Clement* here is dependent on a separate source that had already harmonized the different versions of the saying in the synoptics into its present form here.[2] But this source seems to be part of a post-synoptic development which presupposes the finished gospels of Matthew and Luke.

COMMENTARY

The references to keeping the flesh pure in the previous chapter lead to a small excursus in 9.1–5 (or 9.1–6) on the importance of the flesh, especially in relation to the resurrection.

The opening introduction, 'let none of you say', reminiscent in some ways of the diatribe in Greek rhetoric, may suggest that the author is directing his attention to a specific group and/or problem in his community. Clearly the issue of the resurrection, and specifically the resurrection of the flesh, was a recurring one in early Christianity and a range of authors clearly felt obliged to assert as strongly as they could their beliefs about the resurrection.[3] Early Christians faced a range of objections to their claims, from those who believed in some kind of immortality of a soul (and hence denied the need for any kind of 'resurrection' at all) to those who may have claimed that the resurrection had in some sense already happened (cf. 2 Tim. 2.18). The

---

[1] The version in *Gos. Thom.* 99 is only extant in Coptic and it is thus difficult to compare finer points of detail concerning the construction in Greek in this context. Similarly the version in *Int. Know.* is also only available in Coptic, though the use of the Greek loan word ⲕⲟⲓⲛⲱⲛⲟⲥ there suggests close similarity (not quite agreement) with συγκληρονόμοι in the version in Clement of Alexandria. Thus the version in *Int. Know.* is closer to that of Clement than to *2 Clement*. See Funk, Painchaud, and Thomassen, *L'Interprétation de la* Gnose, 127–8. The text thus provides little evidence for any knowledge of *2 Clement* by the author of *Int. Know.* (*pace* Plisch: cf. p. 12 above).

[2] Köster, *Synoptische Überlieferung*, 79; Donfried, *Setting*, 73; Warns, 'Untersuchungen', 367–9; also Bartlet, in 'II Clement', *New Testament in the Apostolic Fathers*, 134; Gregory, *Reception*, 148.

[3] See variously 1 Cor. 15; 2 Tim. 2.18; *1 Clem.* 23–7; Pol. *Phil.* 7.1; Herm. *Sim.* 5.7.2; Justin, *Dial.* 80.4; Ireneus, *Haer.* 1.23.5; 2.31.2, etc. See the valuable survey in Donfried, *Setting*, 133–46.

precise nature of the problem addressed here is not clear. The dangers of 'mirror-reading' any (mildly) polemical text are well known. However, it would appear that, *if* the response given by the author to the (perceived) problem is apposite, the issue is not so much that some are denying the very idea of resurrection, nor necessarily claiming that resurrection is already present. Rather, the issue seems to be more specific: how far the 'flesh' participates in the (presumed future) resurrection.[4] What seems to be regarded as dangerous here is any denial that the present physical body ('flesh') has any place in the future resurrection life. The author here insists passionately on the full participation of the 'flesh' in the future resurrection life.

'Flesh' for the author of *2 Clement* seems to be simply the physical 'body' of human beings. There are no overtones of any negative associations with the human $\sigma\acute{\alpha}\rho\xi$.[5] If there is any part of the human make-up that is the source of evil, it would seem that for this writer it is the $\psi\upsilon\chi\acute{\eta}$ rather than $\sigma\acute{\alpha}\rho\xi$ (cf. 16.2).

The argument here runs parallel to that of Paul of 1 Cor. 15. There is, however, no clear evidence that the author knew Paul's argument or is referring to it in any way.[6] At one level, the author goes directly against what Paul says: Paul asserts that 'flesh and blood can*not* inherit the kingdom of God' (1 Cor. 15.50). For Paul, resurrection will involve a 'body' ($\sigma\hat{\omega}\mu\alpha$), and Paul insists that resurrection existence without a body is impossible. Nevertheless, the resurrection body will be different from the present body (see 1 Cor. 15.35 ff.) and resurrection existence will involve a radical change from the present order (v. 51 'we shall all be changed', even if 'we shall not all die'). For Paul therefore, resurrection life necessarily involves having a 'body' and as such there is continuity with the present order; but equally too there is discontinuity in that the resurrection body is not the same as the present body. For the author of *2 Clement*, there are no such fine distinctions. The present physical form of existence (summed up in the word 'flesh') will continue into the new order.[7] Further, such continuity is essential as the foundation of his demand for ethical seriousness in the present world of 'flesh'.

---

[4] Against Donfried, *Setting*, 145. See Lindemann, *Clemensbriefe*, 225; Lohmann, *Drohung*, 109; Pratscher, *Zweite Clemensbrief*, 134.

[5] As on some occasions in Paul, cf. his negative references to the 'works of the flesh' in Gal. 5.19–21; cf. also Rom. 8.5–8.

[6] *Contra* e.g. Donfried, *Setting*, 145; see Lindemann, *Paulus*, 269–70.

[7] The author of *2 Clement* may differ from Paul, but he agrees on this score with many other early Christian writers who also make strong claims about the resurrection of the physical body without the distinctions Paul makes between different kinds of bodies: see e.g. *1 Clem.* 23–7; Ign. *Smyrn.* 3.1.; Justin, *1 Apol.* 19–21; *Dial.* 80.4; Tatian, *Orat.* 6; Theophilus, *Autol.* 1.7; Ps.-Justin, *De Res.* 5; Irenaeus, *Haer.* 5.2.3; Tertullian, *Res.*

1 The section starts with the negative command 'let none of you say'. What is opposed here is any claim that flesh might not be 'judged' or 'rise'. The author is adamant that the flesh will 'rise' again, and also will be judged: hence one cannot ignore the physical aspects of life in the present in one's ethical behaviour.

2 The author reminds his addressees of the position they were in when they initially became Christians. The two rhetorical questions echo, perhaps deliberately, the language of 1.4–6 (for being 'saved', cf. 1.4; for 'receiving sight' cf. 1.6). Further, it is notable that here, as in 1.4–8, 'salvation' is again something that is past and already achieved.[8] The assumption is evidently that any conditions in relation to Christian existence will not change: if one is in the state of the 'flesh' at the start of one's life as a Christian, one will stay that way. The possibility that there might be a change in the mode of one's existence (as e.g. Paul asserts in 1 Cor. 15, with a change from one kind of 'body' to another) is simply excluded here as apparently self-evident.

3 The importance of the 'flesh' as the mode of existence which it is assumed will continue unchanged in resurrection existence means that it must be 'guarded'. The analogy here is that the flesh is like 'a temple of God'. In the context here, it seems clear that the main point is primarily ethical: the language of 'guarding the flesh' has been reflected earlier in 8.4, 6 ('keeping the flesh pure') where it evidently means behaving in a morally upright way. The same general meaning thus probably applies here too.

The language comparing human beings (individually or collectively) to God's 'temple' comes in Paul (cf. 1 Cor. 6.19 in relation to individuals' 'bodies', and 1 Cor. 3.16 in relation to the community), though the language is widespread in early Christianity and indeed beyond.[9] Whether the author knows, and takes up, Paul's use of the language is not certain.[10] In any case, the author here does not make as strong a statement of identity as Paul makes ('*you* are God's temple'), nor does he relate the comparison to the presence of the Spirit as Paul does. What is said is simply that the flesh is to be regarded as having the greatest possible value and must not in any way be undervalued or derided as unimportant. As such, it is then a slightly unusual and unexpected comparison; hence it may well be that the analogy has been taken from elsewhere (as a quasi-'citation') and inserted here by the author. But given

---

[8] See above for the variation in the author's terminology in this respect; but for salvation as already past, cf. 1.4, 7; 2.7; 3.3, and v. 5 below. See also Aono, *Entwicklung*, 144.

[9] The closest parallel, explicitly comparing the 'flesh' to the temple of God, is in Ign. *Phil.* 7.2; cf. too 2 Cor. 6.16; Eph. 2.20–1; *Barn.* 6.15, etc.; also the idea of the community as the temple in Qumran (e.g. 1QS 8).

[10] Warns, 'Untersuchungen', 230–6, argues that the (Valentinian) opponents had taken up this Pauline language, but this is not certain. See Lindemann, *Clemensbriefe*, 226; Pratscher, *Zweite Clemensbrief*, 136.

the widespread use of the verbal imagery, it is not possible to identify the immediate origin of the writer's language here.

4 The author now makes clear, and presupposes as something he can assume without really arguing the case, the fundamental continuity in the human condition: those who were 'called in the flesh' will also 'come in the flesh'.[11] The precise nature of the 'coming' is not certain: it could be a reference to the future judgement, or to the coming kingdom.[12] However, the difference between the two may not be very great: the result of a favourable verdict at the last judgement is participation in the kingdom.

5 The opening word εἰς constitutes a possible text-critical problem. All the MSS of the text (A C S) have (or imply) this reading, as does the *Florilegium Edessenum*, whose excerpts from *2 Clement* include this verse.[13] However, many commentators have claimed that this produces a very difficult reading, since the οὕτως καί clause which follows seems to imply a preceding conditional clause. Hence many have postulated a reading εἰ instead of εἰς, a reading which also appears to be read by another Syriac collection of excerpts, the *Excerpta Patrum*, which cites the text of 9.1–5 here in full.[14] However, given that the text with εἰς is so strongly attested, and can be made to make reasonable sense (in terms of ideas and without an impossible grammatical difficulty),[15] it may be preferable to follow the (all but) uniformly attested text in the MSS.

---

[11] S presupposes a reading ἦλθεν, which is probably then a Christological reference to the incarnation. This would link more closely to what is then said in v. 5. However, the combined witness of both Greek MSS is strong evidence for the reading ἐλεύσεσθε.

[12] For the former, see Lightfoot, *Apostolic Fathers*, 2.230; Knopf, *Zwei Clemensbriefe*, 166 and cf. vv. 1, 5 here; for the latter, see Lindemann, *Clemensbriefe*, 226 and cf. v. 6 here.

[13] For the text, see p. 10 above.

[14] See p. 11 above. The reading εἰ is accepted by Lightfoot, *Apostolic Fathers*, 2.230 ('εἰς is quite out of place here'); Gebhardt, Harnack, and Zahn, *Opera*, 39; Bihlmeyer, *Apostolischen Väter*, 77; Knopf, *Zwei Clemensbriefe*, 167; Lake, *Fathers*, 142; Richardson, *Fathers*, 196; Grant and Graham, *Apostolic Fathers*, 120; Warns, 'Untersuchungen', 246. εἰς is accepted by Wengst, *Zweite Clemensbrief*, 249; Lindemann, *Clemensbriefe*, 226; Pratscher, *Zweite Clemensbrief*, 137. According to Lindemann, a clause introduced by καὶ οὕτως would be very unusual after an εἰ clause (though, as Pratscher observes, it is the second clause, introduced by οὕτως καί, which forms the possible apodosis to the first clause!).

Ehrman suggests an emendation of the text, reading εἰ Ἰησοῦς Χριστός to account for the variant: with the use of nomina sacra, this would have been written ΕΙΙΣ, which might then have been corrupted to ΕΙΣ: see B. D. Ehrman, 'Textual Traditions Compared: The New Testament and the Apostolic Fathers', in A. F. Gregory and C. M. Tuckett (eds), *The Reception of the New Testament in the Apostolic Fathers* (Oxford: Oxford University Press, 2005), 16, and Ehrman, *Fathers*, 178. This is somewhat speculative, and his further reason added, that the proposed reading 'preserves the double name Jesus Christ used throughout *2 Clement*'s text', seems to overstate the evidence: cf. 2.7; 5.5; 14.2 (bis); 14.4, where 'Christ' alone is used without an accompanying 'Jesus'.

[15] cf. Lindemann as in the previous note: the reading εἰ may make for an equally difficult reading in terms of the surface grammar.

The qualification of Christ as 'one' is part of a number of confessional quasi-formulae in early Christianity (cf. 1 Cor. 8.6; Eph. 4.5; 1 Tim. 2.5; 1 *Clem.* 46.6; Ign. *Magn.* 7.2; cf. too Ign. *Eph.* 7.2). The further reference, that this 'one Christ' is 'the Lord who saved us', picks up the language of salvation, again (as in v. 2) seen as something already in the past for Christians. However, neither claim constitutes the main thrust of the argument.[16] The main point is only now introduced: this saviour figure 'became flesh', from which the deduction is drawn that 'we shall receive the reward in this (same) flesh'. Prior to 'becoming flesh', Christ 'was first spirit ($\pi\nu\epsilon\hat{v}\mu\alpha$)'. This seems to be an allusion to christological language found elsewhere, equating 'Christ' and 'Spirit'.[17] The language then of 'becoming flesh' clearly echoes John 1.14 for many modern readers,[18] though whether this was so at a conscious level for the author of 2 *Clement* is uncertain: there is no other clear reference to John in 2 *Clement*, and the language here may have become stock and traditional.[19]

The main conclusion to the whole argument based on the incarnation is now drawn (though with a—somewhat massive!—assumption about the nature of the continuities, and the absence of discontinuity, involved): the author concludes that 'we will receive the reward in this flesh'.[20] Hence the condition of the 'flesh' is nothing transitory, but will last into resurrection existence as well.

6 The paraenetic consequences are now drawn, albeit in somewhat general terms: the hearers are bidden to 'love one another' so that 'we may all enter the kingdom of God'. The reference to mutual love within the community has already been mentioned in 4.3. As in the earlier context, the language is very general, though concern for mutual relations within the community does seem to have been a particular issue for the author (see above on 4.3 and below on 13.4). So too talk about the kingdom as the final goal for the Christian is not new and will occur later (cf. 5.5; 11.7; 12.1, 2, 6). Whether there is any slightly pointed polemic in the language about 'all' entering the

---

[16] The nature of the comment as almost a throwaway remark must question seriously any claim that the author here is engaged in explicit polemic against Gnostics who were uneasy about calling Jesus 'Lord': see Introduction §7. Opponents and on 4.2 above. Nor does the 'oneness' of Christ seem to be an issue. The note here that it is 'the Lord' who saved us does not suggest in the slightest way that such language is contestable: in the logic of the argument it is presented as something that can be assumed as common ground to the author and the hearers.

[17] cf. Herm. *Sim.* 5.6.5–7; Theophilus, *Autol.* 2.10; Tertullian, *Marc.* 3.16. Also 1 Cor. 15.45; 2 Cor. 3.17, and 2 *Clem.* 14 below, though there is no development here of the idea in relation to the post-incarnate Jesus.

[18] And such an allusion is widely taken as the reason why C reads $\lambda\acute{o}\gamma os$ instead of $\pi\nu\epsilon\hat{v}\mu\alpha$ here. (The secondary nature of the reading is shown by the neuter τo still retained in C.)

[19] cf. Lindemann, *Clemensbriefe*, 227; Gregory and Tuckett, '2 *Clement*', 253; Pratscher, *Zweite Clemensbrief*, 138.

[20] The logic is scarcely compelling!

kingdom seems somewhat doubtful, given the relatively low-key way in which this is said.[21]

7 The exhortation takes up again the thrust of what was said in 8.1 with the plea for repentance 'while there is still time' (ὡς ἔχομεν καιρόν);[22] here another metaphor is used, this time that of God as a healer or doctor. The language of God 'healing' is a metaphor for God forgiving sins. This takes up the traditional imagery of sin as illness which God heals (cf. Deut. 30.3 LXX; Jer. 3.22; Ps. 41.4; Jas. 5.16; *Diogn.* 9.6; Herm. *Vis.* 1.1.9). The exhortation that we should 'give ourselves over' to God is also striking. The verb used ἐπιδιδόναι can mean almost 'surrender'.[23] The image of the doctor healing then leads on to further development of the image with language of the 'recompense' (ἀντιμισθία, cf. 1.3, 5), which we then should pay him. The image seems to be that of the 'honorarium' which one would pay a doctor for services rendered.[24]

The 'pattern of salvation' which is presupposed here may be noteworthy. One can argue that the author of *2 Clement* has no idea of 'justification by works', for any 'work' that human beings do is simply to offer back to God (the equivalent of some kind of) 'payment' for what God has *already* done (in his act of 'healing'). Any imperative follows, and results from, the indicative of God's saving work.[25] On the other hand, it is made clear that without the ἀντιμισθία, which is here 'repentance', there would be no final salvation!

8 The 'recompense' is now explicitly stated to be 'repentance' (cf. 8.1), stemming from a 'pure heart'. The fact that the 'recompense' logically *follows* the receipt of the gift suggests that, as before (see on 8.1), 'repentance' here is the actual act of changing one's pattern of life. It is not the expression of remorse about the past (which logically precedes the act of forgiveness by God). Healing/forgiveness then requires the change in lifestyle ('repentance') as the proper response to God's grace.

9 The importance of genuine (as opposed to possibly sham) repentance is given a further reason (γάρ): God knows everything beforehand and hence any dissimulation or pretence is impossible. The word προγνώστης does not occur in the NT or in other Apostolic Fathers, though the idea of God knowing all things in advance is widespread in Judaism (cf. Wis. 8.8; 18.6;

---

[21] Warns, 'Untersuchungen', 258–62, argues that the Valentinian opponents had used John 3.5 to argue for the existence of an elite group within the community. Against this, see Lindemann, *Clemensbriefe*, 228; Pratscher, *Zweite Clemensbrief*, 138.

[22] Pratscher, *Zweite Clemensbrief*, 140, notes that the wording is the same as Gal. 6.10 (cf. too Ign. *Smyrn.* 9.1), though the language is scarcely specific enough to suggest literary dependence.

[23] cf. BAG, 292, with further references and examples.

[24] cf. R. Herzog, 'Arzthonorar', *RAC* 1 (1950), 724–5, cited by Lindemann, *Clemensbriefe*, 228, and Pratscher, *Zweite Clemensbrief*, 140.

[25] Argued strongly by Pratscher, *Zweite Clemensbrief*, 140.

cf. too *Teach. Silv.* (NHC VII.4) 116.1–5) and in writings of the Christian apologists where this adjective does occur (Justin, *1 Apol.* 44.11; *Dial.* 16.3; 23.2; Theophilus, *Autol.* 2.15).[26]

10 The exhortation picks up again from what is said in v. 8 to encourage (in the first-person plural) 'praise' (αἶνον)[27] for God. The whole context is very reminiscent of what is said in 1.5. The praise of God must be not only with our mouths, but with our hearts. The sentiment is widespread and reminiscent of the citation of Isa. 29.13 quoted in 3.5 (though there the contrast is 'lips/heart', rather than 'mouth/heart').[28] The 'reward' that is held out as a promise is then that 'he may receive us as sons'. The terminology is as in 1.4, though here the status of divine sonship is held out as a future hope rather than a present reality, as in 1.4. But this lack of consistency at one level, whereby various aspects of existence and relationships to God are sometimes taken to be present realities and sometimes future hopes, is not uncharacteristic of this author.[29]

11 The basis of the promise of divine sonship is now spelt out as a saying of 'the Lord' (clearly in context Jesus rather than God: cf. the reference to 'my Father' in the quotation itself). The quotation (perhaps based, albeit indirectly, on the gospels of both Matthew and Luke: see above) neatly sums up the twin themes of the writer: salvation (or divine sonship) is promised as a gift from God, but only to those who behave in an ethically responsible and upright way ('those who *do* the will of my Father').

---

[26] The final words of the verse are not quite certain. A has ταενκαρδια (in majuscule script—hence without iota subscripts or spaces); C has τὰ ἐγκαρδία (with the spacing clear). However ἐγκαρδία is not attested elsewhere in early Christian literature and hence the A reading (spaced as τὰ ἐν καρδία) is to be preferred. For the phrase, cf. Deut. 8.2 LXX.

[27] Again the text is not quite certain. αἶνον is read or implied by C S; A has αἰώνιον (which on its own makes no sense). Some have postulated an original reading αἶνον αἰώνιον: see Lightfoot, *Apostolic Fathers*, 2.231; Warns, 'Untersuchungen', 226, 370. (Lindemann, *Clemensbriefe*, 229, mistakenly implies this is the reading of A.) If so, the adjective could easily have been omitted by haplography. However, the close parallel to the language here in 1.5 suggests that one should read αἶνον alone (so Pratscher, *Zweite Clemensbrief*, 143), and the A reading may simply be a mistake (not an uncommon feature of A).

[28] cf. e.g. Ps. 61.5 LXX, cited in *1 Clem.* 15.3.

[29] cf. the writer's references to 'salvation', noted many times already, and see Introduction §9.2 on soteriology above.

Chapter 10

COMMENTARY

1 The 'chapter' division here is somewhat arbitrary and slightly misleading (if it is taken as implying a break in the line of thought). The exhortation here follows immediately on from the preceding citation, as indicated by the ὥστε (with the added ἀδελφοί μου, perhaps for some emphasis, cf. 4.3; 7.1; 8.4): if Jesus' 'brothers' are those who do 'the will of my Father', then it is vital that we should indeed do 'the will of the Father'. In one way the new exhortations add nothing to what has already been said,[1] though the author yet again emphasizes the importance (to him) of the general point by using four different cohortative verbs here: ποιήσωμεν, διώξωμεν, καταλείψωμεν, φύγωμεν, although all four are used in fairly general terms.

At another level, a further rider is added in that God as Father is said here to be the one 'who called us'. Elsewhere, the one who 'called us' is Jesus (1.8; 2.4, 7; 5.1; 9.5; here and in 1.4; 16.1 it is God), which is one facet of the general 'functional identity' between Jesus and God (see on 1.1 above). The note reminds the addressees of the element of divine 'grace' in the whole process of salvation: however much Christians can only attain final salvation on the basis of their ethical behaviour in the present, it is still the case that the divine initiative precedes all such human endeavour.[2]

The intended result is 'so that we may live'. Grammatically, it is not clear whether this is related to the cohortative ποιήσωμεν or the immediately preceding τοῦ καλέσαντος ἡμᾶς.[3] In one way, the former would fit the general tenor of a great deal of what is said in *2 Clement*; but equally, the importance of the divine initiative in the process of salvation is never lost. Perhaps it is pressing the logic too far to distinguish clearly between the two possibilities.

---

[1] Pratscher, *Zweite Clemensbrief*, 144.
[2] cf. the references to being 'saved' (in the past) in 9.2, 5; see also on 9.7 above.
[3] It is usually taken as the former: see Knopf, *Zwei Clemensbriefe*, 168; Lindemann, *Clemensbriefe*, 230; Pratscher, *Zweite Clemensbrief*, 144.

The next exhortation, 'let us rather[4] pursue virtue', is striking for the use of the word ἀρετή. The term is relatively rare in the NT (only Phil. 4.8; 2 Pet. 1.5), but was very widely used in Greek philosophical writings and in Hellenistic Jewish texts.[5] Its usage here thus suggests an awareness of the vocabulary of the wider Hellenistic world. However, the exhortation remains very general with no suggestion of what specifically might be in mind. For the non-literal use of διώκω, see e.g. Rom. 9.30; 1 Cor. 14.1; 1 Pet. 3.11 (= Ps. 34 (33 LXX).14); *1 Clem.* 22.5; *Barn.* 20.2.

The negative counterpart of 'pursuing virtue' is now given as 'abandoning evil' (τὴν δὲ κακίαν καταλείψωμεν), again a general statement with no indication of what particular 'evil' is in mind. The 'evil' is said to be the 'forerunner' (προοδοιπόρον)[6] of 'our sins'. So too, the readers are encouraged to 'flee impiety' so that 'evil may not overtake us'. All these exhortations remain extremely general in their wording.[7]

The language here is open to a reading whereby some kind of analysis is being given about the ultimate origin of multiple sins and misdemeanours. As such, this might be similar to what is said in e.g. Jas. 1.15 (desire produces sin), 1 Tim. 6.12 (love of money is the root of all kinds of evil), or Rom. 7.7–11 (Sin, as some kind of demonic power, produced acts of sinning in 'me'). However, the language here seems to be rather imprecise and one probably cannot press the details to gain a clear model of cause and effect. 'Evil' (κακία) is the forerunner of 'sins' (plur.); but also impiety (ἀσέβεια) may lead to 'evils' (κακά plur.) overtaking us. Since 'evil' occurs in both the alleged prior cause and the resulting effect, it is unlikely that any clear analysis is being offered.[8]

2 The fairly general exhortation continues with the promise that 'if we are eager to do good, peace will pursue us'. The new word in the vocabulary is 'peace'. The language is strikingly reminiscent of Ps. 34 (LXX 33).14 ἔκκλινον ἀπὸ κακοῦ καὶ ποίησον ἀγαθόν ζήτησον εἰρήνην καὶ δίωξον αὐτήν, with common references to 'good', 'evil', 'peace', 'pursue'. The verse was used

---

[4] The use of μᾶλλον . . . δέ sets up the contrast between 'pursuing virtue' and the following negative counterparts, rather than the preceding exhortation to do the will of the Father; moreover μᾶλλον expresses exclusion rather than simply a preferable alternative (BDF §245a (2)).

[5] cf. e.g. Wis. 4.1; 8.7; 2 Macc. 10.28; 4 Macc. 7.22; Herm. *Mand.* 1.2; 6.2.3; 12.3.1; *Sim.* 6.1.4; 8.10.3. See Knopf, *Zwei Clemensbriefe*, 168; also O. Bauernfeind, ἀρετή, *TWNT* 1 (1933), 457–61.

[6] The noun is rare, being absent from the LXX and other early Christian texts; the corresponding verb occurs e.g. in Josephus, *Ant.* 3.2; *1 Clem.* 44.5 (though with a slightly different nuance, namely as a euphemism for 'die before now': cf. BAG, 715).

[7] The one word which might be a little more specific might be ἀσέβεια (here 'impiety'), which could have a nuance of worshipping other gods. But there is no suggestion that that was a live danger for the addressees elsewhere in *2 Clement* (and indeed in e.g. 1.6; 2.4, it seems to be assumed that this is part of the past for author and readers/hearers alike).

[8] See e.g. Pratscher, *Zweite Clemensbrief*, 145.

Commentary: Chapter 10

in other early Christian texts, being cited explicitly as part of an extended citation in 1 Pet. 3.10–12 (citing Ps. 34.12–16) and *1 Clem.* 22.1–8 (citing Ps. 34.11–17). On the other hand, there is no explicit indication that any text is being cited here, and it is noteworthy that, unlike the Psalm verse, 'peace' is here the subject of the verb not the object.[9] Nevertheless the verbal agreement, as well as the sudden introduction of the word 'peace' (which is not taken up in what follows), is striking.[10]

3 The text in v. 3a, specifically the phrase οὐκ ἔστιν εὑρεῖν ἄνθρωπον, is difficult to interpret as it stands and some kind of textual corruption has been suspected. There are no significant textual variants between the MSS, and hence any possible corruption must pre-date the MS tradition we have. Without any emendation, probably the best way to make sense of the text as it stands is that of Knopf. He suggests implicitly supplying an extra αὐτήν as the subject of the verb εὑρεῖν (this is the reason why 'it' [peace] does not find 'man'); alternatively, ἄνθρωπον might be the subject and αὐτήν the object (this is the reason why man does not find it [= peace]).[11] Others have suggested emending the text.[12] However, all emendations are necessarily

---

[9] Warns, 'Untersuchungen', 482–3, suggests that the author of *2 Clement* is writing to oppose a Valentinian interpretation of Ps. 34 (referring the first half of the Psalm verse to psychics, and the second half to pneumatics, cf. Clement, *Strom.* 4.109), but this seems somewhat speculative. There is no indication in the text here that the writer is trying to offer an alternative interpretation to one that is presupposed.

[10] If there is an echo of Ps. 34 here, it provides an intriguing possible similarity with *1 Clem.* 22–3: both would then allude to Ps. 34 (in *1 Clem.* 22 it is an explicit citation), and in the next chapter in each text there is a highly distinctive explicit citation (from an unknown source) of what is evidently the same text (*1 Clem.* 23.3–4//*2 Clem.* 11.2–4: see below). It is then just possible that these two texts (Ps. 34 and the unknown citation) were together in some kind of collection of proof texts, or testimonies, and known to both authors: see Warns, 'Untersuchungen', 484; Pratscher, *Zweite Clemensbrief,* 146. On the other hand, there is nothing to indicate that the two texts are linked in either *1 Clement* or *2 Clement* (apart from the fact that the allusions/citations occur relatively close to each other in both): hence the apparent 'agreement' could be simply a coincidence.

[11] Knopf, *Zwei Clemensbriefe,* 168; followed by e.g. Wengst, *Zweite Clemensbrief,* 273; Lindemann, *Clemensbriefe,* 231; Pratscher, *Zweite Clemensbrief,* 146, as the simplest (and hence most preferable) solution to the problem. This proposal is adopted in the English translation here.

[12] For example, Lightfoot, *Apostolic Fathers,* 2.232, suggests reading εἰρήνην εὑρεῖν (which comes to the same as Knopf's suggestion), or εἰρηνεύειν in place of εὑρεῖν, or ('still better') εὐημερεῖν (to prosper). He claims that if the last suggestion is adopted, the author may be continuing the allusion to Ps. 34; but it is hard to see how this suggested emendation makes a big difference: εὐημερεῖν does not occur in the LXX text of Ps. 34 here, so any possible allusion is at the level of sense rather than specific wording.

Warns, 'Untersuchungen', 596–7 suggests supplying the object of the verb as ἀνάπαυσιν (cf. 6.7), which could then explain why C has ἀνάπαυσις in place of ἀπόλαυσις in the immediate context in 10.3, 4; however, this is even more speculative.

Ehrman, *Fathers,* 180–1, follows one of Lightfoot's suggestions and prints εἰρηνεύειν in his text. (He says that this was a conjecture of Knopf. In fact, Knopf mentions it as a possibility (from Lightfoot), but rejects it in favour of his own interpretation of the text as it exists in the MSS.)

speculative, and one may be better seeking to make sense of the text as it currently stands in the MSS. In any case, the general thrust seems clear: it is a negative statement about the possibility of human beings achieving the desired goal for which they strive.

The second half of the verse is also rather unclear in its detail. The introduction to v. 3a states that this is the implied reason why some people do not attain their desired goal (whether 'peace', or 'rest', or 'peace' attaining them): they are not then 'doing good' (v. 2). A possible hint (but no more!) of the people the writer has in mind is given in the rest of the verse. Such people are those[13] who 'bring in human fears', and who 'prefer[14] the pleasures of the present to the promise of the future'. As the end of the chapter makes clear, there appears to be a specific group of people in mind, perhaps well known to both author and audience here: hence no need was evidently felt to spell out more clearly who is in mind. For us, however, the situation is far from clear! In particular, what are the 'human fears' involved? And what are the 'pleasures of the present' which are being advocated by some as apparently worth more than the writer thinks they should be (in comparison with the future promise)?

A number of commentators have suggested that a persecution situation is in mind: the people being attacked here are those who are seeking to avoid persecution, perhaps advocating a quiet refusal to confess their faith when required in order to avoid possible martyrdom (hence the reference to 'fears' and the implied preference for a better situation in the present).[15] However, the language is extremely vague and general; the exhortation immediately preceding has also been in very unspecific terms but seems to relate to concrete ethical behaviour ('doing good', showing 'virtue', not committing 'sins'). It does not seem to refer to specifically religious 'confession' in a context of threatened persecution. So too, it was argued earlier (see on 5.4 above) that it was rather unlikely that the author had in mind a situation of threatening persecution: hence it is unlikely to be the situation here.[16]

---

[13] οἵτινες (plur.), introducing the second half of the sentence, follows immediately after ἄνθρωπον (sing.): the grammar is awkward though not impossible. Cf. Lindemann, *Clemensbriefe*, 231; Pratscher, *Zweite Clemensbrief*, 147.

[14] Reading A's προῃρημένοι as qualifying the οἵτινες as people from whom the writer clearly wishes to distance himself. The first-person plural in the C reading προαιρούμεθα does not fit the context. The S reading (implying προαιρούμενοι), adopted by Wengst, is similar to the A reading.

[15] So e.g. Knopf, *Zwei Clemensbriefe*, 168 (referring to his interpretation of aspects of 4.4–6.7); Wengst, *Zweite Clemensbrief*, 273 (who is very explicit that the primary issue is confession under threat of persecution); Lohmann, *Drohung*, 111; Lindemann, *Clemensbriefe*, 231; also apparently Pratscher, *Zweite Clemensbrief*, 147 (the proposal would provide 'einen gut verständlichen Sitz im Leben' ('a very intelligible Sitz im Leben')).

[16] It is slightly ironical that those such as Lindemann and Pratscher, who distance themselves from Knopf's suggested situation of possible martyrdom to interpret the earlier passage in 5.4 (see above), support the existence of such a context here.

Further, the particular stress on the 'pleasures' of the present life (evidently highly valued by the 'opponents') seems slightly strange language if what is meant is the very existence of the present life itself. Perhaps one has to admit the limits of one's knowledge on the basis of the existing evidence, but it is certainly hard to read into the language here a plea for persecuted Christians to confess their faith publicly at all costs.

4 The author continues by elaborating on the future consequences of the different strategies and/or lifestyles he evidently has in mind. He accuses his 'opponents' of 'not knowing' the real consequences of their actions. Whether the language used by the writer is deliberately loaded is not certain. If they were in some sense Gnostics, claiming to 'know' important things in relation to salvation, the claim that they do '*not* know' is perhaps all the more pointed.[17] But a Gnostic background is not essential to make sense of the language used here.

Those who opt for pleasures in the present will experience great torment (βάσανον). The reference is to the eschatological punishment awaiting the wicked.[18] But the promise in store (by implication for those who eschew the 'pleasures' of the present) is joy or delight (τρυφή).[19] The general point is then the standard apocalyptic motif of the reversal of roles and fortunes in the future eschatological age. Whether the 'opponents' denied any kind of future hope, claiming to have received everything in the present,[20] is not so clear: perhaps they had simply decided to ignore any future consequences for their actions (or might have disputed whether such consequences were quite as certain as is claimed here).

5 It is now made more explicit that the people whom the author has in mind are not only acting for themselves, but are influencing others via teaching: hence presumably in part the danger which the author feels they constitute for the wider community. The author has no sympathy for these people themselves, and indeed seems to have given up on them (cf. v. 5a). But they are teaching[21] and leading others ('innocent souls' τὰς ἀναιτίους ψυχάς) to join them in what the author regards as highly undesirable behaviour. Again the charge against them is that they 'do not know' (οὐκ εἰδότες)—possibly

---

[17] cf. also 1.2 above. The use of slightly understated irony in his language is not untypical of this author.

[18] cf. Wis. 3.1; Luke 16.23, 28. The same word is used in 17.7 here to refer to present, earthly sufferings.

[19] The word is often used in a negative sense: e.g. in the NT in Luke 7.25; 2 Pet. 2.13; also quite often in Hermas, e.g. *Sim.* 6.4.4; *Mand.* 8.3 (τρυφὴ πονηρά); but it can also be used in a positive sense, e.g. *Diogn.* 12.1 (παράδεισος τρυφῆς); Philo, *Cher.* 12. See BAG, 836.

[20] So Donfried, *Setting*, 149.

[21] Κακοδιδασκαλεῖν is a very rare word, though cf. κακοδιδασκαλία in Ign. *Phld.* 2.1; also ἑτεροδιδασκαλεῖν in 1 Tim. 1.3; 6.3; Ign. *Pol.* 3.1.

another understated, but pointed, implicit attack against claims to knowledge on the part of the people concerned (see above on v. 4).

Their ignorance is here said to relate to the fact that they will be liable for a 'double penalty' (δισσὴ κρίσις). How or why the penalty is 'double' is not quite clear: perhaps it is that the punishment in the future will affect not only the (false) teachers but also those who have been seduced by their teaching.[22] Hence the seriousness of the warning by the writer here, since presumably the audience of his words are precisely those in danger of being attracted by these false teachers.

---

[22] cf. Ign. *Eph.* 16.2. There is a similar reference in *Apos. Con.* 5.6.5, which also talks about a διπλοτέραν κρίσιν (in the context of a discussion of possible martyrdom: cf. Wengst, *Zweite Clemensbrief,* 274).

Chapter 11

PARALLELS

2 Clem. 11.2–4	1 Clem. 23.3–4
² λέγει γὰρ καὶ ὁ προφητικὸς λόγος·	³ πόρρω γενέσθω ἀφ' ἡμῶν ἡ γραφὴ αὕτη, ὅπου λέγει
ταλαίπωροί εἰσιν οἱ δίψυχοι, οἱ διστάζοντες τῇ καρδίᾳ, οἱ λέγοντες·	ταλαίπωροί εἰσιν οἱ δίψυχοι, οἱ διστάζοντες τῇ ψυχῇ, οἱ λέγοντες·
ταῦτα πάλαι ἠκούσαμεν καὶ ἐπὶ τῶν πατέρων ἡμῶν,	ταῦτα ἠκούσαμεν καὶ ἐπὶ τῶν πατέρων ἡμῶν,
ἡμεῖς δὲ ἡμέραν ἐξ ἡμέρας προσδεχόμενοι οὐδὲν τούτων ἑωράκαμεν.	καὶ ἰδού, γεγηράκαμεν, καὶ οὐδὲν ἡμῖν τούτων συνβέβηκεν.
³ ἀνόητοι, συμβάλετε ἑαυτοὺς ξύλῳ· λάβετε ἄμπελον· πρῶτον μὲν φυλλοροεῖ,	⁴ ὦ ἀνόητοι, συμβάλετε ἑαυτοὺς ξύλῳ· λάβετε ἄμπελον· πρῶτον μὲν φυλλοροεῖ,
εἶτα βλαστὸς γίνεται,	εἶτα βλαστὸς γίνεται, εἶτα φύλλον, εἶτα ἄνθος,
μετὰ ταῦτα ὄμφαξ, εἶτα σταφυλὴ παρεστηκυῖα.	καὶ μετὰ ταῦτα ὄμφαξ, εἶτα σταφυλὴ παρεστηκυῖα.
⁴ οὕτως καὶ ὁ λαός μου ἀκαταστασίας καὶ θλίψεις ἔσχεν· ἔπειτα ἀπολήψεται τὰ ἀγαθά.	
² For the prophetic word also says,	³ May this scripture be far removed from us that says,
'How miserable are those who are double-minded, who doubt in their hearts, who say	'How miserable are those who are double-minded, who doubt in their souls, who say
"We heard these things long ago, in the time of our fathers, but we have waited day after day and have seen none of these things."	"We have heard these things in the time of our fathers, and behold! We have grown old and none of these things has happened to us."

> ³ Fools! Compare yourselves to a tree. Take a vine: first it sheds its leaves, then a bud comes, after these things an unripe grape, then a full bunch. ⁴ So too my people has had tumults and afflictions; but then it will receive good things.'

> ⁴ Fools! Compare yourselves to a tree. Take a vine: first it sheds its leaves, then a bud comes, then a leaf, then a flower, and after these an unripe grape, then a full bunch.

The author of *2 Clement* here shares a quotation with the author of *1 Clement*: in both texts, there is an introductory formula, explicitly indicating that what follows is a quotation.¹ In *1 Clement*, it is said to be ἡ γραφὴ αὕτη; in *2 Clement*, it is said to be ὁ προφητικὸς λόγος. The use of γραφή in *1 Clement* indicates that what is cited has the status of scripture, and the same is almost certainly true for *2 Clement* too. The phrase ὁ προφητικὸς λόγος occurs in the NT in 2 Pet. 1.19, where it is probably a reference to Jewish scripture in general.² The phrase is used in Philo and elsewhere to refer to individual texts of Jewish scripture.³ The author of *2 Clement* thus probably indicates by this wording that he thinks that this is a quotation from Jewish scripture.

However, the citation here cannot be identified with any known version of a text from Jewish scripture. Lightfoot suggested that the quotation comes from the (now lost) book of Eldad and Modad, mentioned (and briefly cited) in Hermas, *Vis.* 2.3.4,⁴ but this can only remain a conjecture. Perhaps the text illustrates the still fluid nature of the canon of scripture at the time *2 Clement* was written, with some texts not now included in the canon regarded as scriptural.

---

¹ For a full discussion of the issues relating to the citation and its relationship with *1 Clement*, see in addition to the commentaries, Donfried, *Setting*, 52–3; Hagner, *Use*, 87–8; Lindemann, *Paulus*, 266; Warns, 'Untersuchungen', 530–44.

² For a full discussion of the different possible options, see R. J. Bauckham, *Jude, 2 Peter*, WBC 50 (Waco: Word, 1983), 224.

³ See e.g. Philo, *Sobr.* 68 (Gen. 49.22); *Leg.* 3.43 (Exod. 9.24); *Plant.* 117 (Gen. 1.14). Cf. too Justin, *Dial.* 56.6; 77.2; 110.3.

⁴ See Lightfoot, *Apostolic Fathers*, 2.80, 235; cf. too Hagner, *Use*, 74 ('possibly'), 88 ('probable'); Donfried, *Setting*, 53, says that the suggestion is 'worth considering'. The quotation in Hermas is not dissimilar in substance to the quotation here, though much shorter and shows no verbal agreement: it says simply 'The Lord is near those who turn to him' (ἐγγὺς κύριος τοῖς ἐπιστρεφομένοις). For a treatment of the 'text', see E. G. Martin, 'Eldad and Modad', in J. H. Charlesworth (ed.), *Old Testament Pseudepigrapha II* (New York: Doubleday, 1985), 463–5. Martin notes the possibility that the citation in *2 Clement* might be from this text, but observes that others have suggested other origins (e.g. the *Testament of Moses* (Hilgenfeld), or an *Apocryphon of Ezekiel* (Resch))) and says that 'the most prudent course is to leave these verses anonymous'. Cf. too Hagner, *Use*, 87–8; Warns, 'Untersuchungen', 532; Lindemann, *Clemensbriefe*, 233; Pratscher, *Zweite Clemensbrief*, 152.

Commentary: Chapter 11   217

The citations in *1 Clement* and *2 Clement* agree closely with each other in wording. They are not, however, identical, and hence it is unlikely that one has been derived from the other directly.⁵ The differences can be seen in the synopsis above. The most important are the following:

(i)   τῇ καρδίᾳ in *2 Clement*, τῇ ψυχῇ in *1 Clement*;⁶
(ii) πάλαι in *2 Clement*,⁷ no parallel in *1 Clement*;⁸
(iii) the phrase ἡμεῖς δὲ ἡμέραν ἐξ ἡμέρας προσδεχόμενοι οὐδὲν τούτων ἑωράκαμεν in *2 Clement* is broadly parallel in substance with καὶ ἰδού, γεγηράκαμεν, καὶ οὐδὲν ἡμῖν τούτων συνβέβηκεν in *1 Clement*, but quite different in detailed wording;
(iv) ἀνόητοι in *2 Clement*, ὦ ἀνόητοι in *1 Clement*;
(v)   εἶτα φύλλον, εἶτα ἄνθος, καί in *1 Clement* has no parallel in *2 Clement*;⁹
(vi) the whole of the conclusion in v. 4 in *2 Clement* has no parallel in *1 Clement*.¹⁰

The combination of close verbal agreement at times, but also some striking disagreement (including a continuation of the quotation after *1 Clement* stops quoting), suggests that the author of *2 Clement* has had independent access to the quotation here. Certainly the longer ending implies that *2 Clement* is not dependent on *1 Clement*. The reference in v. 4 to 'my people' is often taken as referring most naturally to Israel as God's chosen nation (though now presumably referring to the Christian community), hence

---

⁵ See Warns, 'Untersuchungen', 534–6; Lindemann, *Clemensbriefe*, 233 (in his earlier *Paulus*, 266, he argued that all the differences were due to secondary changes by the author of *2 Clement*); Pratscher, *Zweite Clemensbrief*, 152.

In the context of the citation in *2 Clement* here, there are other agreements with *1 Clement*: as noted above, *2 Clem.* 10.2 may have an echo of Ps. 34.14, which is cited in *1 Clem.* 22 (just before this citation in *1 Clem.* 23: see on 10.2 above); and *2 Clem.* 11.7 may share another unusual 'quotation' with *1 Clem.* 34 (although the 'quotation' is attested more widely in extant texts as well: see the discussion below). But whether these are significant, or simply coincidental, is not certain.

⁶ *2 Clement*'s 'heart' is perhaps more original here: the similar language used in e.g. Jas. 4.8; Herm. *Mand.* 9.5, which also refer to the 'heart', suggests this. See e.g. Warns, 'Untersuchungen', 534, and the discussion below on δίψυχος.

⁷ Lightfoot, *Apostolic Fathers*, 2.235, prints πάντα as the reading of the text, and claims that this is the reading of A. See too Lake, *Fathers*, 144. In the facsimile of A, the extant text reads only the initial πα (the rest is torn away). (Cf. too Bihlmeyer, *Apostolischen Väter*, 76.) Unless the damage to the page is very recent, it would seem that the reading πάντα in A has no justification and should henceforth be ignored.

⁸ It may be that *2 Clement* is here secondary, emphasizing the length of the delay concerned: cf. Warns, 'Untersuchungen', 534.

⁹ Warns, 'Untersuchungen', 535, argues that the longer text of *1 Clement* overloads the line and is secondary.

¹⁰ I have assumed that the citation in *2 Clement* includes v. 4. (The ὥστε ἀδελφοί μου at the start of v. 5 seems to be the start of the application of the citation.) I have also assumed that the words at the end of *1 Clem.* 23.4 are *not* part of the citation in *1 Clement* but constitute the application of the citation by the author (so most commentators: e.g. Lindemann, *Clemensbriefe*, 82–4, and others).

indicating that the text is indeed of Jewish (rather than Christian) origin.[11] However, it is probably impossible to say more on the source of the quotation (and hence also its possible original context).

2 Clem. 11.7	1 Cor. 2.9	1 Clem. 34.8
	ἀλλὰ καθὼς γέγραπται,	λέγει γάρ
ἃς οὖς οὐκ ἤκουσεν	ἃ ὀφθαλμὸς οὐκ εἶδεν	ὀφθαλμὸς οὐκ εἶδεν
οὐδὲ ὀφθαλμὸς εἶδεν,	καὶ οὖς οὐκ ἤκουσεν	καὶ οὖς οὐκ ἤκουσεν
οὐδὲ ἐπὶ καρδίαν	καὶ ἐπὶ καρδίαν	καὶ ἐπὶ καρδίαν
ἀνθρώπου ἀνέβη	ἀνθρώπου οὐκ ἀνέβη,	ἀνθρώπου οὐκ ἀνέβη,
14.5		
ἃ ἡτοίμασεν ὁ κύριος	ἃ ἡτοίμασεν ὁ θεὸς	ὅσα ἡτοίμασεν κύριος
τοῖς		
ἐκλεκτοῖς αὐτοῦ	τοῖς ἀγαπῶσιν αὐτόν.	τοῖς ὑπομένουσιν αὐτόν.[12]

Isa. 64.3 LXX: ἀπὸ τοῦ αἰῶνος οὐκ ἠκούσαμεν οὐδὲ οἱ ὀφθαλμοὶ ἡμῶν εἶδον θεὸν πλὴν σοῦ καὶ τὰ ἔργα σου ἃ ποιήσεις τοῖς ὑπομένουσιν ἔλεον

Ps.-Philo *LAB* 26.13: quod oculus non vidit nec auris audivit, et in cor hominis non ascendit

What eye has not seen nor ear heard, and has not entered into the heart of man

Gos. Thom. 17 (NHC II.2, 36.5–9): ⲡⲉϫⲉ ⲓ̅ⲥ̅ ϫⲉ ϯⲛⲁϯ ⲛⲏⲧⲛ̅ ⲙ̅ⲡⲉⲧⲉ ⲙ̅ⲡⲉ ⲃⲁⲗ ⲛⲁⲩ ⲉⲣⲟϥ ⲁⲩⲱ ⲡⲉⲧⲉ ⲙ̅ⲡⲉ ⲙⲁⲁϫⲉ ⲥⲟⲧⲙⲉϥ ⲁⲩⲱ ⲡⲉⲧⲉ ⲙ̅ⲡⲉ ϭⲓϫ ϭⲙ̅ϭⲱⲙϥ ⲁⲩⲱ ⲙ̅ⲡⲉϥⲉⲓ ⲉϩⲣⲁⲓ ϩⲓ ⲫⲏⲧ ⲣ̅ⲣⲱⲙⲉ

Jesus said 'I shall give you what no eye has seen and what no ear has heard and what no hand has touched and what has never occurred to the human mind'.

The words of *2 Clem.* 11.7 (with perhaps part of 14.5) form a striking parallel with what is given as a citation (apparently of scripture) in 1 Cor. 2.9 and *1 Clem.* 34.8, and which appears as a saying of Jesus in *Gos. Thom.* 17. There are also parallels to the saying in a range of other texts and witnesses.[13] In studies of Paul, the citation (clearly indicated as such by the introductory formula καθὼς γέγραπται) is a well-known crux since the saying in the

---

[11] cf. Warns, 'Untersuchungen', 531; Pratscher, *Zweite Clemensbrief*, 155.

[12] For variants among the MSS of *1 Clement* here, with possible assimilation occurring to the text of 1 Cor. 2.9, see Hagner, *Use*, 204–5.

[13] For full surveys of the evidence, see K. Berger, 'Zum Diskussion über die Herkunft von 1 Kor. II. 9', *NTS* 24 (1978), 271–83; M. E. Stone and J. Strugnell, *The Books of Elijah, Parts 1 & 2* (Missoula: Scholars Press, 1979), 42–73; J. Verheyden, 'Origen on the Origin of 1 Cor 2,9', in R. Bieringer (ed.), *The Corinthian Correspondence*, BETL 125 (Leuven: Peeters, 1996), 491–511; C. M. Tuckett, 'Paul and Jesus Tradition: The Evidence of 1 Corinthians 2:9 and Gospel of Thomas 17', in T. J. Burke and J. K. Elliott (eds), *Paul and the Corinthians: Studies on a Community in Conflict. Essays in Honour of Margaret Thrall*, NovTSup 109 (Leiden: Brill, 2003), 55–73. Apart from the texts given above, see also e.g. *Mart. Pol.* 2.3; Justin, *Baruch* apud Hippolytus *Ref.* 5.24; *Pr. Paul* (NHC I.1), 25–9, etc.

form given by Paul does not correspond with any extant version of a text in Jewish scripture. The closest is probably Isa. 64.3 (see above), though this is not an exact verbal parallel by any means.[14] In *1 Clement*, the words are also introduced as a quotation (λέγει γάρ); the wording is also very close to that of Paul, and it seems highly likely that the author of *1 Clement* is dependent on 1 Corinthians here (given the author's apparent knowledge of this Pauline letter elsewhere).[15] However, it is very unlikely that Paul himself is the originator of the saying: not only does Paul expressly indicate that he (thinks he) is quoting something; there is also a parallel in Ps.-Philo (see above) which cannot be dependent on Paul (though, as with *2 Clement*, the words there are not marked explicitly as a citation).[16] Hence the saying evidently circulated independently in a number of contexts.

Here in *2 Clement*, the words are not marked as a citation by an introductory formula.[17] Also it is not clear whether it is right to bring in the evidence from the wording of the later passage in 14.5 as an indication that the author does indeed know (and use) the full form of the saying as given by Paul. There is no evidence that the author is dependent on *1 Clement* (either for this saying, or more generally);[18] nor is there any evidence that the author of *2 Clement* thinks that this is a Jesus tradition.[19] Perhaps the most one can say is that the words of *2 Clement* here provide further evidence for the widespread use of the saying in a range of different authors.

COMMENTARY

The author continues his general message, looking forward to the future judgement which will bring rewards for those who are ethically upright and dire punishment for those who are not. To back up his argument further, he adduces a citation (from an unknown source: see above). As with some other citations in *2 Clement*, this one fits the general context here only with some difficulty. The situation is made more complex by the fact that, in the form in which it is cited, the citation includes an application already (see below on v. 4); however the application supplied within the citation itself

---

[14] For the phrase 'arising in the heart', cf. Jer. 3:16, though again the parallel in wording is not exact.

[15] cf. Lindemann, *Paulus*, 187–8; Hagner, *Use*, 76, 204–8.

[16] It is widely agreed that Pseudo-Philo has no Christian influence at all.

[17] However, the same has happened in the use of Isa. 54.1 in 2.1 where it clearly is a citation (see the commentary above).

[18] See n. 5 above.

[19] The ascription of the saying to Jesus (in *Gos. Thom.* 17) is probably a feature of the later Christian tradition, not a pre-Pauline development: see Tuckett, 'Paul and Jesus Tradition'. It is not presented here as a Jesus tradition, and hence any dependence on *Gos. Thom.* itself is unlikely, *pace* Aono, *Entwicklung*, 120.

may not be quite the same as the application which the author here wants to make. It seems that the citation itself seeks to allay doubts about eschatological hopes for the future in their entirety. However, nothing elsewhere in *2 Clement* suggests that this is quite the problem which the author is addressing. For example, in ch. 9, the 'problem' was not so much the existence of resurrection hope in itself, but rather the specific issue of whether the future resurrection (apparently accepted by all) involved the 'flesh' or not (see above). The 'problem' which the author is addressing generally is the denial of the seriousness of ethical behaviour in the present in the light of the future judgement to come. He is thus addressing a situation of 'doubt'; but it is not necessarily a doubt which questions all aspects of a future hope; rather, it is the doubt which denies the reality of a future judgement based on one's present behaviour.

To drive home his general message, the author fastens on this citation, attracted perhaps by the reference in it to 'doubting', also put in terms here of being 'double-minded' with an assertion that those who 'doubt' are/will be 'miserable'. He thus repeats the language of being 'miserable' (v. 1) and 'double-minded' (v. 5) from his source (v. 2), to drive home his general message that his addressees should not 'doubt' or 'not believe the promise', i.e. of rewards for the upright and punishment for the wicked. Neither term ('double-minded' or 'miserable') is repeated elsewhere in *2 Clement*. Yet it may well be that part of this 'agreement' with the cited source is at a relatively superficial level of common words. At a slightly deeper level, the author and the source may be using the same words in slightly different ways, and addressing different problems.[20]

1 The author reverts to his general exhortation to his audience. The exhortation to 'serve God' takes up again the language of 6.1; and the reference to a 'pure heart' echoes in part 9.8 ('a sincere heart').[21] The consequence of 'serving God' is that one will be 'righteous' ($\dot{\epsilon}\sigma\acute{o}\mu\epsilon\theta\alpha$ $\delta\acute{\iota}\kappa\alpha\iota\omicron\iota$). The alternative, 'if we do not serve him', is supplied with a reason: 'because we do not believe the promise of God'; and the consequence is that we shall be 'miserable' ($\tau\alpha\lambda\alpha\acute{\iota}\pi\omega\rho\omicron\iota$ $\dot{\epsilon}\sigma\acute{o}\mu\epsilon\theta\alpha$).

Most commentators take the two future $\dot{\epsilon}\sigma\acute{o}\mu\epsilon\theta\alpha$'s as eschatological, with the reference to being 'righteous' as meaning 'justified' or 'acquitted'

---

[20] The use of a citation which can only be made to fit the author's general message with some ingenuity and hermeneutical dexterity is not unprecedented in the text: cf. 2.1; 12.2; 14.2, etc.

[21] The phrase 'pure heart' is widely used in early Christian literature (see Pratscher, *Zweite Clemensbrief*, 150–1). It is, however, perhaps striking that this language occurs elsewhere also in relation to language about being 'double-minded': cf. Jas. 4.8; Herm. *Mand.* 9.7, where in both instances it is said that having a 'pure heart', or 'purifying the heart', is the positive counterpart of being $\delta\acute{\iota}\psi\upsilon\chi\omicron\varsigma$ or showing $\delta\iota\psi\upsilon\chi\acute{\iota}\alpha$. The latter language is unusual (see below), but the author here may already be tapping into the 'language game' associated with being 'double-minded' in this introductory exhortation prior to the citation in v. 2.

(i.e. at the final judgement).²² In relation to the latter, this may be too Pauline a reading: δίκαιος and its cognates in *2 Clement* normally refer to moral behaviour,²³ not as such to the verdict to be received at the final judgement. However, the two are closely connected: those who are (now) 'righteous' will receive a favourable judgement in the future. Hence the first ἐσόμεθα may not itself be strictly eschatological, although it clearly has eschatological implications. The second ἐσόμεθα may, however, be eschatological. It refers to the state of those who 'do not serve' God properly now: they 'will be miserable'. The use of ταλαίπωρος as the binary opposite of δίκαιος is unusual, though is probably prompted by the language of the following citation.²⁴ In the citation itself, the word refers to the present state of those who doubt; here, however, it seems to refer to the future state of those who 'do not believe the promises of God' in that such people will suffer terrible punishment. The words of the citation are thus being pressed to fit the author's own message, perhaps slightly against their 'original' meaning and application. The reference to the 'promise' picks up the language of 10.3–4. Evidently, the 'promise' here refers to the eschatological events which are to come in the future; those who 'do not believe' the promise here have probably not given up all future hope completely; rather, they have chosen to ignore the promise of future punishment for the disobedient (as well as the corresponding positive promise of reward for the righteous).

At one level, the 'problem' addressed is not dissimilar to that addressed in 2 Peter,²⁵ and it is striking that the text here displays a number of verbal similarities and agreements with the language of 2 Peter.

2 The author's claim about the 'miserable' state of those who doubt the future hope is now backed up with a quotation of what the author calls 'the prophetic word' (ὁ προφητικὸς λόγος). As noted above, the text is very close to (but not identical with) the quotation of 'scripture' cited in *1 Clem.* 23.3–4. The origin of the specific text cited here is unknown (see above on Parallels).

---

²² See variously Knopf, *Zwei Clemensbriefe*, 169; Wengst, *Zweite Clemensbrief*, 253; Lindemann, *Clemensbriefe*, 232; Pratscher, *Zweite Clemensbrief*, 151. Commentators refer partly to the wider context (cf. e.g. 10.3–5; 11.6), partly to the contrast drawn with being 'miserable'.

²³ cf. v. 7 here where the author seems to be summarizing what he has just said, saying 'if we do righteousness': 'doing δικαιοσύνη' and 'being δίκαιος' are thus probably synonymous, and the 'doing' indicates that the primary reference is to (human) ethical behaviour in the present, not a divine verdict at the final judgement.

²⁴ In itself it seems slightly weak, e.g. when compared with the reference to 'unquenchable fire' in 7.6 (citing Isa. 66.24). But the vocabulary is probably being taken somewhat woodenly from the source.

²⁵ Though perhaps the similarity is closer at the level of the citation than with *2 Clement* itself in that the citation seems to be addressed to those who have given up all eschatological future hope and are, as a result, now 'miserable' and in despair. There is no hint that *2 Clement* is addressing a situation of despair.

As noted above, the phrase 'prophetic word' is unusual, though not unparalleled. It probably refers to what is taken to be a text from Jewish scripture.

The phrase also occurs in 2 Pet. 1.19. As such, it represents one of a set of parallels between the language here and that of 2 Peter; but whether this is simply coincidental or implies some relation between the two texts is not certain. See further below.

The quotation starts by denouncing those who are 'double-minded' (οἱ δίψυχοι), those who 'doubt' (οἱ διστάζοντες) in their heart.[26] The language is somewhat unusual. Δίψυχος does not occur in the LXX, nor does the cognate verb διψυχέω or noun διψυχία. The adjective occurs in the NT in Jas. 1.8; 4.8, and the root then recurs in later Christian literature.[27] The unusual nature of the vocabulary in these Christian texts led Seitz, in a series of essays, to argue that the language comes from a common source, and he suggested that it was precisely this citation that led to the use of the word-group in James and Hermas as well as the echoes in 1 Clement and 2 Clement.[28] He suggested that the language derives from the Hebrew idiom בלב ולב (e.g. 1 Chron. 12.33; Ps. 12.2), referring to the divided 'heart' showing lack of true commitment to God. In the Christian texts, the word-group is often associated with 'doubt',[29] and also the need to purify the 'heart'.[30] Whether one can identify the origin of the language quite so precisely is perhaps debatable;[31] but the connection in ideas is striking. διστάζω is also lacking in the LXX; in the NT it occurs only in Matt. 14.31; 28.17; again it recurs in later Christian literature, often in connection with references to being 'double-minded' (cf. n. 29 above). In any case, the context here makes it clear that being 'double-minded' refers to 'doubting' the reality of the future hope.

The doubts are now articulated in what such people 'say'. These things (ταῦτα: presumably the 'promises' mentioned earlier) have been heard

---

[26] Whether the 'doubting' phrase defines 'double-mindedness', or adds something more, is not clear: see below.

[27] Apart from the citation here and in *1 Clem.* 23, see *1 Clem.* 11.2; *2 Clem.* 11.5 (presumably from the citation); 19.2; *Did.* 4.4; *Barn.* 19.5; it then occurs very frequently (over 50 times) in Hermas, e.g. *Sim.* 2.2.4, 7; 8.7.1; *Mand.* 9.1, 5–11.

[28] See O. F. J. Seitz, 'Relationship of the Shepherd of Hermas to the Epistle of James', *JBL* 63 (1944), 131–40; Seitz, 'Antecedents and Signification of the Term ΔΙΨΥΧΟΣ', *JBL* 66 (1947), 211–19; Seitz, 'Afterthoughts on the Term "Dipsychos"', *NTS* 4 (1958), 327–34.

[29] See here, also *1 Clem.* 11.2; Herm. *Mand.* 9.5: οἱ γὰρ διστάζοντες εἰς τὸν θεόν, οὗτοί εἰσιν οἱ δίψυχοι ('for those who have doubts towards God, these are the double-minded'), virtually defining the 'double-minded' as those who 'doubt'; also Jas. 1.(6-)8.

[30] cf. Jas. 4.8; Herm. *Mand.* 9.7: καθάρισον οὖν τὴν καρδίαν σου ἀπὸ τῆς διψυχίας ('purify your heart from double-mindedness'; the whole of *Mand.* 9 is concerned with 'double-mindedness': see Osiek, *Hermas*, 30–2 for this theme in Hermas generally, and 130–4 on *Mand.* 9). Hence too the reference to 'heart' here in *2 Clement* is more likely to be original than *1 Clement*'s 'soul': see n. 6 above.

[31] Presumably the author of this citation did not coin the word out of thin air!

about long ago,³² in³³ the time of the 'fathers'; but we have waited 'day after day' (ἡμέραν ἐξ ἡμέρας)³⁴ and seen none of them.

There is a parallel in terms of ideas in the words of the scoffers in 2 Pet. 3.4, doubting the reality of the hope of the parousia.³⁵ However, apart from the common reference to the 'fathers', and the general ideas in common, there is little verbal agreement; hence it is unlikely that the citation itself and 2 Peter are directly related.³⁶ However, it may be noteworthy that the language of *2 Clement* here, precisely at points where it differs from *1 Clement* in relation to this citation, is close to that of 2 Peter elsewhere (cf. above on ὁ προφητικὸς λόγος (cf. 2 Pet. 1.19) and ἡμέραν ἐξ ἡμέρας (cf. 2 Pet. 2.8)). It seems unlikely that the author of 2 Peter would be so influenced by a possible source at his disposal to echo the language associated with it in widely different contexts; but it may be more plausible to envisage the author of *2 Clement* as influenced by the wording of a text such as 2 Peter, perhaps already becoming part of a 'scriptural' 'canon', as influencing the language of a Christian writer. It may be then that *2 Clement* provides a relatively early witness to the existence, and use, of 2 Peter in early Christianity.³⁷

3 The citation continues with an exhortation to consider the natural world, in particular the growth of a vine. The progression from shedding its leaf, forming the bud, the unripe grape, and then the full bunch of grapes is certain. Unlike the use of the citation in *1 Clement* where it is the imminence of the future events that is stressed, here it is their certainty that is the primary focus.

4 The application of the analogy in the citation is now made explicit in relation to the experience of 'my people'. In the original, this may have referred to the nation Israel, perhaps suffering during the exile in Egypt and/or in the wilderness wanderings;³⁸ here it is probably taken as referring to the Christian church (cf. 2.3). However, the reference to the 'tumults and afflictions' (ἀκαταστασίας καὶ θλίψεις) experienced by God's people seems somewhat alien in the present context, both in *2 Clement* and in the rest of

---

[32] For the reading πάλαι here, see n. 7 above.

[33] The καί preceding the ἐπί is probably epexegetic.

[34] The phrase is unusual, though said by Knopf to be 'good Greek' (Knopf, *Zwei Clemensbriefe*, 169, referring e.g. to Euripides, *Rhes.* 445–6; cf. too Gen. 39.10; Num. 30.15). The phrase is also used in 2 Pet. 2.8 and provides another small, but not indistinctive, linguistic parallel between the language of *2 Clement* here and that of 2 Peter.

[35] See e.g. Lindemann, *Clemensbriefe*, 233; Pratscher, *Zweite Clemensbrief*, 154.

[36] *Pace* Bauckham, *Jude, 2 Peter*, 284, who claims that the texts are close enough to suggest that 2 Peter is here dependent on the source cited in 1 and *2 Clement*.

[37] cf. Lightfoot, *Apostolic Fathers*, 2.235, commenting on the phrase ἡμέραν ἐξ ἡμέρας: 'this additional coincidence of the passage quoted with the language of 2 Peter ... is worthy of notice. It seems hardly possible that the two can be wholly independent' (though he then goes on to say 'we have no means of determining their relation').

[38] *If* the text cited was originally of Jewish, non-Christian origin.

the citation itself (the vine is not necessarily 'suffering'!). The idea is not developed either by the author of 2 Clement: this suggests that this verse is still part of the citation (although it has no parallel in 1 Clement), though perhaps within the citation it functions as an explanatory gloss interpreting the 'parable' of the vine.[39] The final assurance that God's people 'will receive' (ἀπολήψεται future) good things is also slightly unexpected: if the analogy was with the people of God in the wilderness, one might have expected an assurance that they *did* receive the promises (in entering the promised land), as then the basis for the assurance given to the contemporary readers/hearers;[40] but one does not know the original context of the citation, so perhaps one cannot speculate too much.[41]

5 The writer now leaves the citation with a typical transitional ὥστε ἀδελφοί μου (cf. 4.3; 8.4; 10.1). He takes up the language of δίψυχος in the citation, exhorting his hearers directly not to be double-minded (μὴ διψυχῶμεν) but rather to be patient in hope, so that they may receive the rewards that are promised. The focus seems to be primarily on the judgement that is to come. The warning against being 'double-minded', and hence 'doubting', seems to relate exclusively to this (see above on v. 1). Thus where the citation may have in mind a more general denial of future hope and offers reassurance about the certainty of that hope, the author of 2 Clement uses the citation to relate, perhaps slightly more narrowly, to the certainty of future rewards (and punishments) on the basis of ethical behaviour now.[42]

6 The basis for the assertion of the reality of the future promise is now given (γάρ) in the claim that 'he who has promised ... is faithful' (πιστὸς γάρ ἐστιν ὁ ἐπαγγειλάμενος). The wording is almost identical with that of Heb. 10.23 (πιστὸς γὰρ ὁ ἐπαγγειλάμενος). However, it is uncertain whether one should make any claim about literary dependence on the basis of the parallel wording.[43] Statements about God/the Lord as faithful (πιστὸς ὁ θεός or πιστὸς ὁ + participle) are frequent in Jewish and Christian texts

---

[39] The reference to suffering experienced by the addressees is a standard part of apocalyptic writing. Cf. e.g. Luke 21.9; Mark 13.19. For v. 4 as (logically) secondary to vv. 2–3, cf. Lindemann, *Paulus*, 266; Pratscher, *Zweite Clemensbrief*, 152. However, this need not imply that the saying in v. 4 is taken by the author of 2 Clement from a source other than that used in vv. 2–3. The 'expansion' may well have occurred in the source already.

[40] Warns, 'Untersuchungen', 537.

[41] An apocalyptic text may have been written for a community suffering hardship in the present, and seeking to give hope for a future resolution of their troubles.

[42] In the immediate context of ch. 11 alone, the focus is all on the positive rewards in store; but in the context of ch. 11 following ch. 10, the focus is clearly also on the negative threat of punishment for the wicked.

[43] Direct dependence on Hebrews is claimed by Knopf, *Zwei Clemensbriefe*, 170; Lake, *Fathers*, 145, gives the English translation of the words in inverted commas. Wengst, *Zweite Clemensbrief*, 274; Lindemann, *Clemensbriefe*, 234; Pratscher, *Zweite Clemensbrief*, 156, and Gregory and Tuckett, '2 Clement', 290, are rather more sceptical.

(cf. e.g. Deut. 7.9; Ps. 144.13 LXX; 1 Cor. 1.9; 10.13; 1 Thess. 5.24, etc). The language has a liturgical sound to it,⁴⁴ and the substance of what is said here is as close to *1 Clem.* 27.1 (τῷ πιστῷ ἐν ταῖς ἐπαγγελίαις) as it is to Hebrews. It is thus doubtful if one can base anything about possible knowledge of Hebrews on this evidence.

God's faithfulness is shown here in being consistent in judging human beings on the basis of their behaviour. Men and women will receive the 'recompense' (ἀντιμισθία) for what they have done. The word has been used earlier for the response that human beings should give to God (1.3, 5; 9.7; 15.2); here it is the response that God will make to human beings.

God will then repay everyone for what they have done (ἀποδιδόναι ἑκάστῳ τῶν ἔργων αὐτοῦ). The language is again fairly stereotypical and parallels are easy to find (cf. e.g. Ps. 62.13; Matt. 16.27; Rom. 2.6): hence it is probably unnecessary to see here any direct literary influence of specific texts. The promise is a two-edged sword, offering both encouragement and threat: for those who behave ethically, there is encouragement; for those who do not, the promised 'recompense' represents a real threat in highly negative terms.⁴⁵

7 The author now sums up his argument of this section (which largely repeats the general theme running through the text as a whole: if we 'do righteousness' (i.e. if we are 'righteous', cf. v. 1 above), we will 'enter the kingdom' (cf. 9.6 for similar language used to refer to the rewards to come in the future for those who deserve them), and we will receive the promises 'which ear has not heard …'. The last phrase uses an apparently semi-proverbial saying widely attested elsewhere in Christian and non-Christian texts (see above) to refer to the wonderful nature of the rewards in store.⁴⁶

---

⁴⁴ So Wengst.
⁴⁵ So, rightly, Pratscher, *Zweite Clemensbrief*, 156, against Lindemann, *Clemensbriefe*, 234, who sees no threat and only 'hope' being expressed here.
⁴⁶ Warns, 'Untersuchungen', 548–9, argues that the 'citation' (if it is such) is used by the author here as part of his polemic against his Valentinian opponents who used the same citation: for this author, however, the 'promises, which eye has not seen and ear has not heard etc.' are for those who act 'righteously', and *not* on the basis of mystical experiences. This is theoretically possible, but it is hard to see any direct evidence for such a theory one way or the other.

Chapter 12

PARALLELS

2 Clem. 12.2, 6	Gos. Eg. (Clement, Strom. 3.92.2)	Gos. Thom. 22 (NHC II.2, 37.23–35)
² ἐπερωτηθεὶς γὰρ αὐτὸς ὁ κύριος ὑπό τινος, πότε ἥξει αὐτοῦ ἡ βασιλεία	πυνθανομένης τῆς Σαλώμης, πότε γνωσθήσεται τὰ περὶ ὧν ἤρετο,	ⲡⲉϫⲁⲩ ⲛⲁϥ ϫⲉ ⲉⲉⲓⲉⲛⲟ ⲛ̄ⲕⲟⲩⲉⲓ ⲧⲛ̄ⲛⲁⲃⲱⲕ ⲉϩⲟⲩⲛ ⲉⲧⲙⲛ̄ⲧⲉⲣⲟ
εἶπεν·	ἔφη ὁ κύριος ὅταν τὸ τῆς αἰσχύνης ἔνδυμα πατήσητε	ⲡⲉϫⲉ ⲓⲏ̅ⲥ̅ ⲛⲁⲩ ϫⲉ
ὅταν ἔσται τὰ δύο ἕν,	καὶ ὅταν γένηται τὰ δύο ἕν,	ϩⲟⲧⲁⲛ ⲉⲧⲉⲧⲛ̄ϣⲁⲣ̄ ⲡⲥⲛⲁⲩ ⲟⲩⲁ ⲁⲩⲱ ⲉⲧⲉⲧⲛ̄ϣⲁⲣ̄ ⲡⲥⲁ ⲛϩⲟⲩⲛ ⲛ̄ⲑⲉ ⲙ̄ⲡⲥⲁ ⲛⲃⲟⲗ ⲁⲩⲱ
καὶ τὸ ἔξω ὡς τὸ ἔσω,		ⲡⲥⲁ ⲛⲃⲟⲗ ⲛ̄ⲑⲉ ⲙ̄ⲡⲥⲁ ⲛϩⲟⲩⲛ ⲁⲩⲱ ⲡⲥⲁⲛⲧⲡⲉ ⲛ̄ⲑⲉ ⲙ̄ⲡⲥⲁ ⲙⲡⲓⲧⲛ̄ ⲁⲩⲱ
καὶ τὸ ἄρσεν μετὰ τῆς θηλείας	καὶ τὸ ἄρρεν μετὰ τῆς θηλείας,	ϣⲓⲛⲁ ⲉⲧⲉⲧⲛⲁⲉⲓⲣⲉ ⲙ̄ⲫⲟⲟⲩⲧ ⲙⲛ̄ ⲧⲥϩⲓⲙⲉ ⲙ̄ⲡⲓⲟⲩⲁ ⲟⲩⲱⲧ ϫⲉⲕⲁⲁⲥ
οὔτε ἄρσεν οὔτε θῆλυ.	οὔτε ἄρρεν οὔτε θῆλυ	ⲛⲉ ⲫⲟⲟⲩⲧ ⲣ̄ ϩⲟⲟⲩⲧ ⲛ̄ⲧⲉ ⲧⲥϩⲓⲙⲉ ⲣ̄ ⲥϩⲓⲙⲉ ϩⲟⲧⲁⲛ ⲉⲧⲉⲧⲛ̄ϣⲁⲉⲓⲣⲉ ⲛ̄ϩⲛ̄ⲃⲁⲗ ⲉⲡⲙⲁ ⲛ̄ⲟⲩⲃⲁⲗ ⲁⲩⲱ ⲟⲩϭⲓϫ ⲉⲡⲙⲁ ⲛ̄ⲛⲟⲩϭⲓϫ ⲁⲩⲱ ⲟⲩⲉⲣⲏⲧⲉ ⲉⲡⲙⲁ ⲛ̄ⲟⲩⲉⲣⲏⲧⲉ ⲟⲩϩⲓⲕⲱⲛ ⲉⲡⲙⲁ ⲛ̄ⲟⲩϩⲓⲕⲱⲛ ⲧⲟⲧⲉ
⁶ ἐλεύσεται ἡ βασιλεία τοῦ πατρός μου		ⲧⲉⲧⲛⲁⲃⲱⲕ ⲉϩⲟⲩⲛ ⲉⲧⲙⲛ̄ⲧⲉⲣⲟ

²For when the Lord himself was asked by someone when his kingdom would come, he said,	When Salome enquired when she would know the things about which she had asked, The Lord said, 'When you tread on the garment of shame, and	They said to him, 'Shall we then, as children, enter the kingdom?' Jesus said to them,
'When the two are one,	when the two become one,	'When you make the two one, and when you make the inside like the outside and
and the outside like the inside,		the outside like the inside, and the above like the below,
and the male with the female	and when the male with the female	and when you make the male and the female one and the same, so that the male not be male nor the
neither male nor female',	is neither male nor female	female female; and you fashion eyes in the place of an eye, and a hand in the place of a hand, and a foot in the place of a foot and a likeness in the place of a likeness;
⁶'the kingdom of my Father will come.'		then will you enter the kingdom

In v. 2, continued in v. 6 (see below), the author of *2 Clement* gives a citation of a response of 'the Lord' to a questioner. The saying cited in v. 2 is then expounded in detail in vv. 3–5. The citation is clearly related to traditions preserved elsewhere in two early Christian texts: one is a saying recorded by Clement of Alexandria who claims that it (*a*) was used by the Gnostic Julius Cassianus to support his own (encratite) views, and (*b*) does not come from any of the four (canonical) gospels but is from the *Gospel of the Egyptians*; the other is a saying recorded in *Gos. Thom.* 22. The synopsis above makes it clear that the three versions are closely related to each other.[1]

---

[1] Discussion of the parallels is found in all the commentaries, especially Pratscher, *Zweite Clemensbrief*, 161–4; also Donfried, *Setting*, 73–7; T. Baarda, '2 Clement 12 and the Sayings of Jesus', in J. Delobel (ed.), *Logia. Les Paroles de Jésus—The Sayings of Jesus*, BETL 59 (Leuven: Peeters, 1982), 529–56; Warns, 'Untersuchungen', 432–7, 457–65; Petersen, 'Textual Traditions', 35–8. Baarda's treatment is the most extensive.

The precise extent of the citation is debated: in particular, opinions are divided on whether to include v. 6 in the citation or not. V. 6a is almost certainly the author's own summary of his interpretation which he gives in vv. 3–5; but the status of v. 6b is less clear. Prior to the discovery of *Gos. Thom.*, this extra clause was sometimes regarded as a conclusion added by the author of *2 Clement*. However, the presence of a similar conclusion (including the reference to the kingdom) in what is clearly an alternative version of the same basic saying in *Gos. Thom.* makes this theory less likely. The use of φησίν in *2 Clem.* 12.6 is ambiguous: it could signify a resumption of the explicit citation of the tradition,[2] or it could indicate the author's own interpretation of the cited tradition. However, the reference here to the kingdom as belonging to '*my* Father' suggests strongly that this is a continuation of the saying. It would be highly unusual for the author of *2 Clement* to refer to God specifically as 'his' Father (rather than e.g. 'our' Father). On the other hand, it fits perfectly well if it is seen as (continuing and resuming) a saying of Jesus (cf. 3.2; 9.11, both in sayings attributed to Jesus). Further, some kind of conclusion seems to be demanded by the structure of the saying: the earlier ὅταν clauses function as an extended protasis which requires an apodosis to complete it. Hence v. 6b should probably be taken as part of the citation here.[3]

The three versions of the saying are close enough to suggest that they reflect a common tradition (e.g. all three agree in having the clauses about 'the two becoming one', and about 'the male with the female' and 'neither male nor female'); however, the differences between them are such that it is very unlikely that there is any direct literary relationship involved. In fact any two pairs of witnesses exhibit agreements against the third. Thus, the version in *2 Clement* agrees with the version in *Gos. Thom.* against *Gos. Eg.* in

(i) framing the citation with references to the kingdom at the start and the finish;
(ii) including the clause about the outside becoming as the inside;
(iii) not including the clause about 'trampling on the garments of shame'. (However, *Gos. Thom.* has a version of this saying elsewhere (*Gos. Thom.* 37), suggesting that the saying may have been originally

---

[2] cf. 7.6 where it is the (sole) introduction to the citation of Isa. 66.24.
[3] See Baarda, '2 Clement 12', 547–9; also e.g. Donfried, *Setting*, 75; Warns, 'Untersuchungen', 436–7; Lohmann, *Drohung*, 121; Ehrman, *Fathers*, 185. *Contra* e.g. Lightfoot, *Apostolic Fathers*, 2.240; Knopf, *Zwei Clemensbriefe*, 171 (in his translation he implies it is a citation, but does not interpret it as such); Lake, *Fathers*, 149; Köster, *Synoptische Überlieferung*, 103; Wengst, *Zweite Clemensbrief*, 274. Lindemann, *Clemensbriefe*, 237, and Pratscher, *Zweite Clemensbrief*, 167, leave the question open. Pratscher says that the issue does not make any substantial difference to the interpretation of the text: this may be so, though the issue does affect the extent to which the text of *2 Clement* here is to be seen as agreeing or disagreeing with the parallel versions.

independent and was only secondarily combined with the present saying in the version in *Gos. Eg.*)[4]

On the other hand, the *2 Clement* version has a number of *dis*agreements with the version in *Gos. Thom.*, and shows more agreement with the version in *Gos. Eg.* in

(i) having the speaker as 'the Lord';
(ii) making the saying a response to an enquiry by an individual ('someone' in *2 Clement*, 'Salome' in *Gos. Eg.*);[5]
(iii) lacking the extra clauses in *Gos. Thom.* about the inside being as the outside (and the outside as the inside), about the above being as the below, the reference to a 'single one', the extra clauses about the eye, hand, foot, and image;
(iv) it also talks about the kingdom 'coming', rather than 'entering' the kingdom.

Given all the disagreements, as well as agreements, it is very hard to claim that there is a direct literary relationship between any of the three texts. The longer version in *Gos. Thom.* may have undergone secondary expansion and is not the source of the version in *2 Clement*.[6] The presence of the extra clause in the version in *Gos. Eg.* (about trampling garments of shame) suggests that this version too has undergone some secondary expansion by combining what were probably two independent sayings earlier in the history of the tradition, as well as by naming the (perhaps previously anonymous) questioner as Salome. We thus have in the three witnesses evidence of a freely floating tradition of a saying of Jesus; and of all the three versions, the version in *2 Clement* probably represents the earliest form.[7]

In particular, the author of *2 Clement* was not dependent on *Gos. Eg.* here. Such a theory has been popular in the past, partly to explain this particular text in *2 Clement*, and sometimes then used to explain other—if not all—quotations of the Jesus tradition in *2 Clement* not deriving from canonical sources.[8] The analysis above suggests that the version of this saying in

---

[4] The existence of a seam in the tradition here may also be indicated by the fact that the verb in this clause is in the second-person plural, whereas in the rest of the saying in *Gos. Eg.*, the verbs are in the third-person singular: see Baarda, '2 Clement 12', 542.

[5] The explicit identification of the questioner in *Gos. Eg.* (as 'Salome', often named as the dialogue partner in some of the extant fragments of *Gos. Eg.*) may be a secondary development: it is often regarded as a feature of the developing tradition to give specific names to anonymous figures.

[6] See Donfried, *Setting*, 76; Baarda, '2 Clement 12', 547.

[7] So Baarda, '2 Clement 12', 547. See too Koester, *Ancient Christian Gospels*, 359; Pratscher, *Zweite Clemensbrief*, 163.

[8] cf. above on the citations in 4.5; 5.2; 8.5, and see p. 41 above and Introduction §8.1.4 above (on Egypt as the place of writing).

Gos. Eg. is rather more developed than that in *2 Clement*: hence it is very unlikely to have been the immediate source of the latter. Whether the sayings cited by the author of *2 Clement* come from a unified single ('gospel') source is another issue (see p. 41 above.) But it is very unlikely that *Gos. Eg.*, at least in any form identifiable on the basis of the extant evidence which we now possess, was any such source used by the author of *2 Clement*.

COMMENTARY

1 The opening exhortation takes up the language of the 'kingdom' from the end of the previous chapter (11.7). The language changes slightly: no longer is it a matter of entering the kingdom, but of waiting for it. This 'waiting' is to be καθ' ὥραν. The precise meaning of the phrase is not certain, and may depend on (and/or determine) how far the author of *2 Clement* had an expectation of the End as imminent. Strictly speaking the phrase would imply this;[9] but elsewhere in the text, the author seems to think in terms of a longer, rather than a shorter, period before the End (cf. 20.3).[10] Also the discussion in the present chapter is about how to behave in the period before the End comes, and this too might fit better if the author were not thinking of a very short time. Hence καθ' ὥραν here may mean something like 'constantly'.[11]

This time of 'waiting' must be one of 'love and righteousness'. This states in general terms the theme running throughout *2 Clement*, emphasizing the importance of ethical behaviour ('righteousness', cf. 4.2; 6.9 for 'righteousness' as the required ethical behaviour), here also clarified as 'love' (cf. 4.3; 9.6 for similar exhortations to 'love'). This emphasis on ethical behaviour is what governs the 'exegesis' of the Jesus saying which now follows.

A further reason is given for the importance of behaving properly: 'we do not know the day' when the End will come. Again, this would fit rather better with a model whereby the author does *not* think that the End is about to come very soon. The End is here said to be 'the day of the appearance of God' (τὴν ἡμέραν τῆς ἐπιφανείας τοῦ θεοῦ). In the NT, the word ἐπιφανεία to refer to the Parousia comes mostly in the Pastorals (e.g. 1 Tim. 6.14; 2 Tim. 4.1, 8; Tit. 2.13) and is always with reference to Christ. (Cf. too 17.4 here, where

---

[9] Cf. e.g. Lindemann, *Clemensbriefe*, 235: 'eine zeitliche Naherwartung' ('a temporally imminent expectation'); also Donfried, *Setting*, 151: 12.1 implies 'the nearness of the kingdom'.

[10] Though this comes in the section 19.1–20.4, which *may* be a secondary addition to the text by another author: see Introduction §5. Literary Unity.

[11] cf. BAG, 904; also Wengst, *Zweite Clemensbrief*, 253; Baarda, '2 Clement 12', 531–2; Lohmann, *Drohung*, 116; Pratscher, *Zweite Clemensbrief*, 159. Lohmann speaks of a 'Stetserwartung' rather than a 'Naherwartung' (a 'constant expectation', rather than an 'imminent expectation', of the End).

the 'appearance' is probably that of Christ.)¹² Whether one should presume the same here and infer an implicit reference to Jesus as 'God' is, however, uncertain. The author generally works with a fairly naïve, and not clearly thought out, identity (at least a functional identity) between Jesus and God (cf. 1.1, and see below on v. 2 on the kingdom as Jesus' kingdom), so that what can be said of Jesus can also be said of God and vice versa (but without necessarily identifying the two ontologically). Hence it may be best to take the words here at face value and see a reference to the End time as involving the ἐπιφάνεια of God (rather than a reference to the appearance of Jesus, with Jesus described as θεός). The question about lack of knowledge of the time of the End is also a feature of a number of traditions in the synoptic gospels, including some of the parables (cf. Mark 13.35–8; Luke 12.35–46; Matt. 25.1–13, etc.), all of which also include exhortations to behave appropriately in the intervening period.

2 Further justification for the answer given to the problem in v. 1, especially the reference to 'love and righteousness', is now given by citing a saying of Jesus about the coming of the kingdom.

The author clearly attributes very great significance to the saying cited, but also may show awareness that the saying is potentially obscure, or perhaps ambiguous in its meaning. He thus provides a detailed, phrase-by-phrase interpretation of each part of the saying in vv. 3–5. The manner of interpretation is very similar to the interpretation of the text from Isa. 54.1 given in 2.1–3. The author thus treats the Jesus tradition in the same way as Jewish scripture, where each phrase has meaning and this meaning is to be carefully expounded. The care with which the saying is interpreted here *may* also be due to the saying's being used by the author's 'opponents' in a rather different way, to justify their own position and views. However, certainty on this is not possible.¹³

It is hard to know what the 'original' intention and meaning of the saying might have been. Much depends on the context in which the saying is placed. It seems very unlikely that the saying is to be traced all the way back to the historical Jesus.¹⁴ The language of the two becoming one, and of there being

---

¹² For the background to the use of the word in the Hellenistic world, see Dibelius and Conzelmann, *Pastoral Epistles*, 104; also D. Lührmann, 'Epiphaneia. Zur Bedeutungsgeschichte eines griechischen Wortes', in G. Jeremias, H.-W. Kuhn, and H. Stegemann (eds), *Tradition und Glaube. Das frühe Christentum in seiner Umwelt. Festgabe für K.G. Kuhn* (Göttingen: Vandenhoeck & Ruprecht, 1971), 185–99. The forward-looking reference distinguishes the Christian usage generally from that in the Hellenistic world.

¹³ See below. However, it has never been suggested that the detailed, phrase-by-phrase interpretation of Isa. 54 in 2.1–3 is due to the presence of competing interpretations of the same text!

¹⁴ *Pace* T. Callan, 'The Saying of Jesus in Gos. Thom. 22/2 Clem. 12/Gos. Eg. 5', *JRelS* 16 (1990), 46–64, whose chief argument is simply that the saying is multiple-attested in three independent sources. For Callan, the 'two becoming one' is simply a call to the unity of all people.

no longer male and female, is paralleled in one way in Gal. 3.28; however, it seems to be more specific here, and apparently refers to the abolition of all real distinctions between the sexes so that human beings become asexual, without gender. This would be congenial to at least some strands of Gnostic and/or encratite thought.[15] As such, this might well fit in the contexts of the saying as preserved by Julius Cassianus and in *Gos. Thom.*

However, any such ideas are quite different from those adopted by the author here. For our author, the saying is interpreted in a radically ethical manner, referring to the ethical behaviour that is expected of Christians living alongside each other. At times, this leads to a highly artificial interpretation that barely fits the wording of the citation (cf. below on v. 4), and seems to be imposed quite forcefully on the text. (This in turn might then fit with the theory that the text was being used by others in a very different way, since the text in itself does not seem very well suited to make the point the author wants to make: hence he may have felt forced to use this text because others are using the same text to say something rather different. This is, however, not at all certain and there is no direct evidence for it.)[16]

3 The first phrase is about 'two' being 'one'. Here this is interpreted in a way unconnected with any abolition of sexual differentiation. Rather, it is (simply) interpreted as relating to one's neighbour with integrity, honesty, and openness. 'Two are one' when the readers/hearers 'speak with one

---

[15] cf. Baarda, '2 Clement 12', 555; Lindemann, *Clemensbriefe*, 236; Pratscher, *Zweite Clemensbrief*, 164.

[16] For such a theory, see Donfried, *Setting*, 152–3; and in massive detail Warns, 'Untersuchungen', esp. 448–51. Both argue that the saying was used in a 'Gnostic' sense, and that the author's interpretation here seeks to counter this. Both appeal to Valentinian ideas of the pneumatics (the 'female') joining with their heavenly angelic counterparts (the 'male') in some kind of syzygy or union, perhaps in some kind of sacramental rite (of the 'bridal chamber'); for Donfried too the emphasis in such Gnostic interpretation would be on the possibility of attaining the kingdom in the present, which the author here vehemently rejects with his insistence that the kingdom is future. Thus, for this author, 'the kingdom is not a present spiritual phenomenon, but . . . it is future'; the author '"de-gnosticizes" the text in terms which are completely on the moral and ethical plane'.

The difficulty of such a theory, especially in the details given, is that so much has to be read into the text. There is no explicit reference to a Valentinian sacrament of the bridal chamber (as Warns himself at one point concedes: cf. p. 450), and there is no hint of such an idea being opposed in what the author here actually says. So too, the issue does not necessarily seem to be specifically the temporal one (the kingdom as future here, as opposed to present as claimed by others): rather, it is *assumed* that the kingdom is to come, and the issue is how to behave in the present. (See too Baarda, '2 Clement 12', 531–2, specifically against Donfried.) Indeed it could be contended that the author himself argues for a potentially present kingdom by the end: if people behave in the way recommended, then the kingdom 'will come': see below on v. 6. In any case, the thrust of the exhortation in v. 5 on how men and women should relate to each other (as well as the general insistence on 'good works' in v. 4) suggests that the author here is more concerned about sexual and/or general moral licence than about esoteric Gnostic sacramental rites (and also encratite sexual abstention).

another[17] in truth', without any hypocrisy, so that the two 'bodies' become 'one soul'.[18] Any idea of 'unity' is thus solely at the level of agreement in thought. As elsewhere in *2 Clement*, the issue of personal relationships within the community seems to be of primary importance (cf. the earlier references to 'loving one another' (e.g. 4.3) and the importance of loving 'one another' quite as much as one's enemies (13.4)).

4 The 'outside being as the inside' is now interpreted by defining the 'inside' as the soul, and the 'outside' as the body. The application that is then made is via the themes of 'good works' and the (assumed) visibility of what is 'outside'. This is also coupled with the assumption that 'good works' are to be ascribed to the soul and not the body. With all these assumptions, the claim is then made that, as the body is visible, so the soul should also be made visible by the 'good works' which it does.

The application is extremely forced. As several have noted, the interpretation seems to presume a text which says the opposite of what the cited text actually says: what the writer needs to make his point is a text which has the 'inside being as the outside'.[19] This might perhaps strengthen the theory that the text being interpreted here is one that is 'given' to the author: it is not of his own choosing and he has to make a highly artificial and forced interpretation of it to make it fit with his own ideas.[20] But, as noted above, the details of any competing interpretation are not hinted at in any way.

5 The clause about male and female is similarly interpreted in a radically ethical way. Any suggestion that the saying might imply the abolition of gender differences is implicitly suppressed. According to this author, what the saying means is that men and women should not have any 'thoughts' about the other sex—by implication one should not have any sexual desires for someone of the other sex.

It is not clear whether this is meant in a totally radical, and hence encratite, way (one should not entertain any sexual thoughts or desires for anyone) or

---

[17] ἑαυτοῖς for ἀλλήλοις: cf. BDF §287.

[18] The thought and language are not far removed from Eph. 4.25, which exhorts readers to 'speak the truth to each other', because they are 'members one of another' (recalling the imagery of the community as the 'body'). See Baarda, '2 Clement 12', 535. But whether the author of *2 Clement* is deliberately echoing the language of 'Paul' is not certain. For classical examples of the language, see Warns, 'Untersuchungen', 569–70.

[19] And indeed the Syriac version 'cites' this part of the saying in this form; but this is almost certainly a secondary alleviation of the difficulty (as well as being poorly attested with both the Greek MSS having the text as given above): see Pratscher, *Zweite Clemensbrief*, 165. Codex C apparently attempts to 'resolve' the difficulty by exchanging the identification of soul/body with inside/outside: it reads that the soul is the 'outside' and the body the 'inside'. But this is equally difficult: the correlation is extremely unnatural, as well as destroying the obvious link between what is 'outside' with what is 'visible'. For the artificiality in the author's 'exegesis' here, see Knopf, *Zwei Clemensbriefe*, 171; Baarda, '2 Clement 12', 535–6.

[20] See 2.1; 11.2–4; 14.2–4, for possibly similar examples of texts having to be forced to make them fit with the author's argument.

in a limited way (one should not entertain such thoughts in an improper way, i.e. outside the limits of marriage—but within marriage normal sexual activity would be accepted and affirmed).²¹ However, nowhere else does the author of *2 Clement* clearly suggest a completely ascetic sexual lifestyle as being the desired norm. And as noted above (on 4.3; 6.4), the condemning of 'adultery' would be odd if full sexual relations within marriage were regarded as undesirable. A radically encratite reading is probably appropriate for the text in the earlier tradition (as well as in the context of *Gos. Eg.* and *Gos. Thom.*).²² But given that the author is interpreting another text whose wording is not his own (and evidently does not easily fit with what he wants to say: see above on v. 4), he may well be struggling to give a rather different interpretation. Hence, in view of the evidence of the rest of *2 Clement*, the author is here probably seeking to condemn (only) *inappropriate* sexual relations, rather than sexual activity in toto.²³

6 The conclusion is now drawn. When men and women do 'these things', then (and apparently only then) the kingdom will come. The words in v. 6b are probably the completion of the citation given in v. 2 (see above).

At one level, this confirms the interpretation offered above of v. 1 as not necessarily implying a vivid expectation of an imminent End. Language about the coming of the kingdom as in some sense conditional upon human behaviour is not unprecedented.²⁴ Others have contested such an idea as present here on the grounds that the author himself has said in v. 1 that the time of the coming of the End is unknown to everyone; and in any case the coming of the kingdom is a gift of God fulfilling his promise, not a matter of any human achievement.²⁵ Perhaps though one should not drive a wedge too strongly between the two. Judaism and Christianity are at times capable of holding together different kinds of language which seem on the surface to be mutually contradictory but nevertheless are both maintained: hence the kingdom's arrival is purely a matter of God's decision and timing, but also, proper human response and behaviour are a necessary prerequisite.

---

²¹ For the former, cf. Knopf, *Zwei Clemensbriefe*, 171; Windisch, 'Christentum', 132; Lindemann, *Clemensbriefe*, 236; Pratscher, *Zweite Clemensbrief*, 166. For the latter, cf. Wengst, *Zweite Clemensbrief*, 231; Baarda, '2 Clement 12', 537; Lohmann, *Drohung*, 120.

²² See e.g. Baarda, '2 Clement 12', 555–6.

²³ cf. too Baarda, '2 Clement 12', 537, who sees the references to love and righteousness in v. 1 as the key to the author's interpretation: men and women are to love each other in a 'righteous' way: which means that full sexual relations and desires are entirely acceptable and appropriate within marriage, but not outside.

²⁴ Knopf, *Zwei Clemensbriefe*, 171, with reference to W. Bousset, *Die Religion des Judentums im späthellenistischen Zeitalter, bearbeitet von H. Gressmann*, HNT 21 (Tübingen: Mohr Siebeck, 1926), 248–9 (with texts such as Sir. 36.10; *1 En.* 47.1; 97.3; *b.Sanh.* 97b: see Pratscher, *Zweite Clemensbrief*, 168).

²⁵ See Lindemann, *Clemensbriefe*, 237; supported by Pratscher (who notes Lindemann's objections as 'correct').

Whether there is any idea here of (at least potentially) a belief in the presence of the kingdom in this life is not certain.[26] It is not at all demanded by the wording here: the coming of the kingdom if/when people 'do' all things specified here does not mean that life lived in this way *is* the presence of the kingdom. The kingdom can still be future and thought of as following on after such a lifestyle is attained.

[26] It is mooted by Pratscher, *Zweite Clemensbrief*, 168.

Chapter 13

PARALLELS

2 Clem. 13.2	Isa. 52.5 LXX	Rom. 2.24
λέγει γὰρ ὁ κύριος·	τάδε λέγει κύριος	
διὰ παντὸς	δι' ὑμᾶς διὰ παντὸς	
τὸ ὄνομά μου	τὸ ὄνομά μου	τὸ γὰρ ὄνομα τοῦ θεοῦ
βλασφημεῖται	βλασφημεῖται	δι' ὑμᾶς βλασφημεῖται
ἐν πᾶσιν τοῖς ἔθνεσιν,	ἐν τοῖς ἔθνεσιν	ἐν τοῖς ἔθνεσιν,
		καθὼς γέγραπται.
καὶ πάλιν· οὐαὶ δι' ὃν		
βλασφημεῖται τὸ ὄνομά		
μου.		

Ign. *Trall.* 8.2: οὐαὶ γάρ δι' οὗ ἐπὶ ματαιότητι τὸ ὄνομά μου ἐπί τινων βλασφημεῖται

For woe to the one through whom my name is blasphemed in vain among some.

Pol. *Phil.* 10.3: vae autem, per quem nomen domini blasphematur

For woe to the one through whom the name of the Lord is blasphemed.

Apos. Con. 1.10.1: οὐαὶ γάρ, φησίν, δι' οὗ τὸ ὄνομά μου βλασφημεῖται ἐν τοῖς ἔθνεσιν (cf. too 3.5.6)

For woe, it says, to the one through whom my name is blasphemed among the Gentiles

2 Clem. 13.2 gives (probably) two citations, introduced as sayings of 'the Lord' which could be a reference to God or to Jesus (see below). The first is a citation of Isa. 52.5, a text also cited by Paul in Rom. 2.24 (see above). Nothing, however, suggests that the author of *2 Clement* was dependent on Paul:[1] the version cited here agrees almost exactly with the wording of

---

[1] See Lindemann, *Paulus*, 238; Gregory, in Gregory and Tuckett, '*2 Clement*', 281.

the LXX.² Certainly the version given in *2 Clement* shows no agreement with Paul in the (very tiny) differences which occur between the LXX version and that of Romans (e.g. 'the name of God' for 'my name'). Thus the author here gives a straightforward quotation of the text in Isa. 52.5, following the LXX wording very closely.

In the second half of v. 2, the author of *2 Clement* gives a second citation, introduced by καὶ πάλιν.³ The saying is in the form of a woe with language very similar to that of Isa. 52.5. There is no known text in Jewish or Christian scripture with precisely this wording. However, a very similar saying is found in other early Christian literature, e.g. Ign. *Trall.* 8.2; Pol. *Phil.* 10.3; *Apos. Con.* 1.10.1; 3.5.6 (see above). It would appear then that a saying in this form was known in early Christian circles, possibly appended to Isa. 52.5 and backing up what is said there with a 'woe' against the people involved in 'blaspheming the name'.

There is also a slight uncertainty, connected with a textual variant, about where the citation ends. At the end of the verse, C reads 'when you do not do what I want' (ἐν τῷ μὴ ποιεῖν ὑμᾶς ἃ βούλουμαι), whereas S implies a reading 'when we do not do what we say' (ἐν τῷ μὴ ποιεῖν ἡμᾶς ἃ λέγομεν). The C reading seems to presume that the citation runs through to the end of the verse (it would be quite out of character for the author suddenly to refer to his own personal 'wishes' in this context). However, the S reading fits better with the author's overall style and ideas (stressing the importance of 'doing', as well as using the first-person plural), and also provides a clear application of the text(s) cited just before. The C reading would leave the citation(s) without a clear application; it would also mean that this version of the second citation was unlike all other attested versions of the saying (which just have the simple woe). Hence it is preferable to accept the S reading,

---

² There is no δι' ὑμᾶς (in C; S has an equivalent, but is probably assimilating to the LXX text). It is possible that the preceding clause in v. 1 reflects these words (S δι' ἡμᾶς, C δι' ὑμᾶς: C has a propensity to change first persons to second persons and hence the S reading here may be preferable). See Warns, 'Untersuchungen', 506. *2 Clement* also has πᾶσιν with 'the Gentiles' (so C; S omits, perhaps assimilating to the LXX wording), but this may be an independent addition, cf. Deut. 4.27; Ps. 81.8 LXX; Tob. 3.4 א etc: see Warns, 'Untersuchungen', 507; Pratscher, *Zweite Clemensbrief*, 172.

³ The text is not absolutely certain. Instead of πάλιν· οὐαὶ δι' ὅν, C has simply διό. This has the effect of making the author virtually repeat the words of the Isaiah text as a single citation repeating the clause about 'my name' being blasphemed. This seems to make less sense, and hence it is very widely accepted that the S reading, implying a second citation with a 'woe' following, is more original. See Lightfoot, *Apostolic Fathers*, 2.241–2; Wengst, *Zweite Clemensbrief*, 254; Lindemann, *Clemensbriefe*, 238; Pratscher, *Zweite Clemensbrief*, 172. The reading is accepted by all the printed editions (e.g. Gebhardt–Harnack, Funk–Bihlmeyer, Lake, Ehrman, etc.).

and to take the second citation (as with the other parallels) as containing only the woe.[4]

2 Clem. 13.4	Matt. 5	Luke 6
... λέγει ὁ θεός· οὐ χάρις ὑμῖν, εἰ ἀγαπᾶτε τοὺς ἀγαπῶντας ὑμᾶς, ἀλλὰ χάρις ὑμῖν,	[46] ἐὰν γὰρ ἀγαπήσητε τοὺς ἀγαπῶντας ὑμᾶς, τίνα μισθὸν ἔχετε;	[32] καὶ εἰ ἀγαπᾶτε τοὺς ἀγαπῶντας ὑμᾶς, ποία ὑμῖν χάρις ἐστίν;
	[44] ἐγὼ δὲ λέγω ὑμῖν,	[27] ἀλλὰ ὑμῖν λέγω τοῖς ἀκούουσιν,
εἰ ἀγαπᾶτε τοὺς ἐχθροὺς καὶ τούς μισοῦντας ὑμᾶς·	ἀγαπᾶτε τοὺς ἐχθροὺς ὑμῶν	ἀγαπᾶτε τοὺς ἐχθροὺς ὑμῶν, καλῶς ποιεῖτε τοῖς μισοῦσιν ὑμᾶς, [28] εὐλογεῖτε τοὺς καταρωμένους ὑμᾶς,
	καὶ προσεύχεσθε ὑπὲρ τῶν διωκόντων ὑμᾶς,	προσεύχεσθε περὶ τῶν ἐπηρεαζόντων ὑμᾶς

The introductory formula here attributes what is said to 'God' (see below). The words which follow provide a clear echo of the demand to love one's enemies in Matt. 5//Luke 6 in the Jesus tradition, though there is clearly no verbatim repetition of the synoptic texts. There is, for example, nothing explicit here of any contrast between those who follow such an ethic and Gentiles or sinners. However, a vestige of the synoptic tradition may still be apparent in the language of χάρις that is used here. Further, this may be of considerable significance in that this language is closely parallel to the Lukan version of the tradition, and moreover, this may well be due to LkR at this point in Luke.[5] Thus the language of *2 Clement* here appears to presuppose Luke's redactional work and hence Luke's finished gospel. In addition, *2 Clement* agrees with Luke in exhorting the readers/hearers to love those who 'hate' them, aligning again with Luke against the wording in Matthew. It is not certain if Luke's language here is redactional or not; but given the earlier

---

[4] The C reading, hence also presuming a longer form of the citation, is accepted by e.g. Schubert, '2. Clemensbrief', 252; Knopf, *Zwei Clemensbriefe*, 172; W.C. van Unnik, 'Die Rücksicht auf die Reaktion der Nicht-Christen als Motiv in der altchristlichen Paränese', in W. Eltester (ed.), *Judentum. Urchristentum. Kirche. Festschrift für J. Jeremias*, BZNW 26 (Berlin: Töpelmann, 1960), 224. The S reading is accepted by Wengst, *Zweite Clemensbrief*, 275; Lindemann, *Clemensbriefe*, 238; Pratscher, *Zweite Clemensbrief*, 172–3. Lightfoot, *Apostolic Fathers*, 2.242, accepts the C reading but says that the last line is no longer part of the citation: however, this makes the first-person singular βούλομαι extremely difficult.

[5] See Robinson, Hoffmann, and Kloppenborg, *Critical Edition*, 68, 70; Schulz, *Spruchquelle*, 129; F. Bovon, *Luke 1*, Hermeneia (Minneapolis: Fortress, 2002), 237, and many others.

agreement between *2 Clement* and the (probably) LkR reference to χάρις, it seems most likely that *2 Clement* is again showing some dependence (direct or indirect) on the Lukan form of the tradition.

It is true that *2 Clement* does not display verbatim agreement with Luke's text,[6] but the most 'economical' interpretation of the evidence is that *2 Clement* is here presupposing Luke's version of the command to love one's enemies, possibly 'citing' it somewhat loosely (perhaps from memory).[7] On the other hand, certainty is impossible and it may be that the immediate origin of the saying for the author of *2 Clement* is another source (perhaps another 'gospel' text); but that source, it would seem, must presuppose the finished gospel of Luke. It cannot be a source which is independent of the synoptic gospel tradition.

COMMENTARY

1 With the introductory ἀδελφοὶ οὖν,[8] the author draws the conclusion from what he has said in 12.1 about the End: we should 'at last' (ἤδη ποτέ cf. Phil. 4.10) 'repent' (cf. 8.1–3; 9.8; 16.1, 4; 17.1; 19.1). As before, the exhortation is primarily to an actual change in behaviour (rather than to remorse about the past, which might then lead to a subsequent change). This is then expanded with an exhortation to be 'sober' or 'self-controlled' or 'alert'[9] (νήψωμεν). The word is used metaphorically in the NT quite often, especially in eschatological contexts, to refer to the readiness which Christians must display in the light of the coming End (cf. 1 Thess. 5.6, 8; 2 Tim. 4.5; 1 Pet. 1.13; 4.7; 5.8; cf. too Ign. *Pol.* 2.3). The exhortation is for 'the good', again probably referring to the actual behaviour required or expected.

The reason is then spelt out: 'we'[10] are full of much 'foolishness and evil' (ἀνοίας καὶ πονηρίας). The latter word is very general. Whether one can read more into the word ἀνοία here is not certain. Donfried argues, on the basis of the parallel use of the word in 2 Tim. 3.8–9 (where the false

---

[6] See Donfried, *Setting*, 78, referring to the differences in order, the fact that Luke has the saying as a question not an affirmation, the much shorter version in *2 Clement*, etc. He thus argues for dependence on an independent apocryphal gospel; cf. too Bartlet, in 'II Clement', *New Testament in the Apostolic Fathers*, 132. Gregory, *Reception*, 139, appears undecided.

[7] Köster, *Synoptische Überlieferung*, 76. Lightfoot, *Apostolic Fathers*, 2.243, takes it as a 'loose quotation from Luke vi. 32, 35'; cf. too Köhler, *Rezeption*, 143. Warns, 'Untersuchungen', 388–92, takes it as coming from his proposed apocryphal gospel, but this seems unnecessary.

[8] The οὖν after the vocative ἀδελφοί is all but impossible, and several have suggested a slip by the author or a primitive scribal error (cf. e.g. Knopf, *Zwei Clemensbriefe*, 172, who suggests it is a mistake for μου; Lindemann, *Clemensbriefe*, 238, calls the reading 'eigentlich unmöglich' ('really impossible')).

[9] cf. BAG, 540.

[10] Perhaps another example of the writer's general modesty, and his non-confrontational style, in using 'we' when he probably means 'you'!

teachers opposed in the Pastoral epistles are explicitly in view) that the same vocabulary here implies that false teachers are also in mind.[11] It may well be that the writer is addressing what he regards as a real problem in his community, and indeed that this is in mind not only here but throughout the whole text; but whether one can deduce this from this one word (on the basis of another text which may well not have been known to the author of *2 Clement*) is doubtful.

Further exhortation is given to 'wipe away from ourselves our former sins'. The language of 'wiping away' ($\dot{\epsilon}\xi\alpha\lambda\epsilon i\phi\omega$) in relation to sins is striking and reminiscent of the language of Acts 3.19, though whether one can build on this is uncertain.[12] The reference to 'former' sins presumably relates to sins committed by Christians after baptism (since pre-baptismal sin would have been thought to have been dealt with by baptism itself). In one way, this may show that the author has no 'theological' problem with the idea of forgiveness for post-baptismal sin. On the other hand, it is striking that the 'wiping away' here is an active verb, with 'we' as the implied subject. There is no reference to the removal (or 'forgiveness') of sins by God here: rather, the action involved is a human action, perhaps simply referring to the change in ethical behaviour which is being encouraged and/or demanded. (The 'wiping away' of sins is hence virtually synonymous with 'repenting', at least as interpreted here.)

This is then buttressed by a further general exhortation to be 'saved', clearly implying that, at this point at least, 'salvation' is future and is not guaranteed, even for the Christian. But equally, such (future) salvation is integrally related to whether or not Christians have 'repented', i.e. changed their behaviour: and what is implied is an almost 'automatic' correlation between 'repenting', changing one's behaviour, and being saved. There is thus at least an element of salvation being 'earned' by the Christian's good behaviour.

What is 'good' is now made a little more specific in the exhortation not to be 'men-pleasers' ($\dot{\alpha}\nu\theta\rho\omega\pi\acute{\alpha}\rho\epsilon\sigma\kappa o\iota$).[13] The sequel is in some ways strange. Elsewhere, the word (or its cognates) is generally used negatively, with the implied (or sometimes explicit) converse that one should rather please God (cf. 1 Thess. 2.4; Ign. *Rom.* 2.1).[14] Here, however, the human beings whom one should not necessarily (or at least not only) please are immediately limited to

---

[11] Donfried, *Setting*, 159.

[12] Clear allusions to Acts are rare in early Christian texts: cf. Gregory, *Reception*, (though he does not discuss this possible allusion). The same verb is used in Col. 2.14, though with $\chi\epsilon\iota\rho\acute{o}\gamma\rho\alpha\phi o\nu$ as the object (though this may be a metaphor for sins).

[13] cf. Col. 3.22; Eph. 6.6. Elsewhere the word is a rare one in the Bible: cf. Ps. 52.6 LXX; *Pss. Sol.* 4.8, 10. Similar ideas in e.g. Gal. 1.10; 1 Thess. 2.4.

[14] See Van Unnik, 'Rücksicht', 221–2, and valuable discussion of the theme here in the whole essay.

'ourselves' or 'one another';[15] rather, one should seek to please those who are 'outside' (τοῖς ἔξω ἀνθρώποις), that is, those outside the Christian community.[16] The motivation is, however, scarcely very altruistic. It seems very doubtful whether there is any sense of a missionary motive here, with the well-being of outsiders as such as the primary aim. The only motivation expressed here is that, if one does not 'please' those outside, then they will 'blaspheme' against the name of God; and the prime reason why this is to be avoided at all costs is primarily *theo*logical, not anthropological: it is that God will be discredited, not that other human beings will be lost for possible salvation.[17]

The (bad) result of failing to please outsiders will be that 'the name' will be 'blasphemed' 'because of us'.[18] The absolute use of 'the name' here is slightly unusual (cf. Acts 5.41; Ign. *Eph.* 3.1),[19] though it is immediately clarified in the citation which follows in v. 2. 'Blaspheming the name' also occurs in Jas. 2.7, where the 'name' is probably the name of Jesus. Whether that is the case here is less certain and depends in part on how one interprets v. 2 (see below). Whether there is any reflection of (Gnostic) speculation about 'the name' is much less certain: the 'name' is simply mentioned here without qualification and then clarified in v. 2 as the name 'of the Lord'.[20]

2 The claim that the name will be blasphemed is now backed up by a citation from Isa. 52.5, stating that this is indeed happening. It is introduced as something that 'the Lord says' (λέγει γὰρ ὁ κύριος). Elsewhere (in 5.2; 8.5), this introductory formula is used to introduce a saying of Jesus. Hence many have assumed that the same is true here: the risen Jesus can be assumed to be the speaker in Jewish scripture as well, and the 'name' which is being blasphemed among the non-believing Gentiles is the name of Jesus (cf. too Jas. 2.7).[21] However, the introductory formulae in *2 Clement* are very variable and inconsistent; hence it might be dangerous to assume that the author always means the same thing by the same words. Thus it may be better to take κύριος here,

---

[15] ἑαυτοῖς may be used here instead of ἀλλήλοις: see on 12.3 above, and see Lightfoot, *Apostolic Fathers*, 2.241; Pratscher, *Zweite Clemensbrief*, 170.

[16] For this use of οἱ ἔξω, cf. Mark 4.11; 1 Cor. 5.12–13; 1 Thess. 4.12.

[17] Hence although in one way the author's argument here is not dissimilar to that of Paul in 1 Cor. 14, the prime motivation seems rather different.

[18] For this reading, see above.

[19] Following the reading of C: S adds 'of the Lord'.

[20] *Pace* Donfried, *Setting*, 156–7, who refers to *Gos. Truth* (NHC I.3) 38.7–41.19. But this seems unnecessary (cf. too Lindemann, *Clemensbriefe*, 238; Pratscher, *Zweite Clemensbrief*, 171). Language about the 'name' of God and/or Jesus is widespread enough in Judaism and early Christianity to render otiose a specifically Gnostic background to make sense of the author's language here.

[21] cf. Knopf, *Zwei Clemensbriefe*, 172; Lindemann, *Clemensbriefe*, 238; Pratscher, *Zweite Clemensbrief*, 171. The possibility that κύριος = 'God' is seen as a possibility by Wengst, *Zweite Clemensbrief*, 275 (though he does not commit himself). More clearly, see Schubert, '2. Clemensbrief', 252.

introducing a citation from Jewish scripture, in its more natural sense as a reference to God,[22] and hence the 'name' that is blasphemed is the name of God, rather than the name of Jesus.

The author here shares the citation of Isa. 52.5 with Paul in Rom. 2.24. As noted above, there is no evidence to suggest that the author was dependent on Paul here; and indeed the citation given operates in part in a rather different way. In Paul, the citation is part of his anti-Jewish polemic, attacking the Jews for their ethical failure; and the 'blaspheming of God's name' is how such ethical failings are interpreted theologically: the Jews themselves are doing the blaspheming.[23] This is certainly at odds with any 'original' sense of Isa. 52, where the verse refers in highly negative terms to the actions of 'the Gentiles' who are holding Israel in exile and as such 'blaspheming God's name'. The interpretation of *2 Clement* here is in one way perhaps closer to the MT of Isa. 52 (though it also shares some features with Paul). There is certainly no hint of any polemic against non-Christian Jews: it is assumed without question that the text refers directly to Christians. In the immediate context of v. 2 here, the application of the citation is similar to Paul's, with the (morally deficient) Christians in place of the Jews: the name is blasphemed insofar as 'we do not do what we say' (cf. v. 2 end here). But there is also a sense in which it is the outsiders' reaction to the Christians which constitutes the blaspheming, as vv. 3 and 4 (end) makes clear: when outsiders mock the Christian claim (as a result of what they see of Christian behaviour) and 'laugh at us, then the name is blasphemed': the blaspheming occurs in the action of the outsiders' mockery. As such, the citation comes closer to the meaning implied in Isa. 52.5 MT. Christian failings lead to *others* blaspheming.

The statement that the (God's) name is blasphemed everywhere is then buttressed by a further[24] citation, pronouncing a woe on those who cause such blasphemy to happen, a sentiment that occurs elsewhere in early Christian literature (see above). The ultimate reason for such blasphemy taking place is now spelt out as being due to the failure of Christians to match their own behaviour with the words they themselves promote.

3 The 'outsiders' are now specified as 'Gentiles'. (It would seem that there is little or no contact between the Christian community reflected in *2 Clement* and any non-Christian Jewish community.) Such people may (and, it is implied, do) 'hear' from Christians 'the oracles of God' (τὰ λόγια τοῦ θεοῦ). The phrase is often used to refer to the words of Jewish scripture (cf. Rom.

---

[22] Though bearing in mind of course that the author is probably working with a (relatively) naïve) equation between the person of Jesus and the person of God: cf. 1.1.
[23] The same text is used similarly with an anti-Jewish thrust by Justin in *Dial.* 17: see van Unnik, 'Rücksicht', 224–5.
[24] Following the S reading against that of C: see above for the textual problem.

3.2; Heb. 5.12; *1 Clem.* 19.1; 53.1). Here, it is striking that an example of one such λόγιον is then given in v. 4 as (probably) a saying of *Jesus*, though still introduced as something that '*God* says': see below. The implied context seems to be not dissimilar to that implied by Paul in 1 Cor. 14: outsiders appear to have access to Christian meetings and gatherings so that what goes on, and what is said, is seen and heard by outsiders. Whether we can deduce more from this about the nature of such early Christian gatherings is not clear.

The initial reaction of outsiders to hearing the 'oracles of God' is thoroughly positive: they marvel at the beauty and greatness of what they hear. The attractiveness of the words of Jewish scripture is attested elsewhere, or at least claimed (perhaps in hindsight) by some: cf. the claims of e.g. Justin Martyr and Theophilus to have been converted to Christianity by reading the words ('prophecy') of Jewish scripture.[25] However, what is said here is that further observations by outsiders of Christian behaviour leads to a rejection of their claims if/when such behaviour does not match the words they proclaim. From an attitude of wonder they turn to one of 'blasphemy',[26] accusing the Christian movement of peddling a 'myth' and 'error' (μῦθόν τινα καὶ πλάνην). The importance of a positive correlation between words and actions was an important one in the ancient world; and the validity of teaching (by philosophers and others) was widely judged on the basis of whether teachers lived out their own teaching.[27]

4 The key illustration is now given by reference to the command to love one's enemies. The saying is well known as a saying of Jesus. Here it is introduced as something which 'God says'. As an introductory formula to a quotation in 2 *Clement*, the language is unusual and striking. It is not clear what the precise force of it is. Is it a reflection of a (relatively naïve) equation between Jesus and God (cf. 1.1)? Or has the Jesus tradition become encapsulated in written form such that it is acquiring the status of scripture, so that what is said there can be regarded as akin to the words of (Jewish) scripture and hence seen as part of 'the oracles of God' (cf. v. 3) and be taken as something that 'God says' (cf. present tense!)? Perhaps the latter is more likely (though certainty is not possible).

The author implies that Christians are failing to live up to their own standards in their relations within their own community: failure to live out the love command in practice is evidently leading to outsiders refusing to

---

[25] cf. Justin, *Dial.* 7; Theophilus, *Autol.* 1.14.

[26] cf. above: the 'blasphemy' is in the first instance what is said/done by the 'Gentiles' here. It is not the Christians' moral failings as such.

[27] See A. J. Malherbe, *Moral Exhortation, A Greco-Roman Sourcebook* (Philadelphia: Westminster, 1986), 38–40; cf. e.g. Epictetus 3.7.17; Ps.-Diogenes 15; Matt. 23.3; Rom. 2.21–3; *1 Clem.* 30.3, etc.

accept the validity of the Christian proclamation, mocking the Christians' claims and as such 'blaspheming the name' (of God).

Just how far all this reflects concrete realities in the Christian community of the writer, and its relationships with outsiders, is not clear. It may be that the reference to outsiders is only brought in here to buttress the specific teaching for those *in*side the community. Certainly nowhere else in *2 Clement* is there much if any concern for non-Christian outsiders or any kind of missionary activity. In terms of relations within the community, the language here does seem to reflect concerns about a lack of respect for others within the community. The real complaint (of the implied outsiders here) is not so much that 'we' are failing to live up to the demand of the saying to love our enemies: it is rather that 'we' are failing even to obey the somewhat easier demand to love 'those who love us' (cf. v. 4b). It is this, it is claimed, which is leading to outsiders mocking us and then 'blaspheming the name'. It is thus internal disagreements and squabbles within the community which are the writer's real concern here. The demand to 'love one another' has been stated earlier (cf. 4.3; 9.6):[28] the language here suggests that this is not just a general platitude, but reflects a real concern about the internal relations within the author's community.

---

[28] cf. too the reference to 'love' in 12.1, and the importance for the writer of respectful inter-personal relations in his interpretation of the saying about the two becoming one in 12.3.

Chapter 14

PARALLELS

2 *Clem.* 14.1	Jer. 7.11
ἐὰν δὲ μὴ ποιήσωμεν τὸ θέλημα κυρίου,	
ἐσόμεθα ἐκ τῆς γραφῆς τῆς λεγούσης·	
ἐγενήθη ὁ οἶκός μου σπήλαιον λῃστῶν	μὴ σπήλαιον λῃστῶν ὁ οἶκός μου

Mark 11.17 Ὁ οἶκός μου οἶκος προσευχῆς κληθήσεται πᾶσιν τοῖς ἔθνεσιν; ὑμεῖς δὲ πεποιήκατε αὐτὸν σπήλαιον λῃστῶν.

The author of 2 *Clement* cites the words from Jer. 7.11 with a clear introductory formula, referring to the text as γραφή (cf. 6.8; 14.2). The text is used in the synoptic gospels as part of Jesus' saying in the story of the 'cleansing' of the temple. There is, however, no evidence to support any suggestion that 2 *Clement* has been influenced by the text of the gospels here. In the gospels, the saying functions as an antithesis to the citation of Isa. 56.7 (the temple should be a house of prayer for all nations).[1] The text of 2 *Clement* here knows nothing of this antithesis; nor does it give any hint of the verse being used as a charge against others for what they have already done (cf. the πεποιήκατε (or equivalent) in the synoptic versions). There is no need to see here anything other than a direct use of the text of Jeremiah itself.[2]

2 *Clem.* 14.2	Gen. 1.27
λέγει γὰρ ἡ γραφή·	
ἐποίησεν ὁ θεὸς τὸν ἄνθρωπον	καὶ ἐποίησεν ὁ θεὸς τὸν ἄνθρωπον ...
ἄρσεν καὶ θῆλυ	ἄρσεν καὶ θῆλυ

---

[1] The differences between the different synoptic accounts here (e.g. Matthew and Luke both lack the 'for all nations') do not affect the present discussion in any way.

[2] See also Wengst, *Zweite Clemensbrief*, 257; Lindemann, *Clemensbriefe*, 241; Pratscher, *Zweite Clemensbrief*, 180. Despite the slight differences between the text form here and that of Jer. 7.11 LXX, there seems also no need to postulate the existence of a different manuscript/version of Jeremiah (other than the LXX), or a collection of testimonia, being used: see Pratscher.

Mark 10.6 // Matt. 19.4: ἄρσεν καὶ θῆλυ ἐποίησεν αὐτούς

This is a further example of a quotation, again referred to as ἡ γραφή, giving a text from the OT which is also cited in the gospels. Once again, however, there is no evidence at all that the text is taken from the NT gospels or the Jesus tradition. The wording agrees verbatim with the text of Gen. 1.27 (or at least those parts which are parallel) and indeed the plural αὐτούς in the NT versions would be quite inappropriate for the use of the citation here. The text is thus almost certainly derived from Genesis alone.[3] Whether it is derived directly from there is probably impossible to say.[4]

COMMENTARY

Ch. 14 is probably one of the most problematic sections of the whole of the text of 2 Clement. At a number of points, the text itself is not entirely certain.[5] Further, the author's argument is at times very difficult to follow, and many have commented on the obscurity (and indeed questioned the sense) of what is said.[6] The situation is not helped by the fact that author may be addressing a specific situation and context which he knows well and does not need to explain, but which is partly hidden from us. Moreover, the author here may well be in part citing materials and/or ideas which are shared by others (cf. v. 2a), and which he may be 'quoting' (or at least alluding to) from his 'opponents'. It certainly seems to be the case that he introduces here ideas and terminology which are highly unusual and unparalleled elsewhere in the text (unless hinted at in 2.1); and his own use of the language seems to be somewhat tangential to the ideas themselves. In particular here, he introduces some highly unusual, and distinctive, ideas and claims about the nature of the 'church'; yet the main aim of the discussion seems to be to reinforce yet again the importance of correct ethical behaviour on the part of individual Christians (cf. v. 4: see below), and the ideas about the nature of the church

---

[3] Pratscher, Zweite Clemensbrief, 181.

[4] What is given here is an abbreviated citation of the fuller sentence in Gen. 1, which includes the reference to 'man' being the 'image' of God. It may be purely coincidental, but it is perhaps worth noting that the same abbreviated form of Gen. 1.27 appears in the citation given in 1 Clem. 33.5 (though there the citation also includes Gen. 1.26, which does have the reference to intention to make man in the image of God: hence the author of 1 Clement clearly does know that part of the text of Genesis).

[5] For the most part, the variants do not affect the meaning very much, but occasionally they do.

[6] e.g. Knopf, Zwei Clemensbriefe, 175, says 'Die Verwirrung im Denken hier ist sehr groß' ('the confusion in thought here is very great', in relation to the thought progression in v. 4); Lightfoot, Apostolic Fathers, 2.248: 'it is almost impossible however to trace the connexion of thought in so loose a writer ... our preacher seems to be guilty of much confusion in his metaphor in this context' (again in relation to v. 4). Others concede implicitly that the referents (e.g. in a key word such as σάρξ) change significantly during the course of the argument.

seem to be, for the author here, only a means to another end, not an end in itself.

As we shall see, some of what is said here may be closely parallel with what is said by other Gnostics; it may well be that the author of *2 Clement* is taking up the ideas of some of those he is addressing (whether directly or indirectly) and seeking to use them, at times with some difficulty, to say what he wants to say. This phenomenon may have happened earlier in the letter (cf. e.g. 1.2; 12.2; etc.). Hence the difficulty in tracing a clear line of thought in the argument here may be in part because the author is using material derived from elsewhere and originally coined for another purpose, and which only supports what he wants to say with some exegetical ingenuity. Where precisely the author's 'traditions' cease and his own ideas come to the fore is not always clear. Further, if the author is indeed using ideas, and/or words, from his 'opponents', he is doing so in a fairly eirenic (or 'diplomatic') way, as indeed is the case throughout his address: he gives no hint that he is disagreeing with anything he says here, nor does he directly contradict anything that is said. Rather, the claims made here which many have seen as relating positively to Gnostic ideas are implicitly affirmed without question.

1 The section starts with a familiar ὥστε, ἀδελφοί. Strictly speaking, this might imply a deduction following on from what has been said in 13.4. What follows is, however, a set of totally new ideas and claims about the nature of the church and its relationship to Christ. However, such speculations are introduced by the (by now) very familiar statement about the importance of 'doing the will of God our Father' (cf. cf. 5.1; 6.7; 8.4; 9.11; 10.1; precisely *whose* will one must obey varies: here it is 'God our Father').[7] This importance is now spelt out in two parallel conditional clauses: 'if we do the will of . . . ; if we do not do the will of . . .'. The second clause refers to doing 'the Lord's will': although elsewhere the author can talk of 'the will of Christ' in similar contexts (6.7), it seems more likely, given the close parallelism between the clauses here, that 'the Lord' is God.[8]

The consequences of doing the will of God are now spelt out in terms which are quite new in the argument thus far, with a focus on the 'church' introduced somewhat abruptly. The author claims that those who 'do' the will of God will belong to 'the' church, which is first described in three ways: it is 'first' (πρώτη), 'spiritual' (πνευματική), and 'created before the sun and moon'. The church is thus a pre-existent entity, created (hence not quite on a par with God himself)[9] before significant elements of the present world.

---

[7] Warns, 'Untersuchungen', 294, sees here a reminiscence of the Lord's Prayer. This seems unnecessary, though the references to θέλημα shortly, and also to the 'name' just before in 13.4, may be noteworthy: see Pratscher, *Zweite Clemensbrief*, 178; Lindemann, *Clemensbriefe*, 240.

[8] See Pratscher, *Zweite Clemensbrief*, 178, *contra* Lindemann, *Clemensbriefe*, 241.

[9] cf. Pratscher, *Zweite Clemensbrief*, 178.

The promise and/or hope that is held out is that we 'shall belong to' (ἐσόμεθα) this first, spiritual church. The reference is probably to a future, eschatological hope (rather than to a reality in this life): the sequel seems to make it clear that, in this life, present existence will be a matter of guarding the church in its capacity as 'flesh' (the 'flesh of Christ': cf. v. 3), and participation in the 'spiritual' church, and/or receiving the Spirit, is a matter of future hope. Yet the future nature of this hope does not of itself seem to be the point at issue (as if some were claiming this as a present reality and the author were insisting on its future status: the future nature of the hope seems to be presupposed).[10]

The description of the church as 'first' is not quite clear. There is no indication that this 'first' church is somehow to be distinguished from the present church: there is no ἐκκλησία δευτέρα.[11] Nor is there much indication that the identification of the two is the key point in the discussion here.[12] Rather, calling the church 'first' may be to stress its pre-existent nature and its pre-eminence. So too the description of it as 'spiritual' heightens its status (as in some sense other-worldly) as well as implying it is filled/infused with God's Holy Spirit.[13] The statement about being created before the sun and moon may be based on the language of Ps. 71.5, 17 LXX (though taken here in a quite different—temporal—sense).[14]

The origins and background of the ideas here are not clear. In one sense, one can parallel much of what is said from the language of Ephesians in the NT: e.g. for the idea of the church as (at least potentially) pre-existent, cf. Eph. 1.4.[15] There is a striking parallel to the idea of the pre-existent church in the vision of the old woman in Hermas, *Vis.* 2.4.1, where Hermas is told that the old woman he sees is the 'church' who πάντων πρώτη ἐκτίσθη

---

[10] See Lohmann, *Drohung*, 122, *pace* Donfried, *Setting*, 160.

[11] Pratscher, *Zweite Clemensbrief*, 178, is somewhat confusing: he says that the description of this church as 'first' *is* to distinguish it from the present church, but then immediately goes on to say that 'die erste und die gegenwärtige Kirche sind trotzdem aller Differenzen ident, sodass nur von zwei Existenzweisen der einen Kirche gesprochen werden kann' ('the first and the present church, despite all their differences, are identical, so that one can only speak of two modes of existence of the one church').

[12] *Pace* Donfried, *Setting*, 160–4, esp. 162, who argues that the author is combating the claims of 'opponents' who believed they were already part of the spiritual church, but had no regard for the present, contemporary church. The author does not appear to be seeking to establish and/or bolster the status of the contemporary church as such.

[13] Similar language is used in 1 Pet. 2.5; *Barn.* 16.10.

[14] The verses from Ps. 71 LXX are used by Justin, *Dial.* 64.5–6 Christologically (cf. Lightfoot, *Apostolic Fathers*, 2.244; Lindemann, *Clemensbriefe*, 241; Pratscher, *Zweite Clemensbrief*, 179).

[15] However, the idea is not quite the same. There it is 'we' who are foreordained in the heavenly places, though whether 'we' as such are pre-existent is surely doubtful; also in *2 Clement* here it seems to be a question of the church having some quasi-independent existence to which 'we' aspire.

('was created the first of all things').¹⁶ There is also a possible background in Gnostic texts, especially those from Valentinian Gnosticism, where ἐκκλησία is one of the primary eight members of the primal Ogdoad emanating in pairs ('syzygies') one after the other: each pair comprises a male and a female partner, with ἐκκλησία as the female partner of the male ἄνθρωπος in the fourth and last syzygy.¹⁷ This too would be relevant for explaining what the author of *2 Clement* says in v. 2 about Christ and the church as the male and female counterparts of a union.¹⁸ If one takes this as a possible background of thought, it might strengthen the theory that the author is debating with those influenced by some kind of Gnostic ideas and speculations (perhaps specifically of Valentinian Gnosticism) and is seeking a dialogue with them. We have seen earlier examples of the author possibly taking up potentially Gnostic language and seeking to adapt it for his own purposes.¹⁹ This then may be another example of the same phenomenon. However, the author here gives no hint that he disapproves in any way of the sentiments or claims being made about the church. Indeed he seems happy to affirm them all fully and positively without any qualms. What is at stake for him is simply how one becomes a member of this church. For the author at least, one will only do so if one 'does the will' of God and/or Christ. The crucial criterion is ethical behaviour in the present.

This last point is then spelt out negatively in the second half of the general claim: if 'we' do not do what we should, then we shall belong to an institution that can *not* claim to be the true church, but will have become a 'den of robbers'. The language is traditional: the wording is taken from Jer. 7.11 (a verse placed on the lips of Jesus in the synoptic gospels, but there is no trace

---

[16] There is also a fragment of Papias (in the work of Anastasius Sinaita) who apparently also interpreted the creation account in relation to Christ and the church: see U. Körtner, *Papias von Hierapolis. Ein Beitrag zur Geschichte des Urchristentums*, FRLANT 133 (Göttingen: Vandenhoeck & Ruprecht, 1983), 67 (frag. 16): cf. Lindemann, *Clemensbriefe*, 240.

[17] See especially Irenaeus *Haer.* 1.1.1; 11.1; also reflections of this, including clear ideas about the pre-existence of the church, in *Tri. Trac.* (NHC I.5) 57.34–5; 58.30–1; *Val. Exp.* (NHC XI.2) 29.25–35. The 'Valentinian' ideas as background for the language here are stressed e.g. by Donfried, *Setting*, 164; Warns, 'Untersuchungen', 207–15, though regarded as 'fraglich' ('questionable') by Lindemann, *Clemensbriefe*, 241. The background may also be relevant for the immediately following speculation about Christ and the church as the 'man, male and female' of Gen 1.27. Pratscher, *Zweite Clemensbrief*, 184, says that the Gnostic language provides the closest parallel. See also below on v. 2.

[18] In the account of Irenaeus, the fourth pair is Anthropos and Ecclesia (man and church), not Christ and church. However, there may have been some variation: e.g. in *Haer.* 1.8.4, Irenaeus cites Ptolemy as using the text from Eph. 5.32, referring to Christ and his church, as justification for his theory of syzygic pairs, possibly then implying that Ptolemy had postulated a Christ–church syzygy. See further Donfried, *Setting*, 164 (with reference to Daniélou).

[19] e.g. in 1.2; also the citation in 12.2 and the somewhat forced interpretation in 12.3–5.

of any influence of Jesus tradition here: see Parallels above). The introduction is expressed somewhat compactly but the sense is clear.[20]

The author now gives an exhortation, implying almost a statement of the obvious: 'let us choose' to belong to the 'church of life'. (Few would presumably choose otherwise!) Whether there is any implied polemic in the language of 'choosing' is not clear: if the 'opponents' claimed that belonging to the true church was dependent on their prior status (e.g. as 'pneumatics'), perhaps then the implicit claim that membership of the church is a matter of individual 'choice' could have added significance. However, there is no explicit indication of this here: the point simply seems to be that we will all want this end result and hence should achieve it by the only way that is possible, i.e. via a life of proper ethical behaviour.[21]

The church is now described as the 'church of life', implying that the church is the place where 'life' (i.e. eschatological, or eternal, life) is to be found.[22] The overall aim is that 'we may be saved'. It is assumed here that 'salvation' is something that is future rather than present (cf. earlier 4.1–2; 8.2; 9.2). Also probably the last two phrases in this final sentence (to belong to the church, to gain salvation) are not meant to refer to strictly consecutive events (as if belonging to the church was a necessary preliminary for gaining salvation) but are two aspects of the same reality (i.e. belonging to the church is the same as gaining ultimate salvation).[23]

2 The author continues with the speculative ideas associated with the church. He starts by a typically modest introduction ('I do not think that you are ignorant'), apparently explicitly referring the addressees to something that

---

[20] cf. Knopf, *Zwei Clemensbriefe*, 173: ἐσόμεθα ἐκ τῆς γραφῆς τῆς λεγούσης seems to be an abbreviation of something like ἐσόμεθα ἐκ τούτων περὶ ὧν λέγει ἡ γραφή. Whether one can deduce, from the fact that the original context in Jer. 7 is about the temple, that the author here has in mind an idea of the church as a 'temple' (cf. 9.3) is not clear.

[21] In another way, the language of 'choice' here is theologically a little strange, as if final salvation is something which it is the power of human beings to be able to choose for themselves. Yet, even in the most radical of theologies of 'grace', there is an ineradicable element of human response that is required.

[22] See Knopf, *Zwei Clemensbriefe*, 173 ('weil sie Leben hat, und Leben mitteilt' ['because it has life and imparts life']), followed by most others. It has been suggested, on the basis of the possible Gnostic background, that since the syzygy of Anthropos-Ekklesia emanates (according to Irenaeus' description) from the prior syzygy of λόγος ('word') and ζωή ('life'), talk about the church as 'of life' may allude to the idea of the church as being born by the prior aeon 'life': see A. Frank, 'Studien zur Ekklesiologie des Hirten, II Klemens, die Didache und die Igantiusbriefe unter beonderer Berücksichtigung der Idee einer präexistenten Kirche' (dissertation, Munich, 1975), 241, as noted by Wengst, *Zweite Clemensbrief*, 275 (Frank's work was not available to me). Wengst himself is, however, dubious about the suggestion. In any case the phrase here is taken up again in v. 2, but as 'the living church': hence 'of life' here probably means exactly the same as 'living' and there is no need to read further Gnostic mythology into the language at this point.

[23] See Pratscher, *Zweite Clemensbrief*, 180.

they already know. This gives strength to the view (cf. above) that the somewhat unusual ideas in this chapter are perhaps arising from the ideas of the partners in the dialogue in which the author is engaged.

The first claim made is that 'the living church is the body of Christ'. The 'living church' is synonymous with the 'church of life' (see above). Whether one should regard the claim that the (living) church is the body of Christ as a 'quotation' is not clear. There is no introductory formula signalling it as a quotation explicitly.[24] Nevertheless, it is a claim introduced somewhat abruptly here and indeed only taken up in the argument that follows with some difficulty. It would seem then to be a 'given' for the author; though whether it is given to him as language used by his dialogue partners, or whether it is part of an authoritative text, is not clear.

The claim is of course attested in a number of places in the Pauline corpus in the NT.[25] Given a number of other similarities with the language of Ephesians in the context here, it is tempting to think of e.g. Eph. 1.23 in the present case.[26] So too the appeal to οἱ ἀπόστολοι shortly as a supporting authority for the claims being made here might fit with a theory that the author knows the Pauline corpus and is appealing to it (but see below). On the other hand, some of what is said in addition here about the church seems to go beyond Ephesians in a significant way. It is, however, still striking that the claim that the church is the 'body' of Christ is somewhat alien to the present context: the author has to change 'body' to 'flesh' to make the point he wants ultimately to make (see below), and the idea of the church as the 'body' of Christ does not easily mesh with the other claims made here where the church is the 'partner' of Christ in a syzygy (quasi-marriage) relationship. The case for the claim being a quotation used by the author of 2 Clement

---

[24] But there are instances elsewhere in 2 Clement of what are widely agreed to be quotations but not explicitly signalled as such: see e.g. 2.1; 11.7; 17.5. The sentence here is taken as a citation (printed with quotation marks) in Lake, Fathers, 151; Richardson, Fathers, 199; Grant and Graham, Apostolic Fathers, 126, though not in Ehrman, Fathers, 187. Lindemann, Clemensbriefe, 241, calls it a 'Zitat' ('citation'), but does not make it clear exactly what it is a citation of. Pratscher, Zweite Clemensbrief, 181, claims that it is not clearly a citation, but that it is certainly 'zitathaft'.

[25] In the genuine Pauline letters, see Rom. 12.5; 1 Cor. 10.16–17; 12.12–27. The motif is considerably developed in the deutero-Pauline letters, cf. Col. 1.18, 24; 2.9 and also many instances in Ephesians.

[26] A reference to Ephesians is assumed by e.g. Donfried, Setting, 161; Grant and Graham, Apostolic Fathers, 125–6 (who see the whole of ch. 14 as 'exegesis' of Ephesians, esp. Eph. 5.22–32); also J. Muddiman, 'The Church in Ephesians, 2 Clement, and the Shepherd of Hermas', in A. F. Gregory and C. M. Tuckett (eds), Trajectories through the New Testament and the Apostolic Fathers (Oxford: Oxford University Press, 2005), 114–15. Warns, 'Untersuchungen', 207–15, argues that Col. 1.24–6 underlies the text here. However, such a direct reference is doubted by e.g. Lindemann, Paulus, 267 (cf. too his Lindemann, Clemensbriefe, 241); also Gregory and Tuckett, '2 Clement', 287–8, both arguing that, although the (deutero-)Pauline language might lie ultimately in the background, it cannot be shown to be the direct source of the language here.

from elsewhere is thus a strong one; but identifying precisely the author's immediate source is not easy.

The claim is now said to be justified ('for') by an appeal to Gen. 1.27 as 'scripture', but with a distinctive interpretation: the statement of the creation of the human race as male and female[27] is interpreted as referring to a single entity ($\tau\grave{o}\nu$ $\check{a}\nu\theta\rho\omega\pi o\nu$) made up of Christ (as the male) and the church (as the female). Quite how this justifies the claim that the church is the 'body' of Christ is not clear. The language is similar to that of Eph. 5.23–32, where Christ is presented as the husband of the church as wife in a ('spiritual') marriage relationship;[28] it is also very close to the language of Valentinian Gnosticism and the theories of aeons emanating in the Pleroma in a series of linked male–female pairs (cf. above), especially in relation to the claim that the church and Christ are pre-existent so that the syzygy relationship is also something that is a matter of pre-existent beings.[29] The writer may then be taking up the ideas and language of others. Certainly not much is made of the gender aspects of the claim here, namely that Christ and the church constitute some kind of primeval androgynous unity. The case then for the writer operating in the context of some kind of (Valentinian?) Gnostic milieu is thus strengthened.

The assertion is now added, perhaps as a further case of something about which the author presumes is not unknown to his hearers/readers,[30] that the

---

[27] In the original of Genesis, the 'man' who is the object of the verb 'made' is clearly generic, referring to human beings generally. The grammatical singular is here exploited for all it is worth!

[28] With analogies drawn between the church and (Christ's) 'body' in vv. 23, 28, 30. Nevertheless, the dominant analogy in the passage is the church as the 'bride', rather than the 'body', of Christ.

[29] cf. Pratscher, *Zweite Clemensbrief*, 184: 'Die Syzygie zwischen den präexistenten Größen Christus und Kirche hat ihre nächste Parallele in der valentinianischen Gnosis.' ('The idea of the syzygy between the pre-existent entities Christ and the church has its closest parallel in Valentinian Gnosticism.')

[30] The text is not certain: at the start C reads $\kappa\alpha\grave{\iota}$ $\ddot{o}\tau\iota$; S implies a reading $\kappa\alpha\grave{\iota}$ $\ddot{\epsilon}\tau\iota$; and towards the end, S implies an extra $\lambda\acute{\epsilon}\gamma o\upsilon\sigma\iota\nu$, absent from C. The S readings are widely accepted: so e.g. Knopf, *Zwei Clemensbriefe*, 174; Lake, *Fathers*, 150; Wengst, *Zweite Clemensbrief*, 256; Lindemann, *Clemensbriefe*, 239; Pratscher, *Zweite Clemensbrief*, 182. Lightfoot, *Apostolic Fathers*, 2.245, claims that the text is corrupt and some words have fallen out: he thus reads $\ddot{o}\tau\iota$ and adds $\lambda\acute{\epsilon}\gamma o\upsilon\sigma\iota\nu$, $\delta\hat{\eta}\lambda o\nu$ at the end of the sentence. However, the sequence of thought is not entirely easy with the S reading: it seems to imply that what is said (about 'the books and the apostles') gives further justification for the claim that the church is the body of Christ: but what the 'books and the apostles' are said here to affirm is the pre-existence of the church, which is not clearly identical with the claim that the church is the body of Christ. It is thus possible that the reading $\ddot{o}\tau\iota$ in C is correct (so too Ehrman, *Fathers*, 160): the claim about what is said by the books and the apostles is not a further justification for the claim that the church is the body of Christ, but a further, separate claim alongside this, with the $\ddot{o}\tau\iota$ clause providing a second example of the things that the writer presumes that the hearers are not ignorant about (hence $\ddot{o}\tau\iota$ here resuming the $\ddot{o}\tau\iota$ earlier in the verse (*not* v. 1a as Pratscher implies). The $\lambda\acute{\epsilon}\gamma o\upsilon\sigma\iota\nu$ implied in S has to be read implicitly, if not explicitly, to make sense of the sentence.

'books (?of the prophets)³¹ and the apostles' attest to the pre-existent nature of the church. The language is somewhat compressed: the statement that the church 'is not just of the present' (οὐ νῦν εἶναι) presumably means that the church's origins are not just a matter of the present. Rather, the church has existed 'from the beginning' (ἄνωθεν).³²

Precisely what authorities the author is referring to here is not clear, the lack of clarity being compounded by uncertainty about the precise wording of the text. Τὰ βιβλία alone would presumably refer to the Jewish scriptures in toto;³³ τὰ βιβλία τῶν προφητῶν might refer more narrowly to the prophetic books of Jewish scripture, but equally might refer to Jewish scripture regarded in its prophetic nature.³⁴

Οἱ ἀπόστολοι would appear to refer most naturally to writings of Christian 'apostles'; the assumption would be then that the author presupposes the existence, and the authoritative nature (cf. 'the apostles' parallel with τὰ βιβλία), of apostolic writings. In one way, the obvious reference would be to some (or all) of the Pauline corpus of letters. However, the reference here is extremely general and unspecific.³⁵ It is also striking that, if this is what οἱ ἀπόστολοι refers to, there is then no mention of any Jesus ('gospel') traditions, whereas elsewhere in *2 Clement* such traditions are regularly cited alongside OT texts, and for the most part Pauline (and/or other 'apostolic' writings) are notable by their absence. This single reference here would then be unique within *2 Clement*.

Whether the author has specific texts in mind is also not clear. From the OT side, some have suggested that perhaps e.g. Ps. 45 or Gen. 1 might be in mind.³⁶ And for the 'apostles', there are various passages in the Pauline corpus

---

³¹ The words 'of the prophets' are not present in C but are implied by S. C has a number of possible omissions in this section (cf. Lindemann, *Clemensbriefe*, 241–2), perhaps indicating some general carelessness by the scribe here. The S reading is accepted by e.g. Wengst, *Zweite Clemensbrief*, 256; Pratscher, *Zweite Clemensbrief*, 182, but not by e.g. Lake, *Fathers*, 150; Ehrman, *Fathers*, 186; Lightfoot, *Apostolic Fathers*, 2.245 calls the S reading 'the obvious gloss of a later age'; cf. too Donfried, *Setting*, 93. The issue may not be ultimately very important overall in the interpretation of the text here. I would incline to include the words, but indicate the textual uncertainty by bracketing the words.

³² It is widely agreed that ἄνωθεν here is used in a temporal sense, not a spatial one. See e.g. Donfried, *Setting*, 162; Lindemann, *Clemensbriefe*, 242; Pratscher, *Zweite Clemensbrief*, 182 (though Pratscher also argues for a possible double meaning for the word: the church is of heavenly origin; but this might, however, overload the meaning too much).

³³ cf. Lightfoot, *Apostolic Fathers*, 2.245; Donfried, *Setting*, 93–4 (with examples from Josephus and other Jewish sources for τὰ βιβλία used to refer to Jewish scriptures: e.g. Josephus, *Ant.* 1.15; 8.159; *Let. Aris.* 28).

³⁴ For the latter view, even with the reading 'of the prophets', cf. e.g. Wengst, *Zweite Clemensbrief*, 276; Pratscher, *Zweite Clemensbrief*, 182.

³⁵ e.g. Wengst, *Zweite Clemensbrief*, 276, argues that the reference here is not to apostolic *texts* as such, but to apostolic *teaching*. This is possible but not easy to show clearly one way or the other.

³⁶ The suggestion originally made by Knopf, *Zwei Clemensbriefe*, 174, and repeated by others since. On the use of Ps. 45 by Justin to stake a claim about the pre-existence of Christ, see *Dial.* 63.4. Gen. 1 is clearly in mind in the present context.

which might be in mind (cf. the references earlier to the church as the body of Christ; though there is nothing very obviously relating to the specific claim about the pre-existence of the church).

Given all the difficulties raised so far, it is very attractive to take the reference here as a more general one, appealing to the authoritative texts which the author has available and generally uses.[37] Further, given the extensive use made of gospel traditions by the author, it is possible that the 'apostles' here is indeed a reference to *gospel* literature, echoing the language used elsewhere (especially by Justin) of the gospels as the 'memoirs of the apostles'.[38] This would then align what is said here with the appeals to authority which the writer does make elsewhere in his text.

The claim about the pre-existence of the church is now expanded and elaborated further with the assertion that the church was 'spiritual' (cf. v. 1), as too was 'Jesus Christ our Lord'[39] himself. The statement is no doubt not intended to be a definitive statement about Christology as such; it does though express the view that Christ is/was of the same status as the church, hence pre-existent and 'spiritual' (cf. 9.5) just as, later, Christ will be said to be 'Spirit' in the present (cf. v. 4).

The end of v. 2 represents a notorious crux in relation to who the subject of the final clause is meant to be. In terms of the surface grammar, the sentence reads more naturally if ἡ ἐκκλησία is the subject. However, the content of what is said (he/she 'was made manifest in the last days so that he/she might save us') is more naturally taken as referring to Jesus, not the church. The phrase ἐπ' ἐσχάτων τῶν ἡμερῶν is used in Heb. 1.2 and 1 Pet. 1.20 to refer to the coming of Christ; and elsewhere in *2 Clement* the work of 'saving' others (whether as a past event or a future hope) is attributed to Christ (and/or God), not the church (cf. 2.7; 9.5; cf. 1.4, 7). Moreover, if the church is the subject of the sentence, then v. 3a provides a possibly awkward repetition of what is said. For this reason, a large number of commentators and editors take Jesus to be the subject.[40]

---

[37] cf. Lindemann, *Clemensbriefe*, 242: 'alle in der Kirche geltenden Autoritäten' ('all valid authorities in the church').

[38] See Just. *1 Apol.* 66.3; 67.3; *Dial.* 100–7, and see further p. 43 above.

[39] C reads here 'our Jesus' (ὁ Ἰησοῦς ἡμῶν), which is extremely unusual. S implies a reading ὁ Ἰησοῦς Χριστὸς ὁ κύριος ἡμῶν which reads much more naturally. If the S reading were original, the C reading would be a simple mistake arising from an omission of three words. Although the C reading could be regarded as the lectio difficilior and as such to be preferred, it seems better to take the S reading as original and to see the C reading as the result of a simple mistake of omission (to which the scribe of C is prone at times: cf. Lightfoot, *Apostolic Fathers*, 1.128). The S reading here is accepted by Wengst, *Zweite Clemensbrief*, 256; Lindemann, *Clemensbriefe*, 242; Pratscher, *Zweite Clemensbrief*, 183. (The C reading is accepted by Lake, *Fathers*, 150; Richardson, *Fathers*, 199; Ehrman, *Fathers*, 186.)

[40] So e.g. the Lake, *Fathers*, 151; Ehrman, *Fathers*, 187; also Lightfoot, *Apostolic Fathers*, 2.246; Knopf, *Zwei Clemensbriefe*, 174; Wengst, *Zweite Clemensbrief*, 276; Lindemann, *Clemensbriefe*, 242; Pratscher, *Zweite Clemensbrief*, 183.

On the other hand, in this section, the author is probably in part citing and referring to views and traditions of others; hence the author's own views elsewhere may not be determinative for the meaning of this one phrase in the present context. Further, what is said in v. 3a is *not* an exact repetition of the clause in v. 2: it is in part abbreviated (ἐπ' ἐσχατων τῶν ἡμερῶν is not repeated nor is the reference to 'saving us'), and in part expanded (by the phrase ἐν τῇ σαρκὶ Χριστοῦ). Moreover, the idea that the church itself has some kind of salvific role in the divine economy would not be entirely out of place with what has been said thus far in ch. 14.[41] Given that the syntax of the sentence reads much more naturally if ἡ ἐκκλησία is the subject, it may then be better to interpret this sentence in v. 2 as a statement about the church (perhaps, as with so much here, taking up language which is coming from others in the dialogue/debate in which the author is engaged), a statement which is then immediately interpreted and glossed in v. 3a.[42]

3 If the interpretation of the previous clause is correct, what now follows is by way of interpretation and/or gloss on what has just been said, not a new claim. In particular, what is now clarified is that the church has been made manifest 'in the flesh of Christ'. The idea implied is very unusual. One might have expected a simple 'in the flesh', i.e. the pre-existent church which existed before as a spiritual entity has been manifested on earth as a tangible reality. But what is said is that it is manifested 'in the flesh of Christ'. It is not clear, for example, whether the author has in mind here the time of Jesus' incarnate life, or the post-Easter period.[43] Perhaps too this is the point at which the author is seeking to bring in his own views. In one sense, there may be an anti-Gnostic thrust to the claim here: the church is made manifest to human beings in the concrete earthly reality of the flesh of Christ, and does not simply remain as a heavenly aeon in the Pleroma. Certainly too the author's key point in the whole discussion here focuses on the 'flesh' (cf. v. 4), and this may be the reason why he changes the categories slightly, from talking about the church as the 'body' of Christ to the church as the 'flesh' of Christ. This manifestation of the church in the 'flesh' of Christ should not, however, be

---

[41] e.g. if it is right to interpret the reference to the 'church *of life*' as implying not only that the church is herself 'living' but also in some sense is the medium through which life is dispensed to others (cf. Knopf as in n. 22 above), then it is not so great a step to talk about the church as 'saving us'. Certainly the language of 'being manifested' *is* clearly applied to the church in v. 3a.

[42] The subject of the sentence here is taken as the church by G. Krüger, 'Zu II. Klem. 14,2', *ZNW* 31 (1932), 204–5; Richardson, *Fathers*, 199; Grant and Graham, *Apostolic Fathers*, 126; Donfried, *Setting*, 163.

[43] The reference to the 'flesh of Christ' might suggest the former: the 'flesh' of Christ refers to his incarnate life; but then the notion that the physical presence of Jesus on earth was also the manifestation of the church itself would be highly unusual. But presumably either way, the claim covers the post-Easter period as well.

seen as compromising the coming of Christ himself 'in the flesh' as well (as if Christ remains, as a 'spiritual' being, in heaven).

The manifestation of the church in the 'flesh' now leads on to the exhortation to which the writer has been heading all along. In particular he plays (quite clearly by the end of v. 3) with two meanings, or rather two referents, of the word 'flesh': the church is related to the 'flesh' of Christ, but 'flesh' also relates to the general human condition and refers to human physical behaviour. 'Flesh' has thus both an ecclesiological and an anthropological sense and the writer seeks to exploit this duality.

This may then make better sense of the next clause. The manifestation of the church in the flesh leads to (the church!) 'showing us' ($\delta\eta\lambda o\hat{v}\sigma a$ $\hat{\eta}\mu\hat{\iota}\nu$) that 'any of us' who keeps the flesh without corruption,[44] will receive her (the church) back in the Holy Spirit. The language is scarcely clear! In particular, what 'keeping the flesh' refers to is obscure. There is, however, a variant reading in S which implies reading an $a\mathaccent"017E{v}\tau o\hat{v}$ after $\sigma a\rho\kappa\acute{\iota}$. This is usually dismissed as impossible as a reference to the flesh of Christ, and the author does not have this in mind at all.[45] However, given the propensity of C to omit words occasionally (both generally and specifically in this section: see above), the S reading should perhaps be taken seriously. Further, an $a\mathaccent"017E{v}\tau o\hat{v}$ here need not refer to Christ, but could just as well refer to the $\tau\iota\varsigma$ as the subject of the clause. The owner of the 'flesh' is thus 'any one of us': it is then *our* flesh that is at issue. This would then mark a transition from the ecclesiological use of 'flesh' to the anthropological (which is clearly made by the end of v. 3), and could thus be the original reading. Keeping/guarding the church is perhaps intended as a metaphor for proper ethical behaviour in the Christian's present; it is certainly this that the author is, via a somewhat tortuous exegesis of various (apparently traditional) claims and statements, struggling to reach as the end of his line of argument in this section.

The reward that is promised is that anyone who does so keep/guard the church 'will receive her back in the Holy Spirit'. Again the language is peculiar in a number of ways. It seems to imply that membership of the church is in one sense a matter of a future reward, not a present experience: at least membership of the church in its capacity for being the 'spiritual' entity it is (and/or will become again) is still future, whereas presumably in the present the church is still 'fleshly', i.e. the 'flesh' of Christ.[46] It is also striking that the

---

[44] The feminine participle $\delta\eta\lambda o\hat{v}\sigma a$ clearly has the church as its subject: hence the church is clearly an active agent in the 'drama' being described; this in turn may make it more plausible to see it as at least possible that the church could be referred to as 'saving' human beings in v. 2 (cf. above).

[45] cf. Lindemann, *Clemensbriefe*, 242; Pratscher, *Zweite Clemensbrief*, 184.

[46] On its own, the claim about the future nature of membership of the 'spiritual church' is simply another way of expressing the claim that 'salvation' is something that is still future. Certainly this kind of argument would do little to address counter claims that the present church is being regarded as too *in*significant and unimportant. Cf. n. 12 above.

reference to the Holy Spirit is entirely related to the future: it would seem that possession of the Spirit is seen by the author here as something to be expected (or hoped for) in the future, not a phenomenon of experienced reality in the present. As such, the viewpoint implied here is quite unlike significant other sections of early Christianity which evidently claimed that present Christian existence was characterized by the presence of the Spirit.[47]

The argument is now developed further by bringing in the categories of an 'antitype' (ἀντίτυπος) and what is true or real (τὸ αὐθεντικόν), with the claim that the 'flesh' is the antitype of the true reality which is the Spirit. The categories seem to reflect the Neoplatonic distinction between the present world of the senses and the heavenly world of ideas.[48] Having made the identification of the categories involved, the writer claims that if one 'corrupts', or does not keep/guard, the antitype, one cannot receive the reality to which it corresponds. The two correspond closely together and one cannot divorce them. Hence there is not necessarily any downgrading of the present world in relation to the heavenly (as might be the case in some applications of such ideas): although in one way, the heavenly is better and greater than the earthly (so that the hope of belonging to the future 'spiritual' church is a genuinely positive hope for the future), the present reality of the church (as fleshly) is no less important and valuable.

The 'application', or conclusion, of the whole argument (from the writer's perspective) is now reached with the exhortation to 'guard the flesh'. The language has been used by the writer before (cf. 8.4, 6). There, and presumably here too, the 'flesh' is used anthropologically, so that 'guarding the flesh' is a synonym for behaving properly in one's everyday life. The move from the ecclesiological to the anthropological use of 'flesh' seems now clear.[49]

4 The author, however, now reverts to his earlier, ecclesiological, use of 'flesh'. As a result, the logic of the section as a whole becomes even more strained: now the church is said to be 'flesh' without qualification, with Christ as the Spirit.[50] Certainly the language is somewhat surprising given what has been said just before: any idea of the church as 'spiritual' (v. 3a) seems to have been

---

[47] See Acts 2.1–11; Rom. 8; 1 Cor. 12.1–11; *1 Clem.* 22.1 etc. Cf. Pratscher, *Zweite Clemensbrief*, 178. See also Introduction §9.3 above.

[48] cf. L. Goppelt, τύπος κτλ., *TWNT* 8 (1969), 248 (cf. Plotinus, *Enn.* 2.9.6).

[49] cf. Wengst, *Zweite Clemensbrief*, 277; Lindemann, *Clemensbriefe*, 243, for the author here 'playing' with different meanings of 'flesh'.

[50] cf. Lightfoot, *Apostolic Fathers*, 2.248: 'here the relation of flesh to spirit represents the relation of the church to Christ, whereas just above it has represented the relation of the earthly Church and Christ to the heavenly Church and Christ'. Thus Lightfoot comments that 'our preacher seems to be guilty of much confusion ...'. Others are slightly more charitable, e.g. Donfried, *Setting*, 163, says that having made his point in the earlier part of the argument, the writer here 'can now switch to another image'. Lindemann, *Clemensbriefe*, 243, states that the ideas here are completely 'new'.

forgotten and lost.⁵¹ The conclusion drawn is that anyone who abuses the 'flesh' (at one level by not behaving in an ethically upright way) abuses the church (which is the manifestation of the 'flesh' of Christ). On the basis of the antitype/reality dualism, such a person cannot hope to receive the Spirit (again assumed to be a solely future experience), which is Christ.⁵² As in v. 2 (and 9.5) there is a virtual equation made between Christ and Spirit.

5 The writer now seeks to bring the (somewhat tortuous) discussion to a conclusion. 'This flesh' (clearly here the human 'flesh', i.e. human beings in their present life, not the church) can receive wonderful things in the future.⁵³ These are life and immortality.⁵⁴ Such can be received if the Holy Spirit is joined ($\kappa o \lambda \lambda \eta \theta \acute{\epsilon} \nu \tau o s$) to it/him/her.⁵⁵ As before, the reference still seems to be entirely future: the receiving, or being joined to, the Spirit is a matter of future hope, not necessarily present reality.⁵⁶

The section then closes with what is probably the conclusion of the saying given earlier in 11.7 (with parallels in 1 Cor. 2.9, *Gos. Thom.* 17, *1 Clem.* 34.8, and elsewhere: see earlier).⁵⁷ In relation to the wording of other versions of

---

⁵¹ Or perhaps the focus is here primarily on the present, when the church is 'flesh' (or 'the flesh of Christ'); the time for the 'spiritual' church is the future.

⁵² The topic under discussion is *not* an abstract treatise on Christology! Hence it would be quite wrong to try to draw conclusions about the writer's Trinitarian (or otherwise) 'theology', or his Christology. Rather, he seems desperate to use, in whatever way he can, the language and ideas of others to make his general point about the importance of ethical behaviour.

⁵³ This might have a possible anti-Gnostic element to it, against any who would deny the value of the (human) 'flesh' (cf. too ch. 9 earlier, insisting on the fact that flesh *will* be raised and participate in resurrection life): cf. Wengst, *Zweite Clemensbrief*, 277–8; Pratscher, *Zweite Clemensbrief*, 188. However, the main point the author seeks to make is as much about the importance of ethical behaviour in the present.

⁵⁴ S implies a reading $\dot{\alpha}\phi\theta\alpha\rho\sigma\acute{\iota}\alpha\nu$, C reads $\dot{\alpha}\theta\alpha\nu\alpha\sigma\acute{\iota}\alpha\nu$. The former is perhaps to be preferred (cf. too 2 Tim. 1.10; Ign. *Pol.* 2.3). The S reading is accepted by Wengst, *Zweite Clemensbrief*, 258; Lindemann, *Clemensbriefe*, 243; Pratscher, *Zweite Clemensbrief*, 189, as well as by all the printed editions; the C reading may be influenced by *1 Clem.* 35.2.

⁵⁵ The language is unusual and represents yet another piece of verbal imagery. It is just possible that this represents a reminiscence of the language of Gen 2.24, perhaps mediated through its citation in Eph. 5.31 where it is applied to the union between Christ and the church: the coming together of 'flesh' and 'Spirit' in the final salvation of human beings is thus analogous to the coming together of 'flesh' = church and 'Spirit' = Christ in the marriage union of the two as alluded to briefly earlier. But as before, it is uncertain whether this is due to direct dependence on Ephesians, or whether it reflects some dependence on a line of tradition which has developed some way already from Ephesians.

⁵⁶ cf. Pratscher, *Zweite Clemensbrief*, 188, *contra* Lindemann, *Clemensbriefe*, 243. Lindemann argues partly on the basis of the change in vocabulary (from 'receiving' to 'being joined to') that a change of reference is implied. But the author here seems notoriously imprecise in his use of language with a wide range of different verbal images being used, apparently virtually synonymously (cf. in relation to the church, there is talk of 'belonging' to it (v. 1), guarding/keeping it and corrupting it (v. 3), receiving it back (v. 3) etc.). It would probably be hazardous to reckon that the author has a very clear vocabulary which he applies strictly and consistently in relation to different periods of the history of salvation.

⁵⁷ Neither in 11.7 nor here are the words signalled as a citation, but this is not necessarily a bar to such a theory: cf. 2.1; 17.5.

the saying, there are a few small differences, though it is not clear if these are significant. For example, in I Cor. 2 and in *1 Clem.* 34, God is the subject, whereas here it is 'the Lord'.[58] What is in store is said here to be not capable of being expressed verbally. In the other versions it is as much about things which cannot even be envisaged or comprehended. The final difference may have a slight significance. In 1 Cor. 2, the rewards are for 'those who love Him', in *1 Clem.* 34, they are for 'those who wait for Him'; here they are for 'his elect' (τοῖς ἐκλεκτοῖς αὐτου). If one is right to see some kind of Gnostic claims in the background in all this discussion, it is just possible that this language is slightly pointed: the rewards for the elect are all in the future, and dependent on proper human ethical behaviour in the present. They are not something on which the elect can rely in any way.

This section is undoubtedly the most complex part of the whole of the text of *2 Clement*. In part its difficulty may be due to the author's taking up the language of others and seeking to interpret it, often with considerable strain, to make it support what he wants to say. Nevertheless, despite the strained and forced line of argument, the conclusions and main point seem to be clear: it is yet again an insistence on the vital importance of proper ethical behaviour in the present (in the author's terminology, 'guarding the flesh') which is the essential prerequisite for sharing in the rewards that are to come in the future (which are variously described as belonging to the pre-existent spiritual church, receiving the Spirit, being joined to the Spirit, receiving the church back, receiving Christ, etc.). The language and verbal imagery vary somewhat alarmingly, but the underlying message remains constant and insistent.

---

[58] However, throughout most of ch. 14, Jesus has been referred to as 'Christ', and 'the Lord' of v. 1 is probably God (see above). Hence 'the Lord' here may be God as well, in which case the difference between the text here and the other parallels is purely verbal.

Chapter 15

PARALLELS

2 Clem. 15.3	Isa. 58.9
τὸν θεὸν τὸν λέγοντα·	ὁ θεὸς εἰσακούσεταί σου
ἔτι λαλοῦντός σου ἐρῶ· ἰδοὺ πάρειμι.	ἔτι λαλοῦντός σου ἐρεῖ· ἰδοὺ πάρειμι

The saying cited here in v. 3 is identical with Isa. 58.9 LXX, with only the tiny difference of ἐρῶ for ἐρεῖ, due to the fact that the first phrase is now a direct address by God. There is no need to presume anything other than that the writer has drawn the text from the LXX.[1]

COMMENTARY

1 The introductory οὐκ οἴομαι is similar to 14.2, as is the slight understatement which follows using litotes. The writer's exhortation so far is summed up as a piece of 'advice' (συμβουλία).[2]

The subject matter of it is said now to be 'self-control' (ἐγκράτεια). An explicit reference to being 'self-controlled' has occurred only once before (cf. the adjective ἐγκρατεῖς in 4.3): hence it is not easy to see the word as encapsulating *the* central aspect of the text as a whole.[3] Nevertheless, it is clear (not least from the way in which the author sums up his address so far in this way) that it is an important idea for the author. The word here probably refers to 'self-control' in a relatively general way, rather than to complete sexual

---

[1] The same slight difference in wording occurs in a number of patristic references, e.g. Irenaeus, *Haer.* 4.17.3; Clement, *Strom.* 5.120.3; *Apos. Con.* 3.7.6. Postulating some influence from Isa. 65.24 (ἔτι λαλούντων αὐτῶν ἐρῶ, τί ἐστιν: so Lightfoot, *Apostolic Fathers*, 2.249; Warns, 'Untersuchungen', 509; Lindemann, *Clemensbriefe*, 246) seems unnecessary: cf. Pratscher, *Zweite Clemensbrief*, 193.

[2] See p. 23 above for the possibility that this is a quasi-technical term referring to the genre of the whole: this seems unlikely, and the word here probably simply means 'advice'.

[3] Hence the difficulty in the theory of Harris, 'Authorship', that 2 *Clement* was the work Περὶ ἐγκρατείας of Julius Cassianus. See p. 15 above and also on 4.3.

abstinence in a technical (encratite) sense.⁴ If anyone follows this advice,⁵ they will have no regrets (οὐ μετανοήσει: the word is used here probably in its secular, everyday sense, without any connotations of the more 'religious' sense of 'repent').

The continuation stresses the importance of the pattern of behaviour for the ultimate salvation of both the person who accepts the advice and the teacher: for the first time the author presents himself in the first person (cf. too 18.2 and perhaps 19.1), though perhaps noticeably, without referring to himself with any kind of 'title' or official position within the community: he is simply 'the one who has given the advice' (κἀμὲ τὸν συμβουλεύσαντα).⁶ The motif of response to a preacher bringing benefit not only to the respondent but also to the preacher may be traditional (cf. Ezek. 3.21; 1 Tim. 4.16; Jas. 5.19–20).⁷ Again the writer uses litotes ('no small reward') to underline the importance of the saving 'a soul that is wandering and perishing'. Precisely who the writer has in mind here is not clear: possibly it is the false teachers who may be in view the whole way through; possibly too it may be others who are influenced by them and follow their teaching (cf. 10.5); possibly it is a further (highly self-deprecatory) self-reference.⁸ But perhaps it is not a case of 'either/or' but of 'both/and': it is a positive outcome if anyone is 'saved'.

2 The saving of these lost souls is now said to be the 'recompense' (ἀντιμισθία) which we can give back to God. The idea of a 'recompense' has occurred before, though with different nuances.⁹ Here it is something seen as both possible and positive, something which can be given to God. Slightly unusually within *2 Clement* as a whole, this is related to God's activity as the creator, not as the one who institutes salvation: nowhere else does the author refer to God as the creator.¹⁰ The reference here slips out as apparently something which can be presumed without question: there is no suggestion that

---

⁴ See above on 4.3: the warnings about 'adultery' would be slightly strange (if all sexual activity were regarded negatively).

⁵ Taking the relative ἥν as qualifying συμβουλία rather than ἐγκράτεια (although the word order might suggest otherwise): see Wengst, *Zweite Clemensbrief*, 259; Lindemann, *Clemensbriefe*, 245; Pratscher, *Zweite Clemensbrief*, 191, and *contra* Knopf, *Zwei Clemensbriefe*, 175.

⁶ cf. on 1.1 above: in line with the rest of the text, the author does not put forward any explicit claim to authority by virtue of an 'office'.

⁷ Noted in all the commentaries: cf. e.g. Knopf, *Zwei Clemensbriefe*, 175; Wengst, *Zweite Clemensbrief*, 259, 278; Donfried, *Setting*, 89; Lindemann, *Clemensbriefe*, 245; Pratscher, *Zweite Clemensbrief*, 191.

⁸ In 18.2, it is clear that the author has a very real sense of his own situation as *not* yet 'saved'.

⁹ cf. 1.3, 5; 9.7–8; 11.6. In 9.8, the 'recompense' is specified as 'repentance'; in 11.6, the recompense is that which God gives to us (in judgement).

¹⁰ Some kind of 'creation' language is used in 1.8, but probably refers there to the establishment of Christians as Christians (i.e. 'salvation'), rather than to their physical existence. See above on 1.8.

this claim about God as the creator might be a contested or controversial one. This is potentially striking if *2 Clement* is written in a context of competing Gnostic claims: for a key feature of Gnostic ideas is usually assumed to be a distinction made between the one true God and the creator God, with the latter as at best ignorant and at worst highly malevolent.[11] In such a context, an appeal to God as the one 'who created us' might be quite polemical and pointed; however the fact that so little is made of it here suggests that perhaps this was not a controversial feature of the situation in which the author finds himself.

The context of such activity must then be speaking and hearing in 'faith and love'. The immediately following reference to ἐφ᾽ οἷς ἐπιστεύσαμεν (v. 3) suggests that the πίστις here is full ('religious') 'faith', rather than simply 'trust'.[12] The word is, however, used here for the first (and only) time in *2 Clement*. For the importance of 'love' within the community, cf. 4.3; 9.6; 13.4. As before, the morality for which the author is battling is not simply an individual matter but involves the well-being of all those in the community as well.

3 The exhortation continues with the (fairly general) plea to be 'righteous and holy' (both words quite common in *2 Clement*),[13] holding fast to the things that we have believed.

Another purpose is then given: so that we may pray to God with confidence (παρρησία);[14] and the confidence is bolstered by the citation from Isa. 58.9 (the only biblical citation in which the speaker is specified as 'God'), where God says that he will be present whenever his people address him.

4 The full significance of this is now underlined: what is said here is the sign of a 'great promise'. This is then backed up by the further claim that 'the Lord' says that he is more ready to give than we are to ask. It is not clear if this represents an expansion or interpretation of the citation just given, or whether it refers to a further citation. (If the latter, it appears here in a very general way and giving the gist, rather than the exact words, of what 'the Lord says'.) Nor is it certain who is meant to be the speaker: is the 'Lord' Jesus or God?[15] Perhaps

---

[11] See pp. 51, 66 above.

[12] cf. Lindemann, *Clemensbriefe*, 246, *contra* Knopf, *Zwei Clemensbriefe*, 175.

[13] For 'righteous', or 'righteousness', cf. 5.7; 6.9; 11.1; 17.7; 4.2; 6.9; 11.7; 12.1; for 'holy', cf. 1.3; 6.9; for the combination together, cf. 5.6; 6.9.

[14] The general sentiment is fairly widespread, but the specific language here (with παρρησία) is reminiscent of 1 John 3.21–2; cf. 5.14. Whether there is any literary dependence is uncertain. Pratscher, *Zweite Clemensbrief*, 193, claims that the sentiment here is quite unlike that of 1 John, where 3.20 makes it clear that God is greater than us and knows us all anyway. This is true, but if one looks only at vv. 21–2, the ideas (at least on the surface) are very similar to those of *2 Clement* here: we have 'boldness' to ask God in prayer, and if we do, he will respond positively.

[15] Lindemann, *Clemensbriefe*, 246, claims that the double γάρ suggests that the same speaker is in mind so that the change from 'God' to 'Lord' is difficult and perhaps an extra καί might have dropped out by mistake.

the change of name does indicate a change of referent, in which case a saying of Jesus, rather than an OT quotation of God, might be in mind. Sayings such as Matt. 6.8; Matt. 7.7//Luke 11.9 are regularly cited as possibilities, though none of them provides an exact parallel to what is said here. It is possible that the saying attributed to Jesus and recorded in Acts 20.35 ('it is more blessed to give than to receive') may be in mind here, but again the parallel is not exact (and it would also have to be taken with an implicit assumption that Jesus himself is one who lives out his own instruction to others.)[16] But whatever the details may imply about the origin of what is said, the substance is clear: God is always present to answer prayers addressed to him.

5 The exhortations are now summed up, though in slightly strange language. The first exhortation is for 'us' to 'accept such great goodness'. (Though why this should need saying is not clear: were there people around who were *not* ready to accept God's goodness? The problem seems to be more a disagreement about when and/or where such goodness is available, not about whether or not to accept it.)

The precise exegesis of the next clause is debated: is the ἑαυτοῖς with φθονήσωμεν a genuine reflexive (= 'ourselves') or an equivalent of ἀλλήλοις (= 'one another')? Both possibilities are attested elsewhere in the text (for the former, cf. 6.9; 9.7; 11.3; 19.1; for the latter, cf. 4.3; 12.3; 13.1; 17.2).[17] Van Unnik has argued that the immediate context of the sentence suggests strongly a genuine reflexive, though also with a tinge of 'irony': he claims that the immediate context is about the addressees' own salvation (or otherwise), not about any concern for others. However, this makes for a somewhat awkward connection with the opening participle μεταλαμβάνοντες, which suggests that the addressees are already in the process of receiving God's goodness or generosity (χρηστότης cf. 19.1); in turn this suggests that what follows relates more easily to others gaining the same benefits.[18] Further, the immediate context does have implied references to the well-being of others as well as the readers/hearers themselves (cf. v. 1, and the reference to 'love' in v. 2: see above). It seems preferable then to interpret the ἑαυτοῖς here as ἀλλήλοις: just as the addressees are receiving the goodness of generosity of

---

[16] Not an unreasonable assumption for the author of *2 Clement*! But it is a further connection in any postulated chain of dependence here which has to be assumed.

[17] For the former, see Lightfoot, *Apostolic Fathers*, 2.249; Lake, *Fathers*, 153 ('ourselves'); Richardson, *Fathers*, 200; Grant and Graham, *Apostolic Fathers*, 128; Lindemann, *Clemensbriefe*, 246; Pratscher, *Zweite Clemensbrief*, 195. For the latter, see Knopf, *Zwei Clemensbriefe*, 176; Ehrman, *Fathers*, 191 ('one another'). The case for the former is argued in detail by W. C. van Unnik, 'The Interpretation of 2 Clement 15,5', *VC* 27 (1973), 29–34.

[18] Van Unnik has to interpret the present participle as a 'conative' present (with reference to BDF §§319, 326, but these refer to the use of the present (and for §326 the imperfect) indicative, not a participle), and he translates it as 'since then we *desire to* share in so great a goodness' (my italics; the implication is that we do not yet share).

God now, so they should not begrudge the same good things for others. As at several points in the address, concern for good relationships within the community is a high priority for the author.

The final exhortation in this section is to note that 'these words' (presumably not just the citation in v. 3 but the whole section here and the assurances about God's readiness to answer prayer and to give generously) lead to 'great joy' ($\dot{\eta}\delta o\nu\dot{\eta}$) for those who 'do' them (with again the emphasis on the importance of putting everything into action), but equally strong condemnation ($\kappa\alpha\tau\acute{\alpha}\kappa\rho\iota\sigma\iota\varsigma$) for those who do not. The word $\dot{\eta}\delta o\nu\dot{\eta}$ as used here is somewhat unusual: elsewhere it is often used in a negative sense (e.g. Luke 8.14; Tit. 3.3; Jas. 4.1, 3; 2 Pet. 2.13). It is just possible that there is another slightly pointed address to possible 'opponents': they find their pleasures in the things of this world/age (cf. 6.3–4), but 'true' $\dot{\eta}\delta o\nu\dot{\eta}$ is to be found in the promises of God.[19] This is possible but one must say that any such 'attack' is very indirect!

---

[19] See Donfried, *Setting*, 169.

Chapter 16

PARALLELS

The chapter contains a number of places where earlier texts may have been taken up and used. However, there is no explicit citation (with an introductory formula) in the chapter. Two of the closest parallels are noted here; for others, see the commentary below.

2 Clem. 16.3	Mal 3.19 LXX (4.1 MT)
γινώσκετε δέ, ὅτι	διότι
ἔρχεται ἤδη ἡ ἡμέρα τῆς κρίσεως	ἰδοὺ ἡμέρα κυρίου ἔρχεται
ὡς κλίβανος καιόμενος	καιομένη ὡς κλίβανος

The words in *2 Clement* are not signalled as a citation (though perhaps the introductory γινώσκετε suggests that what follows is known to the readers/hearers and is not stating anything new). The language has probably been derived from the text in Malachi. It is, however, doubtful whether one can deduce anything about the text form used from the detailed wording here. There are some differences from the LXX text of Malachi: for example, *2 Clement* has ἤδη, the 'day' is the day 'of judgement' rather than 'of the Lord', and strictly it is the oven that is burning, not the day (though the difference in substance in the end is trivial!). But these differences may well be due to the author of *2 Clement*, who in any case makes no claim to be citing anything (and hence makes no implicit claim to accuracy by a 'citation').

2 Clem. 16.4	Tob. 12.8–9a (BA)	Tob. 12.8–9a (ℵ)	Tob. 12.8–9a (106 and 107)
κρείσσων νηστεία προσευχῆς, ἐλεημοσύνη δὲ ἀμφοτέρων·	⁸ἀγαθὸν προσευχὴ μετὰ νηστείας καὶ ἐλεημοσύνης καὶ δικαιοσύνης	⁸ἀγαθὸν προσευχὴ μετὰ ἀληθείας καὶ ἐλεημοσύνη μετὰ δικαιοσύνης	⁸ἀγαθὸν προσευχὴ μετὰ νηστείας καὶ ἐλεημοσύνη μετὰ δικαιοσύνης ὑπὲρ ἀμφότερα

2 Clem. 16.4	Tob. 12.8–9a (BA)	Tob. 12.8–9a (ℵ)	Tob. 12.8–9a (106 and 107)
	ἀγαθὸν τὸ ὀλίγον μετὰ δικαιοσύνης ἢ πολὺ μετὰ ἀδικίας· καλὸν ποιῆσαι ἐλεημοσύνην	μᾶλλον ἢ πλοῦτος μετὰ ἀδικίας· καλὸν ποιῆσαι ἐλεημοσύνην μᾶλλον	κρεῖσσον ποιεῖν ἐλεημοσύνην
	ἢ θησαυρίσαι χρυσίον	ἢ θησαυρίσαι χρυσίον	ἢ θησαυρίζειν χρυσίον
ἀγάπη δὲ καλύπτει πλῆθος ἁμαρτιῶν, προσευχὴ δὲ ἐκ καλῆς συνειδήσεως ἐκ θανάτου ῥύεται.	⁹ἐλεημοσύνη γὰρ ἐκ θανάτου ῥύεται,	⁹ἐλεημοσύνη ἐκ θανάτου ῥύεται,	⁹ἐλεημοσύνη γὰρ ἐκ θανάτου ῥύεται,
ἐλεημοσύνη γὰρ κούφισμα ἁμαρτίας γίνεται	καὶ αὐτὴ ἀποκαθαριεῖ πᾶσαν ἁμαρτίαν	καὶ αὐτὴ ἀποκαθαίρει πᾶσαν ἁμαρτίαν	καὶ καθαρίζει ἀπὸ πάσης ἁμαρτίας

1 Pet. 4.8 = *1 Clem.* 49.5 ἀγάπη καλύπτει πλῆθος ἁμαρτιῶν

As with the previous example, this is not formally a citation in that there is no explicit introductory formula to indicate this. However, the author suddenly introduces a number of previously unmentioned categories, including prayer, fasting, and ἐλεημοσύνη,[1] as well as a rather strange ranking of the three in a relative order of importance; in addition, there is an equally abrupt introduction of the theme of 'love'. The words on love here agree almost verbatim with the words of 1 Pet. 4.8 and also *1 Clem.* 49.5 which in turn are close to those of Prov 10.12 ('love covers all offences').[2] The reference to the three activities of prayer, fasting, and ἐλεημοσύνη together, including possibly a relative ranking of the three in an order of importance, followed also by a reference to 'saving from death' and then in turn by a statement that ἐλεημοσύνη deals with sin and/or its effects in some way, is strikingly paralleled in Tob. 12.8–9. The abrupt way in which these categories are suddenly intro-

---

[1] For the possible meaning of this word, see below.
[2] So NRSV. The LXX here seems to have used a different Hebrew text at this point. Hence the wording in 1 Peter and *2 Clement* cannot be derived from the LXX version of Proverbs. The saying is attested in a number of later writers: cf. *Gos. Phil.* (NHC II.3) 78.11; Clement, *Strom.* 4.3.3; *Paed.* 3.12.91; *Quis div.* 38.1; *Didasc. Apos.* 2.3. See Hagner, *Use*, 240; Warns, 'Untersuchungen', 274.

duced may well then be due to the author of *2 Clement* making an allusion to, or echoing, these traditions.³

The 'love' saying can be dealt with fairly briefly here. The common allusion to the verse from Proverbs in 1 Peter, *1 Clement*, and *2 Clement*, with common wording which agrees strikingly against the LXX version, suggests a common tradition circulating in some early Christian circles, including the provenances of these writings; but it is probably impossible to say more.⁴

The link with the text of Tobit is more complex. All text-critical study of the book of Tobit is notoriously complicated, with two main textual traditions often distinguished, represented by LXX codices BA and codex א respectively. In addition, for part of the text (6.9–12.22), a third textual tradition (represented in MSS 106 107) has been isolated.⁵ *2 Clement* here agrees with the text of Tobit in mentioning the three activities together; on the other hand, it differs in relation to some of the relative ordering in importance which is implied here, and it also differs in relation to some of what is ascribed to them.

The relative ranking in importance of the three activities in *2 Clement* is very striking: fasting is better than prayer and ἐλεημοσύνη is better than both. The first has no parallel in any known text of Tobit and is (as far as I know) unparalleled elsewhere. However, the claim that ἐλεημοσύνη is better than 'both' (prayer and fasting) does have a possible parallel in one strand of the textual tradition of Tobit 12.8, namely the text as found in MSS 106 and 107 (see above), which, unlike the BA and א texts, also says that ἐλεημοσύνη is better than 'both' (apparently prayer and fasting).⁶

---

³ The link with Tob. 12 is noted in all the commentaries: cf. Knopf, *Zwei Clemensbriefe*, 176–7; Wengst, *Zweite Clemensbrief*, 278; Lindemann, *Clemensbriefe*, 248–9; Pratscher, *Zweite Clemensbrief*, 201, as is the parallel in 1 Pet. 4//1 *Clem.* 49 on the 'love' saying. The triad of prayer, fasting, and ἐλεημοσύνη are often said to be fundamental forms of Jewish religious piety (cf. too Matt. 6.1–18), though they only occur together in Jewish scripture in Tob. 12: see J. A. Fitzmyer, *Tobit* (Berlin: De Gruyter, 2003), 292. Hence the case of seeing some kind of 'echo' or 'allusion' to Tobit here is strengthened. The link between Tob. 12 and *2 Clem.* 16 is also regularly noted in editions and commentaries on Tobit: see e.g. R. Hanhart, *Tobit. Septuaginta. Vetus Testamentum Graecum Auctoritate Academiae Scientiarum Gottingensis editum. Vol. VIII,5* (Göttingen: Vandenhoeck & Ruprecht, 1983), 158; Fitzmyer, *Tobit*, 292.

⁴ There is scarcely enough evidence to suggest that the author of *2 Clement* knew 1 Peter itself and derived the words from there, though of course this remains a possibility. The same applies to *1 Clement*. In the immediate context of *1 Clem.* 49, there is a clear allusion to Paul's chapter on love in 1 Cor. 13. For a common oral tradition, cf. Wengst, *Zweite Clemensbrief*, 278; Pratscher, *Zweite Clemensbrief*, 202. For dependence on 1 Peter here, cf. Lightfoot, *Apostolic Fathers*, 2.251; Hagner, *Use*, 25, 240; Donfried, *Setting*, 92 ('or a similar tradition').

⁵ See the discussion in Hanhart, *Tobit*, 31–6.

⁶ There is some doubt about the punctuation: e.g. S. Weeks, S. Gathercole, and L. Stuckenbruck (eds), *The Book of Tobit. Texts from the Principal Ancient and Mediaeval Traditions* (Berlin: De Gruyter, 2004), 208, give the text here with a break after δικαιοσύνης in v. 8a, and then take ὑπὲρ ἀμφότερα with what follows rather than with what precedes. This, however, makes the verse say all but nonsense: prayer with fasting, and ἐλεημοσύνη with righteousness are good; better than both is to do ἐλεημοσύνη . . .: hence doing ἐλεημοσύνη is better than ἐλεημοσύνη!

Thus *2 Clement* here links with one version of the text of Tob. 12.8.⁷ The text of *2 Clement* then also has an assertion about 'rescuing from death', as in Tob. 12.9a; however in *2 Clement* this is ascribed to prayer, whereas in all the textual traditions of Tob. 12, this is ascribed to ἐλεημοσύνη. Further, the final clause of the chapter here refers to ἐλεημοσύνη 'lightening' sin, which is roughly parallel (though not identical) with the clause in Tob. 12.9b about ἐλεημοσύνη 'purging away' or 'cleansing' sin.⁸ Clearly the 'parallels' are not close enough to label this a 'quotation' in any strict sense; but there is enough similarity between the texts, in the content and in the general sequence of the sayings, to suggest that some allusion to (at least one version of) the text of Tobit is present here.

What this tells us about the status of the book of Tobit in the eyes of the author is impossible to say with certainty. What is said here stands on its own, with no explicit indication that this is any kind of allusion, let alone a citation. Hence the words are not explicitly ascribed any ('scriptural') authority. Nevertheless, the fact that the author has gone to the trouble of using this tradition (if indeed he has!) suggests that the tradition was thought to be useful, valuable, and worth using. It would seem likely (though one cannot say more) that Tobit was accepted as a book whose words could be used and exploited in the same way as the words of other scriptural books were used. But whether this implies that Tobit was regarded as (fully) scriptural must remain uncertain.

It thus seems best to take ὑπὲρ ἀμφότερα with v. 8a and the verse then makes sense (at one level): prayer with fasting is good, but ἐλεημοσύνη (with righteousness) is better than both: mooted as a possibility also by S. Weeks, 'Some Neglected Texts of Tobit: The Third Greek Version', in M. Bredin (ed.), *Studies in the Book of Tobit* (Edinburgh: T. & T. Clark, 2006), 37; cf. also NRSV 'Prayer with fasting is good, but better than both is almsgiving with righteousness. A little with righteousness is better than wealth with wrongdoing' (though this is somewhat 'eclectic' in relation to the MSS apparently used: it takes the first clause from 106 and 107, the first half of the second clause from the BA text, and the second half from the ℵ text!).

⁷ The fact that this reading in the Greek MSS is not simply a very late variant in medieval (14th-cent.) MSS may be indicated by the Old Latin version which also seems to attest the reading, albeit indirectly: bona est oratio cum ieiunio et eleemosuna cum iustitia: super utrumque autem melius est modicum cum iustitia quam plurimum cum iniquitate. The super utrum(que) seems to reflect the 106 and 107 reading above, though clearly taking it with the following clause (cf. the -que and autem): but as with the Greek text of 106 and 107, this makes virtual nonsense: eleemosuna with iustitia is good, but then a little (of anything?) with iustitia is better than both, including eleemosuna with iustitia! The comparative super utrem would make better sense if taken with the previous clause, asserting that eleemosuna is better than both prayer and fasting. Hence the Old Latin version may indirectly witness to a reading like that of the 106 and 107 version lying behind it.

The link between *2 Clem.* 16.4 and this version of the text of Tob. 12.8 was noted by J. R. Harris, 'The Double Text of Tobit', *AJT* 3 (1899), 546–8. The link is doubted by Weeks, 'Neglected Texts', 14, who suggests possible influence of Sir. 40.24; but he does not refer to the Old Latin version, and the verse from Sirach is quite different in substance. (NRSV 'Kindred and helpers are for a time of trouble, but almsgiving rescues better than either.')

⁸ The MSS of Tobit vary slightly in the verb used, but none of them corresponds exactly to *2 Clement's* 'lightening'.

COMMENTARY

1 The writer draws out his conclusions from the previous section in 15.3–5 with the initial ὥστε here. In many respects, what follows immediately is nothing new and largely repeats in summary form what has been said earlier, e.g. in 8.1–3; 9.7–8: while there is time, we should then 'repent' and turn to God who calls us (cf. 10.1).[9] The motif of 'while there is still time' recalls what was said in the earlier passages.

The final phrase spells out this 'while we have time' in slightly different wording, though the precise sense is not clear. The translation is in one way reasonably clear: 'while we still have the Father[10] who accepts us'. What is meant precisely by the statement that 'we still have' the Father is slightly unclear. Is a future time envisaged when we will not 'have' the Father? Perhaps though the sense is that the present time is one when we still have the Father as a receiving and accepting figure, whereas in the future he may be rather different (e.g. a stern judge). Perhaps then a 'translation' (or slight paraphrase) such as 'while we still have the Father as someone who is still ready to accept us' might capture the sense of what is intended.

2 The author now spells out in slightly more detail what it might mean in practice to undertake 'repentance'. Unfortunately (for us), the details still remain vague! The requirements are set out in a long conditional clause (ἐὰν γάρ). First, the readers are implicitly encouraged to bid farewell to 'these pleasures'. The noun used here is ἡδυπάθεια (also in 17.7). The word is used only here in early Christian literature, and in the LXX only in 4 Macc. 2.2, 4. Bauer's *Lexicon* gives a meaning 'enjoyment, comfort in the sense of a luxurious mode of life'.[11] Elsewhere, in secular Greek, it is used uniformly

---

[9] Though elsewhere it is sometimes Christ who 'calls' Christians: cf. 2.4, 7; other instances are ambiguous (e.g. 1.2; 9.4, *pace* Pratscher, *Zweite Clemensbrief*, 197, who says all these refer to Christ).

[10] Many editions and texts read here τὸν παραδεχόμενον instead of τὸν πατέρα δεχόμενον. Some even claim that this is the reading of C, with S adding the extra reference to the Father. So e.g. Wengst, *Zweite Clemensbrief*, 258 (with the critical apparatus); Bihlmeyer, *Apostolischen Väter*, 78, and Ehrman, *Fathers*, 190 (C reads τὸν παραδεχόμενον, the longer S reading resulting from treating παρα as π̄ρ̄ᾱ and taken as a *nomen sacrum*); Gebhardt, Harnack, and Zahn, *Opera*, 42, and Lake, *Fathers*, 154, print τὸν παραδεχόμενον with no variant noted in the critical apparatus. The facsimile of the relevant passage in C (readily available as an appendix in Lightfoot, *Apostolic Fathers*, 1.471) makes it quite clear that C reads τὸν π̄ρ̄ᾱ δεχόμενον. Hence both the MSS agree in reading 'father' here and there is no basis for a reading τὸν παραδεχόμενον which would be a conjectural emendation. For a correct statement of the evidence, see Lindemann, *Clemensbriefe*, 247; Pratscher, *Zweite Clemensbrief*, 197. Lightfoot, *Apostolic Fathers*, 2.250, correctly states the MS evidence, but prints τὸν παραδεχόμενον (without 'father') in his text without any discussion.

[11] BAG, 345.

negatively.¹² Clearly the exhortation is directed against some kind of overindulgence, though precisely what is in mind is not stated. (The ταύταις suggests that something specific is in mind, but precisely what is unclear.)

The further exhortation is that we should 'conquer our soul' by no longer 'doing its evil desires'. Again the language is rather unspecific. In general terms, it is in line with what has been said about ἐγκράτεια in the previous chapter: evidently some kind of self-control is being urged on the listeners and a readiness to resist those parts of the human make-up that might be tempted to some kind of indulgence ('evil desires'). But once again the language remains vague and unspecific. It is striking too that here the 'soul' is identified as the responsible part of the human make-up that is singled out for mention. A similar negative view of the 'soul' occurs in 17.7 ('pleasures of the soul'). Elsewhere the 'soul' is generally regarded positively (cf. 5.4; 6.2; 10.5; etc.). However, as with a number of other features in his language and thought, the author is not always consistent in his terminology; and perhaps here it would be asking too much to expect a clear, well-defined anthropology.¹³

The promise held out for those who fulfil the requirements implied in the conditional clause is that they will share in 'the mercy of Jesus'.¹⁴ In 3.1, the 'mercy' which Jesus has bestowed on 'us' evidently relates to something that has already happened. However, to try to make 3.1 the hermeneutical key to the language here would probably be mistaken: the context seems to imply clearly that this sharing in the 'mercy of Jesus' is something that is future and dependent on the readers/hearers fulfilling the requirements just spelled out, i.e. bidding farewell to the pleasures mentioned, conquering their souls, and giving up its evil desires. The eschatology here seems entirely future.¹⁵

3 The wholly futurist eschatology here is now buttressed with a further claim in the form of a brief, pregnant statement about the fact that the final Day (implying the end of at least the present world order) will come—both inevitably and (perhaps) soon (cf. ἤδη).

The introductory γινώσκετε, and the closeness of the language to that of Mal. 3.19 LXX (4.1 MT), suggest that this is virtually a 'citation' (see Parallels above). There is, however, no introductory formula as such. It is therefore uncertain how far one can make anything of small differences between

---

¹² e.g. Xenophon, *Cyr.* 7.5.74; Plutarch, *Mor.* 132c; Marcus Aurelius 10.33.

¹³ See earlier on whether 'salvation' is past/present or future etc. On anthropology, the author seems to work with a 'body/soul' dichotomy in ch. 5, but then insists on the future resurrection of the 'flesh' (meaning apparently the physical body) in ch. 9. On the general lack of consistency here, see Lindemann, *Clemensbriefe,* 247; Pratscher, *Zweite Clemensbrief,* 197.

¹⁴ The reference to the name 'Jesus' alone is unusual; the S reading ('our Lord Jesus Christ') is probably a secondary attempt to ease the slight difficulty.

¹⁵ So rightly Pratscher, *Zweite Clemensbrief,* 198, *contra* Lindemann, *Clemensbriefe,* 248. Cf. too Lohmann, *Drohung,* 124–5.

Commentary: Chapter 16 271

the text of Malachi and the words here, whether at the level of text form presupposed or of conscious changes made by the author. Some differences might well fall into the latter category: e.g. the fact that the 'day' is here the day 'of judgement' (rather than 'the day of the Lord') underlines the fact that what is coming will bring judgement, and it is precisely this that the author wishes to emphasize here. The other difference concerns the word ἤδη, not present in our versions of the text of Malachi. Whether this indicates a vivid expectation that the End is imminent is not clear. At face value it might; but other parts of *2 Clement* suggest an opposite point of view (e.g. especially 20.3). It may be that the ἤδη here is simply part of the writer's concern to show how pressing the issue is: the End is coming (already!) with such certainty that action now is imperative.[16]

The allusion to Malachi is followed by words that contain a notorious crux: 'some (τινες) of the heavens will melt'. The MSS agree on the wording of the text, but it has always been regarded as extremely difficult to have an idea that (only) 'some' of the heavens will melt in this context. Lightfoot suggested a textual corruption and proposed emending τινες to (αἱ) δυνάμεις, with a possible allusion to the words of Isa. 34.4 LXX (BLO*) καὶ τακήσονται πᾶσαι αἱ δυνάμεις τῶν οὐρανῶν.[17] This must, however, remain conjectural, though if one sticks with the text we have in the MSS, the idea of only a partial conflagration of the heavenly world seems somewhat strange.[18] The picture of a final end of the present cosmic world order is completed with the claim that the earth will be caught up in this cosmic destruction by melting like lead in the fire.

The image of the end of the present world order in the form of a cosmic conflagration is widespread. In early Christianity, the idea occurs only in the NT at 2 Pet. 3.7, 10.[19] The motif also occurs in Jewish texts such as 1 QH 3.29–36, *Syb. Or.* 3.84–7; 4.172–80, as well as being reflected in some Gnostic circles,[20] and also in Greek philosophical thought, especially the

---

[16] See Pratscher, *Zweite Clemensbrief*, 198.

[17] Lightfoot, *Apostolic Fathers*, 2.250. There is similar wording in *Apoc. Pet.* as recorded in Macarius of Magnesia 4.7: καὶ τακήσεται πᾶσα δύναμις οὐρανοῦ ('every power of heaven will be shaken'). See Kraus and Nicklas, *Petrusevangelium*, 93. (The text does not occur in the text of *Apoc. Pet.* in the Akhmim codex.)

[18] Lake, *Fathers*, 155, in a footnote defends the text 'as a reference to the early Christian belief in seven concentric heavens surrounding the Earth'; but he gives no more detail and, even with this belief, it is still strange to posit someone thinking of (only) *some* of these being destroyed. Lindemann, *Clemensbriefe*, 248 admits defeat: 'Die Aussage muß uns wohl unverständlich bleiben.' ('The saying must remain unintelligible to us.')

[19] Other later Christian writers who attest the idea include Justin, *1 Apol.* 20.1–2; 60.8; Tatian, *Orat.* 25.6; Tertullian, *Spect.* 30; Clement, *Strom.* 5.121–2. For a good summary discussion, see Bauckham, *Jude, 2 Peter*, 300.

[20] cf. Irenaeus, *Haer.* 1.7.1: according to Valentinians, after the pneumatics are separated from others and enter the Pleroma, the rest of the earth will be consumed by fire. It is just possible that this is hinted at in the τινες reading (cf. Warns, 'Untersuchungen', 510–11); but it is hard then to see this as *anti*-Valentinian as Warns does: it might be another case of the author adopting 'Gnostic' language positively as his own.

Stoics.²¹ Here the apocalyptic speculation is, however, firmly linked to the paraenetic exhortation by linking the speculation about the end-time fire with the theme of judgement: the great conflagration at the End will also have as a result the making visible the 'secret and open' deeds of men and women.²² Thus *2 Clement* here shares with *Syb. Or.* a timescale where the final conflagration is not quite the End itself, but precedes the final judgement which then follows. The whole point of the reference to the final judgement is to reinforce the seriousness of the ethical exhortations in the present with the threat of divine punishment in the future if nothing is done now.²³

4 The consequences of what has just been said are now (apparently) drawn (cf. οὖν). What follows is, however, somewhat strange with unexpected ideas and language appearing very abruptly and with a line of argument that many find unsustainable. We suddenly hear about 'charity' (ἐλεημοσύνη: see below), fasting, and prayer. Moreover, these three are put into some kind of ranked order, with fasting better than prayer and charity better than both (see above on Parallels). But then what is said about the lower-ranked prayer (as rescuing from death) seems to be greater and better than what is said about the higher-ranked 'charity' (as (only?) lightening sin). So too a slightly abrupt reference to 'love' also appears. The logic seems strained at best; and the sudden appearance of categories that have barely been mentioned before, as well as the all but total absence of reference to the one theme that does seem to be important in this section of the text, namely repentance,²⁴ has given rise to some fairly harsh comments about the writer's abilities or about the reliability of the present text.²⁵

The sudden introduction of language about 'charity', prayer, and fasting might, however, be better explained if a tradition is being incorporated here, at times with some difficulty and in a strained way; but it may be that the confusion is arising in part by the attempt to incorporate, and adapt, earlier tradition(s) that was/were not originally coined for the present context. As noted above (on Parallels), there is a striking parallel (though also some disagreement) with (one version of) the text of Tob. 12.8 in what is said about the relative merits of 'charity', prayer, and fasting; and Tob. 12.9 then also

---

[21] cf. Diogenes Laertius 7.142 (= *SVF* 1.102); Nemesius 309.5 ff. (= *SVF* 2.625). See Tuckett, *Gospel of Mary*, 139.

[22] For the motif, cf. Rom. 2.16; 1 Cor. 3.13.

[23] The threatening nature of the language is rightly emphasized by Lohmann, *Drohung*, 125.

[24] cf. 16.1; also when the argument is resumed after this mini-section in 16.4, it is in terms again of repentance: 17.1 'so then let us repent', as if what has gone just before gives the basis for this exhortation.

[25] cf. Lightfoot, *Apostolic Fathers*, 2.251, who thinks that the text might have been corrupted. Schubert, '2. Clemensbrief', 254, calls this section 'höchst unklar' ('extremely unclear') and 'in großen Durcheinander' ('in great confusion'); Pratscher, *Zweite Clemensbrief*, 203, talks about 'Verwirrung' ('confusion').

mentions rescuing from death (though ascribing it to ἐλεημοσύνη rather than to prayer, as here), and alleviating sin(s) (though again with slightly different language used). It is possible that the introduction of the category of ἐλεημοσύνη is linked with the earlier reference to the 'mercy' (ἔλεος) of Jesus in v. 2: just as the addressees hope to receive, and share in, the ἔλεος of Jesus, so too perhaps they are called on to exhibit ἐλεημοσύνη in their own lives. It may then have been this which led the author to a form of the tradition in Tob. 12.8, extolling the supreme value of ἐλεημοσύνη along with the associated activites of prayer and fasting.

There is first the problem of the precise meaning of ἐλεημοσύνη. The noun is usually translated as 'almsgiving', i.e. giving money to the poor. However, Heiligenthal has shown that the word is used at times in a rather broader sense, referring to a wide range of acts of kindness or compassion shown to those in need.[26] Given that the specific issue of money may not be paramount for the author of *2 Clement*,[27] there is a lot to be said for the possibility that the author understands the word here in this broader sense of 'good works' or 'charity'.[28] This might also fit better with the way the word is actually used here in v. 4 (see below).

It is frequently noted that the three activities of prayer, fasting, and charity constitute fundamental forms of Jewish religious piety. They are mentioned (and apparently rejected as religiously worthless) in *Gos. Thom.* 6, 14.[29] They are also treated together in Matt. 6.1–18. However, Tob. 12 seems to be the closest parallel; in all forms of the text, a very high status is given to ἐλεημοσύνη, and in one form it is explicitly said to be 'better' than prayer and fasting (see on Parallels above).

---

[26] See R. Heiligenthal, 'Werke der Barmherzigkeit oder Almosen? Zur Bedeutung von ἐλεημοσύνη', *NovT* 25 (1983), 290–1. For a broader use, Sir. 3.14; Tob. 1.16; 4.16 are probably the clearest examples (e.g. in the context, the passages in Tobit imply that doing ἐλεημοσύνη involves far more than simply giving money: it involves a wide range of acts of kindness to those in need—clothing the naked, feeding the hungry, etc. (cf. Isa. 58.6–7)); other instances are more ambiguous.

[27] Though it may not be irrelevant: cf. the warnings against 'love of money' in 4.3; 6.4; and the reference to the unrighteous enjoying wealth in 20.1.

[28] There is no obvious translation equivalent as a single word in English for the idea; I have used 'charity' as perhaps the least unsatisfactory, though it is not ideal. Cf. BAG, 249, give 'kind deed', especially 'alms, charitable giving' as the meaning; LSJ, 531, give 'pity, mercy . . . 2. charity, alms'.

[29] This is exploited by Donfried, *Setting*, 170–1, arguing that there is a direct link between these texts and that *2 Clement* is here directly opposing the view represented in *Gos. Thom.* 6, 14; cf. too Aono, *Entwicklung*, 130. This seems to press the evidence too far. *2 Clement* does not seem to be pressing the positive value of these three activities against those who would deny them any value at all. And Donfried's claim (p. 171) that 'these are the only two pieces of literature in Christian circles that combine the three elements of charity, prayer and fasting' is surely contradicted by the example of Matt. 6.1–18, where the three activities are clearly connected and treated together: see Wengst, *Zweite Clemensbrief*, 278.

The existence of such a text (or a tradition) lying behind *2 Clement* here might explain the author's somewhat strained line of argument (perhaps not dissimilar to what appears to have happened in ch. 14). This may be hinted at in the opening clause, which states that charity is good 'as repentance from sin'. The precise force of the ὡς is not clear. It is often translated as 'almsgiving is good, just as repentance is good'. This, however, makes the mini-section on ἐλεημοσύνη into something of a diversion, and fails to explain how the author can claim at the start of the next chapter (as he does) that what he has just said is the basis for, and can be summed up in, the exhortation to repent (17.1).

It would, however, fit the overall line of argument of this section of the text as a whole better if the ὡς were translated as 'ἐλεημοσύνη is good, *as being* repentance from sin'.[30] What the author may be doing is then *identifying* ἐλεημοσύνη as repentance. This would also fit better if ἐλεημοσύνη is taken with the broader meaning of 'good works/charity' (rather than just almsgiving), and also if μετάνοια is taken as referring to the actual change (of behaviour) that is being demanded (rather than simply remorse about the past: see on 8.1 above). What then is being equated here is not giving of money with remorse, but the broader activity of good works in general with the change in behaviour that is expected and demanded of the Christian: the change in behaviour involves now being engaged in ἐλεημοσύνη, i.e. showing practical loving care and concern for one's neighbour.

If this is combined with an existing tradition which commends the value of 'charity' as being pre-eminent, even over such apparently self-evidently worthy activities such as prayer and fasting, then the argument of the writer would become appropriate and germane: since ἐλεημοσύνη is the supreme 'virtue' or activity, then with the equation being implied here between ἐλεημοσύνη and repentance, the point is made that the change in behaviour ('repentance') to one of doing good to one's neighbour ('charity') is the supremely important thing which the addressees should undertake as a matter of the utmost urgency. And this then would explain how and why the author can then summarize his previous argument at the start of ch. 17 with the exhortation 'so then let us repent'. Certainly, if ἐλεημοσύνη here does refer to works of love and mercy more broadly (rather than just 'almsgiving'), then the pre-eminent position which such activity has here would fit well with rest of *2 Clement* which stresses the importance of practical ethical behaviour, with so much emphasis also placed on the importance of relationships with one's immediate neighbours (mostly within the community).[31]

---

[30] The two alternatives are given by Lightfoot, *Apostolic Fathers*, 2.251. He takes the first as all but self-evident: 'the sense will hardly allow us to translate "as being repentance from sin"'.

[31] It must, however, be conceded that, although an appeal to one version of the text of Tob. 12.8 goes some way to explaining the pre-eminent position given to ἐλεημοσύνη here, the relative ranking of prayer and fasting remains unexplained. There is no extant version of the text

The meaning suggested above for ἐλεημοσύνη may also explain what others have seen as a rather abrupt introduction of the motif of 'love' and the claim that 'love covers a multitude of sins'. For if ἐλεημοσύνη has the broader meaning of 'good works', then it could be seen as synonymous with love.[32] Further, the claim that ἐλεημοσύνη can function in an atoning way for sins is already stated in Tob. 12.9.[33] Hence the introduction of 'love' in its capacity for somehow dealing with sin and its consequences is not as arbitrary as might appear initially.

The language may also be traditional within early Christian circles, the saying being also attested (in almost identical language) in 1 Pet. 4.8 and *1 Clem.* 49.5 (see above). What is striking here is that, in its present context, and unlike the contexts in 1 Peter and *1 Clement*, the 'sins' that are 'covered' seem to be one's own sins, not the sins of others.[34] But it may be that the 'covering' here refers not so much to any 'forgiveness', but to the elimination of sin: the exercise of love involves practical action and concern for others being put into practice, and the resulting life will no longer be characterized as sinful.

Fasting is not mentioned again after the comparison and relative order of importance of the three activities is stated. However, prayer is mentioned: provided it is from the 'good conscience',[35] it 'rescues from death'. The same is said about ἐλεημοσύνη in Tob. 12.9a (cf. too 4.10; Prov. 10.2; 11.4 of 'righteousness').[36] Whether this is a deliberate attempt to amend what is said in Tob. 12 is not clear. Certainly there is no clear parallel elsewhere to ascribing this function to prayer. Some have seen this as giving prayer a very high status, and hence all but contradicting what has just been said about ἐλεημοσύνη being better than (fasting and) prayer.[37] However, there may be an element of consistency in what is said. Whatever one makes of the comparison between the three activities at the start of v. 4, the author does not deny the value of either prayer or fasting (unlike *Gos. Thom.* 14): both are

---

of Tob. 12.8 which might account for this. The author here makes nothing more of fasting, or of the relative merits of fasting in relation to the other two. It may have been part of his tradition here and left hanging; but there is no way we can identify that tradition more precisely.

[32] cf. Lindemann, *Clemensbriefe*, 249.

[33] On this see K. Berger, 'Almosen für Israel', *NTS* 23 (1978), 183–6. On p. 185, Berger refers to the 'unevangelische Natur' ('unevangelic nature') of the way in which a number of early Christian texts, including *2 Clem.* 16, took over this idea from Judaism. Certainly the absence of any reference here to Jesus, and/or Jesus' death, in the whole process of forgiveness and atonement is surprising.

[34] See Lightfoot, *Apostolic Fathers*, 2.251–2.

[35] cf. Heb. 13.18; for the opposite, see *Did.* 4.14; *Barn.* 19.12.

[36] cf. also Pol. *Phil.* 10.2 for a 'citation' (or allusion: there is no explicit introductory formula) of this verse from Tobit. This comes just before the 'citation' (though again with no introductory formula) in 10.3 of the 'woe' found in *2 Clem.* 13.2. The 'agreement' is intriguing, though one cannot say more.

[37] e.g. Lightfoot, *Apostolic Fathers*, 2.251; Schubert, '2. Clemensbrief', 254.

good, and it is simply that ἐλεημοσύνη is better. Hence implicitly ascribing a high status to prayer (by saying that it rescues from death) may give an even higher status to ἐλεημοσύνη, which is what the author seems to want to do overall in this section.

It is not clear what precisely is in mind in this assertion about prayer. In one way, it is a claim that is manifestly false: prayer does not obviate the inevitability of physical death. In the context of Tob. 12, the reference seems to be to *premature* death. Perhaps one can import that meaning into the present context (though one has to admit that it is not stated). So too, it may be worth noting that rescuing from death may not be the most important thing for the author of *2 Clement*: in ch. 5 he has argued that (physical) death should not be regarded as a matter of overriding importance and Christians should not worry about it. Hence in one way, it may be that the author regards 'rescuing from (premature?) death' as in one way very good and praiseworthy. But more important is perhaps the final judgement which Christians must face; and in order to face that prospect with hope (rather than dread), the most important factor is how one behaves ethically in the present, whether one 'does' ἐλεημοσύνη or whether one remains engulfed in 'sin'. And for this writer, the way of dealing with it is summed up in the idea of 'repentance', which involves above all changing one's whole lifestyle: cf. v. 2 above!

There may be then no intention of downplaying prayer (and fasting) as such: hence the beatitude expressed here—'blessed' is every person who is found to be full of (all!) these things. But the most important thing for the writer is perhaps saved up for the last. The final clause is sometimes taken as something of an afterthought, after the main substance of the section has ended with the beatitude.[38] But it may be that this is the real 'last word' which the author wishes to emphasize: ἐλεημοσύνη 'lightens sin'. The language is unusual: for κούφισμα (or the cognate verb) cf. 1 Esd. 8.84; 2 Esd. 9.13. The normal translation is to 'lighten', but not perhaps in any half-hearted way (as if 'lightening' involves a lessening of a load but the load is still present).[39] Rather, the 'lightening' of sin may mean dealing with sin radically, in the sense of maybe simply eliminating it, by replacing it with works of ἐλεημοσύνη. The idea that ἐλεημοσύνη has beneficial effects for the giver as well as the recipient, including dealing with the effects of sin, is present already in Tob. 12.9 ('For charity saves from death and purges away every sin';[40] see above on Parallels). It is this which the writer wants to emphasize above all,

---

[38] So e.g. Lindemann, *Clemensbriefe*, 249; Pratscher, *Zweite Clemensbrief*, 203.

[39] 2 Esd. 9.13 makes it clear that language about 'lightening' sin can be taken very radically: ἐκούφισας ἡμῶν τὰς ἀνομίας καὶ ἔδωκας ἡμῖν σωτηρίαν. 'Lightening' sins and/or wickedness has led to 'salvation'. By implication, the 'lightening' has involved dealing with sin definitively.

[40] The NRSV translation (though changing 'almsgiving' to 'charity' for the translation of ἐλεημοσύνη). Cf. too Sir. 3.30: 'almsgiving will expiate sins'; also Dan. 4.24. See Fitzmyer, *Tobit*, 171, 292, and see above on Berger.

having staked the claim that the change in lifestyle ($\mu\epsilon\tau\acute{a}\nu o\iota a$) which is demanded is to a life characterized by good works and acts of mercy and kindness to one's neighbours, i.e. as $\dot{\epsilon}\lambda\epsilon\eta\mu o\sigma\acute{v}\nu\eta$. In this sense it may well be that the writer does genuinely think that $\dot{\epsilon}\lambda\epsilon\eta\mu o\sigma\acute{v}\nu\eta$ is better even than prayer (which rescues from death) because the most important thing above all is the change in lifestyle, and the resulting new way of behaving, that is required in the face of the imminent judgement.

The line of argument is not easy to follow. However, it may also be that, if one posits a tradition (a form of Tob. 12.8–9) being taken up and exploited by the writer for his own argument here, there may be a little more 'logic' than appears at first sight. There are clearly times when the author's logic and train of thought is somewhat confused. But as with ch. 14, the argument here may have more than an element of its own logic and sense.

Chapter 17

PARALLELS

2 Clem. 17.4, 5	Isa. 66.18
εἶπεν γὰρ ὁ κύριος·	
ἔρχομαι συναγαγεῖν πάντα τὰ ἔθνη, φυλὰς καὶ γλώσσας . . .	ἔρχομαι συναγαγεῖν πάντα τὰ ἔθνη καὶ τὰς γλώσσας
	καὶ ἥξουσιν
καὶ ὄψονται τὴν δόξαν αὐτοῦ	καὶ ὄψονται τὴν δόξαν μου

The wording here is almost identical with that of Isa. 66.18, with the last part of the sentence in Isaiah apparently quoted at the start of 2 Clem. 17.5. The extra reference to 'tribes' in 2 Clem. 17.4 may derive from Dan. 3.2, 7 LXX, where ἔθνη, φυλαί, and γλωσσαί occur together. There is no need necessarily to presuppose use of a different text of Isa. 66, or a testimonium collection, or a citation from an apocryphal gospel here.[1] The αὐτοῦ for μου at the end is presumably due to the fact that the author of 2 Clement has split the citation up into two parts with the second part no longer as direct speech by 'the Lord'.

2 Clem. 17.5	Isa. 66.24
καὶ ὁ σκώληξ αὐτῶν οὐ τελευτήσει καὶ τὸ πῦρ αὐτῶν οὐ σβεσθήσεται, καὶ ἔσονται εἰς ὅρασιν πάσῃ σαρκί	ὁ γὰρ σκώληξ αὐτῶν οὐ τελευτήσει καὶ τὸ πῦρ αὐτῶν οὐ σβεσθήσεται καὶ ἔσονται εἰς ὅρασιν πάσῃ σαρκί

The words here are not introduced as a citation with an introductory formula, but they agree verbatim with the words of Isa. 66.24 LXX. The same words are also used (with the brief introductory φησίν) in 7.6. Clearly the verse was well known to the author. The verse is used in the gospels (Mark 9.48), but there is no evidence that the words have come to the author of 2 Clement via the gospels rather than from Isa. 66 direct (see above on 7.6).

---

[1] Contra e.g. Warns, 'Untersuchungen', 408.

COMMENTARY

The final section of the exhortation proper in the 'letter' reverts again to the stringent need for repentance on the part of the readers/hearers, with renewed reference to the threats posed by the coming judgement for those who refuse to repent.

1 Repentance 'with our whole heart' is enjoined (cf. 8.2). The exhortation is yet again in the first-person plural: as much as the author no doubt thinks that he is speaking *to* some of his readers/hearers, he includes himself among the group of those who need to repent (cf. more explicitly 18.2). This is part of the author's overall rhetorical stance of not being overly polemical and identifying with his audience/readership. The aim of this repentance is that 'none of us' should perish (παραπόληται).[2] The immediate concern (as is spelt out shortly) is to ensure that no member of the *Christian* community ('us') should be lost.

The wider purview is mentioned briefly: 'since' (εἰ)[3] we have commandments and[4] do 'this' (presumably what is specified in the 'commandments'). . . . The 'commandments' evidently relate to 'tearing away' others from idols and 'instructing' them. This seems to be a reference to missionary activity, 'converting' people from being non-Christians to Christians (cf. 'turning from idols'). What 'commandments' are in mind is not clear, and not specified. Some have suggested that possibly the mission charge of Matt. 28.19–20 (or possibly Mark 16.15) is presupposed here.[5] But the language used, about tearing others away from idols, does not relate to anything said in Matt. 28 or Mark 16. If anything such language is closer to texts such as 1 Thess. 1.9; 1 Cor. 12.2. Donfried argues that the reference here might be to the saying cited in 2.4 about calling sinners,[6] but again there is no mention there of idols. Perhaps then the words here constitute a rather general reference to the presupposition that Christian mission to outsiders is

---

[2] A fairly rare word, at least in early Christian literature, but not unprecedented in wider Graeco-Roman literature (e.g. Aristophanes, *Vesp.* 1228; Lucian, *Nigr.* 13). See Knopf, *Zwei Clemensbriefe*, 177.

[3] Εἰ expressing a condition in accordance with fact.

[4] This is the reading of C καὶ τοῦτο πράσσομεν. S presupposes a reading ἵνα καὶ τοῦτο πράσσωμεν. The S reading is accepted by Lightfoot, *Apostolic Fathers*, 2.252; also Bihlmeyer, *Apostolischen Väter*, 75; Lake, *Fathers*, 156; Richardson, *Fathers*, 200. The C reading is accepted by Gebhardt, Harnack, and Zahn, *Opera*, 43; Wengst, *Zweite Clemensbrief*, 260; Lindemann, *Clemensbriefe*, 250; Ehrman, *Fathers*, 192; Pratscher, *Zweite Clemensbrief*, 205. The S reading, implying a demand (rather than expressing a statement after the εἰ), fits rather awkwardly with the following infinitives. The C reading is thus followed here.

[5] Lightfoot, *Apostolic Fathers*, 2.253; Knopf, *Zwei Clemensbriefe*, 177; Grant and Graham, *Apostolic Fathers*, 129; mentioned as possible by Pratscher, *Zweite Clemensbrief*, 205.

[6] Donfried, *Setting*, 173.

part and parcel of Christian existence as a (divine) demand.[7] The reference to 'instructing' (κατηχεῖν) may reflect a more technical sense of catechetical instruction given to catchumens.[8]

However, such a wider purview is almost immediately forgotten and attention is once more focused on the problems with*in* the Christian community:[9] it is the duty of 'us'[10] to save from perishing someone[11] who 'already knows God' (cf. 3.1). The reference is clearly to those inside the community who the writer believes are in danger of rejection at the final judgement. Clearly too, the author believes that profession of the Christian faith in itself provides no guarantee of final salvation. The wording in the final phrase may also be somewhat pointed: the danger is for those 'who already know God' (or perhaps who think/claim they know God!). This might then be a quiet reference to some kind of Gnostic claims to 'know' God and the writer is indirectly questioning the sufficiency of any such claims.[12] But, as always, any possible polemic is very muted, and the language may simply refer in a general way to errant Christians.

2 The reference to the intra-community situation is now clear: we must help 'one another',[13] but evidently especially those who are 'weak in goodness'. Talk about the 'weak' occurs only here in 2 Clement, though the verbal image seems to be presupposed as known (for similar uses cf. Rom. 14.1–2; 1 Cor. 8.11–12; *1 Clem*. 38.2, though whether this implies knowledge by the author of *2 Clement* of any of these *texts* is not certain).[14] The 'good' is presumably the correct manner of ethical behaviour which has been the concern of the author throughout.

The aim is that we may 'all' be saved. Being 'saved' presumably refers to the eschatological salvation at the End time. Whether one should see any quiet polemic in the 'all' is not certain: it is just possible that the author is speaking against (possibly Gnostic) claims that excluded certain classes of human beings from final salvation; however, it is equally possible that the author is

---

[7] See Lindemann, *Clemensbriefe*, 250.

[8] See H. W. Beyer, κατηχέω, *TWNT* 3 (1938), 639.

[9] cf. Wengst, *Zweite Clemensbrief*, 261. Cf. too Lindemann, *Clemensbriefe*, 251: concern for right teaching and behaviour within the community evidently has precedence over any concern for external missionary activity.

[10] The first-person plural is now rather less inclusive: it refers to 'us' who can 'save' others with*in* the community.

[11] Literally 'a soul': as in 16.2, the author does not hesitate to speak negatively of a human being as ψυχή.

[12] cf. Warns, 'Untersuchungen', 310.

[13] ἑαυτοῖς used for ἀλλήλοις (cf. 4.3; 12.3; 13.1), as is made clear by the use of ἀλλήλους in v. 2b.

[14] However, for Paul, the 'weak' are generally those who apparently are over-stringent in their behaviour (e.g. in relation to Jewish food laws); for *2 Clement*, the 'weak in goodness' are those who *dis*regard ethical requirements.

Commentary: Chapter 17   281

simply expressing his concern that everyone in the community, including the teachers who are the immediate object of his concern, should be saved. Further exhortations are also given:[15] we should 'bring back' (to the right way) and 'exhort' one another. For the use of ἐπιστρέφειν here, cf. Pol. *Phil.* 6.1.[16] 'Exhorting' each other is in context very similar in meaning.

3 The actual situation of the community seems to come into view more clearly. The context is a community gathered together for some kind of worship receiving an exhortation of the 'elders', to be followed by a return to daily life at home. The meaning is clear at one level: we should not only pay lip service to what we hear at the time in the 'exhortation'; we must also take this back into our everyday lives and live out the consequences in practical daily living.

Further details about what may have been going on in such a context remain tantalizingly hidden from us. The one thing that is mentioned is that 'we' are being 'exhorted by the elders'. It may well be that the present text of *2 Clement* constitutes precisely this kind of address to the community, given in the context of some kind of liturgical gathering of the community (cf. too 19.2), with perhaps the author as one of the 'elders' involved. In general terms, this fits with the description we have in Justin, *1 Apol.* 67.4, where some kind of 'sermon' is given after readings (from scripture and/or the 'memoirs of the apostles'), and this is referred to in part as 'exhorting' (νουθεσία).[17] However, any status claimed by the author himself remains unclear. At the surface level of the language, he includes himself among the *recipients* of the exhortation, not stating that he is the author.[18] Whatever theological and/or philosophical or logical problems the author may suffer from in grappling with the problems he is seeking to resolve, any tendency to pride or standing on an 'office' is not one of them! Either the author is exhibiting a zeal for self-effacing modesty, or he is referring to exhortations ('sermons') other than his own appeal in the text here.

When going back to one's daily life, the author urges the addressees to remember 'the commandments[19] of the Lord'. Whether the 'Lord' here is God

---

[15] The verbs ἐπιστρέψωμεν and νουθετήσωμεν are probably not dependent on the ὅπως: they are not the aims of the 'helping' activity, but part of that help itself: see Lindemann, *Clemensbriefe*, 251; Pratscher, *Zweite Clemensbrief*, 206.

[16] See BAG, 301. The sense is not necessarily that of 'convert' (*pace* Lake, *Fathers*, 157).

[17] The sermon is given by the προεστώς, who delivers τὴν νουθεσίαν καὶ πρόκλησιν τῆς τῶν καλῶν τούτων μιμήσεως. See p. 21 above.

[18] See Aono, *Entwicklung*, 157. Cf. too the general use of first-person plurals in the exhortations, and see above on 1.1; 15.1.

[19] The word used here is ἐντάλματα, which is only rarely used in the LXX, and used in a bad sense in e.g. Isa. 29.13 (= Mark 7.6 pars) to refer to the human (as opposed to divine) teaching. Here it is clearly parallel to the more normal ἐντολαί later in the same verse and the different word may be used simply to avoid duplication. The variation does show that the author's vocabulary is not necessarily monochrome: see Introduction §5. Literary Unity, p. 32 above.

or Jesus is not clear; for the author there was doubtless little difference in status, and certainly no difference in real substance, between the commands of Jesus (from gospel traditions) and the commands of God (from scripture).

The negative side is expressed in terms of not being dragged away ($ἀντιπαρελκώμεθα$)[20] by 'worldly desires' (cf. Tit. 2.12 for the same phrase). The sentiment is similar to what was said in 5.6 (cf. too 16.2 'evil desires'), though as so often throughout *2 Clement*, what precisely might be in mind is not clear. More positively, the readers/hearers are encouraged to come[21] 'more frequently'. A similar exhortation occurs in e.g. Ign. *Eph.* 13.1; *Pol.* 4.2. What is probably in mind is not a greater frequency for gatherings as such (as e.g. in Ign. *Pol.* 4.2) but reliable attendance at those which are already arranged. How far this is stock language, or whether it reflects the real situation of the writer (with perhaps some attending Christian gatherings only infrequently) is not clear.

The overall aim is now expressed more positively: to make 'progress' in the 'commands of the Lord' (presumably exactly the same as those mentioned earlier in this verse). Presumably what is intended is a progression in successfully fulfilling such commands in one's ethical behaviour. Further, the goal is that, being 'all of one mind' ($τὸ αὐτὸ φρονοῦντες$),[22] we are all gathered together 'for life'. The aim is then to ensure that (eternal) life is the outcome for all members of the Christian community.

4 The focus of attention now shifts to the eschatological judgement. There is verbal play on the verb 'gather together' ($συναγαγεῖν$) as the author moves from the gathering together of the community in worship (v. 3b) to the gathering together of the nations by God/Christ in the final judgement.[23]

The ideas are put in the words of a citation from Isa. 66.18, introduced as words which 'the Lord said'. The 'Lord' here may be God or Christ. Elsewhere, citations introduced as sayings of 'the Lord' are clearly Jesus traditions (cf. 4.5; 5.2; 6.1; 8.5; 9.11; 12.2), so that it is natural to assume that here too

---

[20] The verb appears to be a *hapax* in the whole of Greek literature, though the simpler forms $παρέλκειν$ and $ἕλκειν$ are relatively common.

[21] For C's $προσερχόμενοι$, S has $προσευχόμενοι$ ('pray'). The S reading is suggested as possibly original by Lightfoot, *Apostolic Fathers*, 2.254; cf. too Schubert, '2. Clemensbrief', 254; however, it would introduce a rather different theme into the discussion at this point. See Pratscher, *Zweite Clemensbrief*, 209.

[22] The language occurs quite often in Paul: cf. Rom. 12.16; 2 Cor. 13.11; Phil. 2.2; 4.2. Lake, *Fathers*, 157, prints the words in English in quotation marks; cf. also Richardson, *Fathers*, 200. But whether this shows any dependence on Paul (as a quasi-'citation') is doubtful: cf. Pratscher, *Zweite Clemensbrief*, 209.

[23] Whether this is more than a connection via relatively simple implicit wordplay is uncertain: e.g. A. O'Hagan, *Material Re-Creation in the Apostolic Fathers*, TU 100 (Berlin: Akademie, 1968), 74, postulates a more self-conscious idea of 'present earthly meetings [as] an image of the eschatological one to come', but this may read too much into the language and progression here.

'the Lord' is meant to be Jesus rather than God. The same might also be suggested by echoes of the scene in Matt. 25.31–46 (where the nations appear for judgement before the throne of the Son of Man = Jesus), and by the reference to 'his' parousia later in the sentence, an idea which relates more easily to Jesus than to God.[24] If so, then it is striking that a citation (of God) from Jewish scripture is put on the lips of Jesus (just as, conversely, words from the Jesus tradition can be ascribed to 'God', cf. 13.4).

The words from Isa. 66 express the expectation that God/Christ will gather all peoples together for the final judgement. The purpose of the gathering is not explicitly mentioned in the text cited, but is clarified in the subsequent interpretative gloss τοῦτο δὲ λέγει. The event concerned is the 'day of his ἐπιφανεία', a reference to the final end time and the appearance of Christ.[25] Moreover, what will happen then is spelt out: he will come and 'rescue' (λυτρώσεται) each person according to their works. The language of 'rescuing' (or 'ransoming') here is very strange and unexpected, not only in relation to itself in this context (referring to the final judgement), but also in the context of the sentence, where 'according to their works' scarcely fits as supplement to the activity of 'rescue/ransom'. More normal would be a verb implying judging.[26] The vocabulary of 'rescue/ransom' can refer to the payment of a price (e.g. to buy back slaves or prisoners) though it is also used extensively, especially in Deuteronomy, to refer to God's act of 'rescue' of the nation Israel at the time of the Exodus (cf. Deut. 7.8; 9.26; 13.6; 15.15; 21.8; 24.18). Certainly here there seems to be no idea at all of any ransom price being paid, so that the word should probably be translated simply as 'rescue'.

Language of 'rescue' does not occur elsewhere in *2 Clement*, nor does it generally occur elsewhere in early Christian literature with reference to the final judgement.[27] Clearly the writer wants to emphasize the salvific aspect of the coming future judgement, at least for some, and to contrast it with the negative results in store for others (cf. v. 5).[28] The phrase provides yet another example of the author transferring so much to do with 'salvation' to

---

[24] cf. Wengst, *Zweite Clemensbrief*, 217; Lindemann, *Clemensbriefe*, 252; Pratscher, *Zweite Clemensbrief*, 210. Knopf, *Zwei Clemensbriefe*, 178, is undecided.

[25] If the κύριος at the start is indeed Jesus rather than God. The language of ἐπιφανεία is more normally applied to Jesus in Christian literature; cf. 12.1 above (where it is referred to God, but this is very unusual in Christian texts).

[26] For judging, or 'repaying', according to one's works, cf. Ps. 62.13; Matt. 16.27 (alluding to Ps. 62); Rom. 2.6; *1 Clem.* 34.3; etc.

[27] Much more 'normal' (in a Christian context) would be to use such language in relation to Jesus' death, cf. Mark 10.45 pars; Rom. 3.24; 1 Cor. 1.30; Eph. 1.7; Col. 1.14. However, cf. e.g. Luke 21.28; Eph. 4.30 for the Eschaton as signifying 'redemption' (ἀπολύτρωσις). O'Hagan, *Material Re-Creation*, 75, seeks to exploit the word as implying a 'this worldly' idea of the eschatological age to come; but this may press the language too far. Warns, 'Untersuchungen', 87, sees here polemic against a Valentinian sacrament of 'redemption', but this seems to read a lot into one word.

[28] See Lindemann, *Clemensbriefe*, 252; Pratscher, *Zweite Clemensbrief*, 211.

the eschatological future: whereas for other Christian writers, some kind of 'ransoming' or 'rescuing' might have been achieved in and through the death of Jesus in the past, for this author it is sometimes hard to see what at all has already been achieved by Jesus' life or death in the past: almost all the 'good things' and/or 'benefits' that provide positive 'good news' for the Christian lie in the future. Nevertheless, it is still striking that the language here is above all positive, referring to saving and rescuing rather than to rejection and condemnation.[29]

5 After the interpretative gloss of the first part of the citation of Isa. 66.18 in v. 4, the writer continues with what is almost certainly intended to be the completion of the citation with the words that (some) 'will see his glory'. However, the gloss introduces a distinction not present in Isa. 66 itself: in Isaiah, all those assembled will see God's glory. Here, however, the focus is specifically on the 'unbelievers' (ἄπιστοι) who will see God's glory, and their response.

Who the 'unbelievers' are is not certain. Most argue that it is other (Christian) 'opponents' who are in mind.[30] However, it is unusual to refer to other Christians as 'unbelievers', the description usually being applied to (Gentile) non-Christians.[31] However, Ignatius sometimes uses such language of his (Christian) docetic opponents (*Trall.* 10.1; *Smyrn.* 2; 5.3); moreover, the continuation in v. 6, which probably has the same people in view, seems to refer clearly to other Christians (see below on v. 6): hence despite the unusual terminology here, it may be best to take the 'unbelievers' here as (other) 'Christians'.[32]

These people will be amazed when they see the kingly power (cf. 6.9) over the world 'given to Jesus'. The precise reason (if there is one!) why 'Jesus' (simpliciter) is mentioned explicitly is not clear. In one way, the proper name seems unnecessary (though by no means impossible) after the αὐτοῦ earlier in the sentence, especially if the whole of vv. 4–5 is about what Jesus (rather than God) has said (see above on ὁ κύριος in v. 4). Further, if it is correct to take the 'unbelievers' as other Christians, it is not clear why such people would be astonished that cosmic sovereignty is in the hands of Jesus.[33]

---

[29] See more generally Introduction §9.1 God, p. 67 above.

[30] So e.g. Schubert, '2. Clemensbrief', 253; Knopf, *Zwei Clemensbriefe*, 178; Donfried, *Setting*, 172; Wengst, *Zweite Clemensbrief*, 261, 263 (with reference to v. 6b as well); Lohmann, *Drohung*, 127; Pratscher, *Zweite Clemensbrief*, 212, seems undecided.

[31] See Lindemann, *Clemensbriefe*, 252.

[32] The inverted commas here are intended to reflect the probable view of the author that, despite their claim to be Christians, these people are ultimately not!

[33] It is just possible that, if these people were Gnostics of some kind, they had a docetic Christology, possibly distinguishing the earthly Jesus from the heavenly Christ: hence what they are astonished about is the fact that it is the earthly Jesus (hence the name 'Jesus' alone mentioned here), rather than a heavenly Christ figure, who receives such glory and honour. But this must be rather speculative; and elsewhere it is difficult to find any clear evidence for such a belief being addressed (see e.g. above on 1.1–2).

The people concerned express their surprise and astonishment at what they see and their realization that they are now lost (cf. 'woe to us'). The first phrase is not entirely clear. They say 'it was you' (σὺ ἦς). Possibly this reflects an original ἐγώ εἰμι on the lips of Jesus,[34] though this is by no means certain: if the people concerned claimed to be Christians, it is hard to see how they would have expressly denied that Jesus made such a claim for himself; and in any case, the past tense ἦς suggests that the reference is back to the earthly activity of Jesus, not to any transcendent (perhaps quasi-divine) status possibly implied by the words ἐγώ εἰμι.[35]

They also confess that they did not 'know or believe', and were not obedient to the elders when told of 'our' salvation. The reference to not 'knowing and believing' might take on added point if the people concerned had already been claiming that they did know God in some special way (cf. above on v. 1): they would now realize that any special 'knowledge' which they thought they had is in fact worthless. The author seems to have in mind a continuous process of (what he takes to be) continuous disobedience (cf. the verbs in the imperfect) and a refusal to listen to the teaching of the elders in his community. Probably too the reference to 'our' salvation is not to the fact that 'we' have been saved, but rather to the particular form of the salvation preached by the elders, resulting in salvation for 'us' but the opposite for those who have disregarded what they were told.

The consequence is now drawn with another citation (though not marked as such explicitly). It is an exact repetition of the words of Isa. 66.24, cited (explicitly) in 7.6.[36] The words express the terrible fate awaiting those who fail to respond positively while there is yet time. As well as seeking to drive home the seriousness of the message the author is trying to get across to the people concerned about their behaviour and/or their beliefs, the citation also functions as assurance to those who may feel threatened by (and/or tempted to join) these people in the author's own day, showing how any promises of ultimate well-being which others might offer are illusory.

6 Again an explicit interpretation is offered (with a similar λέγει as in v. 4b). The reference is explicitly said to be to the 'day of judgement', when others will see 'those who were ungodly among us' (the reference seems to be clearly to people claiming to be inside the Christian community), but who 'distorted the commandments of Jesus Christ' (again presumably referring to Christians, i.e. those who accepted the validity of the teaching of Jesus). If

---

[34] cf. Knopf, *Zwei Clemensbriefe*, 178; Lindemann, *Clemensbriefe*, 252.

[35] See Pratscher, *Zweite Clemensbrief*, 212. However, the precise implications of ἐγώ εἰμι are notoriously difficult to determine.

[36] Whether this is the reason for the lack of introductory formula (so Knopf, *Zwei Clemensbriefe*, 179) is not certain. This is by no means the only occasion where the author cites a text without introducing it as such: cf. 2.1; 11.7; 16.3.

these people are the same as the 'unbelievers' of v. 5, then the language here (especially e.g. the 'among us') suggests that other Christian claimants are in mind. If the 'unbelievers' of v. 5 are not Christians, then one has to presume that a different group has suddenly come into view.[37] However, there seems to be a seamless transition from v. 5 to v. 6: the 'unbelievers' will be astonished, the words of Isa. 66 will apply (clearly to them), and this in turn is expounded in more detail in v. 6, clarifying who is referred to in the words of Isa. 66 just cited. Hence it is probably a single group of people in mind in both v. 5 and v. 6, and the language of v. 6 suggests strongly that these are Christians.

These people have been 'ungodly' and 'perverted the commandments of Jesus Christ'. The disobedience to the commands of Jesus suggests an ethical failing on the part of these people. This would fit with the theory that they were 'libertines'.[38] Whether these people will only be 'seen' as such at the final judgement itself is, however, not so clear.[39] More likely they will primarily be seen as then receiving their final punishment.

7 In contrast, the 'righteous' will give glory to God. The δίκαιοι are here described in various ways. They are those who have 'done good' (εὐπραγ-ήσαντες), and have 'endured torments' (ὑπομείναντες τὰς βασάνους). Βάσανος is a fairly general word, which can refer to specific torture (e.g. 1 Macc. 9.26; 4 Macc. 17.10) but equally more generally to sufferings which are not specifically inflicted by other human beings (cf. Matt. 4.24 of illnesses). Nowhere else in 2 Clement is a persecution situation clearly implied;[40] hence it may be that the reference here is to more general, unspecified sufferings undergone by Christians.[41] The 'righteous' have also 'hated the desires of the soul' (μισήσαντες τὰς ἡδυπαθείας τῆς ψυχῆς). The language picks up that of 16.2, especially the reference to the ἡδυπαθείαι (also here ascribed to the ψυχή). Those who are 'righteous' are thus those who have behaved properly in their lifetime, even to the point of suffering, and certainly not indulging themselves.

The writer continues with the description of the 'righteous' now seeing the others suffering torment. The latter are described as people who have done wrong, and above all 'denied Jesus' whether by word or by deed. How

---

[37] So e.g. Lindemann, *Clemensbriefe*, 252.

[38] Emphasized strongly by Donfried, *Setting*, 172, 175–6.

[39] This is argued by Lindemann, *Clemensbriefe*, 252, who then claims that Donfried's suggestion cannot be right: these people presented themselves earlier in a different light and will only be 'seen' in their true colours at the End; hence they cannot have been libertines. This may, however, press the 'seeing' here too far. What others will 'see' is these people receiving (what is presumed to be) the justified punishment for their failures; it does not necessarily imply that others will only 'see' these people as the charlatans (which the author believes) they are at the End too. Presumably at least the author himself claims to be able to 'see' who these people are now!

[40] 5.1 perhaps comes closest, possibly also 10.3, but it is not clear (see the commentary there).

[41] See Lindemann, *Clemensbriefe*, 253; Pratscher, *Zweite Clemensbrief*, 214.

precisely, or why, they are thought to have 'denied Jesus' is not explicit. The same language is used in 3.1, with an allusion to the gospel saying Matt. 10.32//Luke 12.8. There the language of 'denying Jesus' is clearly applied to the ethical behaviour which others are engaged in. Probably then the same applies here: rather than any doctrinal issues (e.g. involving a docetic Christology), the criterion is above all one of ethical behaviour.[42]

The vision is then painted in yet more lurid colours; these people will be seen as suffering terrible torments in 'unquenchable fire' (picking up the language of Isa. 66.24 just cited in v. 5).

The 'righteous', in contrast to the 'unbelievers', will give glory to God, and say that there will be hope for those who have served God wholeheartedly. The language picks up significant elements of what has been said earlier in the text.[43] However, the words placed on the lips of the righteous here (after λέγοντες) fit somewhat awkwardly into the present context: the future tense ἔσται, together with the reference to 'hope', seems odd in the context of things allegedly said by those apparently at the final judgement itself; and the singular participle δεδουλευκότι seems strange after all the plural references preceding. Thus several have suggested that what we have here is a quotation taken from another context.[44] What the quotation is, or where it is from, is, however, unclear. There is no scriptural text giving the words here exactly, though similar sentiments can be found in a number of passages.[45] Maybe it is a citation from a biblical passage in a version otherwise unknown to us, and/or perhaps another example of our author's willingness to cite a very wide range of texts, some of which were not included in the (later) canon, in the course of his own argument and discussion.

---

[42] Unless the reference to being astonished at seeing Jesus in a position of glory (v. 5) refers to some kind of docetic ideas, separating the earthly Jesus from the heavenly Christ: see above.

[43] For 'serving', cf. 6.1; 11.1; for 'with the whole heart', cf. 3.4; 8.2; 17.1. See Donfried, *Setting*, 173.

[44] Warns, 'Untersuchungen', 167–74; Lindemann, *Clemensbriefe*, 253; Pratscher, *Zweite Clemensbrief*, 32, 216.

[45] e.g. Isa. 54.17 LXX (though it is by no means exact); also *T. Jud.* 26.1 (but again by no means an exact parallel). Warns and Pratscher (see previous note) suggest a citation from a possible liturgical context, perhaps from a burial rite. But this must remain speculative and uncertain.

Chapter 18

COMMENTARY

1 The author sums up with a positive exhortation to his addressees, drawing together the threads of the preceding appeals. (The 'chapter' division here is particularly misleading: the exhortation flows on relatively seamlessly from ch. 17.) 'We' should seek to belong on the side of those who will be treated favourably in the final judgement. Here this is put positively in terms of 'those who give thanks' (ἐκ τῶν εὐχαριστούντων) and those 'who have served God' (δεδουλευκότων τῷ θεῷ), and negatively in terms of not being 'the ungodly who are judged' (μὴ ἐκ τῶν κρινομένων ἀσεβῶν). Εὐχαριστεῖν is not used elsewhere in *2 Clement*. Its precise overtones are not certain: is there, for example, any sense in which it implies that 'we' are those who join in a/the Eucharist (with perhaps a quiet but pointed remark against possible 'opponents' who are absenting themselves from regular Christian gatherings, cf. 17.3)?[1] Alternatively, it could simply mean 'give thanks'. The language of 'those who have served God' picks up what was said in the saying (possibly a quotation) in 17.7 ('the one who has served God'). The negative exhortation not to belong to the wicked who are judged picks up the judgement references in 17.6 and 17.7. Whether the 'wicked' here are erring Christians, or non-Christians, is not certain;[2] but maybe the issue is immaterial: the point is that 'we' do not want to belong to any group who will be condemned and punished.

2 The author now concludes his peroration with a sudden interjection about himself and his own situation. He has mentioned himself very briefly earlier (cf. 15.1), but what is said here goes rather further. As noted already by things that are not said, or only implied, the tone is extremely self-deprecating. There is no appeal by the writer to his authority or status, and certainly not to

---

[1] *Did.* 14.1 *might* be a possible example of εὐχαριστεῖν used in this more technical sense of 'celebrate the Eucharist', rather than simply 'give thanks', though this is debated.

[2] Knopf, *Zwei Clemensbriefe*, 179, claims they are false Christians. Lindemann, *Clemensbriefe*, 253, suggests both Christians and non-Christians; similarly Pratscher, *Zweite Clemensbrief*, 217.

any particular 'office'. Rather all that is said is to underline his sinfulness and, at one level, unworthiness. He starts by saying that he is 'completely sinful' ($\pi\alpha\nu\theta\alpha\mu\alpha\rho\tau\omega\lambda\acute{o}s$).[3] He himself has not yet managed to 'flee' temptation/testing.[4] The 'temptation/testing' might be the period of suffering and tribulation thought to precede the End (as probably in the petition in the Lord's Prayer in Matt. 6.13 par.); but more likely it refers to the individual, moral 'temptation' to sin.

He also says that he is 'surrounded by the instruments ($\grave{o}\rho\gamma\acute{a}\nu o\iota s$) of the devil'. What these 'instruments' are is not clear. The word $\mathring{o}\rho\gamma\alpha\nu o\nu$ can be used of military equipment (2 Macc. 12.27), as well as for instruments of torture (4 Macc. 6.5; 9.20, 26). However, the precise reference here remains obscure. Whether, for example, the writer is hinting at the fact that he is suffering violent persecution is not certain; more likely it is simply a vivid way of saying that he had not yet achieved any kind of ethical perfection. (The context is primarily one of ethical behaviour fully achieved or not achieved: it is not one of persecution.)

Nevertheless, despite this, he is striving to 'pursue righteousness',[5] that is, struggling to behave in the way he believes he should and achieve ethical uprightness. The overall aim is then at least to be able to 'draw near to it'. Similar language occurred earlier in 7.3. The sentiment is very similar to that of Paul in Phil. 3.12–14, though apart from the verb $\delta\iota\acute{\omega}\kappa\omega$, there is no verbal overlap. Further, as Pratscher notes, there is no equivalent to Paul's claim that Christ has already made him his own (Phil. 3.12).[6] The emphasis here is solely on the (apparently unaided) human effort to behave ethically and properly. The negative incentive is, as in ch. 17, the fear of the coming judgement which will condemn those who fail.[7]

Nevertheless, the thrust of the whole of the rest of the text is that the author, and the 'we' he associates himself with, will be finally saved. (Cf. 17.1–2 above: final rejection is primarily for others, not for 'us'.) Hence, despite the author's own self-awareness of his total sinfulness and unworthiness, he can—and does—look forward to the future with hope rather than simply

---

[3] The word is a *hapax* in Greek of this period, though cf. $\pi\alpha\nu\theta\alpha\mu\acute{a}\rho\tau\eta\tau os$ in *Did.* 5.2; *Barn.* 20.2.

[4] For 'fleeing' passions etc. cf. 2 Tim. 2.22 $\tau\grave{a}s \ldots \grave{\epsilon}\pi\iota\theta\upsilon\mu\acute{\iota}\alpha s \ \phi\epsilon\tilde{\upsilon}\gamma\epsilon$, with also the phrase $\delta\acute{\iota}\omega\kappa\epsilon \ \delta\grave{\epsilon} \ \delta\iota\kappa\alpha\iota o\sigma\acute{\upsilon}\nu\eta\nu$ immediately following (as later in this verse here: see the following note).

[5] The phrase occurs in the Pastorals, in 1 Tim. 6.22; 2 Tim. 2.22. The similarity earlier with other language in 2 Tim. 2.22 is noteworthy, but whether this suggests that the author knew the Pastorals is uncertain.

[6] Pratscher, *Zweite Clemensbrief*, 218.

[7] It is just possible that the author's language here has been influenced by that of Paul (including the Paul of the Pastorals): for the claim that he is a terrible sinner, cf. Paul himself in 1 Cor. 15.9; Gal. 1.13; and 'Paul' in 1 Tim. 1.13. For the possible echoes of verses such as 2 Tim. 2.22, see above. However, this must be weighed against the apparent lack of knowledge of Paul and Paul's letters shown generally by the author of *2 Clement*. See pp. 43–5 above.

fear. Thus despite his (at times) one-sided ethical perfectionist stance, apparently demanding ethical perfection with a threat of dire consequences for those who do not attain such standards, he is also apparently a realist, fully able to include within his thinking (or 'theology') an assumption that, even for those who fail to achieve such perfection, there is still hope (provided perhaps they at least *try* to do what [the author believes] they should!)

Chapter 19

COMMENTARY

For the status of chapters 19–20 within the text as a whole, see Introduction §5. Literary Unity above and the discussion of whether the section here may be a later addition to chs. 1–18 (and perhaps 20.5).

1 The address of the readers/hearers as 'brothers and sisters' marks this section off from the rest of *2 Clement* where the standard address is simply ἀδελφοί. It has been suggested that the double address here reflects a seating plan where men and women were expected to sit separately,[1] though this is not certain. The different address is perhaps one of the strongest arguments for taking this section as written by someone other than the author of the main part of the text.

The context is now spelled out in a highly cryptic phrase μετὰ τὸν θεὸν τῆς ἀληθείας, literally 'after the God of truth'. The phrase 'God of truth' is reminiscent of the slightly more unusual 'Father of truth' in 3.1; 20.5; 'God of truth' occurs in Jewish scripture in Ps. 30.6 LXX; 1 Esd. 4.40. The similarity in language with 3.1 represents one of the points of continuity (albeit not identity) between this section and the rest of *2 Clement*. The cryptic 'after the God of truth' is usually taken as an ellipsis for something like 'after the God of truth has spoken', or 'after you have heard the God of truth', with an implied reference to an immediately preceding reading from scripture: hence after you have heard the word of the God of truth read out loud in a scriptural reading.[2] As such, it probably attests to the way in which a 'sermon' or 'homily' in early Christian worship gatherings (following the example in Judaism) followed on from a scriptural reading.[3] What the specific scriptural

---

[1] So Parvis, '*2 Clement*', 34.

[2] See Lightfoot, *Apostolic Fathers*, 2.257; Knopf, 'Anagnose', 266; Wengst, *Zweite Clemensbrief*, 216; Lindemann, *Clemensbriefe*, 256; Pratscher, *Zweite Clemensbrief*, 220.

[3] cf. Luke 4.20–1; Acts 13.15; cf. too 1 Tim. 4.13; in more detail, Just. *1 Apol.* 67.3.

reading might have been is probably not possible to determine on the basis of the evidence available.[4]

The author here now goes on to say that he is 'reading' them an ἔντευξις. An ἔντευξις is a 'request',[5] the same word being used in *1 Clem.* 63.2 to refer to the appeal made through the text of *1 Clement* and also as part of the opening of Justin's *1 Apol.* 1 as a description of his work.[6] Presumably the reference here is to the text of the 'sermon' which constitutes chs. 1–18 and which is now being 'read'.[7] The request is that the hearers will attend to 'what is written' (τοῖς γεγραμμένοις). The absolute perfect participle might be most naturally seen as a reference to scripture (cf. Luke 18.31; John 12.16; 2 Cor. 4.13; *1 Clem.* 13.1).[8] On the other hand, however much the author (of both the rest of *2 Clement* and presumably the 'reader' here as well) clearly values scripture, it is hard to see (on the basis of the rest of *2 Clement*) how paying attention specifically to scripture will lead to the desired result stated here, namely the 'salvation' of the readers and the 'reader' himself. The argument of the rest of *2 Clement* is that this result will follow if, and only if, the readers act in a way that is morally upright and proper. Scripture is adduced on several occasions to back up parts of this general message; but its function is mostly ancillary. With the exception perhaps of ch. 2 (and its detailed, phrase-by-phrase, interpretation of Isa. 54.1), scripture itself and its interpretation is not the primary concern (or way of arguing) of this writer.[9] It may thus be preferable to see here a reference to the text of (the rest of) the sermon in *2 Clement* itself (perhaps as well as a reference to scripture).[10]

---

[4] See pp. 21–2 above for the theory Knopf, 'Anagnose', that Isa. 54–66 might have been the scriptural text on which *2 Clement* as a sermon is based (as well as other suggestions).

[5] See BAG, 268. Cf. e.g. *Let. Aris.* 252; Josephus, *Ant.* 15.79. In some contexts the word is used for 'prayer' or intercession: cf. e.g. 1 Tim. 2.1; 4.5, and on occasions in Hermas (e.g. *Mand.* 5.1.6; 10.3.2–3; 11.9, 14; *Sim.* 2.5–7), though that seems inappropriate here.

[6] Whether the verbal link with *1 Clem.* 63 is distinctive enough to establish any kind of link between the two contexts must remain doubtful, *pace* e.g. Donfried, *Setting*, 14–15. See Introduction §5. Literary Unity above and also the discussion of the theories of Stegemann.

[7] The language suggests a fairly formal 'reading' of at least part of the sermon. Whether sermons were generally written down and then read out is not certain. The reference to the practice of Origen writing down his sermons (see Eusebius, *Hist. eccl.* 6.36.1) applies only to the context of his old age (and hence may imply that his earlier practice was different).

[8] cf. Knopf, *Zwei Clemensbriefe*, 180; Wengst, *Zweite Clemensbrief*, 216.

[9] See Introduction §4. Genre, p. 22 above.

[10] See Pratscher, *Zweite Clemensbrief*, 221. Salzmann, *Lehren*, 222, sees here a reference to *2 Clement* alone; also Stegemann, 'Herkunft', 101. The interpretation of Schüssler, 'Zweite Klemensbrief', who sees here a reference to *2 Clem.* 1–18 regarded *as scripture* seems very unlikely: would the text of *2 Clement* have acquired scriptural status so early? The attempt by Donfried, *Setting*, 14–15, to see in τοῖς γεγραμμένοις a reference to *1 Clement*, especially to *1 Clem.* 63.2, seems very unconvincing: this depends in part on making a great deal out of possible verbal agreements between *1 Clement* and *2 Clement* here, not all of which are convincing. (See p. 16 above.) Moreover, the stated aim here ('so that you may save yourselves') fits far better if the reference is to (the rest of) *2 Clement* than if it is a reference to *1 Clement*.

The aim—'so that you may save yourselves and also the one who is reading among you'—corresponds closely with what is said in 15.1, both in its reference to 'salvation', and also in the reference to saving both the addressees themselves and also the one who is purveying the message to them. The language of 'saving yourselves' comes perilously close to making salvation a human achievement (though in some theological tension with other passages where 'salvation' is the work of God or Christ, and cf. v. 3 below).[11] The inclusion of the reader himself in the process parallels what is said in 15.1, though whether the two people concerned are the same or different is uncertain (see on the literary problem of the status of this section of *2 Clement* within the rest of the text).[12]

The success in enabling others to achieve this salvation will result in a 'reward' for the reader (cf. too 15.1 for similar claims). The reader here thus begs the hearers to 'repent' and to do so 'with all their heart'. Both themes are prominent in the earlier part of *2 Clement*, and come together in e.g. 8.2; 17.1. The exhortation here thus summarizes well a central theme in the rest of the sermon. By such repenting, the hearers will give themselves 'salvation and life'.[13] Once again, the language is all but claiming an idea of salvation as something one achieves by one's own efforts: certainly any idea of salvation as divine gift is at best only implicit here.

A further overall aim is now added, bringing in rather new ideas and themes: the repentance of the hearers will set a mark ($\sigma\kappa o\pi\acute{o}\nu$)[14] for 'all the younger people' ($\tau o\hat{\iota}\varsigma\ \nu\acute{e}o\iota\varsigma$) who wish to work for ($\phi\iota\lambda o\pi o\nu\epsilon\hat{\iota}\nu$)[15] piety and the goodness of God. The mention of the younger people is slightly unexpected: they have certainly not been mentioned before. Normally the word $\nu\acute{e}o\iota$ is used to refer to people who are younger in age so one assumes the same is meant here (rather than e.g. those who have only become Christians more recently, i.e. 'younger in their faith'). But who they are is not

---

[11] Pratscher, *Zweite Clemensbrief*, 222, says that 'saving' here is to be understood 'im Sinn der Ermöglichung der göttlichen Rettung durch das entsprechende Handeln' ('in the sense of making possible divine salvation through the appropriate behaviour'), though this may represent a certain amount of theological wishful thinking!

[12] S implies an additional $\dot{\epsilon}\mu\acute{e}$ qualifying $\tau\grave{o}\nu\ \dot{a}\nu a\gamma\iota\nu\acute{\omega}\sigma\kappa o\nu\tau a$. The reading is accepted by Wengst, *Zweite Clemensbrief*, 264, but not by most other editors of the text. As Lindemann, *Clemensbriefe*, 256, says, the implied meaning is probably the same. Probably S is simply clarifying (secondarily) what is implicit in the C reading.

[13] For the two connected together, cf. too *Barn.* 2.10.

[14] The reading of S over against $\kappa o\pi\acute{o}\nu$ ('trouble') in C: the latter is almost universally accepted as an error, and the S reading makes much better sense in context.

[15] The scribe of C originally wrote $\phi\iota\lambda o\sigma o\phi\epsilon\hat{\iota}\nu$ ('philosophize'), and then corrected it with πo (but not $\pi o\nu$) above the line. Hilgenfeld suggested that $\phi\iota\lambda o\pi o\iota\epsilon\hat{\iota}\nu$ ('make friends') was the intended correction, though Lightfoot, *Apostolic Fathers*, 2.206, is adamant that $\phi\iota\lambda o\pi o\nu\epsilon\hat{\iota}\nu$ is the intended correction. The latter does agree then with S and gives a good sense (and is universally accepted as the reading here), though whether one can be so certain that C's correction reads this may be slightly doubtful.

clear. The language may presuppose a community with a wide age range, including perhaps some younger people who (the speaker seems to think) may be more impressionable.

The presumption is that they want to work in the cause of piety and the goodness of God. Again, the precise reference is obscure to us at such a temporal distance. (What is it that they are wanting to do specifically? And how will the repentance of the immediate audience of the speaker affect them?) 'Piety' ($εὐσέβεια$) is widely used in Jewish and Christian writings of the time (though mostly in relatively late NT texts) to refer to the correct relationship to God (cf. 1 Tim. 2.2; 3.16; Tit. 1.5; *1 Clem.* 1.2; 32.4).[16] Such language is absent from the rest of *2 Clement*, but comes to the fore in this small final section (cf. 19.1, 4; 20.4): as such it *may* provide an indication of a different author.[17] For the 'goodness' of God, cf. 15.4–5.

2 The exhortation continues with a plea not to be angry or resentful if one is admonished by someone else. Such a reaction would make one 'foolish' ($ἄσοφος$).[18] The aim of the admonishment is to turn people from 'unrighteousness'[19] to 'righteousness'. Part of the reason for such admonition is then said to be because sometimes we do not even know that what we are doing is wrong. Again the idea is somewhat surprising in the context of the rest of *2 Clement* where it seems to be assumed that any failure to behave properly is *not* the result of any ignorance (or if it is, it has not been mentioned before).[20]

Such ignorance is here said to arise from possible $διψυχία$ and/or $ἀπιστία$. Again both 'reasons' are slightly surprising in relation to the rest of *2 Clement*. Being 'double-minded' has occurred in 11.2, 5 (originally as part of the citation of unknown origin in 11.2–4 and then repeated in v. 5), though with no suggestion there that it might imply ignorance about the moral status of disputed behaviour. There is also a reference to $ἄπιστοι$ in 17.5: they are people who have refused to obey the elders, rather than being ignorant about what is right or wrong. In both instances, the words used here show an element of continuity with the rest of *2 Clement* in that the same words are repeated; but also there is some difference in the way they are used. It may be then a case of a secondary writer taking up language from the text (of someone else) he has and using the same words in slightly different ways.

---

[16] See p. 30 above and the reference in n. 13 there to Dibelius and Conzelmann, *Pastoral Epistles*, 39, for the use of the word group in Hellenistic writings.

[17] See p. 28 above.

[18] A relatively rare word: only here and Eph. 5.15 in early Christian literature.

[19] $ἀδικία$ used here for the only time in *2 Clement*. Again this might be a sign of a different author from the rest of the text, though the author elsewhere by no means has a fixed, rigid vocabulary that brooks no variation!

[20] And hence perhaps another indication that a different author is present in this section.

The final description of possible ignorance suggests that 'we'[21] might be 'darkened in our understanding'[22] by 'vain desires'.[23]

3 The positive side of the exhortation is then given in terms that are by now standard in the vocabulary of *2 Clement*: we should 'do' 'righteousness'. Righteousness seems to be clearly right behaviour (what one 'does': cf. 4.2; 11.7).[24] The purpose of such behaviour is 'that we may be finally saved'. Despite what is said earlier (e.g. in 1.4, 7) about salvation as something already achieved, it seems that at least 'final' salvation is still future and not guaranteed even for the Christian (cf. similarly 8.2; 14.1). However, unlike v. 1, salvation here does *not* seem to be something that is achieved by one's own efforts: the passive verb implies that someone else (presumably God or Christ) is the agent of the saving activity.

The exhortation continues with a blessing on those who take notice of what is said: 'blessed are those who obey these commandments' (μακάριοι οἱ τούτοις ὑπακούοντες τοῖς προστάγμασιν). The vocabulary is slightly unusual for *2 Clement*: ὑπακούειν does not occur elsewhere in *2 Clement*, nor does πρόσταγμα, though both are quite common in *1 Clement*.[25] On the other hand, it is not simply a case of claiming that the author here uses a different word (e.g. ἐντολή in 3.4; 4.5) and hence deducing a different authorship:[26] in the other passages (as indeed in *1 Clement*), the 'commands' are those of God or of Christ, whereas here 'these instructions' are presumably those of the author himself. The addressees are to take note of, and obey, what the preacher himself is saying. The slightly different vocabulary may thus simply reflect a slightly different reference.

The gaze now shifts to the eschatological future and the promises in store for those who are not condemned but who do obey the instructions given. It

---

[21] Like the author of the rest of *2 Clement*, the writer here does use the first-person plural, including himself (at least on the surface) with those he is directly addressing and implicitly criticizing: the general approach is conciliatory, not directly polemical.

[22] There is a possible allusion to the language of Eph. 4.18, but it is hard to say if this is intentional or simply coincidental. Similar language is also used in *1 Clem.* 36.2.

[23] In 16.2, the bad ἐπιθυμίαι are said to be πονηραί rather than μάταιαι as here. For some this might be a further indication of a different author; on the other hand, the context here is of describing people who do not realize that what they are doing might be wrong: hence their 'desires' might be less obviously 'evil' (which might imply clear intentionality).

[24] Though the use of πράσσειν, rather than e.g. ποιεῖν, is unusual and the use of this verb here with δικαιοσύνη is not attested elsewhere in early Christian literature.

[25] For ὑπακούειν, cf. *1 Clem.* 7.6; 9.1; cf. 9.3; 10.2, 7. For πρόσταγμα, cf. *1 Clem.* 2.8; 3.4; 20.5; etc. See on Literary Unity above (p. 29) for possible links with *1 Clement* and Pratscher, *Zweite Clemensbrief*, 19, 225.

[26] One should not assume that the vocabulary of one author is absolutely monochrome. The use of πρόσταγμα is regularly cited as an example of a difference in vocabulary from chs. 1–18 (see p. 28 above), where the author uses ἐντολή; but then in 17.3 the same author uses ἔνταλμα. Clearly the author of chs. 1–18 does not have a monochrome vocabulary that never varies.

is conceded that they will 'suffer' (κακοπαθεῖν) for a 'short' time in this[27] world. Quite what 'suffering' is in mind is not clear. References have been made earlier in *2 Clement* to possible suffering by Christians (e.g. 5.1–4; 10.3; 17.7; *possibly* 18.2), though the theme does not seem to dominate elsewhere, and any real 'problem' seems much more focused on the issue of ethical behaviour than on any threat from persecution. Whether too one can make much of the reference to the 'short' time of such suffering as implying a vivid eschatological awareness is also uncertain: the language is in one way fairly stereotyped (cf. Mark 13.20; 2 Cor. 4.17; 1 Pet. 1.6; 5.10). However, the language does presuppose a two ages scheme.[28] Hence if the author does move to a more individualistic idea in what follows (see above), he seems capable of holding the two broad ideas together (as indeed Luke and Paul may do).

The promise in store is that such people will 'gather in the immortal fruit of resurrection'. The language is unusual in a number of ways. 'Fruit' (καρπός) is used here of the final reward in store for the righteous, elsewhere in *2 Clement* for the human behaviour that is required of the Christian in the present (cf. 1.3). The reward is said to be 'resurrection'.[29] 'Resurrection' now seems to be not a universal future cosmic event, but the individual reward for the righteous, perhaps received at the moment of an individual's death.[30] The

---

[27] C adds τούτῳ to κόσμῳ while S omits it. The S text is followed by Lightfoot, *Apostolic Fathers*, 2.258, and the reading is accepted too by Pratscher, *Zweite Clemensbrief*, 225. Lindemann, *Clemensbriefe*, 254, 257, seems uncertain (in his translation he has 'in (dieser) Welt' ('in (this) world')). The C text is read by Lake, *Fathers*, 160; Richardson, *Fathers*, 201; Wengst, *Zweite Clemensbrief*, 266; Ehrman, *Fathers*, 196. The decision depends in part on how far the author here has in mind a 'two worlds' apocalyptic scheme, or how far he has moved to a completely individualistic idea of each individual obtaining eternal life immediately after physical death. Lindemann and Pratscher both imply the latter, referring to 19.4 and 20.2; but at least 20.2 still keeps the language of a 'coming' life, which could fit with (even if it does not demand) an apocalyptic 'two-age' scheme. But in any case, some oscillation (between an 'apocalyptic' two-age scheme and a more 'individualistic' eschatology) might well be evidenced in writers such as Luke and Paul in the NT to mention but two. See p. 32 above. I have followed the C text here, partly on the basis of its witness in the (only) Greek MS we have, partly because of the fit with other language in *2 Clement*.

[28] cf. Lindemann, *Clemensbriefe*, 257; Pratscher, *Zweite Clemensbrief*, 225.

[29] The genitive is presumably one of apposition: the 'fruit of resurrection' is the 'fruit which consists of resurrection'. *Contra* e.g. Pratscher, *Zweite Clemensbrief*, 226.

[30] It might be that the author is still working with a corporate idea, with resurrection as the reward for (all) the righteous. On the other hand, the idea of judgement, and punishment, for the wicked, which has dominated the earlier appeals in *2 Clement*, seems then implicitly to have disappeared from sight if only the righteous are resurrected. O'Hagan, *Material Re-Creation*, 82–5, argues that the ideas here are very different from elsewhere in *2 Clement* (an individualized eschatology, and a belief in an other-worldly existence rather than a renewal of the present world order), but appealing in part to the presence of a different author for this section to account for the differences. Similarly, Lindemann, *Clemensbriefe*, 255, for the difference in ideas here from the rest of *2 Clement*. However, other early Christian writers may display similar differences in their eschatological views: see p. 32 and n. 19 above on Luke and Paul.

use of the word 'immortal' (ἀθάνατος) also suggests a less apocalyptic, and perhaps more 'hellenistic', way of talking and/or thinking.[31]

4 Talk about the joys which the righteous can look forward to is developed further (or perhaps effectively repeats what has been said in v. 3 in slightly different vocabulary). Those who can look forward to such good things are the 'pious' (εὐσεβής).[32] The pious should not 'grieve' (μὴ οὖν λυπείσθω): the vocabulary, and idea, is similar to Paul in 1 Thess. 4.13 (μὴ λυπῆσθε). The 'grieving' arises in part presumably from the conditions of present experience, but perhaps not as such: the issue may be more that one should not 'grieve' by lacking hope in a future that will put right the conditions of the present.

The hope then is spelt out by asserting a contrast between 'the present time' (τοῖς νῦν χρόνοις) and a glorious future time (μάκαριος ... χρόνος). The talk of a 'blessed' time is somewhat unusual: perhaps it is taking up the vocabulary of the preceding verse and the beatitude there in a slightly mechanical way. The language of the 'present' time in contrast with the (implicitly future) blessed time to come still assumes a two ages schema in some sense.[33] However, what follows is certainly open to a more 'individualistic' eschatological idea: the pious will 'live again with the fathers above'. The language of 'above' seems to move to a more spatial, rather than temporal, distinction: the new life is something that already exists in another place. However, such language, existing alongside more temporally orientated distinctions is not unprecedented in early Christian texts (cf. e.g. Col. 3.1; Eph. 2.6; in Jewish texts, cf. e.g. 4 Macc. 17.5, 18).

The language of 'living again' is also unusual. The verb ἀναβιοῦν does not occur in early Christian literature elsewhere.[34] Who the 'fathers' are is also not clear: it could be the righteous of Jewish history (cf. Acts 13.36), or it could be Christian figures of the writer's past (cf. 2 Pet. 3.4). This new life will be one where the righteous will 'rejoice' (εὐφρανθήσεται)[35] in the age to come which will be 'without sorrow' (τὸν ἀλύπητον αἰῶνα). Again the languge is unusual, though may be again determined in part by the author's

---

[31] The word is common in Graeco-Roman literature, though rare in Jewish texts and not used in the NT (apart from a variant reading in 1 Tim. 1.17).

[32] cf. εὐσέβεια in v. 1 (also θεοσέβια in 20.4) and the discussion there about whether this vocabulary implies a different author from chs. 1–18.

[33] So Pratscher, Zweite Clemensbrief, 226, against Lindemann, Clemensbriefe, 257, who says that the idea here is 'ganz individualistisch' ('completely individualistic').

[34] 2 Macc. 7.9 talks of αἰώνιος ἀναβίωσις. Josephus, Ant. 18.14 uses the verb in his account of Pharisaic eschatological beliefs. Philostratus, Vit. Apoll. 1.1.1 uses the verb of the post-mortem existence of Pythagoras.

[35] Again a somewhat unusual word to refer to the joy of the eschatological life. The word is a key one in the citation of Isa. 54.1 used in 2.1 above; it is possible that there is a verbal echo of the earlier passage here.

tendency to take up vocabulary used just before and repeat it (ἀλύπητος here echoing μὴ λυπείσθω at the start of the verse).³⁶ The general sentiment is of course very similar in general terms to the description in Rev. 7.14–17.

---

³⁶ If so, then this tendency of the author of this small section is remarkably similar to that of the author of the rest of *2 Clement*. Such a stylistic similarity might then suggest common, rather than different, authorship of the two sections.

Chapter 20

COMMENTARY

1 The theme of encouragement and exhortation continues (the chapter division is somewhat misleading and/or unnecessary). However, a new note is introduced here, with the reference to the unrighteous apparently enjoying material prosperity while the righteous are oppressed. The language changes again slightly: from being troubled or grieving, the author now says 'neither let it disturb our[1] mind'.[2] What brings about such anxiety is seeing the 'unrighteous' enjoying wealth. By contrast, those who are at present suffering are said here to be 'the servants of God'. Probably all Christians concerned are involved, not just an elite group of office-holders (cf. Tit. 1.1). Who then the 'unrighteous' are is not so clear: if the 'servants of God' are all Christians, it might make more sense to interpret the 'unrighteous' as non-Christians; however, it could be a reference to other Christians of whom the author disapproves. It is not possible to decide with any certainty. Whether we can deduce that the 'opponents' who are in mind in the rest of *2 Clement* are implicitly then socially well-off and relatively rich is also not clear.

The theodicy question arises here out of nowhere and is not paralleled elsewhere in *2 Clement*. The issue is of course a perennial one, and certainly keenly felt as a problem in both Judaism and Christianity, as well as in a wide range of other writers of the time. The problem is simply raised here: the wicked (appear to) prosper while the righteous suffer. Apart from the reference to future rewards for the righteous (see below on v. 2), there is no

---

[1] C has ὑμῶν, whereas S implies a reading ἡμῶν. The C reading is accepted by most editors (e.g. Lightfoot, *Apostolic Fathers*, 2.259; Lake, *Fathers*, 160; Ehrman, *Fathers*, 198). However, C does have a marked tendency to replace first-person pronouns with second persons (cf. Lightfoot, *Apostolic Fathers*, 1.128); moreover, the whole of the rest of this sentence here is couched in the first-person plural. It is not the author's style to speak *to* his audience, but to identify himself with them. The S reading is therefore to be preferred (with Wengst, *Zweite Clemensbrief*, 266; Lindemann, *Clemensbriefe*, 258; Pratscher, *Zweite Clemensbrief*, 227).

[2] If indeed all these verbal references are parallel, it would suggest that any 'suffering' being experienced by the community at present is relatively low key, and in part brought about by feelings and thoughts, rather than by external physical pressures or persecution.

real theologizing about the issue, and certainly no discussion of, or polemic against, the value of wealth and money as such (unlike perhaps e.g. Luke 6.24, or James).

2 All that is said in response to the 'problem' raised is a reference to the future rewards in store for the righteous, and hence by implication an assessment of the present life as a preparation for that. The author takes up the image of the present life as an athletic contest (developed more in ch. 7). And in particular, he refers to the 'crown' that is in store. Issues about how many people might win such a crown (as in ch. 7) are not raised here. Nor is there a reference here to the possibility of not gaining the crown (cf. 7.3 and the reference there to coming near it). Whether this is an indication of a different author[3] is not clear: at one level, the common use of the athletic metaphor serves to tie this section closely with the earlier chapter of *2 Clement*.

3 The author now says that any such reward will not necessarily come quickly. The idea is similar to that in Jas. 5.7, though it is slightly at variance with what seems to be implied in 19.3 with the talk there of the present time in this world being 'short'. The reward in store is again referred to as καρπός which is slightly unusual (see above on 19.3), though close in language to that of Jas. 5.7 (καρπὸς τίμιος).[4] Unlike 19.3, the author here seems to want to impress on his hearers the possibility, if not certainty, of an ongoing period in this life which will *not* necessarily be short-lived, but which will still be followed by a time of blessedness etc.

4 The assertion of v. 3 is now substantiated and expanded further (γάρ). The issue is still the simple temporal one: will the righteous receive their reward *soon*, or might they have to wait? The issue is not whether the righteous will be rewarded at all (see below). The argument to back this up is, however, a strange one. The author claims that, if the righteous were to be rewarded quickly, the relationship between God and human beings would be one based on commercial transactions, and not on the basis of the righteous exhibiting 'godliness' (θεοσέβια).[5] However, the language is still of 'reward' (μισθός) and elsewhere in *2 Clement* there is an all but 'automatic' correlation between human action and behaviour on the one hand and 'reward' on the other: those who do what they are meant to do will receive eschatological rewards, those who do not will not receive. Hence, in one way, one could say that the model *is* that of commerce rather than of any 'grace'. Hence Lindemann's comment, that the author here 'weist also den

---

[3] So e.g. Pratscher, *Zweite Clemensbrief*, 230.
[4] Though there it is part of a wider verbal image of a farmer harvesting: such is not the case here.
[5] See above on 19.1, 4 for this word group and the distinctive language of this section of *2 Clement* in this respect.

Gedanken zurück, der Mensch könne sich das Heil "verdienen"' (the author 'thus rejects the idea that men and women can "earn" salvation') is perhaps a little optimistic![6] The issue here seems to be solely the immediacy of any receiving of rewards. It is true that elsewhere salvation is sometimes a gift of God or Christ (e.g. 1.3); but equally there are other passages where salvation is apparently thought of as following almost automatically from 'righteousness', that is, correct human behaviour (cf. 19.3).[7] Maybe the author has simply not thought through the issue clearly (or perhaps not even seen it as a problem: there is always the danger of modern interpreters viewing early Christian texts through post-Reformation spectacles!).

The final sentence of v. 4 present a notorious crux and the precise interpretation, and/or reference, is notoriously obscure. The first verb ἔβλαψεν is in the aorist and most naturally refers to a (single) event in the past (though it is taken by some as a gnomic aorist to refer to a general situation).[8] In particular the identity of the πνεῦμα here is not clear either. Nor is it very clear how or why this reference (to God punishing a spirit that is not righteous) backs up what has just been said in v. 3 (despite the introductory διὰ τοῦτο): the theme of reward may implicitly imply judgement (and hence punishment if such judgement is negative), but it is at best implicit and not really related to the issue of whether rewards come quickly (as in a commercial setting) or demand patience.

Some have suggested that the reference is to a particular instance in the community of an individual member, known perhaps to be 'not righteous' who has fallen ill and/or died.[9] On the other hand, it is not clear why such a (human) figure would be referred to as a πνεῦμα.[10] Also the language of being 'bound' by 'chains' is also problematic. Others have suggested that what is said here may presuppose the story of the fallen angels in Jewish interpretations of Gen. 6.1–4. Here the 'sons of God' are interpreted as angels who have illegitimate sexual relations with women on earth and are cast in chains into darkness (cf. *Jub.* 5.10; *1 En.* 10.4; cf. too Jude 6 etc.). But, as others have pointed out, the reference to a single 'spirit' is unexpected and unusual. Others too have suggested that a singular devil figure (e.g. 'Satan') might be in mind, though what the precise event in mind might be is also not clear (the 'binding of Satan' is usually thought of as something which will happen in an eschatological future, not an event to look back on in the past). Perhaps one simply has to admit ignorance!

5 The final doxology is usually assumed by those who ascribe 19.1–20.4 to another hand to be by the original author of 1–18. The language is certainly

---

[6] Lindemann, *Clemensbriefe*, 259. [7] See Pratscher, *Zweite Clemensbrief*, 232.
[8] So e.g. Lake, *Fathers*, 163; Richardson, *Fathers*, 202; Ehrman, *Fathers*, 199, who use a present tense in their translations.
[9] Suggested tentatively by Knopf, *Zwei Clemensbriefe*, 183.
[10] As Knopf himself concedes.

very similar to what comes elsewhere in *2 Clem.* 1–18, e.g. for 'Father of truth' cf. 3.1; for Jesus as the 'saviour', cf. references to Jesus' saving activity in 2.7; 9.5; for reference to ἀφθαρσία, cf. 7.5; 14.5. The language clearly has a quasi-liturgical flavour, invoking praise to God, and is not so clearly part of any explicit argument from earlier in the text.[11]

The opening phrase describes the being of God. He is 'only' (μόνος), 'invisible' (ἀόρατος), and the 'Father of truth' (cf. 3.1). The language is very close to that of 1 Tim. 1.17 τῷ ... ἀοράτῳ μόνῳ θεῷ, ... δόξα εἰς τοὺς αἰῶνας τῶν αἰώνων, ἀμήν, though it would be difficult to claim any literary dependence: both are probably reflecting quasi-liturgical formulations.[12] The description of God as μόνος is standard terminology in the Judaeo-Christian tradition.[13] Whether this is meant as a pointed claim made against (Gnostic) opponents is perhaps doubtful: the context is of an expression of praise to God, implicitly shared by all, not part of a theological argument directed against others.[14] Similarly, the claim that God is 'invisible' is standard fare.[15] For God as the 'Father of truth', cf. 3.1; and although this is a description of God widely used in Gnostic texts (see on 3.1 above), it is uncertain if the usage here is deliberately targeted at rival Gnostic claims: nothing in the language suggests that the claim here is contested or polemical.

The next phrase spells out significant aspects of what God has done. 'Sending' Jesus into the world uses the same language as in Gal. 4.4, and is also used frequently in John (related there to God as Father and/or Jesus as Son: cf. John 3.17; 5.36; 6.57; etc.). Here it is related to Jesus in his capacity as 'saviour' (σωτήρ). The noun is applied to Jesus in the NT mostly in the later writings;[16] and although the noun as such has not occurred earlier in

---

[11] I have followed the text as in C throughout. The longer readings at various points in the doxology in S are almost certainly typical secondary 'flowery' expansions of the language in the same quasi-liturgical vein as the rest.

[12] 1 Tim 1.17 also refers to God as ἀφθάρτος, which links with the note here later of Jesus as the ἀρχηγὸν τῆς ἀφθαρσίας.

[13] In the Jewish tradition, cf. the opening of the Decalogue in Exod. 20.3; Deut. 5.7; and then a range of texts such as Isa. 37.20; 2 Kgs 19.15, 19; *Let. Aris.* 132.1; *Sib. Or.* 3.629; Josephus, *Ant.* 8.335; etc. (though with perhaps varying levels of the extent to which such a claim is thought of in terms of an 'ontological' monotheism (God alone exists), or 'henotheism' (our God is supreme)). The language is then taken over by Christian writers, cf. John 17.3; Rom. 16.27; 1 Tim. 1.17; Jude 25; *1 Clem.* 59.4.

[14] In any case, such a claim on its own would scarcely engage with Gnostics since all would presumably agree that 'God' is unique: the differences might emerge in relation to claims about the status, and/or identity, of the creator God of the Hebrew Bible in relation to this unique God.

[15] cf. *Sib. Or.* 3.12; Col. 1.15; 1 Tim. 1.17; Ign. *Magn.* 3.2; Ign. *Pol.* 3.2.

[16] In Paul, only in Phil. 3.20; for the Pastorals, cf. 2 Tim. 1.10; Tit. 1.4; 2.13; 3.6; also Luke 2.11; John 4.42; Acts 5.31; 2 Pet. 1.1, 11; 2.20; 3.18. In the Apostolic Fathers, see Ign. *Eph.* 1.1; *Magn.* Prescr.; *Philad.* 9.2; *Smyrn.* 7.1. The description has often been linked with the use of the same language in Graeco-Roman mystery cults and/or the emperor cult: see Dibelius and Conzelmann, *Pastoral Epistles*, 100–3. But whether such possible overtones are in mind here is very doubtful: nothing has indicated this earlier in the text.

2 *Clement*, the verb σώζειν has occurred in relation to Jesus in 2.7 and 9.5. Jesus is also called here the ἀρχηγὸν τῆς ἀφθαρσίας. ἀρχηγός (cf. Acts 3.15; 5.31; Heb. 2.10; 12.2) can be taken as a 'pioneer' or 'leader' (going ahead of others and showing the way), or as an 'originator' or 'founder'.[17] The fact that the doxology as a whole is primarily theo-centric might suggest that the former is more appropriate; though the fact that Jesus is here the 'saviour', i.e. has engendered 'salvation' for other human beings, may make a meaning 'founder' (Jesus has then also engendered the possibility of immortality) more likely.[18] The purpose of God's action in sending Jesus is to produce salvation and immortality for those who will respond. Through Jesus God has also revealed the 'truth' and the 'heavenly life'. Neither term as such has occurred earlier in the text. The 'truth' probably refers here to the divine reality and the truth about God (cf. John 1.17; 8.32). 'Heavenly life' is presumably the same as 'eternal life' (5.5; 8.4, 6) or simply 'life' (14.5; 17.3). To a certain extent, and in a way typical of liturgical prayers, the language tends to redundancy and wordiness: the last phrase essentially says no more than what has been said already in the first. However, it is perhaps noteworthy that 'salvation' seems to be primarily conceived in terms of revelation and knowledge.[19]

The final clause of the doxology uses wording found frequently elsewhere in such contexts (cf. 4 Macc. 18.24; Phil. 4.20; 1 Tim. 1.17; 2 Tim. 4.18; *1 Clem.* 50.7). It provides a fitting climax as the end of the address. To this is added simply the word 'Amen', perhaps reflecting a liturgical practice whereby all say the word and thereby express their agreement with, and commitment to, all that has been said.[20]

---

[17] See BAG, 112.

[18] *Contra* Lindemann, *Clemensbrife*, 261; Pratscher, *Zweite Clemensbrief*, 235, suggests that both ideas might be in mind.

[19] What is said here thus correlates closely with the verbal imgery used in 1.6.

[20] A colophon is added in S, but there is none in C, which simply gives the number of *stichoi*. The 'colophon' printed in the editions of Lake, *Fathers*, 162–3, and Ehrman, *Fathers*, 198–9 (both print Κλήμεντος πρὸς Κορινθίους ἐπιστολὴ β 'The Second Letter of Clement to the Corinthians' at the end of the text) appears to be produced on the basis of the colophon to *1 Clement* in codex A. However, the end of *2 Clement* is not extant in A and there is no colophon in C: the text as we have it in our (only!) extant Greek witness ends with the simple 'Amen'.

Bibliography

Aasgaard, R., *'My Beloved Brothers and Sisters'. Christian Siblingship in Paul*, JSNTSup 265 (London: T&T Clark, 2004).

—— '"Brotherly Advice": Christian Siblingship and New Testament Paraenesis', in Starr and Engberg-Pedersen (eds), *Early Christian Paraenesis*, 237–65.

—— 'Brothers and Sisters in the Faith. Christian Siblingship as an Eccelesiological Mirror in the First Two Centuries', in J. Ådna (ed.), *The Formation of the Early Church*, WUNT 183 (Tübingen: Mohr Siebeck, 2005), 285–316.

Abramowski, L., 'The "Memoirs of the Apostles" in Justin', in P. Stuhlmacher (ed.), *The Gospel and the Gospels* (Grand Rapids: Eerdmans, 1991), 323–35.

Aono, T., *Die Entwicklung des paulinischen Gerichtsgedankens bei den Apostolischen Vätern* (Bern: Peter Lang, 1979).

Baarda, T., '2 Clement 12 and the Sayings of Jesus', in J. Delobel (ed.), *Logia. Les Paroles de Jésus—The Sayings of Jesus*, BETL 59 (Leuven: Peeters, 1982), 529–56.

Baasland, E., 'Der 2.Klemensbrief und frühchristliche Rhetorik: "Die erste christliche Predigt" im Lichte der neueren Forschung', *ANRW* 2.27.1 (1993), 78–157.

Barr, J., *Holy Scripture. Canon. Authority, Criticism* (Oxford: Clarendon Press, 1983).

Bartlet, J. V., 'The Origin and Date of 2 Clement', *ZNW* 7 (1906), 123–35.

—— Carlyle, A. J., and Benecke, P. V. M., 'II Clement', in *The New Testament in the Apostolic Fathers. By a Committee of the Oxford Society of Historical Theology* (Oxford: Clarendon Press, 1905), 124–36.

Barton, J., *Holy Writings, Sacred Text. The Canon in Early Christianity* (London: SPCK, 1997).

Bauckham, R. J., *Jude, 2 Peter*, WBC 50 (Waco: Word, 1983).

Bauernfeind, O., ἀρετή, *TWNT* 1 (1933), 457–61.

Bellinzoni, A. J., *The Sayings of Jesus in the Writings of Justin Martyr*, NovTSup 17 (Leiden: Brill, 1967).

Bensly, R. L., *The Epistles of S. Clement to the Corinthians in Syriac. Edited from the Manuscript with Notes* (Cambridge: University Press, 1899).

Berger, K., 'Almosen für Israel', *NTS* 23 (1978), 180–204.

—— 'Zum Diskussion über die Herkunft von 1 Kor. II. 9', *NTS* 24 (1978), 271–83.

Betz, H. D., *Galatians*, Hermeneia (Philadelphia: Fortress Press, 1979).

Beyer, H. W., κατηχέω, *TWNT* 3 (1938), 638–40.

Bihlmeyer, K., *Die Apostolischen Väter. Neubearbeitung der Funkschen Ausgabe* (Tübingen: J. C. B. Mohr (Paul Siebeck), 1956).

Bousset, W., *Die Religion des Judentums im späthellenistischen Zeitalter, bearbeitet von H. Gressmann*, HNT 21 (Tübingen: Mohr Siebeck, 1926).

Bovon, F., *Luke 1*, Hermeneia (Minneapolis: Fortress, 2002).

Brox, N., *Der Hirt des Hermas*, KAV 9 (Göttingen: Vandenhoeck & Ruprecht, 1991).

Bultmann, R., *The Theology of the New Testament* (2 vols; London: SCM, 1952–5).

—— *History of the Synoptic Tradition* (Oxford: Blackwell, 1968).

Callan, T., 'The Saying of Jesus in Gos. Thom. 22/2 Clem. 12/Gos. Eg. 5', *JRelS* 16 (1990), 46–64.
Chadwick, H., 'Enkrateia', *RAC* 5 (1962), 343–65.
Cureton, W., *Corpus Ignatianum: A Complete Collection of the Ignatian Epistles, genuine, interpolated, and spurious, together with numerous extracts from them, as quoted by ecclesiastical writers down to the tenth century* (London: Rivington, 1849).
Davies, W. D., and Allison, D. C., *The Gospel according to Saint Matthew*, ICC (3 vols; Edinburgh: T&T Clark, 1988–97).
DeConick, A. D., *Seek to See Him: Ascent and Vision Mysticism in the Gospel of Thomas*, VCSup 33 (Leiden: Brill, 1996).
Dibelius, M., and Conzelmann, H., *The Pastoral Epistles*, Hermeneia (Philadelphia: Fortress, 1972).
Di Pauli, A., 'Zum sog. 2. Korintherbrief des Clemens Romanus', *ZNW* 4 (1903), 321–9.
Donfried, K. P., 'The Theology of Second Clement', *HTR* 66 (1973), 487–501.
——. *The Setting of Second Clement in Early Christianity*, NovTSup 38 (Leiden: Brill, 1974).
Dunderberg, I., *Beyond Gnosticism: Myth, Lifestyle, and Society in the School of Valentinus* (New York: Columbia University Press, 2008).
Ehrman, B. D., *The Apostolic Fathers I*, LCL (London and Cambridge Mass.: Harvard University Press, 2003).
—— 'Textual Traditions Compared: The New Testament and the Apostolic Fathers', in A. F. Gregory and C. M. Tuckett (eds), *The Reception of the New Testament in the Apostolic Fathers* (Oxford: Oxford University Press, 2005), 9–27.
Fitzer, G., σφραγίς κτλ., *TWNT* 7 (1964), 939–54.
Fitzmyer, J. A., *Tobit* (Berlin: De Gruyter, 2003).
Foster, P., *The Gospel of Peter. Introduction, Critical Edition and Commentary* (Leiden: Brill, 2010).
Freede, J. H., *The Library of Photius*, vol. I (London: SPCK, 1920).
Funk, W.-P., Painchaud, L., and Thomassen, E., *L'Interprétation de la Gnose (NH XI,1)*, BCNH Textes 34 (Louvain: Peeters, 2010).
Gebhardt, O. de, Harnack, A. von, and Zahn, Th., *Patrum Apostolicorum Opera. Textum ad Fidem Codicum et Graecorum et Latinorum adhibitis praestantissimis editionibus* (Lipsiae: J. C. Hinrichs, 1900).
Goppelt, L., τύπος κτλ., *TWNT* 8 (1969), 246–60.
Grant, R. M., and Graham, H. H., *The Apostolic Fathers. A New Translation and Commentary*, vol. 2: *First and Second Clement* (New York: Thomas Nelson & Sons, 1965).
Gregory, A. F., *The Reception of Luke and Acts in the Period before Irenaeus*, WUNT 2.169 (Tübingen: Mohr Siebeck, 2004).
Gregory, A. F., and Tuckett, C. M., '*2 Clement* and the Writings that Later Formed the New Testament', in A. F. Gregory and C. M. Tuckett (eds), *The Reception of the New Testament in the Apostolic Fathers* (Oxford: Oxford University Press, 2005), 251–92.
—— —— 'Reflections on Method: What Constitutes the Use of the Writings that Later Formed the New Testament in the Apostolic Fathers?', in A. F. Gregory and C. M. Tuckett (eds), *The Reception of the New Testament in the Apostolic Fathers* (Oxford: Oxford University Press, 2005), 61–82.

Grundmann, W., ἐγκράτεια, TWNT 2 (1935), 338–40.
Hagner, D. A., *The Use of the Old Testament and the New Testament in Clement of Rome*, NovTSup 34 (Leiden: Brill, 1973).
Hanhart, R., *Tobit. Septuaginta. Vetus Testamentum Graecum Auctoritate Academiae Scientiarum Gottingensis editum. Vol. VIII, 5* (Göttingen: Vandenhoeck & Ruprecht, 1983).
Harland, P. A., 'Familial Dimensions of Group Identity: Brothers (ΑΔΕΛΦΟΙ) in Associations of the Greek East', *JBL* 124 (2005), 491–513.
Harnack, A. von, 'Über den sogenannten zweiten Brief des Clemens an die Korinther', *ZKG* 1 (1873), 264–83, 329–64.
—— *Geschichte der altchristlichen Litteratur bis Eusebius. I: Die Überlieferung und der Bestand* (Leipzig: J. C. Hinrichs'sche Buchhandlung, 1893).
—— *Geschichte der altchristlichen Litteratur bis Eusebius. II: Die Chronologie der altchristlichen Litteratur bis Eusebius. Band 1: Die Chronologie der Litteratur bis Irenaeus* (Leipzig: J.C. Hinrichs'sche Buchhandlung, 1897).
—— 'Zum Ursprung des sog. 2. Clemensbriefs', *ZNW* 6 (1905), 67–71.
Harris, J. R., 'The Double Text of Tobit', *AJT* 3 (1899), 541–54.
—— 'The Authorship of the so-called Second Epistle of Clement', *ZNW* 23 (1924), 193–200.
Heiligenthal, R., 'Werke der Barmherzigkeit oder Almosen? Zur Bedeutung von ἐλεημοσύνη', *NovT* 25 (1983), 289–301.
Hennecke, E., *New Testament Apocrypha 1* (London: SCM, 1963).
Hilgenfeld, A., *Clementis Romanae Epistulae. Edidit, commentario critico et adnotationibus instruxit.* (Lipsiae: T.O. Weigel, 1876).
Jefford, C. N. (with K. J. Harder and L. D. Amezaga Jr.), *Reading the Apostolic Fathers: An Introduction* (Peabody, Mass.: Hendrickson, 1996).
Kenyon, F. G., *The Codex Alexandrinus (Royal MS 1 D V–VIII) in reduced photographic facsimile* (London: British Museum, 1909).
King, K. L., *What is Gnosticism?* (Cambridge, Mass.: Harvard University Press, 2003).
Knopf, R., 'Die Anagnose zum zweiten Clemensbriefe', *ZNW* 3 (1902), 266–79.
Knopf, R., *Die Lehre der zwölf Apostel. Die zwei Clemensbriefe*, HNT Ergänzungsband (Tübingen: J. C. B. Mohr, 1920).
Koester, H., *Introduction to the New Testament*, vol. 2: *History and Literature of Early Christianity* (Philadelphia: Fortress, 1982).
Koester, H., *Ancient Christian Gospels* (London: SCM, 1990).
Köhler, W.-D., *Die Rezeption des Matthäusevangeliums in der Zeit vor Irenäus*, WUNT 2.24 (Tübingen: Mohr Siebeck, 1987).
Körtner, U., *Papias von Hierapolis. Ein Beitrag zur Geschichte des Urchristentums*, FRLANT 133 (Göttingen: Vandenhoeck & Ruprecht, 1983).
Koskenniemi, H., *Studien zur Idee und Phraseologie des griechischen Briefes bis 400 n. Chr.* (Helsinki: 1956).
Köster, H., *Synoptische Überlieferung bei den Apostolischen Vätern*, TU 65 (Berlin: Akademie, 1957).
Kraus, T. J., and Nicklas, T., *Das Petrusevangelium und die Petrusapokalypse*, GCS NF. 11 (Berlin: De Gruyter, 2004).
Krüger, G., 'Zu II. Klem. 14,2', *ZNW* 31 (1932), 204–5.

Lake, K., *The Apostolic Fathers I*, LCL (London and Cambridge, Mass.: Heinemann and Harvard University Press, 1965).

Lampe, G. W. H., *The Seal of the Spirit* (London: SPCK, 1967).

Layton, B. (ed.), *Nag Hammadi Codex II, 2–7 together with XIII,2, Brit. Lib. Or. 4926(1) and P. Oxy. 1, 654, 655*, vol. I, NHS 20 (Leiden: Brill, 1989).

Lightfoot, J. B., *The Apostolic Fathers. Part 1. S. Clement of Rome* (2 vols; London: Macmillan, 1890).

Lindemann, A., *Paulus im ältesten Christentum. Das Bild des Apostels und die Rezeption der paulinischen Theologie in der frühchristlichen Literatur bis Marcion*, BHT 58 (Tübingen: Mohr Siebeck, 1979).

Lindemann, A., *Die Clemensbriefe*, HNT 17 (Tübingen: Mohr Siebeck, 1992).

Lohmann, H., *Drohung und Verheissung. Exegetische Untersuchungen zur Eschatologie bei den Apostolischen Vätern*, BZNW 55 (Berlin and New York: De Gruyter, 1989).

Lührmann, D., 'Epiphaneia. Zur Bedeutungsgeschichte eines griechischen Wortes', in G. Jeremias, H.-W. Kuhn, and H. Stegemann (eds), *Tradition und Glaube. Das frühe Christentum in seiner Umwelt. Festgabe für K.G. Kuhn* (Göttingen: Vandenhoeck & Ruprecht, 1971), 185–99.

—— *Die apokryph gewordenen Evangelien*, NovTSup 112 (Leiden: Brill, 2004).

Luz, U., *Matthew 1–7* (Minneapolis: Fortress, 1989).

Malherbe, A. J., *Moral Exhortation, A Greco-Roman Sourcebook* (Philadelphia: Westminster, 1986);.

Marjanen, A. (ed.), *Was there a Gnostic Religion?* (Helsinki: Finnish Exegetical Society, 2005).

Markschies, C., *Valentinus Gnosticus? Untersuchungen zur valentinianischen Gnosis mit einem Kommentar zu den Fragmenten Valentins*, WUNT 65 (Tübingen: Mohr Siebeck, 1992).

Markschies, C., 'Gnosis/Gnostizismus', RGG^4 iii (2000), 1045–53.

—— *Gnosis: An Introduction* (London: T&T Clark, 2003).

Martin, E. G., 'Eldad and Modad', in J. H. Charlesworth (ed.), *Old Testament Pseudepigrapha II* (New York: Doubleday, 1985), 463–5.

Massaux, E., *Influence de l'Évangile de saint Matthieu sur la littérature chrétienne avant saint Irénée*, BETL 75 (Leuven: Peeters, 1986).

Meeks, W. A., *The First Urban Christians. The Social World of the Apostle Paul* (New Haven: Yale University Press, 1983).

Mitchell, M., *Paul and the Rhetoric of Reconciliation* (Louisville: Westminster, 1993).

Muddiman, J., 'The Church in Ephesians, *2 Clement*, and the *Shepherd of Hermas*', in A. F. Gregory and C. M. Tuckett (eds), *Trajectories through the New Testament and the Apostolic Fathers* (Oxford: Oxford University Press, 2005), 107–21.

O'Hagan, A., *Material Re-Creation in the Apostolic Fathers*, TU 100 (Berlin: Akademie, 1968).

Osiek, C., *The Shepherd of Hermas*, Hermeneia (Minneapolis: Fortress, 1999).

Parvis, P., '*2 Clement* and the Meaning of the Christian Homily', in P. Foster (ed.), *The Writings of the Apostolic Fathers* (London and New York: T&T Clark, 2007), 32–41.

Pearson, B., 'Gnosticism as a Religion', *Gnosticism and Christianity in Roman and Coptic Egypt* (New York and London: T&T Clark International, 2004), 201–23.

Petersen, W. L., 'Textual Traditions Examined: What the Text of the Apostolic Fathers tells us about the Text of the New Testament in the Second Century', in A. F. Gregory and C. M. Tuckett (eds), *The Reception of the New Testament in the Apostolic Fathers* (Oxford: Oxford University Press, 2005), 29–46.

—— 'Patristic Biblical Quotations and Method: Four Changes to Lightfoot's Edition of *Second Clement*', *VC* 60 (2006), 389–419.

Pfitzner, V. C., *Paul and the Agon Motif. Traditional Athletic Imagery in the Pauline Literature*, NovTSup 16 (Leiden: Brill, 1967).

Plisch, U.-W., *Die Auslegung der Erkenntnis (Nag-Hammadi-Codex XI,1)*, TU 142 (Berlin: Akademie, 1996).

Plisch, U.-W., 'Die Auslegung der Erkenntnis (NHC XI,1)', in H.-M. Schenke, H.-G. Bethge, and U. U. Kaiser (eds), *Nag Hammadi Deutsch 2. Band: NHC V,2–XIII,1, BG 1 und 4*, GCS NF 12 (Berlin: De Gruyter, 2003), 734–43.

Pratscher, W., *Der zweite Clemensbrief*, KAV 3 (Göttingen: Vandenhoeck & Ruprecht, 2007).

—— 'Der zweite Clemensbrief', *Die Apostolischen Väter* (Göttingen: Vandenhoeck & Ruprecht, 2009), 83–103.

Richardson, C. C., *Early Christian Fathers*, LCC 1 (London: SCM, 1953).

Robinson, J. M., Hoffmann, P., and Kloppenborg, J. S., *The Critical Edition of Q* (Minneapolis/Leuven: Fortress Press/Peeters, 2000).

Rousseau, A., *Irénée de Lyon. Contre les Hérésies. Livre III. Tome I Introduction, Notes justificatives, Tables*, SC 210 (Paris: Cerf, 1974).

Rucker, I. (ed.), *Florilegium Edessenum anonymum (syriace ante 562)*, SBAW. PH 1933 Heft 5 (Munich: Verlag der Bayerischen Akademie der Wissenschaften, 1933).

Salzmann, J. C., *Lehren und Ermahnen, Zur Geschichte des urchristlichen Wortgottesdienstes in den ersten drei Jahrhunderten*, WUNT 2.59 (Tübingen: Mohr Siebeck, 1994).

Sanders, E. P., *Paul and Palestinian Judaism* (London: SCM, 1975).

Schlarb, E., and Lührmann, D., *Fragmente apokryph gewordener Evangelien in griechischer und lateinischer Sprache*, MTS 59 (Marburg: Elwert, 2000).

Schubert, H. von, 'Der sogen. zweite Clemensbrief, eine Gemeindepredigt', in E. Hennecke (ed.), *Neutestamentliche Apokryphen. In Verbindung mit Fachgelehrten in deutscher Übersetzung und mit Einleitungen* (Tübingen: Mohr Siebeck, 1904), 172–9.

—— 'Der sogen. 2. Clemensbrief, eine Gemeindepredigt', in E. Hennecke (ed.), *Handbuch zu den Neutestamentlichen Apokryphen* (Tübingen: Mohr Siebeck, 1904), 248–55.

Schulz, S., *Q—Die Spruchquelle der Evangelisten* (Zurich: TVZ, 1971).

Schüssler, W., 'Ist der zweite Klemensbrief ein einheitliches Ganzes?' *ZKG* 28 (1907), 1–13.

Seitz, O. F. J., 'Relationship of the Shepherd of Hermas to the Epistle of James', *JBL* 63 (1944), 131–40.

—— 'Antecedents and Signification of the Term $\Delta I\Psi YXO\Sigma$', *JBL* 66 (1947), 211–19.

—— 'Afterthoughts on the Term "Dipsychos"', *NTS* 4 (1958), 327–34.

Stanton, G. N., *Jesus and Gospel* (Cambridge: Cambridge University Press, 2004).

Stanton, G. R., '2 Clement VII and the Origin of the Document', *Classica et Mediaevalia* 28 (1967), 314–20.

Starr, J., and Engberg-Pedersen, T., (eds), *Early Christian Paraenesis in Context*, BZNW 125 (Berlin: De Gruyter, 2004).

Stegemann, C., 'Herkunft und Entstehung des sogenannten zweiten Klemensbriefes' (Bonn: doctoral dissertation, 1974).

Stewart-Sykes, A. , *From Prophecy to Preaching. A Search for the Origin of the Christian Homily*, VCSup 59 (Leiden: Brill, 2001).

Stone, M. E., and Strugnell, J., *The Books of Elijah, Parts 1 & 2* (Missoula: Scholars Press, 1979).

Streeter, B. H., *The Primitive Church* (London: Macmillan, 1929).

Taylor, C., 'The Homily of Pseudo-Clement', *Journal of Philology* 28 (1903), 195–208.

Tite, P., *Valentinian Ethics and Paraenetic Discourse: Determining the Social Function of Moral Exhortation in Valentinian Christianity*, NHMS 67 (Leiden: Brill, 2009).

Torrance, T. F., *The Doctrine of Grace in the Apostolic Fathers* (London: Oliver & Boyd, 1948),.

Tuckett, C. M., 'Paul and Jesus Tradition: The Evidence of 1 Corinthians 2:9 and Gospel of Thomas 17', in T. J. Burke and J. K. Elliott (eds), *Paul and the Corinthians: Studies on a Community in Conflict: Essays in Honour of Margaret Thrall*, NovTSup 109 (Leiden: Brill, 2003), 55–73.

—— *The Gospel of Mary* (Oxford: Oxford University Press, 2007).

—— 'Moses in Gnostic Writings', in A. Graupner and M. Wolter (eds), *Moses in Biblical and Extra-Biblical Traditions*, BZAW 372 (Berlin: De Gruyter, 2007), 227–40.

—— 'Lightfoot's Text of *2 Clement*: A Response to W. L. Petersen', *VC* 64 (2010), 501–19.

Unnik, W. C. van, 'Die Rücksicht auf die Reaktion der Nicht-Christen als Motiv in der altchristlichen Paränese', in W. Eltester (ed.), *Judentum. Urchristentum. Kirche. Festschrift für J. Jeremias*, BZNW 26 (Berlin: Topelmann, 1960), 221–34.

—— 'The Interpretation of 2 Clement 15,5', *VC* 27 (1973), 29–34.

Verheyden, J., 'Origen on the Origin of 1 Cor 2,9', in R. Bieringer (ed.), *The Corinthian Correspondence*, BETL 125 (Leuven: Peeters, 1996), 491–511.

—— 'Assessing Gospel Quotations in Justin Martyr', in A. Denaux (ed.), *New Testament Textual Criticism and Exegesis. Festschrift J. Delobel*, BETL 161 (Leuven: Peeters, 2002), 361–77.

Vielhauer, Ph., 'Anapausis. Zum gnostischen Hintergrund des Thomasevangeliums', *Apophoreta. Festschrift für Ernst Haenchen*, BZNW 30 (Berlin: Töpelmann, 1964), 281–99.

—— *Geschichte der urchristlichen Literatur. Einleitung in das Neue Testament, die Apokryphen und die Apostolischen Väter* (Berlin and New York: De Gruyter, 1975).

Warns, R., 'Untersuchungen zum 2. Clemensbrief' (Marburg: doctoral dissertation, 1989).

Weeks, S., 'Some Neglected Texts of Tobit: The Third Greek Version', in M. Bredin (ed.), *Studies in the Book of Tobit* (Edinburgh: T&T Clark, 2006), 1–42.

Weeks, S., Gathercole, S., and Stuckenbruck, L. (eds), *The Book of Tobit: Texts from the Principal Ancient and Mediaeval Traditions* (Berlin: De Gruyter, 2004).

Wengst, K., *Didache (Apostellehre). Barnabasbrief. Zweite Clemensbrief. Schrift an Diognet. Eingeleitet, hg., übertragen und erläutert* (Darmstadt: Wissenschaftliche Buchgesellschaft, 1984).

Williams, M. A., *Rethinking 'Gnosticism': An Argument for Dismantling a Dubious Category* (Princeton: Princeton University Press, 1996).

Windisch, H., 'Das Christentum des zweites Clemensbriefes', *Harnack-Ehrung. Beiträge zur Kirchengeschichte, ihrem Lehrer Adolf von Harnack zu seinem siebzigsten Geburtstage (7. Mai 1921) dargebracht von einer Reihe seiner Schüler* (Leipzig: Hinrichs'sche Buchhandlung, 1921), 119–34.

Windisch, H., 'Julius Cassianus und die Clemenshomilie (II Clemens)', *ZNW* 25 (1926), 258–62.

Index of Ancient Sources

Old Testament and Apocrypha

Genesis
 1 253
 1.14 216
 1.26 246
 1.27 36, 39, 73, 245–6, 249, 252
 2.24 258
 6.1–4 301
 39.10 223
 49.22 216

Exodus
 9.24 216
 20.3 302

Numbers
 30.15 223

Deuteronomy
 4.27 237
 5.7 302
 6.5 150–1, 155
 7.8 283
 7.9 225
 8.2 208
 9.20 185
 9.26 283
 13.6 283
 15.15 283
 21.8 283
 24.18 283
 30.3 207

Joshua
 21.43–4 176

2 Kings
 19.15 302
 19.19 302

1 Chronicles
 12.33 222

1 Esdras
 4.40 291
 8.84 276

2 Esdras
 9.13 276

Psalms
 6.9 LXX 159, 160
 12.2 222
 30.6 LXX 291
 30.20 219
 34.12–17 211
 34.12–16 211
 34.14 210
 41.4 207
 45 253
 52.6 LXX 240
 61.5 208
 62.13 225, 283
 71.5 LXX 248
 71.17 LXX 248
 81.8 LXX 237
 106.7 LXX 190
 106.28 152
 135.15 135
 144.13 LXX 225

Proverbs
 2.13 190
 10.2 275
 11.4 275
 10.12 265
 20.11 190

Isaiah
 29.13 35, 38, 151–2, 155, 156, 208, 281
 34.4 35, 36, 271
 37.20 302
 44.9–20 135
 52.5 36, 236–7, 241, 242
 54–66 21, 140, 292
 54.1 21, 22, 35, 42, 45, 137, 138, 140, 141, 142, 143, 144, 145, 219, 231, 292, 297

Isaiah – *Contd.*
  54.17 287
  56.7 245
  58.6–7 273
  58.9 22, 36, 142, 260, 263
  64.3 218–19
  66.18 22, 36, 37, 68, 278, 282, 284
  66.24 22, 35, 36, 67, 187, 192, 221, 228, 278, 285, 287

Jeremiah
  3.16 219
  3.22 207
  6.16 184
  7.11 36, 245, 249
  18.4–6 196

Ezekiel
  3.20 185
  3.21 261
  14.13–20 36, 181, 184
  14.16 181
  14.18 181
  14.20 181
  33.13 185

Hosea
  6.6 154

Daniel
  3.2 278
  3.7 278
  4.24 276
  5.4 135
  5.23 135

Malachi
  4.1 265, 270

Tobit
  1.16 273
  3.4 237
  4.10 275
  4.16 273
  6.9–12.22 267
  12.8–9 35, 36, 38, 265–8, 277
  12.8 265–8, 272–7
  12.9 265–8, 272, 275, 276

Wisdom
  3.1 213
  4.1 210
  8.7 210

  8.8 207
  13–14 135
  13.10–19 135
  13.10 135, 152
  15.17 152
  18.6 207

Sirach
  3.14 273
  3.30 276
  36.10 234
  40.24 268

1 Maccabees
  9.26 286

2 Maccabees
  7.9 297
  7.28 136
  10.28 210
  12.27 289
  17.10 286

4 Maccabees
  2.2 269
  2.4 269
  6.5 289
  7.22 210
  9.20 289
  9.26 289
  17.5 297
  17.18 297
  18.24 303

Pseudepigrapha and other extra-biblical Jewish literature

2 Baruch
  44.9–12 182

1 Enoch
  10.4 301
  47.1 234
  97.3 234

4 Ezra
  7.50 182
  8.1 182

Joseph and Aseneth
  8.9 176
  15.7 176

Josephus
  Antiquities
    1.15 253
    3.2 210
    8.102 175
    8.159 253
    8.335 302
    15.79 292
    18.14 297

  Jewish War
    1.415 190

Jubilees
  5.10 301

Letter of Aristeas
  28 253
  132.1 302

Mishnah
  m. Aboth
    3.1 131

Odes of Solomon
  22.12 176
  26.12 176
  28.3 176
  37.4 176
  41.9 153

Philo
  De agricultura
    119–21 188
    120–1 190

  De cherubim
    12 213

  De confusione linguarum
    77–80 172

  In Flaccum
    33 175

  Legum allegoriae
    3.18 165
    3.43 216
    3.72 188

  De plantibus
    117 216

  De sobrietate
    68 216

  De specialibus legibus
    1.149 165
    1.173 165
    2.91 188
    2.195 165
    4.112 165
    4.187 136

  De virtutibus
    180 165

Psalms of Solomon
  2.6 181
  4.8 240
  4.10 240

Pseudo-Philo
  LAB
    26.13 218–19

Qumran literature
  1QH
    3.29–36 271

  1QS
    8 204

Sybilline Oracles
  3.12 302
  3.84–7 271
  3.629 302
  4.172–80 271

Talmud
  b. Sanh.
    97b 234

Testament of Judah
  26.1 287

Testament of Naphtali
  2.2–5 196

New Testament

Matthew
  3.8 132
  4.24 286
  5.44 238

Matthew – Contd.
  5.45 134
  5.46 238
  6.1–18 273
  6.8 263
  6.24 178
  7.5 159, 161
  7.7 263
  7.21 36, 155, 157–8, 162
  7.22 160
  7.23 36, 157, 159–60
  9.13 35, 42, 137–8, 154
  10.16 36, 167, 168–71
  10.28 36, 166, 167, 168, 174
  10.32 35, 148–9, 287
  11.29 184
  12.50 12, 201–2
  14.31 222
  15.8 35, 151–2
  16.26 179
  16.27 67, 225, 283
  18.11 139, 140
  19.4 246
  22.14 145
  23.3 243
  25.1–13 231
  25.31–46 283
  28.17 222
  28.19–20 279

Mark
  1.5 198
  1.15 185
  2.17 35, 137–8
  3.35 36, 37, 201–2
  4.11 241
  7.6 35, 151–2, 281
  8.36 12, 36, 179–80
  9.48 187, 192, 278
  10.6 246
  10.30 182
  10.45 283
  11.17 245
  12.30 151
  13.19 224
  13.20 296
  13.35–8 231
  16.15 279

Luke
  1.75 177
  2.11 302
  4.20–1 291
  5.32 137
  6.24 300
  6.27 238–9
  6.28 238–9
  6.32 36, 238–9
  6.46 155, 157–8
  7.25 213
  8.14 264
  8.21 201–2
  9.25 179
  10.3 36, 168–70
  11.2 134
  11.7 263
  12 32
  12.4–5 36, 168–70, 174
  12.8 35, 148–9, 287
  12.9 149
  12.35–46 231
  13.25 160
  13.26 160
  13.27 36, 159–60,
  16.10–12 36, 179
  16.10 40, 193–4,
  16.12 193–4
  16.13 36, 179, 181
  16.14 166
  16.23 213
  16.28 213
  17 32
  18.1 142
  18.7 142
  18.31 292
  19.10 139, 140, 147
  21 32
  21.9 224
  21.28 283
  22.32 146
  23.43 32

John
  1.4 134
  1.14 206
  1.17 303
  3.5 207
  3.17 302
  4.42 302
  5.36 302
  6.57 302
  8.12 134

8.32 303
8.41 144
12.16 292
12.35 134
12.36 134
14.7 154
16.3 154
17.3 154, 302

Acts
2.1–11 257
2.38 195
3.15 303
3.19 240
5.31 302, 303
5.41 241
7 32
10.42 129
13.10 190
13.15 291
13.36 297
18.23 146
20.35 263
24.25 165
26.20 196

Romans
1.8 152
1.18–32 135
1.21 154
1.27 132
1.29–31 163
1.30 164
2.6 225, 283
2.16 272
2.21–3 243
2.24 236–7, 242
3.2 152, 243
3.24–31 186
3.24 283
4.11 191
4.17 44
6.22 132
7.7–11 210
8 257
8.5–8 203
8.14 134
9.21 44, 196
9.26 134
9.30 210
12.5 44, 251

12.16 282
14.1–2 280
16.25 146
16.27 302

1 Corinthians
1.9 225
1.14–17 185
1.30 283
2.1–5 20
2.9 35, 36, 39, 40, 45, 218–19, 258–9
3.13 272
3.16 44, 204
4.15 127
5.12–13 241
6.9–10 163
6.19 44, 204
7.9 165
8.6 206
8.11–12 280
9.2 191
9.24–27 44, 188
9.24 190
10.1–13 185
10.13 225
10.16–17 251
10.16 44
11.18 152
12.1–11 257
12.2 279
12.3 77
12.12–27 251
12.27 44
13 163, 267
13.4 164
14 243
14.1 210
15 32, 202–3, 204
15.9 289
15.45 72, 206
15.50 56, 203
15.51 203

2 Corinthians
1.22 191
3.17 206
4.4 182
4.13 292
4.17 296
5 32
6.13 132

2 Corinthians – *Contd.*
  6.16 204
  13.11 282

Galatians
  1.4 182
  1.10 240
  1.13 289
  3.28 232
  4.4 302
  4.7 134
  4.27 45, 137, 141
  5.5 71
  5.14 163
  5.19–23 163
  5.19–21 203
  5.19 164
  5.22 132
  5.23 165
  6.10 196, 207

Ephesians
  1.7 283
  1.13 191
  1.21 182
  1.23 44, 251
  2.1 135
  2.6 297
  2.16 44
  2.20–1 204
  4.4 44
  4.5 206
  4.12–16 44
  4.18 135, 295
  4.24 177
  4.25 233
  4.30 191, 283
  5.3 164
  5.14 135
  5.15 294
  5.23–32 252
  5.23 252
  5.28 252
  5.30 44, 252
  5.31 258
  5.32 249
  6.6 240

Philippians
  1.23 32
  2.2 282

  3.12–14 289
  3.12 289
  3.13–14 188
  4.2 282
  4.8 210
  4.10 239
  4.20 303

Colossians
  1.12 134
  1.14 283
  1.15 302
  1.18 44, 251
  1.24 44, 251
  2.9 251
  2.13 135
  2.14 240
  2.19 44
  3.1 297
  3.5 164
  3.15 44
  3.22 240
  4.1 144

1 Thessalonians
  1.9 279
  2.4 240
  2.10 177
  4 32
  4.12 241
  4.13 297
  5.6 239
  5.8 239
  5.24 225

1 Timothy
  1.3 213
  1.13 289
  1.15 138, 139, 140, 147
  1.17 297, 302, 303
  2.1 292
  2.2 294
  2.5 206
  3.2 165
  3.16 22, 294
  4.5 292
  4.13 291
  4.16 261
  6.3 213
  6.10 166
  6.12 210

6.14 230
6.22 289

2 Timothy
 1.10 258, 302
 2.18 202
 2.22 289
 2.25 195
 2.5 188
 3.2 166
 3.8–9 239
 4.1 129, 230
 4.5 239
 4.7–8 188
 4.8 230
 4.18 3–3

Titus
 1.1 299
 1.4 302
 1.5 294
 1.8 165
 2.13 230, 302
 3.3 264
 3.6 302

Hebrews
 1.2 254
 2.10 303
 5.12 243
 6.1 196
 6.6 78, 198
 10.23 224
 12.1 136, 188
 12.2 303
 13.15 142
 13.18 275

James
 1.8 222
 1.25 210
 2.7 241
 4.1 263
 4.2 164
 4.4 263
 4.8 217, 220, 222
 4.11 164
 5.7 300
 5.16 207
 5.19–20 261

1 Peter
 1.6 296
 1.13 239
 1.17 172
 1.20 254
 2.1 164
 2.5 142, 248
 2.9 134
 3.10–12 211
 3.11 210
 4.5 129
 4.7 239
 4.8 35, 36, 266, 275
 5.4 146
 5.8 239
 5.10 296

2 Peter
 1.1 302
 1.5 210
 1.6 165
 1.19 216, 222, 223
 2.8 223
 2.13 213, 263
 2.15 190
 2.20 302
 3.4 223, 297
 3.7 271
 3.10 271
 3.18 302

1 John
 2.1 186
 2.3 155
 3.1 134
 3.20 262
 3.21–2 262
 5.14 262

Jude
 25 302

Revelation
 2.5 195
 2.16 195
 2.21 195
 3.1 135
 3.5 148
 7.14–17 298
 9.20 135
 15.1 146
 15.3 146

Index of Ancient Sources

Apostolic Fathers

Barnabas
2.10 293
3.5 142
4.11 72
4.14 127, 145
5.5 127
5.9 137–8
6.4 146
6.15 127, 204
7.2 129
9.6 191
12.7 142
16.10 248
19.5 222
19.12 198, 275
20.1–2 163
20.1 164
20.2 164, 210

1 Clement
1.2 29, 294
2.3 29
2.4 188
2.8 295
3–6 164
3.4 295
4.7 127
5.5 188
6.2 134
7.6 295
8.5 146
9.1 295
9.3 294
10.2 295
10.7 295
11.1 29
11.2 222
13.1 127
14.1 164, 177
13.1 292
13.3 146
15.1 29
15.2 35, 151–2
15.3 208
18.12 146
19.1 243
20.5 295
22–3 211
22.1–8 211
22.1 257
22.5 210
23–7 202, 203
23.3–4 14, 36, 39, 59, 60, 211, 215–8, 221
26.1 146
27.1 225
29.1 185
30.1 163, 164
30.3 164, 243
32.4 294
33.1 127
33.5 246
34.3 283
34.7 142
34.8 36, 218–19, 258–9
35.2 165, 258
35.4 188
35.5 163
35.8 164
36.2 295
38.2 280
43.2 164
44.5 210
46.6 144, 206
48.4 177
49 163
49.5 266, 275
50.1 146
50.5 29, 30
50.7 303
51.3 198
53.1 243
57.1 195
59.2 134
59.4 302
61.2 29
62.1 29
62.2 165, 195
63.2 16, 24, 29, 30, 164, 292
64.1 165

2 Clement
1–18 24, 27, 28, 29, 30, 31, 32, 33, 291, 292, 295, 301, 302
1.1–2 10, 48, 52, 284
1.1 9, 11, 22, 27, 37, 39, 52, 56, 63, 68, 74, **127–9**, 130, 136, 156, 167, 231, 242, 243, 261, 281
1.2 49, 52, 53, 54, 68, 69, 129, **130–2**, 185, 213, 247, 249

1.3 28, 70, 76, **132–3**, 134, 135, 207, 225, 261, 262, 296, 301
1.4–8 70, 78, 133, 136, 204
1.4–6 204
1.4 23, 56, 66, 68, 70, 133, **134**, 135, 158, 162, 204, 208, 209, 254, 295
1.5 28, 76. 133, **134–5**, 155, 207, 208, 225, 261
1.6–8 140
1.6 17, 28, 32, 66, 69, 71, 134, **135–6**, 153, 210, 303
1.7 56, 68, 70, **136**, 139, 152, 158, 162, 204, 254, 295
1.8 44, 68, 70, **136**, 153, 173, 204, 209, 261
2.1–3 22, 42, 140, 231, 292
2.1 21, 35, 37, 45, 73, **137**, **140–2**, 219, 220, 233, 246, 251, 258, 285, 297
2.2 142, 145
2.3 66, **142–4**, 223
2.4–7 76
2.4 35, 37, 42, 68, 70, 71, 136, **137–9**, **144–5**, 154, 184, 209, 210, 279
2.5 134, **145–6**, 158, 162
2.6 146,
2.7 23, 49, 56, 68, 70, 133, 138, **139–40**, 145, **146–7**, 158, 162, 204, 209, 254, 302, 303
3.1 17, 31, 48, 49, 51, 53, 69, 70, **152–4**, 165, 270, 280, 287, 291, 302
3.2 35, 39, 41, 66, 69, **148–50**, 154, 184, 228
3.3 23, 31, 56, 70, 133, **154–5**, 158, 204
3.4 28, 55, 66, 68, 71, 76, 80, 81, **150–1**, 153, **155–6**, 158, 197, 199, 287, 295
3.5 35, 37, 38, 41, 59, **151–2**, **156**, 184, 208
4.1–2 77, 134, 250
4.1 158, **162**,
4.2 36, 37, 39, 40, 41, 53, 80, 155, **157–8**, 162–3, 167, 206, 230, 262, 295
4.3 27, 55, 81, 82, 127, **163–6**, 167, 177, 183, 188, 199, 206, 209, 224, 230, 233, 234, 244, 260, 261, 262, 263, 280
4.4–6.7 212
4.4–5.4 67
4.4 **166–7**, 173, 174
4.5 28, 36, 37, 41, 66, 68, 76, 77, **159–61**, 167, 169, 199, 229, 282, 295
5 54, 276
5.1–4 296
5.1 27, 70, 76, 127, **172–4**, 175, 184, 198, 199, 209, 247, 286

5.2–4 36, 40, 41, 150, 162, 167, **168–71**, **174–5**,
5.2 37, 41, 174, 229, 241, 282
5.3 171
5.4 37, 67, 77, 167, 173, 174, 270
5.5–6 172
5.5 27, 49, 53, 54, 74, 127, **175–6**, 177, 184, 199, 206, 303
5.6 77, 176, **177**, 262
5.7 **177**, 262
6.1–2 35, 41
6.1 35, 36, **178–9**, 180, **181–2**, 184, 282, 287
6.2 12, 35, 36, **179–80**, **182**, 270
6.3–6 52
6.3–4 263
6.3 181, **182**, 183
6.4 81, 82, 164, 166, 177, **183**, 234
6.5 74, 182, **183**,
6.6 28, 182, **183–4**,
6.7 28, 49, 53, 66, 68, 74, 76, 77, 80, 173, 184, 199, 247
6.8 36, 37, 41, 75, 145, 181, **184–5**, 245
6.9 74, 81, 158, **185–6**, 192, 194, 230, 262, 263, 284
7 31, 44, 300
7.1 4, 16, 27, 60, 127, **188–90**, 209
7.2 74, **190**,
7.3 28, 60, 189, **190–1**, 289, 300
7.4 191
7.5 191
7.6 7, 22, 37, 67, 74, 77, 81, **187**, **191–2**, 194, 197, 199, 200, 221, 228, 278, 285
8.1–3 77, 239, 269
8.1–2 8
8.1 77, **194–6**, 207, 274
8.2–3 194
8.2 31, 44, 70, 134, **196–8**, 250, 279, 287, 293, 295
8.3 196, **198**, 199
8.4 27, 28, 66, 67, 68, 76, 81, 127, 164, 192, 194, **198–200**, 204, 209, 224, 247, 257, 303
8.5 36, 40, 41, 162, 179, **193–4**, **200**, 229, 241, 282
8.6 73, 81, 192, 194, **200**, 204, 257, 303
9.1–5 11, 48, 55, 202–3, 205, 220, 258, 270
9.1 47, 55, 56, 69, 74, **204**, 205
9.2 56, 133, **204**, 206, 209, 250
9.3 44, 192, **204–5**, 250
9.4 70, **205**,
9.5–6 74

2 Clement – Contd.
9.5 5, 10, 31, 48, 53, 56, 68, 69, 70, 72, 133, 136, 204, **205–6**, 209, 254, 258, 302, 303
9.6 49, 66, 74, 77, 81, 163, 205, 225, 230, 244, 262
9.7–8 269
9.7 23, 28, 32, 66, 70, 76, 77, 132, **207**, 209, 225, 261, 263
9.8 77, 194, **207**, 220, 239, 261
9.9 66, **207–8**,
9.10 66, 67, 74, 134, **208**
9.11 12, 27, 36, 37, 41, 66, 67, 68, 69, 76, 127, 199, **201–2**, **208**, 228, 247, 282
10.1 27, 66, 67, 68, 69, 70, 76, 80, 81, 127, 134, 136, 188, 199, **209–10**, 224, 247, 269
10.2 28, 74, **210–11**, 212, 217
10.3–5 221
10.3–4 221
10.3 **211–12**, 286, 296
10.4–5 49
10.4 211, **213**, 214
10.5 47, 55, 57, **213–14**, 261, 270
11.1–4 56
11.1 **220–1**, 224, 225, 262, 287
11.2–4 14, 36, 39, 56, 59, 60, 74, 211, **215–18**, 233, 294
11.2 37, 220, **221–3**, 294
11.3 **223**, 263
11.4 39, 217, **223–4**
11.5 27, 127, 188, 217, 220, 222, **224**, 294
11.6–7 74
11.6 28, 32, 41, 132, 221, **224–5**, 261
11.7 35, 36, 39, 40, 44, 59, 66, 67, 74, 77, 80, 158, 206, 217, **218–19**, 221, **225**, 230, 251, 258, 262, 285, 295
12 49, 54
12.1 66, 68, 74, 128, 158, 206, **230–1**, 234, 239, 244, 262, 283
12.2 15, 36, 37, 40, 41, 43, 49, 54, 56, 59, 61, 62, 74, 82, 162, 164, 206, 220, **226–30**, **231–2**, 247, 249, 282
12.3–5 49, 227, 228, 231, 249
12.3 81, 163, **232–3**, 241, 244, 263, 280
12.4 232, **233**, 234
12.5 4, 6, **233–4**,
12.6 40, 41, 66, 74, 206, **226–30**, **234–5**
13 81
13.1 27, 70, 77, 127, 134, 158, 194, **239–41**, 263, 280

13.2 36, 41, **236–7**, **241–2**, 275
13.3–4 22
13.3 128, **242–3**
13.4 36, 37, 39, **41**, 51, 55, 68, 128, 130, 145, 163, 206, 233, **238–9**, **243–4**, 247, 262, 283
14 53, 54, 59, 73, 141, 206, 274, 277
14.1–2 569
14.1 27, 36, 37, 67, 68, 70, 76, 80, 127, 134, 145, 184, 199, **245**, **247–50**, 258, 259, 295
14.2–4 39, 233
14.2 6, 36, 37, 39, 42, 43, 44, 45, 63, 73, 134, 145, 183, 184, 220, **245–6**, **250–5**, 258, 260
14.3–4 73
14.3 27, 48, 74, 127, 164, 192, 248, **255–7**, 258
14.4 69, 72, 246, 254, 255, **257–8**
14.5 44, 218, **258–9**, 303
15.1 15, 17, 23, 24, 28, 31, 70, 82, 127, 128, 134, 166, 183, **260–1**, 263, 281, 288, 293
15.2 19, 28, 51, 52, 66, 70, 76, 132, 225, **261–2**, 263
15.3–5 269
15.3 22, 36, 37, 66, **260**, **262**, 263
15.4–5 76, 294
15.4 **262–3**
15.5–17.3 33
15.5 66, 80, 81, 163, **263–4**
16.1 27, 66, 68, 70, 77, 127, 128, 136, 144, 194, 209, 239, **269**
16.2–3 28
16.2 81, 165, **269–70**, 273
16.3 7, 28, 35, 36, 67, 74, **265**, **270–2**, 285
16.4 29, 35, 36, 38, 52, 59, 70, 81, 82, 239, **265–8**, **272–7**
17.1 31, 49, 76, 77, 194, 239, 272, 274, **279–80**, 285, 287, 289, 293
17.2 70, 81, 134, 163, 263, **280–1**, 289
17.3–4 74
17.3 17, 19, 28, 32, 64, 66, 76, 127, 128, **281–2**, 288, 295, 303
17.4–7 28, 74, 129
17.4 22, 36, 37, 41, 49, 67, 68, 230, **278**, **282–4**, 285
17.5–6 12
17.5 7, 12, 22, 35, 36, 41, 49, 67, 77, 185, 251, 258, **278**, **284–5**, 286, 287, 294
17.6 28, 66, 68, 74, 76, 284, **285–6**, 288

17.7   77, 213, 262, 269, 270, **286–7**, 288, 296
18.1   **288**
18.2   17, 28, 74, 78, 158, 261, 279, **288–90**, 296
19.1–20.4   16, 17, 27, 28, 29, 30, 31, 32, 33, 230, 301
19.1   6, 16, 17, 19, 21, 24, 27, 28, 29, 30, 31, 33, 53, 54, 127, 134, 194, 239, 261, 263, **291–4**, 295, 300
19.2   28, 31, 32, 81, 222, **294–5**
19.3–4   12, 74
19.3   28, 29, 30, 31, 32, 70, 80, 134, 158, 293, **295–7**, 300, 301
19.4   28, 33, 294, 296, **297–8**, 300
20.1   28, 29, 166, **299–300**
20.2   27, 31, 66, 74, 127, 296, 299, **300**
20.3   28, 32, 230, **300**, 301
20.4   28, 31, 67, 294, **300–1**
20.5   27, 31, 51, 53, 66, 69, 291, **301–3**

Didache
3.3   164
3.5   166
4.4   222
4.14   198, 275
5.1–2   163
5.1   164
6.3   152
7.1   72
11.7–12   72
14.1   288
15.3   195

Diognetus
9.6   207
12.1   213

Ignatius
  Ephesians
  1.1   127, 302
  3.1   241
  7.2   206
  9.1   72
  12.1   146
  13.1   282
  16.2   214

  Magnesians
  Praescr.   302
  3.2   302
  7.2   206

  12.1   144

  Philadelphians
  2.1   213
  7.2   204
  9.2   302

  Romans
  2.1   240
  6.2   127, 134

  Smyrneans
  2   284
  3.1   203
  5.3   284
  7.1   302
  9.1   207

  Trallians
  8.2   236–7
  10.1   284

  Polycarp
  2.3   239, 258
  3.1   213
  3.2   302
  4.2   282

Polycarp
  Philippians
  2.1   129
  2.2   166
  4.3   166
  6.1   166, 281
  7.1   202
  10.2   275
  10.3   236–7, 275

Martyrdom of Polycarp
2.3   218

Shepherd of Hermas
  Mandates
  1.2   210
  4.1.4–8   164
  4.1.5   164
  4.1.8   198
  4.3.5   198
  5.1.6   292
  6.1.1   165
  6.2.3   210

Shepherd of Hermas – Contd.
  Mandates – Contd.
    8.3 163, 164, 213
    8.4 164
    9.1 222
    9.5–11 222
    9.5 217, 222
    9.7 220, 222
    10.3.2–3 292
    11.9 292
    11.14 292
    12.3.1 210
    12.6.3 169

  Similitudes
    2.5–7 292
    5.6.5–7 206
    5.7.2 202
    6.1.4 210
    6.4.4 213
    6.5.5 163, 164
    8.2.2–4 191
    8.10.3 210
    9.16.3–7 191
    9.16.4 191
    9.17.4 191

  Visions
    1.1.9 207
    2.2.4–5 198
    2.2.5 59, 78
    2.3.2 165
    2.3.4 216
    2.4.1 248
    2.4.3 15
    3.7.5–6 198
    3.8.4 165

Nag Hammadi Texts

Preaching of Paul (NHC I.1)
  25–9 218

Gospel of Truth (NHC I.3)
  16.31–3 153
  22.5 131
  22.14–15 131
  24.20 176
  40.3 176
  38.7–41.19 241
  40.30–42.35 131
  41.13 176

Tripartite Tractate (NHC I.5)
  57.34–5 249
  58.30–1 249
  87.1–10 146

Apocryphon of John (NHC II.1)
  26.12–19 146
  26.31 176
  31.23–25 191

Gospel of Thomas (NHC II.2)
  2 176
  6 273
  14 273, 275
  17 40, 218–19, 258
  22 36, 226–30
  47 178–9
  50 176
  60 176
  99 201–2

Gospel of Philip (NHC II.3)
  78.11 266

Hypostasis of the Archons (NHC II.4)
  86.20–2 153

On the Origin of the World (NHC II.5)
  103.22 196

Second Treatise of the Great Seth (NHC VII.2)
  53.3–4 153

Teaching of Silvanus (NHC VII.4)
  92.11–14 131
  116.1–5 208

Interpretation of Knowledge (NHC XI.1)
  9.31–3 12, 201–2
  9.33–5 12, 179–80

Valentinian Exposition (NHC XI.2)
  29.35–35 249

Other Early Christian Writings

Acts of Paul and Thecla
  5 199
  6 185

Apocalypse of Peter 271

Index of Ancient Sources

Apostolic Constitutions
  1.10.1 236–7
  2.14.4 181
  3.5.6 236–7
  3.7.6 260
  5.6.5 214
  8.47.85 9

Athenagoras
  Legatio
    15.2–3 196

Clement of Alexandria
  Excerpta ex Theodoto
    3 169
    14.3 169
    78.2 131

  Paedagogus
    3.12.91 266

  Quis dives salvetur
    38.1 266

  Stromateis
    3.6.1–9.3 164
    3.92.2 226
    4.3.3 266
    4.109 211
    5.120.3 260
    5.121–2 271
    6.41.2–6 143
    6.112.3 179–80

Didascalia Apostolorum
  2.3 266

Epiphanius
  30.14.5 201

Epistula Apostolorum
  33 141

Eusebius
  Historia ecclesiastica
    3.28.2 185
    3.38.4 8
    4.7.7 174
    4.23.9–11 15
    6.36.1 292
    7.17.2 185

Excerpta Patrum 11, 205

Florilegium Edessenum 10, 205

Gospel of the Ebionites 201

Gospel of the Egyptians 36, 40, 41, 54, 61, 62, 194, 226–30

Gospel of Mary
  15–16 131

Gospel of the Nazarenes 36, 161, 169

Gospel of Peter 170
  14.60 170

Hippolytus
  Refutatio monium haeresium
    5.24 218

Hilary
  Epistula seu libellus
    1 193–4

Irenaeus
  Adversus haereses
    1.1.1 249
    1.1.3 48, 162
    1.6.4 144
    1.8.4 249
    1.10.3 141
    1.11.1 249
    1.23.5 185, 202
    2.31.2 202
    2.34.2 193–4
    3.3.3 7
    3.18.5 169, 174
    4.17.3 260
    4.33.9 174
    5.2.3 203

Jerome
  De viris illustribus
    15 9

Justin
  1 Apology
    1 292
    15.8 138
    15.12 179
    16.6 150

Justin – *Contd.*
    16.11 159, 160
    19–21 203
    19.7 168, 170
    20.1–2 271
    44.11 208
    53.5–6 143
    53.5 137, 141
    60.8 271
    66.3 43, 254
    67 21
    67.3 43, 254, 291
    67.4 281

    Dialogue with Trypho
    7 243
    13.8 141
    16.3 208
    17 242
    23.2 208
    44.2 181
    45.3 181
    56.6 216
    64.5–6 248
    76.5 160
    77.2 216
    80.4 202, 203
    93.2 150
    93.3 150
    100–7 43, 254
    110.3 216
    140.3 181

Origen
Commentarii in evangelium Joannis.
    2.34.207 8

Homiliae in Jeremiam
    18 8

Photius
    Bibliotheca
    126 11

Pseudo-Clementine Homilies
    17.5.2 169

Pseudo-Justin
    De resurrectione
    5 203

Sacra Parallela 12

Serverus of Antioch
    Adversus Johannem Grammaticum 10

Tatian
    Oration
    6 203
    25.6 271

Tertullian
    Adversus Marcionem
    3.16 206

De resurrectione carnis 203

Scorpiace 174

De spectaculis
    30 271

Theophilus
    Ad Autolycum
    1.7 203
    1.14 243
    2.10 206
    2.15 208
    2.26 196

Others

Aristophanes
    Vespae
    1228 279

Aristotle
    Rhetorica
    I.3.1ff. 23

Dio Chrysostom
    8.11–12 188
    9.11–12 188

Diogenes Laertius
    6.57 188
    7.142 272

Epictetus
    3.7.17 243
    3.22.57 188
    4.11.27 196

Euripedes
Rhesus
445–6 223

Lucian
Nigrinus
13 279

Marcus Aurelius
10.33 270

Nemesius
309.5ff. 272

Philostratus
Vita Apollonii
1.1.1 297

Plotinus
Enneades
2.9.6 257

Plutarch
Moralia
132c 270

Ps.-Diogenes
15 243

Seneca
Epistles
78.16 188

Xenophon
Cyropaedia
7.5.74 270

Memorabilia
1.5.1 165

Index of Modern Authors Cited

Aasgaard, R. 127
Abramowski, L. 43
Ådna, J. 127
Allison, D. C. 149, 158, 160, 170
Aono, T. 17, 55, 59, 61, 64, 69, 70, 71, 74, 77, 79, 157, 170, 204, 219, 273, 281

Baarda, T. 227, 228, 229, 230, 232, 233, 234
Baasland, E. 18, 19, 20, 22, 23, 24, 27, 61, 62, 80, 127, 128
Barr, J. 34
Bartlet, J. V. 41, 59, 61, 140, 150, 194, 202, 239
Barton, J. 34
Bauckham, R. J. 216, 223, 271
Bauernfeind, O. 210
Bellinzoni, A. J. 40, 160, 170
Benecke, P. V. M. 136
Bensly, R. L. 5, 150, 173
Berger, K. 218, 275, 276
Bethge, H.-G. 12
Betz, H. D. 141, 165
Beyer, H.W. 280
Bieringer, R. 218
Bihlmeyer, K. 130, 149, 205, 217, 237, 269, 279
Bousset, W. 234
Bovon, F. 238
Bredin, M. 268
Brox, N. 198
Bultmann, R. 79, 138, 149, 158
Burke, T. J. 218

Callan, T. 231
Chadwick, H. 165
Charlesworth, J. H. 216
Conzelmann, H. 30, 231, 294, 302
Cureton, W. 10

Davies, W. D. 149, 158, 170
DeConick, A. D. 131
Delobel, J. 227
Denaux, A. 150
Dibelius, M. 30, 231, 294, 302
Di Pauli, A. 27, 29

Donfried, K. P., 4, 14, 16, 17, 18, 19, 20, 23, 24, 27, 29, 34, 48, 49, 55, 56, 60, 68, 71, 78, 79, 128, 133, 138, 141, 143, 148, 149, 153, 154, 155, 157, 158, 160, 161, 164, 165, 169, 172, 174, 176, 180, 182, 185, 188, 189, 192, 193, 194, 195, 197, 202, 203, 213, 216, 227, 228, 229, 232, 239, 240, 241, 248, 249, 251, 253, 255, 257, 261, 264, 267, 273, 279, 284, 286, 287, 292
Dunderberg, I. 59, 131

Ehrman, B. D. 64, 130, 133, 149, 150, 173, 179, 180, 189, 192, 200, 205, 211, 228, 237, 251, 252, 253, 254, 263, 269, 279, 296, 299, 301, 303
Elliott, J. K. 218
Eltester, W. 238
Engberg-Pedersen, T. 24, 25

Fitzer, G. 192
Fitzmyer, J. A. 267, 276
Foster, P. 9, 171
Frank, A. 250
Freede, J. H. 11
Funk, W.-P. 12, 179, 180, 202

Gathercole, S. 267
Gebhardt, O. de 130, 149, 205, 237, 269, 279
Goodspeed, E. J. 15
Goppelt, L. 257
Graham, H. H. 19, 187, 205, 251, 255, 263, 279
Grant, R. M. 19, 187, 205, 251, 255, 263, 279
Gregory, A. F. 35, 39, 43, 136, 138, 140, 148, 158, 161, 169, 184, 187, 194, 202, 205, 206, 224, 236, 240, 251
Grundmann, W. 165

Hagner, D. A. 152, 216, 218, 219, 267
Hanhart, R. 267
Harland, P. A. 127
Harnack, A. von 8, 9, 10, 15, 19, 58, 62, 130, 143, 149, 205, 237, 269, 279
Harris, J. R. 15, 260, 268

Index of Modern Authors Cited

Heiligenthal, R. 273
Hennecke, E. 161
Herzog, R. 207
Hilgenfeld, A. 15, 293
Hoffmann, P. 149, 158, 160, 170, 178, 238

Jefford, C. N. 48, 192
Jeremias, G. 231

Kaiser, U. U. 12
Kenyon, F. G. 3
King, K. L. 50, 55, 131, 155
Kloppenborg, J. S. 149, 158, 160, 170, 178, 238
Knopf, R. 19, 21, 48, 58, 130, 132, 140, 141, 142, 152, 154, 155, 156, 158, 163, 167, 174, 181, 187, 188, 189, 191, 192, 195, 197, 199, 205, 209, 210, 211, 212, 221, 223, 224, 228, 233, 234, 238, 239, 241, 246, 250, 252, 253, 254, 261, 262, 263, 267, 279, 283, 284, 285, 288, 291, 292, 301
Koester, H. 48, 61, 160, 161, 174, 194, 229
Köhler, W.-D. 139, 140, 149, 158, 159, 161, 169, 179, 180, 184, 239
Körtner, U. 249
Koskenniemi, H. 19
Köster, H. 39, 42, 138, 139, 140, 149, 151, 152, 158, 160, 169, 170, 180, 193, 194, 202, 228, 239
Kraus, T. J. 171, 271
Krüger, G. 255
Kuhn, H.-W. 231

Lake, K. 130, 149, 150, 173, 175, 179, 180, 192, 200, 205, 217, 224, 237, 251, 252, 253, 254, 263, 269, 271, 279, 281, 296, 299, 301, 303
Lampe, G. W. H. 192
Layton, B. 178
Lightfoot, J. B. 3, 4, 5, 6, 8, 10, 11, 12, 18, 19, 20, 60, 143, 149, 150, 158, 161, 169, 173, 188, 189, 192, 205, 208, 211, 216, 217, 223, 228, 237, 238, 239, 241, 246, 252, 253, 254, 257, 260, 263, 267, 269, 271, 272, 274, 275, 279, 291, 293, 296, 299
Lindemann, A. 8, 9, 19, 20, 27, 31, 41, 43, 48, 54, 56, 61, 64, 68, 69, 128, 129, 130, 131, 133, 136, 141, 143, 144, 145, 146, 149, 151, 152, 155, 156, 158, 161, 165, 166, 167, 169, 172, 174, 175, 179, 180, 182, 183, 186, 187, 188, 189, 192, 193, 194, 195, 197, 199, 200, 203, 204, 205, 206, 207, 208, 209, 212, 216, 217, 219, 221, 223, 224, 225, 228, 230, 232, 234, 236, 237, 238, 239, 241, 245, 247, 248, 249, 251, 252, 253, 254, 256, 257, 258, 260, 261, 262, 263, 267, 269, 270, 271, 275, 276, 279, 280, 281, 282, 283, 284, 285, 286, 287, 288, 291, 293, 296, 297, 299, 301, 303
Lohmann, H. 56, 128, 166, 173, 174, 183, 199, 203, 212, 230, 234, 248, 270
Luz, U. 158, 228
Lührmann, D. 41, 170, 171, 231

Malherbe, A. J. 243
Marjanen, A. 50
Markschies, C. 50, 59
Martin, E. G. 216
Massaux, E. 139, 149, 158, 160, 161, 169, 180, 194
Meeks, W. A. 127
Mitchell, M. 25
Muddiman, J. 251

Nicklas, T. 171, 271

O'Hagan, A. 282, 283, 296
Osiek, C. 198

Painchaud, L. 12, 179, 180, 202
Parvis, P. 9, 19, 47, 64, 291
Parsons, P. J. 170
Pattie, T. S. 4
Pearson, B. 50
Petersen, W. L. 149, 150, 160, 161, 180, 227
Pfitzner, V. C. 188
Plisch, U.-W. 12, 202
Pratscher, W. 5, 8, 9, 12, 17, 18, 19, 20, 23, 27, 28, 29, 31, 37, 48, 51, 59, 61, 62, 63, 64, 68, 69, 72, 77, 80, 82, 128, 129, 130, 131, 133, 135, 142, 143, 144, 146, 149, 151, 153, 155, 158, 166, 167, 169, 173, 174, 175, 177, 179, 180, 183, 184, 185, 187, 188, 189, 190, 192, 193, 194, 195, 196, 197, 198, 199, 203, 204, 205, 206, 207, 208, 209, 210, 211, 212, 216, 217, 218, 220, 221, 223, 224, 225, 227, 228, 229, 230, 232, 233, 234, 235, 237, 238, 241, 245, 246, 247, 248, 250, 252, 253, 254, 256, 257, 258, 260, 261, 262, 263, 267, 269, 270, 271, 272, 276, 279, 281, 282, 283, 284, 285, 286, 287, 288, 289, 291, 292, 293, 295, 296, 297, 299, 300, 301, 303

Richardson, C. C. 7, 19, 48, 205, 251, 254, 255, 263, 279, 296, 301
Robinson, J. M. 149, 158, 160, 170, 178, 238
Rousseau, A. 7
Rucker, I. 10

Salzmann, J. C. 22, 27, 33, 54, 292
Sanders, E. P. 71
Schlarb, E. 41
Schenke, H.-M. 12
Schubert, H. von 41, 59, 130, 162, 169, 194, 238, 241, 272, 275, 282, 284
Schulz, S. 149, 170
Schüssler, W. 22, 27, 292
Seitz, O. F. J. 222
Shedinger, R. F.
Stanton, G. N. 43
Stanton, G.R. 189
Starr, J. 24, 25
Stegemann, C. 3, 12, 14, 20, 22, 27, 29, 30, 31, 60, 64, 166, 189, 292
Stegemann, H. 231
Stewart-Sykes, A. 23
Stone, M. E. 218
Streeter, B. H. 61
Strugnell, J. 218
Stuckenbruck, L. 267
Stuhlmacher, P. 43

Taylor, C. 7
Thomassen, E. 12, 179, 180, 202
Tite, P. 24

Torrance, T. F. 79
Tuckett, C. M. 35, 39, 43, 50, 52, 80, 131, 136, 149, 150, 161, 180, 181, 184, 187, 205, 206, 218, 219, 224, 236, 251, 272

Unnik, W.C. van 238, 240, 263

Verheyden, J. 150, 218
Vielhauer, Ph. 18, 27, 61, 79, 161, 176

Warns, R. 3, 8, 12, 17, 23, 24, 27, 30, 34, 41, 48, 49, 50, 51, 53, 61, 129, 131, 139, 142, 143, 145, 146, 150, 151, 154, 157, 161, 167, 169, 175, 179, 180, 181, 186, 189, 194, 202, 204, 205, 207, 208, 211, 216, 217, 218, 224, 225, 227, 228, 232, 233, 237, 239, 247, 249, 251, 260, 266, 271, 278, 280, 287
Weeks, S. 267, 268
Wengst, K. 5, 9, 18, 19, 30, 38, 41, 48, 54, 61, 79, 80, 82, 130, 132, 133, 142, 143, 145, 149, 152, 153, 166, 167, 181, 183, 187, 188, 189, 190, 192, 195, 197, 205, 211, 212, 214, 221, 224, 225, 228, 230, 234, 237, 238, 241, 245, 250, 252, 253, 254, 257, 258, 261, 267, 269, 273, 279, 280, 283, 284, 291, 292, 293, 296, 299
Williams, M.A. 50, 55, 155, 164
Windisch, H. 15, 47, 79, 234

Zahn, Th. 130, 149, 205, 269, 279